Creating
a Successful
Christian
Marriage

Creating a Successful Christian Marriage

THIRD REVISED EDITION

Cleveland McDonald

BAKER BOOK HOUSE
Grand Rapids, Michigan 49506

First Edition

First printing, April 1975
Second printing, September 1976
Third printing, September 1977
Fourth printing, May 1978
Fifth printing, February 1980

Revised Edition

First printing, April 1981
Second printing, September 1982
Third printing, October 1983
Fourth printing, January 1985

Third Revised Edition

First printing, January 1986

to
Ruth Smelser Boalt
Alberta Graham Carr
Sandra Millikin Entner
who constituted my first class
in Marriage and the Family
and to
the hundreds of students
in succeeding classes
who have made my teaching
career so enjoyable

ACKNOWLEDGMENTS

I am indebted to many people for their assistance in writing this book. I owe a special word of thanks to Clifford Johnson, Academic Dean of Cedarville College, for his encouragement which gave impetus to my desire to write the text. I am grateful to James Jeremiah, President of Cedarville College, and to the Trustees for the leave of absence with salary during the Winter Quarter of 1971 which enabled me to begin the actual writing.

I owe a great deal to Cornelius Zylstra, editor of Baker Book House, for the encouragement and answers to numerous questions which arose in the planning for the publishing of this book.

I am obligated to many teachers and authors who have stimulated my thinking and enlarged my views in the area of marriage and the family. I wish to thank the many publishers who gave permission to use extended quotations, and have acknowledged their permission in the appropriate footnotes.

I also am grateful to the hundreds of students who have reassured me through the years by their enthusiastic response to a Christian view of marriage and the family. Many have taken part in surveys, and some have done research for me in their Independent Study in Sociology.

Last, but not least, I am grateful for Helen Marie, my loving wife (and typist) for twenty-nine years, who never grew weary of typing and proofreading seemingly endless revisions. Due to an eye tumor, she was unable to help during one stage of the typing, and the Lord providentially sent home our daughter Rebecca Ann, who was a tremendous help in typing the final copy of the manuscript. This volume would never have been published without their aid and support.

PREFACE

Solomon said, "Of making many books there is no end; and much study is a weariness of the flesh." Although there are many books published today covering various phases of Christian courtship and marriage, and many Christian high schools, colleges, seminaries, and Bible institutes offer courses in this area, there is no textbook written specifically for such courses.

The author has studied the subject at the University of Pittsburgh and Ohio State University and has been teaching a course in Marriage and the Family for seventeen years in a Christian liberal arts college. He believes this volume will help to fill this void in Christian literature that has existed so many years.

Those teaching in the field know there are two different ways of approaching a course on the family—the functional and the institutional. The functional course is primarily designed as a preparation-for-marriage course which attempts to give students some instruction in the process of mate selection, and of the interaction which takes place in marriage and family life. The institutional course treats the family from a sociological perspective and is concerned with the relationship of the family to the other institutions of society.

This text is definitely written for the functional course in a Christian institution. Hopefully, it will enable the student to make a wise choice of a mate and to make the adjustments needed to live happily together. Most any young person can learn to drive an automobile, but the insurance companies have discovered that a course in driver's education makes him a better and safer driver. Similarly, any fellow or girl can date and get married, but it can be a much more enjoyable experience if they know something about the interaction that takes place. As one married student said to the writer, "I wish I had taken this course five years ago, for our marriage could have been so much happier if I had known these things when we began our married life."

There is a real need for more and better premarital counseling. Part of the problem has been the lack of a single volume covering the many areas which the pastor wishes to treat in his limited time with the engaged couple. The pastor can now recommend the purchase and reading of this volume by the young couple prior to the counseling sessions. He may even require the completion of the personality inventories to discover significant differences which can form the basis for some of the counseling sessions. A premarital counseling program based on the text should prepare the couple to enter marriage with a realistic view of what is involved in family living.

Another purpose in writing this book is to provide a comprehensive volume that will be a source of information to the many pastors, Christian Education directors, and youth leaders who have not had the privilege of systematically studying these subjects in a classroom setting, but are often called upon to counsel young people, since they often establish a relationship which encourages the young person to share his problems with them. Hopefully, these counselors will be better prepared to deal with questions concerning dating, courtship, and marriage after reading this volume.

The sociological basis used in organizing the text is modern role theory. This theory is very compatible with the Bible, for Jesus said, "As ye would that men should do to you, do ye also to them likewise" (Luke 6:31). Certainly one must be aware of his own role if he is going to interact with another. Many of the difficulties of courtship and marriage adjustment arise because the roles of male and female are no longer clearly defined in American culture. Also, very little education is given the youth of our society to help them successfully play the roles of lover, spouse, or parent. Someone has stated, "The only course in marriage and family living most young people ever get is the one they receive in their parental home." Unfortunately, many Christian young people do not receive very much help from their parents. On the other hand, much of the so-called "sex education" in public schools presents a negative view of family roles and values. Consequently, much of the learning in marriage and family living is through trial and error in an "on the job" setting, a factor which helps to account for the high rate of marriage failure. This text emphasizes the necessity for the individual to know his spiritual, psychological, and emotional needs in order to fulfill his role expectations, and to meet the various needs of those with whom he interacts.

Another aim of this volume is to alert the young person to subtle cultural pressures that bear upon him. For example, Christian young people are not immune to the romantic love complex foisted on our culture by Hollywood and television. An attempt is made in these pages to counteract this by stressing the importance in courtship of seeking psychological compatibility rather than physical compatibility, since the major part of marital interaction is psychological rather than physical. It may be idealistic to think that most young people will choose their mates on the basis of psychological rather than physical compatibility, but even if only a few follow this suggestion their marriages will be happier. The author hopes no couple having studied this text will face each other after the honeymoon year is over and say, "Why did we ever get married to each other?"

Another cultural influence of which Christian young people are often unaware is the pressure for social status conformity—the "keep up with the Joneses" syndrome of American life. This "status seeking," as Vance Packard terms it, is intertwined with the materialism that is seriously affecting Christian homes and churches today. Inasmuch as conflict over financial problems is a major cause of unhappiness in many homes, two chapters of this text are devoted to money management. If young people learn their roles as Christian stewards well, many of the financial situations that cause unhappiness can be avoided.

The author realizes that the first attempt to write a full-length textbook has its shortcomings, and he welcomes criticism and suggestions that will help to make any future edition more useful to its readers.

PREFACE TO REVISED EDITION

It is a delightful experience to send forth another edition of a book that has been so well received. In view of the problems that Christian families are facing in the secular society, young people need all the instruction and encouragement they can get in order to successfully create a strong Christian marriage. The home is never stronger than the marriage, so it is incumbent upon the couple entering matrimony to prepare themselves as fully as possible for the challenge they will face in seeking to fulfill God's design that they become "one flesh."

Although the difficulties facing Christian young people have never been greater, it is also true that the opportunities and rewards received from a Christian marriage relationship have never been more fulfilling. The couple who is willing to work at building a close relationship with Jesus Christ, and who is able to make Him the Lord of their lives and their home, can receive blessings innumerable. Because so many Christian homes are being broken indicates that some couples are not willing to put forth the effort it takes to build a strong relationship that will stand the stresses of the day in which they live.

The principles set forth in the text are those Biblical axioms that have stood the test of time and experience. Thus, the revisions of this edition are mainly in the area of statistics and bibliography. Books on family relationships continue to pour off the presses and students are advised to take advantage of the splendid helps available in every area of family life.

This third edition is sent out with the fervent desire and prayer that many young people will find it useful as they follow the Biblical injunction to "leave, cleave, and become one flesh."

Cleveland McDonald
Cedarville, Ohio

CONTENTS

1

THE BIBLICAL BASIS
OF MARRIAGE

Marriage is honourable in all.
Hebrews 13:4

RECENT TRENDS IN MARRIAGE

Marriage as an institution is being assailed on every side by its critics. The so-called new morality has affected the concept of marital as well as premarital behavior. When the "sexual revolution" first attracted the attention of the national news media in the early part of the 1960s, some observers felt there was only a change in attitude toward standards of sexual conduct, but not in behavior. Recent research indicates behavior was liberalized in the late 1960s so that there is actually more immoral sexual activity today than ever before.[1]

An article in *Time* Magazine indicated the rapid growth of illicit cohabitations in place of marriage.[2] On secular college campuses, the "apartment marriage" (where a fellow and girl temporarily live together until one partner tires of the other) has become popular. Bigamous liaisons (two women living with one man) are found in some circles. Some "liberated" individuals practice "communal living" (no husband-wife relationships). Such perversions of marriage have always occurred, particularly in some segments of the lower

1. Ira E. Robinson, Karl King, Jack O. Balswick, "The Premarital Sexual Revolution Among College Females," *The Family Coordinator*, April 1972, pp. 189-194.
2. *Time*, Dec. 28, 1970, "American Family: Future Uncertain," pp. 34-39.

social classes, but in today's secular society they are becoming more respectable. This trend makes it mandatory to emphasize the true Biblical concept of the origin and nature of marriage.

THE DIVINE ORIGIN OF MARRIAGE

As recorded in Genesis 2:18-25, the family as an institution was originated by God in the beginning of the human race:

> *And the Lord God said, It is not good that the man should be alone; I will make him an help meet for him.*
>
> *And out of the ground the Lord God formed every beast of the field, and every fowl of the air; and brought them unto Adam to see what he would call them: and whatsoever Adam called every living creature, that was the name thereof.*
>
> *And Adam gave names to all cattle, and to the fowl of the air, and to every beast of the field; but for Adam there was not found an help meet for him.*
>
> *And the Lord God caused a deep sleep to fall upon Adam, and he slept: and he took one of his ribs, and closed up the flesh instead thereof;*
>
> *And the rib, which the Lord God had taken from man, made he a woman, and brought her unto the man.*
>
> *And Adam said, This is now bone of my bones, and flesh of my flesh: she shall be called Woman, because she was taken out of Man.*
>
> *Therefore shall a man leave his father and his mother, and shall cleave unto his wife: and they shall be one flesh.*
>
> *And they were both naked, the man and his wife, and were not ashamed.*

Humanists deny this truth as they do the rest of Scripture and substitute their own theory of the origin of the family. To them the family is merely a social institution that has evolved through the ages. One proponent of such a view writes, "It is not known when the family originated, although it was probably between two million and a hundred thousand years ago. It is not known whether some kind of embryonic family came before, with, or after the origin of language. . . The chances are that language and the family developed together over a long period, but the evidence is sketchy."[3] The writer then attempts to explain how the family developed from primates and the ancestors of *homo sapiens*.[4] Since evolutionists reject divine revelation, they are forced to "speculate" as to the beginning of the human family.

3. Kathleen Gough, "The Origin of the Family," *Journal of Marriage and the Family*, November 1971, p. 760.
4. Ibid., pp. 760-770.

The Christian has no such doubts about the origin of the family, for God very carefully gave an inspired record of the first marriage and the first family. Genesis 2:18 tells us that God created man with a social nature: "It is not good that the man should be alone; I will make him an help meet [fit] for him." In the verses which follow survey is made of the animal world, but a mate "fit" or "worthy" or "suitable" for Adam was not found. Consequently, by direct creation, God produced Eve as a companion "suitable for Adam." Quite often the phrase, "help meet for him" has been termed "helpmate for him." It is true that Eve was a helpmate, but she was not created to be merely a servant, but a help "fit" or "worthy" of Adam. Saint Augustine remarked that God did not take a bone from Adam's head from which to create Eve that she might be above him, nor a bone from his foot that she might be beneath him, but from his side that she might be beside him. Apparently this relationship was changed by the fall of man into sin.

The Bible does not indicate how long the blissful union of Adam and Eve lasted before Eve succumbed to the temptation of Satan. It is clear that sin entered the world, and Adam and Eve were placed under the curse. God said to Eve, "I will greatly multiply thy sorrow and thy conception; in sorrow thou shalt bring forth children; and thy desire shall be to thy husband, and he shall rule over thee" (Gen. 3:16). This implies that the relationship Adam and Eve enjoyed before the Fall was changed by the curse. It seems to say that whereas she may have enjoyed an equal status with him at Creation, she now is to submit to his rule. In I Peter 3:7 husbands are exhorted to "dwell with them according to knowledge, giving honour unto the wife, as unto the weaker vessel . . . ," which indicates that the husband is the stronger of the two sexes. He is under divine obligation to treat the wife with great consideration due to her weaker nature. This view of the husband-wife relationship is rejected by members of the Women's Liberation Movement, which stresses the equality of women with men. It is true that in Christ "there is neither male nor female" (Gal. 3:28) in reference to the position of believers before the Lord, but the Bible in I Corinthians 11:3 does give a divine order of authority in the Christian home: "But I would have you know that the head of every man is Christ, and the head of the woman is the man; and the head of Christ is God."

This truth is also clearly stated in Ephesians 5:22-23: "Wives, submit yourselves unto your own husbands, as unto the Lord. For the husband is the head of the wife even as Christ is head of the church." The wife is to submit to the headship of a husband who loves her as "Christ loved the church" (Eph. 5:25). Although some Christian women have rejected the headship of the husband, this fact does not change God's plan for the transmission of His authority in the home. The greatest blessing is found in those homes where the husband and wife are obedient to God and His Word.

Genesis 2:18, "It is not good that the man should be alone," emphasizes that Eve was created to be a companion for Adam and not just a bearer of children, as is taught in some churches. God created Adam with a social nature that craved companionship. This need could only be fulfilled by the creation of another human being to share her life with Adam. From this beginning, the greatest fulfillment of social needs in both men and women has been found in the institution of marriage.

The command, "Be fruitful and multiply, and replenish the earth" (Gen. 1:28), came after the creation, indicating that procreation is a secondary purpose of marriage rather than its primary purpose. "Children are an heritage of the Lord" and are included in the plans of most couples when they marry, but it is a misunderstanding of the Scriptures and of the sexual nature of man to insist that the only legitimate reason for the sexual union of husband and wife is to beget children. God endowed men and women with complementary sexual drives, and these are gratified in the sexual relationship in which a couple most fully express their love for one another.

The phrase "they shall be one flesh" is evidence that sex is God-given and only becomes sinful when it is misused and perverted. God intends for the husband and wife to express their love through the sexual relationship. This is explicitly stated in I Corinthians 7:4-5: "The wife hath not power of her own body, but the husband; and likewise also the husband hath not power of his own body, but the wife. Defraud ye not one the other, except it be with consent for a time, that ye may give yourselves to fasting and prayer; and come together again, that Satan tempt you not for your incontinency." The husband or wife can only receive legitimate sexual satisfaction from the marriage partner, and the exhortation here is to be careful to meet each other's needs unless there is a mutual consent to abstain in order to achieve some spiritual goal.

The monogamous nature of marriage is indicated in Genesis 2:24. A man is to leave his father and mother, cleave unto his wife, and the "two" are to become "one flesh." While it is true that in other Old Testament passages there is evidence of concubinage, such was not the case in the beginning. The highest, purest, and happiest form of marriage has always been that which God instituted—the union of one man and one woman for life. When a Christian couple take vows to live with each other "till death do us part," they are affirming the truth of Genesis 2, which teaches that God intended one man to live with one woman for life.

Walter Trobisch, in his excellent little book *I Married You*, indicates that Genesis 2:24 contains the three elements necessary for a truly Biblical marriage: there must be a "leaving", a "cleaving", and a fusion into "one—flesh."[5] Unless all three of these take place, there is no true marriage between the two people involved. Consequently two young people who engage in a premarital sex act are not married even though physically there is a "one-flesh" because there is no "leaving" and no "cleaving." They are guilty of what the Bible calls "fornication," sexual union between two unmarried persons.

There is a great amount of publicity given today to various experimental marriage styles. These alternatives to marriage and the family range from homosexual unions to groups cohabiting in communes. Many of these are not new, since they have appeared at other times in different societies.[6]

In spite of all the publicity about the impending death of the family, Lester Velie, who spent a year studying the state of the American family for *Reader's Digest*, concludes that the family "is very much alive but under heavy attack."[7] That an institution so sacred as monogamous marriage is under attack is no surprise to the Bible believer, for he has the assurance it will survive the assault. The Lord Jesus Christ predicted that at His second coming the multitudes would be "marrying and giving in marriage" as they were in the days of Noah (Matt. 24:38).

MOSAIC LAW AND THE FAMILY

Additional evidence from the Old Testament for the divine origin of marriage is found in the Law given by Moses to the children of Israel. God had a plan and purpose in His choice of Israel, and stable family life was a necessity for their fulfillment. After the giving of the "great commandment" (Deut. 6:4-5), the faithful Israelite is exhorted to teach all the commandments "diligently unto thy children."

Three of the Ten Commandments have direct reference to the family. The fifth commandment, "Honor thy father and thy mother: that thy days may be long upon the land which the Lord thy God

5. W. Trobisch, *I Married You* (New York: Harper & Row, 1971), p. 12.
6. Nena and George O'Neill, "Open Marriage: A Synergic Model." *The Family Coordinator*, October 1972, p. 403. This entire issue of the *Coordinator* is composed of articles following the theme, "The Meaning of Variant and Experimental Marriage Styles and Family Forms in the 1970's."
7. Lester Velie, "The War on the American Family," *Reader's Digest*, January 1973, p. 106.

giveth thee" (Exod. 20:12), was accompanied by severe sanctions on those who disobeyed (Exod. 21:17; Deut. 21:18-20). R. W. Dale, in his treatise *The Ten Commandments*, explains the necessity of such sanctions: "If parental authority came to be generally disregarded, the whole structure of society would be dissolved. The discharge of filial duty was the condition of the permanence of national existence."[8]

As sexual sins are so very disruptive to family life, two of the commandments are prohibitions against such sins: the seventh, "Thou shalt not commit adultery," and part of the tenth, "thou shalt not covet thy neighbor's wife" (Exod. 20:14,17). Capital punishment was also meted out to those who transgressed the seventh commandment. Dale again writes,

> The dignity and sanctity of human nature, and the consequent inviolability of human life, are protected by a penalty, not less severe than that which vindicates the majesty of God and as there is a divine idea to be fulfilled in the relations between parents and children which makes the relationship sacred—as there is a Divine idea to be fulfilled in the character and history of every individual man which makes man and man's life sacred—so there is a Divine idea to be fulfilled in marriage, in all the offices of mutual love and service which it creates, and in all the happiness which it renders possible; and therefore marriage is sacred too.[9]

Additional safeguards for family life are found in the Levitical laws. Incest, homosexuality, and sexual relationships with members of the kin group are condemned in Leviticus 18:6-24. Prostitution is forbidden in Leviticus 19:29. In the following chapter, verse 10, the death penalty is reiterated as the judgment upon those guilty of adultery. The right of a pregnant woman to be protected from bodily harm is set forth in Exodus 21:22. Property rights of the family and the exhortation to care for widows and orphans are delineated in Exodus 22. There are many other laws regulating marriage and the family, and some of these have been codified to form the basis of civil and criminal laws in most Western nations.

THE SONG OF SOLOMON

Space does not permit the citing of many other Old Testament passages which support the thesis that marriage was originated by

8. R. W. Dale, *The Ten Commandments* (New York and London: Hodder and Stoughton, n.d.), p. 133.
9. Ibid., pp. 162-163.

God and has His divine approval. Nevertheless, some mention must be made of the Song of Solomon. Clarence Mason, Dean Emeritus of the Philadelphia College of the Bible, has stated that this exquisite gem of the Bible was written to show "God's approval of rapturous, blessed human relationships in marriage, and His disapproval of asceticism."[10] The book is a series of "love poems" describing true love between a bride and bridegroom. The book is difficult to understand since these poems are not in chronological order, but the reader who follows an outline such as that found in the *Pilgrim Bible* or the *New Scofield Reference Bible* will be highly rewarded.

The Song describes the bliss of love in terms that are offensive to some readers. Mason points out that the "problem of objectionable language is solved since the scenes described take place after marriage."[11] Solomon, in his wisdom and under the inscription of the Holy Spirit, has recorded for us the emotions that accompany true love. The inclusion of the Song of Solomon in the canon of sacred Scriptures (under the superintendency of the Holy Spirit) is God's seal of approval upon its contents. It is divine illustration of Solomon's exhortation in Ecclesiastes 9:9, "Live joyfully with the wife whom thou lovest all the days of the life of thy vanity."

The Song is also a picture of the love between Christ, the divine Bridegroom, and the church, the bride of Christ. One writer summarizes it as follows:

> Shall we not claim to trace, in the noble and gentle history thus presented, foreshadowings of the infinite condescensions of incarnate love?—that love which, first stooping in human form to visit us in our low estate in order to seek out and win its object (Ps. 136:23), and then raising along with itself a sanctified humanity to the heavenly places (Eph. 2:6), is finally awaiting there an invitation from the mystic bride to return to earth once more and seal the union for eternity (Rev. 22:17).[12]

CHRIST ON THE PERMANENCE OF MARRIAGE

When we turn to the New Testament, we discover that marriage, as God intended it, is reinforced by the teachings of the Lord Jesus Christ, as recorded in Matthew 19:3-6:

10. Sermon by Dr. Clarence Mason, Dean Emeritus of the Philadelphia College of the Bible, delivered at the Kamp Kidron Bible Conference, Kidron, Ohio, August 1971.
11. Ibid.
12. R. A. Redford, "Song of Solomon," *Pulpit Commentary* (London and New York: Funk and Wagnall's Co., 1909), p. XXII.

> *The Pharisees also came unto him, tempting him, and saying unto him, Is it lawful for a man to put away his wife for every cause?*
> *And he answered and said unto them, Have ye not read that he which made them at the beginning, made them male and female;*
> *And said, For this cause shall a man leave father and mother, and shall cleave to his wife, and they twain shall be one flesh?*
> *Wherefore they are no more twain, but one flesh. What, therefore, God hath joined together, let not man put asunder.*

Here Jesus repeats the words of Genesis 2:24 and adds the phrase so often used in our marriage ceremony, "What therefore God hath joined together, let not man put asunder." The corollary passages in the synoptic Gospels of Mark (10:1-12) and Luke (16:18) clearly denote the permanence of the monogamous marriage bond.

If these were the only references made by Christ concerning marriage, it would not be necessary to discuss divorce. Although the subject of divorce is treated in more detail in chapter 16, it will be helpful to point out that Jesus' remarks in Matthew 19 are made in answer to the question of the Pharisees, "Is it lawful for a man to put away his wife for every cause?" (v.3). Their response to His restatement of Genesis 2:24 was to point out that the Mosaic law permitted divorce. The Lord Jesus replied, "Moses, because of the hardness of your hearts suffered you to put away your wives, but from the beginning it was not so. And I say unto you, Whosoever shall put away his wife, except it be for fornication, and shall marry another, committeth adultery, and whosoever marrieth her which is put away doth commit adultery." The right of the so-called "innocent party" to secure a divorce and to remarry is deduced from this passage. In view of the emphasis put upon the permanence of the marriage bond, and the fact that the right of remarriage is not specifically stated here nor elsewhere in the New Testament, many Bible scholars reject this interpretation of the passage. They teach that this text along with many others prohibit divorce and remarriage for the Christian.

THE APOSTLE PAUL ON MARRIAGE

The apostle Paul certainly commended marriage, though there is some question as to whether he ever married. In Ephesians 5:22-33 he compares the union of husband and wife to that of the believer and Christ. It is interesting that Paul also quotes Genesis 2:24 to emphasize the oneness of husband and wife: "and they twain shall be one flesh." This passage clearly sets forth the proper role of the husband as head of the wife who lovingly submits to him because of his unselfish and wholehearted love for her. Then they both walk in complete loving submission to Christ as Head of the church.[13]

In I Corinthians 7 Paul approaches the marriage relationship from a practical viewpoint. The Corinthian believers had been saved out of a culture that practiced immorality as part of the pagan temple worship. In chapter 6:9-20 Paul deals with the problems of fornication and adultery, stating that the Christian's body is a temple of the Holy Spirit and as such should be kept pure and holy. He proceeds in chapter 7 to point out that one way to avoid fornication is for each person to have a spouse, and to enjoy sexual relationships within marriage. The partners are not to withhold themselves from each other except it be with mutual consent, so that there will be no temptation to commit adultery.

In view of such statements, it is difficult to see how some scholars believe that Paul exalted the state of celibacy. Robert C. Williamson writes, " . . . both Jesus and Paul preached the necessity of celibacy. Physical pleasures, including sex, were not deemed worthy of the good life." [14] It is true that our Lord Jesus in Matthew 19:12 speaks of those who "have made themselves eunuchs for the kingdom of heaven's sake," indicating that some individuals forego marriage in order to do the will of God; but He does not imply this is the norm for all believers or even for Christian workers. This same truth is expressed by Paul in I Corinthians 7:8, where he writes, "I say therefore to the unmarried and widows, It is good for them if they abide even as I," and in verse 32, "He that is unmarried careth for the things that belong to the Lord, how he may please the Lord." It is a fact that single persons do not have many of the distractions that married couples do, and many such individuals have rendered great service to the Church of Christ. However, the late P. B. Fitzwater, Professor of Theology at Moody Bible Institute for many years, used to draw attention to verse 26: "I suppose therefore that this is good for the present distress, I say, that it is good for a man so to be." The phrase "present distress" is the key to interpreting the entire chapter. The Corinthians were undergoing persecution, and in such circumstances the unmarried individual had definite advantages over the family person. A similar situation existed in the present generation when Communists in the Congo persecuted and martyred Christians for their belief in Christ. Entire congregations had to flee to the

---

13. The subject of proper role concepts is amplified in Chapter 3.

14. Robert C. Williamson, *Marriage and Family Relations* (New York: John Wiley & Sons, 1966), p. 30.

"bush" and hide for their lives. Certainly those families with children had a more difficult time eluding the enemy than the unmarried.

Charles Hodge in his great commentary on First Corinthians also held that this passage must be interpreted in the light of the situation that prevailed for the Corinthian church:

> If these verses and others of like import, are to be understood of men generally, and not of men in the peculiar circumstances of the early Christians, then it must be admitted that Paul depreciates marriage, and that he represents it as scarcely having any higher end than the sexual intercourse of brutes. This cannot be his meaning; not only because it is contrary to Scripture, but also because Paul elsewhere, in Ephesians 5:22-33, represents marriage as a most ennobling spiritual union; which raises a man out of himself and makes him live for another. . . . Marriage . . . does for man in the sphere of nature, what union with Christ does for him in the sphere of grace. The truth is that the apostle writes to the Corinthians as he would to an army about to enter on a most unequal conflict in an enemy's country, and for a protracted period. He tells them, "This is no time for you to think of marriage. You have a right to marry. But in your circumstances marriage can only lead to embarrassment and increase of suffering."[15]

Additional passages could be cited to show that the Bible stresses the divine origin of marriage and the family.

The Christian family has undergone periods of great persecution and stress in previous eras and has emerged victorious. First John 4:4 states, "Ye are of God, little children, and have overcome them: because greater is he that is in you, than he that is in the world." In the light of such a promise, we can predict that the Christian family will overcome every assault against it and fulfill God's plan for this age.

15. Charles Hodge, *First Epistle to the Corinthians* (New York: Robert Carter and Bros., 1878), pp. 111-112.

QUESTIONS FOR DISCUSSION AND REVIEW

1. What Scripture references, other than those cited in the chapter, support the view that marriage is ordained by God?

2. What alternatives to marriage are being encouraged by certain groups in society?

3. What evidence do evolutionists present for their explanation of the origin of the family?

4. What effect did the fall of man have on the relationship of Adam and Eve?

5. Give Scriptural evidence for the statement, "Sex is a gift of God."

6. Why was the transgression of the fifth and seventh commandments punishable by death?

7. What are the themes of the Song of Solomon?

8. Discuss the phrase, "What therefore God hath joined together, let no man put asunder" (Matt. 19:6).

9. How does the present moral state of American society compare with that of the Corinthian society of Paul's time?

10. What are the arguments for and against celibacy for Christians?

2

SOCIAL CHANGE
AND THE CHRISTIAN FAMILY

. . . He changeth the times and the seasons. . .
Daniel 2:21

The Christian family is not immune to cultural forces which have effected great changes in American society in the last century. In order to successfully play their respective roles, young people need to know how the family structure has been and is being influenced by these forces.

URBANIZATION AND CHANGES IN THE FAMILY

These influences may be listed in general as urbanization, industrialization, and secularization. Herman R. Lantz and Eloise C. Snyder speak of urbanism as a cultural influence and then list five sociohistoric factors—secularism, humanism, democracy, female emancipation, and the American frontier.[1]

Lacy Hall in an article on "Changing Homes, Changing Nation," cites eleven different forces that have helped to change American families. In addition to urbanization, he writes of mobility, working wives, family size, sexual promiscuity, early marriage, divorce, schooling, senior citizens, leisure, and changing roles.[2] Thus, the lists

---

1. Herman R. Lantz and Eloise C. Snyder, *Marriage* (New York: John Wiley & Sons, Inc., 1962), p. 24.
2. Lacy Hall, "Changing Homes, Changing Nation," *The Marriage Affair*, J. Allan Petersen, ed. (Wheaton: Tyndale House Publishers, 1971), pp. 235-240.

differ, depending on the perspective of the writer. Nevertheless, certain factors are generally accepted by most scholars. A few of these will be amplified in the following pages.

America has changed from a rural to an urban society within the last century, due to the rapid growth of industry. As factories multiplied, many of the needed workers came from the rural areas. As Robert F. Winch states, "In the forty-nine years from 1920 through 1968 the total population of the United States nearly doubled; during the same interval the number of people on farms shrank by two-thirds, with the consequence that the farm population diminished proportionally from 30 percent of the total in 1920 to 5 percent in 1968."[3] They moved from the villages and towns, where religious and primary group controls were strong, to the cities and suburbs, where secular and weak secondary group controls predominated. Inevitable modifications of family life took place.

In the city crowded living conditions replace the spaciousness of the country. Families are housed in small homes and apartments with little rooms and little or no privacy. A tour of the countryside in the East or Midwest, where many of the large old farm houses still stand, graphically illustrates the change. Many of these homes have five bedrooms to accommodate the large number of children plus a "hired man." Children were an economic asset because of the labor they provided as they grew up. In the city they are a liability, so families tend to become smaller. On the farm the family worshiped, worked, and played together, but in the city their activities are fragmented to the extent that each member goes his own way. The church ceased to be the center of religious and recreational activity. Instead of attending a covered-dish supper at the church, Dad has his bowling game, Mom her PTA meeting, sister her Campfire Girls pow-wow, and brother his Boy Scouts meeting. The city churches develop activities for the various age groups so that there are few times when the family functions as a unit. This is true in most churches today where there are Women's Missionary Societies, Men's Missionary Societies, Boy's Brigade, Pioneer Girls, Awana Clubs, and athletic teams for the men and boys, etc.

Opportunities where the family can work together are few. Occasionally there are small businesses such as the neighborhood grocery store, where each member can share in its operation. More often the father performs some specialized work in a factory which fails to provide any opportunity for family togetherness as the farm did

3. Robert F. Winch, *The Modern Family* (New York: Holt, Rinehart and Winston, Inc., 1971), p. 86.

when the sons helped dad in its operation. Even today in many situations such as apartment living, there are no "chores" for the boys to perform. With automatic dishwashers more common, tasks around the home are not too numerous for girls either.

This specialization of labor proved to be particularly valuable as craft and labor unions arose to gain increased wages and benefits for their members. As wages and salaries increase, so does the standard of living, accompanied by a growth in a materialistic philosophy of life. Though this philosophy has spread to our rural areas today, its major impact is on the city dweller.

American materialism puts greater emphasis on material possessions than on spiritual values and ideals. It is perhaps epitomized by the "American Dream," which seems to entitle every family to a split-level home, a new car (or perhaps two), and an eighteen-foot boat with trailer. The fact that both parents have to work, or that father must "moonlight" by working a second job, while children are raised by baby sitters, does not seem too important as long as the "American Dream" is realized.

This materialism is encouraged by high pressure advertising and easy credit. Vance Packard writes that advertisers "sometimes playfully call themselves 'merchants of discontent.' They talk profoundly of the 'upgrading urge' of people, and search for appeals that will tap that urge."[4] After the "urge to buy" has been generated, then the "easy credit" system makes it possible for the family to purchase the new product even if their budget cannot afford it. One of the greatest challenges facing Christian families today is finding the balance between material and spiritual values.

URBANIZATION AND ROLE CHANGES

One of the most important effects in this shift from rural to urban living has been on the roles played by husband and wife. In the agrarian society, these roles were clearly defined. The husband was usually the authority in the family, and quite often used his power in a dictatorial manner. His word was law and he demanded unquestioned obedience from wife and children. Family members subordinated their desires to the needs of the family. It was impossible for an intelligent young man to leave the farm to study medicine if the father decided he was needed to help keep the farm operating. Even

4. Vance Packard, *The Status Seekers* (New York: Pocket Books, Inc., 1959), p. 272.

though the wife rebelled against her husband, she stayed with him "for the sake of the children," because she had no other means of support, and divorce was taboo.[5]

This situation changes when the family moves to town. Girls receive more education, and more women are working outside the home. This source of income makes them more independent, so the wife no longer feels it necessary to remain in an incompatible union. She can now work and care for her children. The number of divorces increases and divorce becomes more acceptable, since the individual is not known by too many people in the city. There is no longer the primary group pressure of, "What will the relatives and neighbors think?" because they are separated from the kin group and often they do not know their neighbors! The authoritarianism of the father is replaced by democratic individualism, whereby each member of the family becomes important as a person and has a part in determining his future and that of the family.

It is often necessary for the wife and mother to seek employment to augment the family income so that they can maintain the standard of living dictated by the materialistic society. This trend has continued so that today 53 percent of all married women are employed outside the home. Unfortunately, "over one-half of all mothers with children under eighteen are working."[6] Although many of these working mothers are very conscientious in attempting to provide adequate care for their children, many are left without supervision. Between 1975 and 1983 the ranks of working mothers with children under six swelled from 38.9 percent to 50.5 percent.[7] The social problems created by working mothers and unsupervised children help to create the demand for the government to provide day care centers on a nationwide scale.[8] Many Christian homes are experiencing difficulties because of a mother who's absent when the children need her. Even churches must face the issue of whether the pastor's wife should be allowed to take either full or part-time employment.

5. Gail Putney Fullerton, *Survival in Marriage* (New York: Holt Rinehart & Winston, Inc., 1971), p. 18.
6. *Information Please Almanac*, (New York: Houghton-Mifflin Co., 1985), p. 59.
7. Ibid.
8. Report on the White House Conference on Children, *Behavior Today*, December 28, 1970, p. 4.

GEOGRAPHIC MOBILITY AND THE FAMILY

Another change affecting the family is the increasing amount of geographical mobility since the Great Depression. During those difficult years families began to move in search of employment. This trend was accelerated by World War II and continues, with approximately 20 percent of American families moving each year. The result is a "generation without roots," since children grow up in families that move every two or three years. They never have an opportunity really to know their relatives, nor to establish lasting relationships with neighborhood or peer groups. In rural society, if one parent were missing, there were the members of a close-knit kin group with which the child could identify. Today, large numbers of boys are raised by widowed or divorced mothers, without male models from which the growing boy can learn his masculine roles. "The father is the primary male model for his young son," and if the father is missing from the family it is most difficult for the boy to learn his male role.[9] Constant moving also makes for insecurity in the child's personality, and may account for many of the maladjusted children receiving treatment in child guidance centers and mental health clinics.

This isolation from the kin group through mobility means that the marital partners are forced to depend more heavily upon each other for fulfillment of emotional needs. The wife cannot run home to mother whenever there is a disagreement, nor can the husband consult with his father whenever he faces a major decision. Each move of the family from one community to another, results in a period of time when the partners have only each other until new friends are made. Thus, the family that has to change residence frequently because of the father's occupation has added dimensions of stress and will have to work harder to make the marriage a success. This includes Christian businessmen, pastors, missionaries, Christian education directors, and others whose employment requires mobility for promotion, or to fulfill the will of God for their lives.

SECULARISM AND THE FAMILY

A major influence on the American family is secularism, defined by Webster as "a system of doctrines and practices that rejects any

---

9. Fullerton, *Survival in Marriage* p. 150. The absence of male models may be part of the explanation for the tendency of many rebellious young men to grow long hair, wear beads, carry purses, and exhibit other feminine traits.

form of religious faith and worship." American society is gradually becoming more secular in attitude and practice. Christianity no longer has the predominance that it once enjoyed in the home, school, and church, the major institutions of socialization.

Robin M. Williams, Jr., writes "A broad hypothesis worthy of intensive study, is that the main result of modern secularization of organized religion is the destruction of the belief in a transcendental being, which removes both the supernatural sanctions for our ethical system and a central value focus for the established beliefs."[10] This means that in a secular society the authority of the Biblical norms is rejected, for men establish their own standards of behavior. Usually these are different from, and often opposed to, those of the revealed Word of God.

Values surrounding the family and sexual behavior are changing. Monogamous marriage as instituted by God is rejected, and divorce is widely accepted by the secularist.

The so-called sexual revolution attempts "to free from any penalty any and all sexual relations between freely consenting adults."[11] The interpretation of such a norm of the "new morality" is most difficult. For example, Carle C. Zimmerman asks,

> ... *what is a free consenting adult*? [italics his] If he is a husband or she is a wife, or either is a parent, or an adult child (over sixteen years of age) then can the individual be a free consenter? .... To take a most extreme case, why should a man, who as a freely consenting adult can do as he wishes, not expect the same rights to apply to his wife, to his sixteen year old son or daughter, his young father or even his mother?"[12]

The secular view of man and society, with its denial of Biblical moral authority and the sinful nature of man, makes possible such changes as the sexual revolution of the "new morality," the "situation ethics" of Joseph Fletcher, and the hedonistic "Playboy Philosophy" of Hugh Hefner.[13] The demands of the radical feminists of the Women's Liberation Movement for the legalization of abortion and the abolition of marriage can only occur in a secular society.[14]

10. Robin M. Williams, Jr., *American Society* (New York: Alfred A. Knopf, 1960), p. 347.
11. Carle C. Zimmerman, "The Future of the Family in America," *Journal of Marriage and the Family*, May 1972, p. 324.
12. Ibid.
13. See Fritz Ridenour, *It All Depends* (Glendale, CA: G/L Publications, 1969) for a "Comparison of situation ethics and the Playboy philosophy with what the Bible teaches about morality."
14. Betty Friedan, "Our Revolution Is Unique," *Voices of the New Feminism* ed. Mary Lou Thompson (Boston: Beacon Press, 1970), pp. 31-43.

The believer in Bible prophecy is not surprised to see these trends in society. The apostle Paul wrote in II Timothy 3:1-5:

> *This know also, that in the last days perilous times shall come.*
> *For men shall be lovers of their own selves, covetous, boasters, proud, blasphemers, disobedient to parents, unthankful, unholy, Without natural affection, trucebreakers, false accusers, incontinent, fierce, despisers of those that are good,*
> *Traitors, heady, high-minded, lovers of pleasures more than lovers of God,*
> *Having a form of godliness, but denying the power of it; from such turn away.*

ADDITIONAL CULTURAL INFLUENCES

Many other cultural changes affecting the American family could be described. Governmental policies concerning the family such as Aid to Dependent Children certainly have both beneficial and detrimental effects.[15] The shortened work week, greater amount of leisure time, and the increase in disposable family income provide for new occupations and patterns of family recreational activities.[16]

The increasing number of high school graduates taking advantage of the expanding opportunities for higher education results in a large number of marriages subsidized by parents. Zimmerman makes the point that this generation is different from previous ones in that it must help the children through high school and college. This means that by the time the last child is through college the parents do not have enough time to save for their retirement. This factor coupled with that of inflation, results in financial difficulties in their old age.[17]

Retirement and old age are posing problems peculiar to this generation. Those now retiring passed through the difficult years of the Great Depression of the thirties. Many have not been able to provide adequately for their declining years. One writer asserts

> ...we are now in a period of transition. A system in which the responsibility for the care of the aged rested with the family has now changed to one in which the responsibility rests either with the individual himself, by "planning for retirement," or with the state.

15. Winch, *Modern Family* pp. 93-94.
16. Richard L. Roe, from CRM Books, *Society Today*, copyright 1971 by Ziff-Davis Publishing Co., p. 190. Used by permission.
17. Zimmerman, "Future of the Family," p. 323.

In the meantime, the present generation of aged persons and that about to retire are caught between the expectations they held in their own youth and the expectations of their children and grand-children.[18]

Today's care of aged parents, including adequate housing and health care, represents one of the more significant changes in the family patterns in this century.

THE CHRISTIAN FAMILY IN SECULAR SOCIETY

The secular home may be simply defined as one which pays no attention to God. The members simply leave Him out of their individual lives, and He receives no recognition in the activities of the family. Home life is conducted as though God does not exist.

The only time God and the church are thought of is at a time a pastor is needed to perform a wedding or a funeral. With the increase in humanism, more individuals are even omitting these ceremonies. A justice of the peace takes care of the wedding, and the funeral is eliminated by cremation of the body, or by giving the body to a medical school. Judged by these criteria, many American homes could be classified as secular.

Unfortunately, many nominal Christian homes are not much different from their secular neighbors. When members of a college class in Marriage and the Family were asked to tell how their homes differed from the unsaved family next door, one young man wrote:

> My parents are both professing Christians, but the only difference between them and the next door neighbors is that my parents do attend church regularly on Sunday morning. They do not feel any obligation to be present at the evening service nor on Wednesday night unless it is a very special occasion. I do not know if they have private devotions, but we have never had worship together as a family. Several times we have started saying grace before meals, yet it has never become established as a regular practice. One more thing. My folks don't swear, drink, or smoke, and the neighbors do.[19]

This young man did not find his home too different from the secular home next door.

18. Roe, *Society Today*, p. 35. Used by permission. See also pages 59-60.

19. Anonymous male response to the question, "How does your home differ from the unsaved family next door?" in Marriage and Family class, Cedarville College, March 30, 1972.

Most of the responses to the question were positive. The following answers are those of two young women:

> *The relationship between my father and mother is such that my father is head of the house and God is the head of his life. Because he is guided by the Lord, the decisions he makes are usually right. My mother is submissive to my father and even though he is the head, he loves and takes care of his family well and uses his authority with love and guidance from the Lord.*

> *Our home life is different from that of a family of non-Christians because we have a basic trust and personal relationship with Christ. Because of this our language is different, our habits are different also. More than this there is a stronger bond between our family which helps us to meet and defeat trials and temptations which come along. Christ is the head of our household and has His protecting hand on all of our family. I personally feel that if more families had a Christian basis, there would be less homes splitting up and more homes being truly happy.*[20]

The responses of these young women indicate that they come from homes that are truly Christian, whose secular neighbors are able to see visual evidence of Christianity as it applies to family life.

The gist of the seventy-four responses identify a truly Christian home as one marked by a quality of life and of love (for the Lord and each family member) that makes the marriage relationship and home distinctively different from the secular home. Students sense a bond between their parents and themselves that is missing in the home next door. This bond of love for the Lord Jesus manifests itself in various ways: harmonious family relationships, family worship, regular church attendance, active witness to friends and neighbors, and service to the Lord in the local church.

The Christian family faces many difficulties in a rapidly changing secular society as it seeks to live for Christ and establish a strong Christian home. The testimonies of these young people reared in godly homes show that it can be done. Although society may become more decadent each passing day, the couple has all the resources of the supernaturally inspired Word of God and the supernatural power of His indwelling Holy Spirit to enable them to build a Christian home that glorifies the Heavenly Father.

---

20. Anonymous female responses, Questionnaire, Cedarville College, March 30, 1972.

QUESTIONS FOR DISCUSSION AND REVIEW

1. How does life in your family today differ from that of your grandparents when they were your age?

2. Discuss the statement, "Children are an economic liability today."

3. In what ways has the "American Dream" affected the average Christian home?

4. How has the changing role of women in American society affected the stability and permanence of marriage?

5. List and discuss some effects of geographical mobility on the average American family.

6. What effects has secularism had on the American family?

7. What is the basic difference between secularism and theism?

8. How has the expansion of opportunities for higher education affected the young family and the parental family?

9. Contrast a secular home with a truly Christian home.

10. How can a Christian young person utilize a knowledge of the changes in American family structure to increase his opportunities for success in his own family living?

3

REQUIREMENTS FOR
A SUCCESSFUL
CHRISTIAN MARRIAGE

Submitting yourselves one to another
in the fear of God
Ephesians 5:21

The guests at a wedding reception usually admire first the beauty and then the taste of the bridal cake. Pictures are made as the couple make the first cut. No one would be foolish enough to say that such a beautiful creation just "happened." They know that the necessary ingredients are blended in the correct proportions and then baked. After this, it is decorated by skillful hands before the final product is ready for display. Yet many a couple cuts the wedding cake and have not given as much thought to what is required to create a lovely marriage relationship as the baker has given to producing the cake. There are certain prerequisites necessary if young people expect to achieve the greatest success in their marriage. The spiritual, physical, and emotional elements of each partner are blended together so that the "two become one" in Christ.[1]

FOUR CRITERIA OF SUCCESS

Successful marriage in our culture is usually gauged by the amount of "happiness" that the relationship brings to the individual partners. Marriage for any other reason than to bring happiness is frowned

1. Mike Mason, *The Mystery of Marriage* (Portland, OR: Multnomah Press, 1985), p. 71.

upon by most Americans. If a great amount of "happiness" ensues, then the marriage is termed successful. On the other hand, if "unhappiness" results from the union, then the marriage is judged a failure, and at least one partner will usually seek a divorce.

Happiness is a difficult term to define since it refers to a subjective emotional state, "a feeling of great pleasure, contentment, etc." *(Webster's Dictionary)*. An event or experience which brings pleasure to one partner may be interpreted differently by the other; hence, happiness at best is a relative term. However we define it in marriage, there are those pleasant experiences, cumulative in nature, which give a positive emotional response that is called happiness, so that we term the relationship a "happy" one. When the unpleasant experiences which give a negative emotional response accumulate, then unhappiness results and the relationship is a failure.[2] This is true not only in marital unions, but in any other human relationship, such as those of student-teacher, employee-employer, or pastor-parishioner.

In earlier days, marriage did not demand as much emotional satisfaction from the partners, as there were other criteria by which to judge the success of the relationship.[3] The wife was very much concerned about the ability of the husband to provide for the family, and if he succeeded well in this role, his failure to provide personal happiness was overlooked. The husband wanted a wife who would be a good housekeeper and a good mother to rear his children. If she succeeded in these areas, the marriage was still a success. As seen from the changes in the family described in chapter 2, these basic roles of husband and wife have been altered. The wife can now be a breadwinner and the husband can hire a babysitter.

These changes, plus the Hollywood emphasis on romantic love, mean that if happiness is lost, the marriage is a failure and the couple will divorce. Paul Popenoe writes, "Much of the failure of marriage is based on the adolescent type of fantasy, well named Romantic Infantilism by the psychologist."[4] Such easy abrogation of marriage vows is contrary to the Bible, yet our Christian young people are succumbing to this secular view. It is true that they expect happiness from marriage and should experience it. But it is not true that because they encounter periods of strain and unhappiness, they are free to break the relationship. Most marriages face

---

2. J. L. Hirning and Alma L. Hirning, *Marriage Adjustment* (New York: American Book Co., 1956), p. 7.

3. Robert O. Blood, Jr., *Marriage* (New York: Free Press of Glencoe, 1962), p. 9.

4. Louis H. Evans, *Your Marriage—Duel or Duet* (Old Tappan, NJ: Fleming H. Revell Co., 1962), p. 10. The statement quoted is by Dr. Paul Popenoe who wrote the introduction for this excellent little book.

these unpleasant periods, and it is then that the resources of God's Word, prayer, and godly counseling should be utilized.

Any problem in Christian marriage is capable of solution if the couple will sincerely seek the help of God. As one writer asserts, ". . . there is no necessity for marriage failure. God has given us the responsibility and the spiritual resources to carry it out."[5] When a Christian marriage does fail, it is usually because one or both partners are so backslidden they do not respond to the Holy Spirit's workings. Many times the difficulties arise because the couple have not really considered what it takes to make a successful marriage, and do not realize that a real effort must be made to blend these ingredients into a harmonious relationship.

In addition to happiness and a permanent union, a third criterion of success in a Christian marriage is how well the couple performs the will of God for their relationship. This again is a subjective measurement that each couple must make for themselves. From God's view marriage is not successful simply because a couple enjoys a measure of happiness; God judges how well they complete the life plan He reveals to them. Ephesians 2:10 reads, "For we are his workmanship, created in Christ Jesus unto good works, which God hath before ordained [planned] that we should walk in them." This does not mean that all are to engage in full-time Christian service, but to find the plan of God and to do the will of God should be the supreme desire of every couple who follow Chirst. He is to be Head of the home and at His judgment seat an accounting will be made by every husband and wife, in relation to His will.

A fourth criterion for successful marriage has been suggested in recent years. David Olsen states,

> Increasingly, individuals are seeking a relationship that will provide growth for them as individuals and as a couple. . . . Ideally, the successful marriage is seen as a relationship context in which growth and development of both partners is facilitated to a greater extent than it could be for either of these individuals outside the relationship. . . . Ironically, most couples have been unable to achieve this type of relationship.[6]

Olsen says they fail because of inability to relate in a "meaningful way" or because one partner experiences greater growth which leads to frustration in the relationship.

5. J. Allen Petersen, "Opportunity Unlimited," *The Marriage Affair*, J. Allen Petersen, ed. (Wheaton, IL: Tyndale House Publishers, 1971). p. 8.
6. David H. Olsen, "Marriage of the Future: Revolutionary or Evolutionary Change?" *The Family Coordinator*, October 1972, p. 390.

However, as a couple seek the plan of God for their lives, they often discover that His plan includes growth and stimulation in other areas, such as the intellectual. For some this may mean more formal education in a college or university. For others, it may mean attending evening classes of a local Bible institute. The growth of community colleges and adult education classes provide many opportunities for learning in a wide diversity of subjects at very little cost. Correspondence courses and educational television classes are available for those who cannot leave home.[7] Public libraries have a wealth of information available for those who like to read. The local newspaper and a weekly news magazine help to keep a couple informed on current events.

A Christian couple active in a local church and in the community have many opportunities for social development. Sometimes one partner is more outgoing or has more capable leadership qualities than the other. In this situation the less favored person can grow through the emotional support given to the more active spouse. The latter must guard against becoming so involved that he or she neglects to provide adequate opportunities to participate in social events with the mate.

Christian marriage offers the greatest potential for growth and fulfillment. "It is not like a coat that is put on, but like a flower that grows. . . The art of marriage, it has been said, is in maintaining equilibrium through the various changes and adjustments of life together."[8] As the couple submit to the Lordship of Christ in their lives, they can experience the richness of His grace in every area of their relationship.

NECESSITY OF THE NEW BIRTH

Certain requirements must be met if the couple are to have a successful Christian marriage. The first of these is that both individuals must be born again. They must experience the new birth as described in John 3:5,7: "Jesus answered and said unto him [Nicodemus], Verily, verily, I say unto thee, Except a man be born

---

7. Clyde M. Narramore, *A Woman's World* (Grand Rapids: Zondervan Publishing House, 1963), pp. 12-22. These pages suggest several ways in which the Christian woman can grow intellectually and aesthetically.

8. G. R. Slater, "When the Wine Runs Out," *Marriage Is for Living*, Bruce Larson, ed. (Grand Rapids, Zondervan Publishing House, 1968), p. 59.

again, he cannot see the kingdom of God. . . . Marvel not that I said unto you, Ye must be born again." Jack Wyrtzen says:

> God does not bless marriages unless they are between believers. Centuries ago Joshua warned against marriage with unbelievers. He told the Israelites that if they married unbelievers, the unbeliever would be "a snare and trap unto you, and a scourge in your sides, and thorns in your eyes. . ." (Josh. 23:13). I don't care how pretty she may be, or attentive he may be during the courtship, the unbeliever will pull one way when the Christian wants to go the opposite way. I warn you![9]

Both partners may be religious and attend church regularly and theirs may be called a Christian marriage, but it cannot be that in reality if they are not born again. This type of relationship will be more successful than that of a nonchurch going couple, but they will miss the joy and blessing that comes only from knowing the Lord Jesus Christ as a personal Savior.

Personal relationship to Christ is merely the beginning, for the couple who desires the most happiness in marriage should also be consecrated to God. This means that each individual surrenders himself to God and sincerely seeks to do the will of God in the marriage relationship. This is very important because a disparity in the degree of submission to God can cause great unhappiness. Consider the case of Joe and Jane:

> *Joe (25 years) and Jane (24 years) met in the local church in the young people's meeting. They both came from nominal Christian homes, had been baptized as teenagers, and regularly attended church. However, Jane seemed more inclined toward spiritual things than did John. He had agreed they would have a Christian home, but a few months after the marriage, he became lax in attending church services and did not wish to lead in family devotions. At the same time, Jane was faithful in hearing the Word preached, received it with faith, and grew in grace and knowledge of the Lord Jesus. The spiritual gulf widened between them until it affected other areas of the relationship.[10]*

It is easy to see that although both were saved, the unhappiness in this home occurred because Jane did not wait for a mate who had the same degree of consecration that marked her life.

9. Jack Wyrtzen, *Sex is Not Sinful* (Grand Rapids: Zondervan Publishing House, 1970), pp. 45-46. Used by permission.
10. The names and facts have been altered in order to disguise the identity in all case histories used in this text.

IMPORTANCE OF PERSONALITY COMPATIBILITY

Good basic character and personality certainly are necessary. All saved and consecrated young people do not have the same characteristics. It is important to remember that personalities can be changed, but it does take a great amount of self-effort to effect any desired change. By the time a person reaches marriage age, the personality and its patterns are pretty well fixed.

Judson T. and Mary G. Landis affirm the following:

> The wedding does not change basic personality structure... It is true that a good marriage promotes growth in both partners, so that over a period of time, people do change in many ways, but probably not in the kinds of ways that a hopeful fiancee may have in mind.... The growth changes that occur under the impact of a good marriage will be gradual and will require time, sometimes a lifetime. The changes will also tend to go in the directions and remain within the limits set ... by the early developmental experience of each person. For this reason people choosing mates need to be alert to traits of marriageability or unmarriageability already developed in themselves and others, for such traits are significant indications concerning the potential quality of a future marriage.[11]

Any girl who marries a fellow with the idea she will change undesirable traits after the ceremony, is inviting disaster. If a person is not honest and trustworthy, the words of the marriage ritual will not change him. If a young woman is self-centered and vain during courtship, she will continue these traits into marriage. If a person is loose with the truth while dating, the same behavior can be expected later. The individual who is not concerned about his dress or is slovenly in his speech will be the same person unless some miracle happens. The girl who is shy and afraid of her own voice will not become the life of the party simply because she marries. The young man who is careless in handling his money, or who exhibits instability by failure to hold a steady job, can be expected to behave the same way after the ceremony. It is very important that a young person seek a mate with sound character and a personality that complements his own if he wishes the greatest happiness in his marriage.

J. L. and Alma Hirning in their book *Marriage Adjustment* write, "Permanency of marriage ... depends increasingly upon the judgment of the two persons involved, and success or failure in marriage

---

11. Judson T. Landis and Mary G. Landis, *Building a Successful Marriage* (Englewood Cliffs, NJ: Prentice Hall, Inc., 1968), p. 95. Used by permission.

is becoming a personal responsibility. This fact becomes highly significant when it is realized how adequate personal adjustment is increasingly required to meet the demands of modern marriage." [12] Since marriage does place such great demands upon the personalities involved, it is incumbent upon each Christian young person to develop the personality to the best of his ability.

"Personality Inventories" are found at the end of several chapters to encourage the reader to assess the level of his development. Areas of weakness discovered through the use of these "Inventories" can be strengthened through diligent effort and the wise use of spiritual resources. Henry P. Brandt suggests the daily use of the Bible for personal development:

> The writer to the Hebrews describes the Bible as a "discerner of the thoughts and intents of the heart" (Heb. 4:12). Approaching it with this attitude, you will be guided by the Bible into finding and maintaining a realistic understanding of yourself, your attitudes, thoughts, feelings and desires. The psalmist expresses the attitude that leads to understanding of self: Search me, O God, and know my heart: try me, and know my thoughts: and see if there be any wicked way in me, and lead me in the way everlasting. (Ps. 139:23-24). [13]

INFLUENCES OF THE CULTURAL BACKGROUND

A common cultural background is another requirement for a successful Christian marriage. The challenge to partners in marriage is to harmonize the individual personalities so that the majority of emotional responses from their interaction are pleasurable. The honeymoon period (usually the first year) is a time when many of the adjustments are made. It is axiomatic that the fewer the differences in backgrounds, the fewer the adjustments in marriage. Conversely, the greater the differences, the more numerous the adjustments that will need to be made. Other things being equal, the differences to be resolved will be fewer and the marriage happier when backgrounds are more nearly homogeneous.

Many elements constitute the cultural background. One of the greatest influences is the economic or social class level. In spite of the widespread popular belief that America is classless or that 90 percent

12. Hirning and Hirning, *Marriage Adjustments*, p. 13.
13. Henry P. Brandt and Homer E. Dowdy, *Building a Christian Home* (Wheaton: Scripture Press Publications, Inc., 1960), p. 31. Used by permission.

of the population are middle class, our country does have a highly stratified society.[14] Each stratum is characterized by its own speech, dress, lifestyle, and value patterns. The general rule is that the greater the distance that divides the individuals on the social scale, the more difficult the adjustments. Robert C. Williamson states, "Subcultures of class, religion, and national background operate to draw individuals apart. If class boundaries, for instance, fade in the moonlight, they are plainly visible the next morning. These subcultures are fortified by parents and peers."[15] Richard H. Klemer cites the research of Ernest Burgess and Leonard Cottrell, who "stated that the more similar the spouses were in social-class background, the better their marital adjustment would be." Later studies by Julius Roth and Robert Peck came to the same conclusion.[16] Popular literature likes to dwell on the rich upper-class man marrying the poor girl from the other side of the tracks, but in real life this type of union does not succeed very well.

Most Christians are found in the middle or working class, and our churches and Christian schools and colleges often reflect such stratification. A fellow and girl who meet at a Christian college are generally of the same socio-economic level. However, there are exceptions: Christian young people from upper-middle-class homes often attend a Christian college, and with the extension of higher education to lower-income groups, there is an increasing number of Christian young people from this group who enroll in Christian colleges. If young people are aware of these class differences and values, and have a knowledge of their very pervasive influence on human behavior, they can marry across class lines and make the necessary compromises to achieve happiness.

NECESSITY FOR SIMILAR EDUCATIONAL EXPERIENCES

The educational level of the partners should be similar, for any great disparity can create problems. The girl with only a high school education and the fellow with a college degree have different experiences, and there will be many parts of his life that she cannot enter into because she has not attended college. It is very rare for a woman with a college education to marry a man who has had only a high

14. Jack L. Roach, Llewellyn Gross, and Orville R. Gursslin, *Social Stratification in the U.S.* (Englewood Cliffs, NJ: Prentice-Hall, Inc., 1969), p. 154.
15. Robert C. Williams, *Marriage and Family Relations* (New York: John Wiley & Sons, Inc., 1966), p. 312.
16. Richard H. Klemer, *Marriage and Family Relationships* (New York: Harper & Row, 1970), p. 99.

school education. A study made in Madison, Wisconsin, "discovered that 67 percent of the grooms and 87 percent of the brides with some college education had married college educated partners." [17] When a girl does marry a person with less education, and happiness results, it is because the wife is very careful to encourage the husband and not flount her educational superiority. One college student described such a relationship when he wrote the following about his parents' difference in education:

> *My father is a mechanic who graduated from high school. My mother not only has her bachelor's degree but also a master's degree in education. She is a principal of an elementary school. My parents get along very well. Father runs the garage and mother does the bookkeeping for him. A stranger observing their interaction would never know my mother has a master's degree.*

One problem encountered on college and university campuses today is the "intellectual gulf" that occurs when the couple get married at the end of the freshman or sophomore year, with the wife dropping out to help support the husband in his studies. Quite often this aid includes not only the bachelor's degree, but also the master's and doctor's degrees. Unless the young wife continues to read and keep herself informed in her husband's field, it is not too long before she is unable to communicate with him in his area of specialization. Propinquity puts him in contact with attractive single women who are in his classes and who talk his language. All too often triangular affairs develop and the poor wife who slaved to put her husband through college and graduate school is divorced, and he marries the girl with the M.A. or the Ph.D. This does not mean that all wives to be successful need an M.A. or Ph. D., but it does mean that the wife who drops out will have to make extra effort to keep herself informed so that she can communicate with her husband about his work. Certainly the pleasurable emotional responses will be greater in the relationship if she manifests an interest and understanding of the demands and pressures to which he is subjected each day.

RELIGION AND THE CHOICE OF A MARRIAGE PARTNER

Similarity of religious home life can contribute much to the happiness of a marriage. Preferably, a young person should look for a mate within his own denomination. While it is true that saved young

17. William M. Kephart, *The Family, Society, and the Individual* (Boston: Houghton-Mifflin Co., 1966), p. 274.

people from different denominations have many common beliefs, they also have some very real denominational distinctives. A couple may agree on the new birth but hold widely varying views regarding such doctrines as baptism, church government, eternal security, or others. These difficulties are avoided if marriage is within the denomination.[18] Again, marriage may take place across denominational lines, but the individuals will have to work harder to make it a success.

FAMILY SIZE AND COMPATIBILITY OF MARRIAGE PARTNERS

Ordinarily, a young person does not think of the size of the family from which he or his spouse came as having any connection with success or failure in marriage. Yet the number of siblings in a family has a definite effect upon the personality development of each child. The individual reared in a home where there are brothers and sisters has a very different experience than the only child. He has had to learn to share his possessions and the affections of his parents with his siblings. This should give him an advantage over the only child in interacting on a favorable basis with other people. However, the only child is very often stereotyped as selfish and egotistical, which is not always true, as many are generous and humble in attitude.

The union of two young persons who have been reared as the only child in their respective families will necessitate some very real adjustments. If they have lived in college dormitories, many of the rough edges of their personalities will have been rubbed off by the close personal interaction of dorm life. Whenever an only child marries a person reared in a large family, the intermeshing of their personalities will be more difficult to achieve. Ideally, each child should have siblings to help prepare them for marriage, but this is not always possible. Much thought should be given to this aspect whenever choosing a mate.

AGE AT TIME OF MARRIAGE

The age at which young people marry also has a bearing on the success of the marriage. Fifty percent of young women are married

18. Reference here is not to "mixed marriages" where one partner is saved and the other is not. The emphasis in this chapter is on "Christian" marriage as defined at the beginning of the chapter. The question of mixed marriages will be considered in chapter 14.

by the time they are twenty-four years old, and fifty percent of the men by the time they are twenty-three years old.[19] Teen-age marriages are much more frequent than before World War II. The unfortunate fact is that the estimated one-third to one-half of the teen-age marriages involve a premarital pregnancy.[20] If young people marry before they are emotionally mature enough to carry the responsibilities of marriage, then unhappiness and divorce occur. Vladimar De Lissovoy conducted a three-year longitudinal study of forty-eight couples who married in high school. He states, "The self-ratings and the interview data support the well-documented findings of difficulties in marital competence and satisfaction in young marriages. . . ."[21]

Dating at earlier ages, the stress on saving sex for marriage, increased affluence, and willingness of upper and middle-class parents to subsidize early marriages are factors that contribute to the increase in teen-age marriages. Yet, a person should give himself time to mature if he expects to achieve a successful marriage.

Since the median age for marriage is approximately twenty-three for women and twenty-five for men, it is apparent that the average fellow likes to marry a girl that is about two years younger. This age differential arises because there are the beliefs (whether proven or not is debatable) that young women in our society mature two or three years sooner than young men, and that it may take the male longer to prepare for his role as "chief breadwinner" in the family.[22] Consequently, young women are reluctant to marry men who are younger. There is no evidence of a correlation between the age of marriage (excluding teen-age marriages) and subsequent happiness. Whether the bride is older or younger than the groom is not the decisive factor. The Landises write, "The studies showing the relationship between marriage success and age at marriage underline the truth that most people require years of living before they develop the maturity adequate for marriage success."[23] If the couple are mature, are well mated, and face the situation realistically, then the age differential is not too important as a determinant of success in marriage.

19. *Information Please Almanac* (New York: Houghton-Mifflin Co., 1985), p. 773.

20. *Ibid.*, p. 124. One study cited of high school marriages in Iowa found the rate of premarital pregnancy was 87 percent if both partners were students at time of marriage.

21. Vladimar De Lissovoy, "High School Marriages: A Longitudinal Study," *Journal of Marriage and the Family*, May, 1973, p. 245.

22. Paul C. Glick, *Marriage and Divorce, A Social and Economic Study* (Cambridge, MA: Harvard University Press, 1970), p. 87.

23. Landis and Landis, *Successful Marriage*, p. 125.

ETHNIC BACKGROUND

The question of nationality as a background factor is not as important today as it was a couple of generations ago when America was receiving a large number of immigrants who brought with them their own culture and became a subculture within the American system. For a native-born American to marry a first generation Italian or German meant a meeting of two cultures. In some instances such a situation still prevails today: Puerto Rican citizens settling in our large cities, Cuban refugees arriving in Florida, and the Mexicans moving into the southwestern United States. These all bring a Latin-American culture with them. Young men in military service overseas often marry nationals of the country where they serve and bring their brides home. Greater adjustments will be necessary in any case where a native-born individual marries a person from another culture.

RACIAL BACKGROUND

A similar situation exists in reference to interracial marriage. The white and black communities each constitute a subculture within our society.

Strong cultural influences oppose this type of union, and Christian young people contemplating such a marriage should give serious thought to all the factors involved. Several of the issues the couple must consider are mentioned by Robert K. Kelly. These include the motivation for such a marriage, the reactions of family and friends to the union, the possibility of differences in social, ethical, educational, and religious values, the question of permanence of the marriage, and finally, the opportunity for the couple's children to "have a normal and emotionally healthy childhood." He further states, "Life should be easier for the coming generation in interracial marriage. But this progress is slow and uneven. Prejudice dies hard and those of minority groupings still feel many harsh reminders of discrimination and injustice."[24]

Most churches still exhibit and practice racial discrimination in spite of lip service paid to integration. The couple in a mixed racial marriage is not fully accepted by either culture, which means that they must find more of their satisfactions within the family unit, thereby placing the relationship under more stress than the homoge-

24. Robert K. Kelley, *Courtship, Marriage and the Family* (New York: Harcourt, Brace, and World, Inc., 1969), pp. 270-273.

neous marriage. The children in such a family perhaps pay the greatest price because neighborhood children can be very cruel in their attitudes and actions toward those of mixed blood. The problems of identification for the children is also a very real one. The story of Paul illustrates this difficulty:

> Paul was the son of an interracial marriage. The family lived in a large Eastern city where such marriages were tolerated. The parents were born-again Christians and Paul was saved at an early age. After graduation from high school, he enrolled in a small Christian college. He was nominally accepted by the fellows, but the girls refused to date him. After being rebuffed several times, he went to the Dean of Students and cried bitterly, "Who am I?"

Kelley gives a digest of an analysis made by David H. Heer of Negro-white intermarriage in the four states of Hawaii, Michigan, Nebraska, and California, with relation to status differences. Heer discovered that in these states many Negro families have risen in status and have more opportunities to meet potential white partners. He postulates that "more tolerant and liberal attitudes toward Negroes in general is probably a factor in this increase." His conclusion is most interesting: "Heer does not think, however, that the combination of these factors will produce any dramatic increase in the rate of Negro-white marriages in the next 100 years."[25] Undoubtedly, there have been successful interracial marriages, but the obstacles facing the couple are enormous and will require much greater effort to make the marriage a successful one.

COMMUNICATION

The ability to communicate with each other is considered by some authorities to be the most important element in any marriage. A. Donald Bell in the preface to his book *The Family in Dialogue* writes, "After twenty-one years of experience in the field of marriage and family counseling, I still find communication the basic problem in this area. . . . We call this problem basic, because it is fundamental to all other areas." He demonstrates whether the problem in a family is immorality or lack of spirituality in the home, the basic cause is lack of communication for "communication and its exercise is the secret of spiritual health within the family."[26]

25. Ibid., pp. 263, 268.
26. A. Donald Bell, *The Family in Dialogue* (Grand Rapids: Zondervan Publishing House, 1970), p. 9.

The importance of young people establishing frank and open communication early in the dating relationship cannot be over-emphasized. If a person is unable to talk about certain subjects to the dating partner after the relationship becomes serious, it is evident that a problem exists. If it cannot be resolved, then the person ought to break the relationship and look for another partner with whom he can freely communicate. Some people are by nature or socialization more reticent than others in the initial stages of a courtship, but as it progresses they ought to be able to express their feelings freely on the wide variety of subjects concerning the couple and marriage.

It is necessary for the couple contemplating marriage to discuss and come to agreement on several matters before the wedding. They need a clear understanding as to their role concepts, and what each expects of the other after the ceremony. The use and control of money can be determined in order to avoid the conflicts experienced by so many couples in this area. The number, spacing, and discipline of children merits serious discussion. Young people must also discuss their views concerning the use of leisure time. Married couples today have much more free time and they need to know how they are going to spend it.

The relationship of the couple to the parental families needs to be explored. If there are problems, they must be worked through until the couple is united in their own minds as to how the relationship can be handled. Any unhappiness by either of the in-laws with the impending marriage can have an adverse effect on the young people themselves. Although many young people may not think so, they do marry into their respective families and cannot easily cut themselves off from the parental families.

Another important area for discussion and agreement concerns the values and goals in the life of the partners. Reference is made in the beginning of this chapter to the necessity of harmony in spiritual matters. If there is serious disagreement or conflict in the spiritual realm, the couple must resolve these. If they cannot, they face the possibility of missing much of the blessing that comes in Christian marriage to a couple united in their spiritual views.

Values and goals in life are often linked together because the goals usually reflect the values held by the person. For example, if a person greatly values money and high social status, he will undoubt-edly avoid the goal of becoming a teacher or Christian worker. His values will more likely direct him toward a career in business or medicine since our society provides greater monetary rewards to those filling these roles.

Young people reared in Christian homes have widely different value systems and goals in life. Therefore, two young people who are building a serious dating relationship need to discuss their values and goals to see if they are compatible. If the fellow values money highly and plans a career in business, and the young lady does not value money but is more interested in full-time Christian work, there is little to be gained in continuing the relationship. It will be better for both to seek a partner with values and goals more compatible to the individual.

After a couple are married, the necessity arises to set goals for the family. A. Donald Bell indicates that

> many of these goals must be spiritual in nature. . . . A healthy family needs goals to keep interest, stimulation, and devotion in the family circle. All of this finds its consummation in one final spiritual point. . . . The family should be living toward the goal of becoming the maximum Christian home. Many homes break down because the ultimate goals are material and financial. [27]

This does not mean that material goals are not important, but they must always be subservient to the major spiritual goal of the family.

The young couple who discuss and come to agreement on these and other matters concerning their marriage, have built a large amount of happiness into their relationship.

THE COHESIVE NATURE OF LOVE

The final ingredient is love which, like leaven, "leaveneth the whole lump." If most of the previously mentioned requirements are present in a relationship, then it will not be difficult for love to take root and grow. A very necessary part of love as will be discussed in chapter 6 is physical attraction, but it is only a part and not the whole. One of the great problems in American courtship and marriage is that the mass media so often present a view that equates physical attraction between the sexes as constituting the sum and substance of love. Often a fellow and girl meet, are physically drawn to one another by very natural God-given desires, and conclude they are "in love," and therefore should get married. They give little or no thought to the factors that contribute to compatibility in marriage, and they fail to realize that it is possible to be sexually attracted to many persons who would not make good partners in a marriage to last for a lifetime.

27. Ibid., p. 11.

COMPATIBILITY

Dating partners will find it most helpful to discover something of each other's background, values and goals in life and test their psychological compatibility before they become emotionally involved with each other. Whenever the physical predominates in the relationship, it becomes very difficult to make clear judgments on the basis of reason.

Robert O. Blood has an interesting discussion concerning the meaning of "compatibility." The usual definition refers "to the level of adjustment a couple achieve after marriage by giving a little here and compromising a little there." He rejects this and prefers to define it as "the goodness of fit that exists between the partners' intrinsic characteristics." Thus, "compatibility . . . either exists or doesn't exist . . . it varies by degrees . . . is something to be discovered between people. When sufficient compatibility is found, it provides the basis for the first main choice in marriage—whom to marry." He proceeds to indicate that compatibilities will change as the marriage matures. It is necessary for the couple to be willing to change as they face new incompatibilities.[28]

When God created Eve for Adam, He made her a "help fit for Adam," or she was "compatible" with Adam, i.e., there was a "good fit between the partner's intrinsic characteristics." It is more difficult for the young person today to find a compatible mate or one that "fits" his personality. With so many potential partners he must date many different individuals in order to find one that is most compatible with him. To quote Blood, " . . . compatibility between marriage partners determines how easily a personal relationship can be established. For a highly compatible couple love blossoms easily. The less compatible they are, the harder it is to achieve success."[29] The task then is to find a compatible partner. Young people need to realize there are no perfect prospective mates, but if they will attempt to choose a compatible mate as carefully as possible, in the will of God, then work to make the many adjustments and compromises which are needed, they can have a successful Christian marriage with His help and blessing.

28. Blood, *Marriage*, p. 11.
29. Ibid.

QUESTIONS FOR DISCUSSION AND REVIEW

1. What is meant by the phrase used in Matthew 19:5, "they twain shall be one flesh"?

2. Name four criteria by which the success of a Christian marriage may be judged?

3. Define *happiness*. How is it related to *joy*?

4. What effect did the change from a rural to an urban society have on the criteria for judging the success of a marriage?

5. Why is it important for a couple to have the same degree of consecration to God?

6. List and discuss the elements that constitute a "common cultural background."

7. Why do teen-age marriages have such a high divorce rate?

8. How much change in basic personality is an individual capable of making at twenty-one years of age?

9. What are some of the factors that need to be discussed by a couple considering an interracial marriage?

10. Why do some couples enter marriage without being psychologically compatible?

11. How are values related to goals in life?

12. Define and discuss compatibility as it relates to Christian marriage.

4

ROLE CONCEPTS
IN CHRISTIAN MARRIAGE

For the husband is the head of the wife . . .
Ephesians 5:23

DEFINITION OF ROLES

One of the most important factors in intelligent selection of a mate by young people is a correct understanding of role concepts. Each person must know how he feels about the roles he expects to play. He also must find a mate whose role concepts are compatible with his. The happiest marital interaction takes place between individuals who are well matched in this area, for they avoid much of the conflict caused by improper matching of roles. The couple with complimentary role concepts have fewer role differences to work out. It is this "working out of role differences" that causes much of the unhappiness in marriage.[1]

The term *role* refers to the behavior expected from a person who occupies a given position or "status." A man who is a husband (status) is expected to perform the duties (roles) which the society assigns to that position. A woman who is a wife (status) also is expected to fulfill her obligations (roles) which society expects from her.

The idea of roles is borrowed from the field of drama, and just as

1. Henry R. Brandt and Homer E. Dowdy, *Building a Christian Home* (Wheaton: Scripture Press Publications, Inc., 1960), pp. 40-42. Case histories are given of a businessman and factory worker whose role differences caused conflict in the homes.

the actors must know their parts in order to play them, so the person with a given status must know how society expects him to play the role if he is going to succeed.[2] The child begins learning these roles in the home, and his knowledge is increased as he has contacts with other socializing agencies such as play groups, church, school, peer groups, and others.[3] Each young person approaching marriage has received a socialization different from that of every other person. Thus, each one has a different conception of the roles he or she is to play as a husband or wife. One of the tasks of dating and courtship is for the individual to find a partner whose role concept matches his, rather than clashes with it.

CONFUSION OF ROLES IN AMERICAN SOCIETY

As indicated in chapter 2 the roles of husband and wife are changing and are not clearly defined in our society. This leads to much confusion and misunderstanding on the part of young people assuming these roles. E. E. LeMasters describes the situation in these words: "In the modern American family male and female roles have been shifted and reorganized extensively since about 1920, and some families appear to be disorganized in that nobody seems to know who is supposed to do what."[4]

Some writers in the family life area of study believe that many of the problems in marital adjustment arise from ignorance by the husband and wife of the correct way to play their roles. Robert C. Williamson makes this comment "In some cases the inability or failure to carry out a given role or a number of roles proves disastrous to the marriage. Differences in role perception are illustrated when the husband prefers the patriarchal pattern, and the wife looks forward to an equalitarian one. Divorce may be the only outcome for these role discrepancies."[5]

One major factor influencing these role changes is the Women's Liberation Movement. David H. Olsen makes the point that the

2. Alfred R. Lindesmith and Anselm R. Strauss, *Social Psychology* (New York: Henry Holt & Co., 1956), p. 371-398. The authors use the scene in a typical Sunday morning church service to introduce and to illustrate the subject of "roles."

3. Francis E. Merrill, *Society and Culture* (Englewood Cliffs NJ: Prentice-Hall, Inc., 1965), pp. 172-183.

4. E. E. LeMasters, *Parents in Modern America* (Homewood, IL: The Dorsey Press, 1970), p. 51.

5. Robert C. Williamson, *Marriage and Family Relations* (New York: John Wiley & Sons, Inc., 1966), p. 332.

changing role relationships between husband and wife are being encouraged by the Women's Liberation Movement. He indicates that historically the women have been strong defenders of the institutions of marriage.[6]

The Women's Liberation Movement received renewed impetus in 1966 with the founding of the National Organization of Women (NOW). The movement is highly fragmented today, with the radical groups apparently dominating the scene. The radicals have accepted the view of Marx and Engels that "the first condition for the liberation of the wife is to bring the whole female sex back into the public industry, and that this in turn demands the abolition of the monogamous family as the economic unit of society."[7] A more recent statement by Shelia Cronan is quoted by Margaret M. Poloma and T. Neal Garland: "Since marriage constitutes slavery for women, it is clear that the Women's Movement must concentrate on attacking this institution. Freedom for women cannot be won without the abolition of marriage. Attack on such issues as employment discrimination is superfluous."[8] There is no doubt that these groups want monogamous marriage eliminated.

The more moderate groups in the Women's Liberation Movement are interested in full political, economic, and civil rights for all women. They have been active in supporting the Equal Rights amendment to the United States Constitution. The amendment reads, "Equality of rights under the law shall not be denied or abridged by the United States or by any state on account of sex." It was first introduced in Congress in 1923 but was not passed until March 22, 1972.[9] It was strongly opposed by conservative groups and failed to be ratified by the required thirty-eight states.

In their demands for change, the moderates are more realistic than the radical feminists. Betty Friedan, who wrote *The Feminine Mystique*, which gave renewed interest to the feminist movement, is representative of the moderates. She takes issue with the radicals who want to do away with sex and marriage and who do not want to

---

6. David H. Olsen, "Marriage of the Future: Revolutionary or Evolutionary Change?" *The Family Coordinator*, October 1972, pp. 389-390.

7. Friedrich Engels, "Bourgeois Marriage," *The Family and the Sexual Revolution*, ed. Edwin M Schur (Bloomington, IN: University Press, 1964), p. 261.

8. Margaret M. Poloma and T. Neal Garland, "The Married Professional Woman: A Study in the Tolerance of Domestication," *Journal of Marriage and the Family*, August 1971, p. 533.

9. Robert A. Diamond, ed.,*Current American Government, Congressional Quarterly*, Fall 1972, p. 75.

deal with reality. She wants women to use their power to begin to change society "*now*, so all women can move freely as people in it."[10] The changes desired by this group are not as radical, but it is apparent they want definite changes in society "now."

The majority of the American women are not in favor of the Women's Liberation Movement. In a Roper poll, September 1971, 69 percent of the women surveyed did not believe that they are treated as second-class citizens in the United States.[11] Rather than feeling themselves to be second-class citizens, many women realize that in many areas they enjoy privileges denied to men. Elsieliese Thorpe expressed her attitude toward the Women's Liberation Movement in the May 1972 *Reader's Digest*, "If they don't stop their commotion, their rumblings of discontent and pleas for equality, we might end up getting what they are asking for. And who wants equality when we women are doing so much better now? Biologically, legally, temperamentally, and just about every other way that matters, we women are the favored sex."[12]

Recently instituted "women's studies" courses at the college and university level also contribute to the confusion about roles in family living. Lester Velie remarks, "In large part, the ideological ammunition for these courses comes from Kate Millett's *Sexual Politics*, a powerful and coherent attack on the family. Millett's book, in turn, derives much of its intellectual muscle from the master of ideology, Friedrich Engels."[13] He states that "last year some 200 colleges and universities were teaching an estimated 800 to 1000 women's studies courses. While many of these are objective explorations of the roles that women play in society, many others attack the institutions of marriage and the family with all the fury of a Kate Millett."[14] Such courses belittle the traditional values of marriage and the roles ordinarily played by husbands and wives.

When one understands these widely publicized attitudes that are opposed to the Christian view of role concepts, he has little difficulty realizing why Christian young people are also confused about their roles. When women are seeking equality, and the Bible clearly speaks

10. Betty Friedan, "Our Revolution is Unique," *Voices of the New Feminism*, ed. Mary Lou Thompson (Boston: Beacon Press, 1970), pp. 38-43.

11. *The San Francisco Chronicle*, September 28, 1971, as quoted in Gene Marine's *Male Guide to Women's Liberation* (New York: Holt, Rinehart and Winston, 1972), p. 5.

12. Elsieliese Thorpe, "But Women Are the Favored Sex," *Reader's Digest* (Pleasantville, NY: The Reader's Digest Assn., Inc., May 1972), p. 82.

13. Lester Velie, "The War on the American Family," *Reader's Digest*, January 1973, p. 109.

14. Ibid.

of the wife being submissive to her husband (Eph. 5:22) and in subjection to him (Eph. 5:23), it creates uncertainty for some as to the role of the wife even in Christian marriage. Henry R. Brandt says that the wife is to be

> ... submissive and in subjection. Somehow, many men and women in our day consider these words to mean disrespect, disregard for the abilities of the woman. Thus, in deference to the democratic spirit, the word 'obey' is eliminated from many marriage ceremonies with the magnaminous consent of the bridegroom, because to obey is an unreasonable expectation of a wife.[15]

It is possible for a Christian couple to face "role confusion" also, and to confront problems in their marriage. Therefore, it is very important for Christian young people to study God's Word and to heed what He has to say concerning the proper roles for the husband and wife. The Bible does not change to accommodate the desires of a degenerate culture which changes from time to time. The young person who finds his role concept in the Scriptures, and seeks a mate who also accepts the Scriptural role will have a solid basis for interaction in Christian marriage.

SCRIPTURAL ROLE CONCEPTS FOR THE WIFE

The major passages in the New Testament concerning the roles of husband and wife are Ephesians 5:18-33; Colossians 3:18; I Peter 3:1-7. Jack Wyrtzen makes the point, "This truth is important enough for the Bible to flatly state it three times, as well as to imitate it by example throughout the entire text."[16]

In the passage in Ephesians, Paul exhorts the Christian to "be filled with the Spirit" (v. 18). Many writers begin the discussion of roles with verse 22, "Wives, submit yourselves unto your own husbands," but this submission is only possible as the wife knows the power of a life yielded to, and filled with the blessed Holy Spirit. Before a husband can love his wife (v. 25) as God intends, he, too, must be filled with the Spirit of God.

It is necessary to note that these verses are introductory not only to the proper relationships between husband and wife, but also to those between parents and children and to those between servants and masters. A Christian man must be filled with the Holy Spirit

15. Brandt and Dowdy, *Building a Christian Home*, p. 52.
16. Jack Wyrtzen, *Sex Is Not Sinful* (Grand Rapids: Zondervan Publishing House, 1970), p. 45.

before he can properly play his role in any of the three most important areas of human relationships. The family that endeavors to establish the best Christian home can only do so as they are empowered by the Holy Spirit. He is pleased to exalt the Lord Jesus in the life of the believer, and He is pleased to exalt Christ in the home where two believers "have become one flesh."

The exhortation in Ephesians 5:22, "Wives, submit yourselves unto your own husbands, as unto the Lord," is a very definite command for the wife to submit herself to the Lordship of Christ in her daily life. She is to follow the example of the church who as the bride of Christ submits to His leadership. Norman V. Williams comments, "In this commandment we have the divine key to any woman's being a happy, fruitful, and successful wife."[17]

In view of the concerns of the Women's Liberation Movement, W. G. M. Martin has an interesting statement concerning this command:

> The sentiment of this verse is so far removed from, and contrary to, the common thought of the world today that it must seem to some the very essence of retrogression in civilized social relationships. Have not women attained by the onward march of civilization an equality with man that has always been their natural right, but has only recently come to be recognized? The answer is that in many things, for example, spiritual qualities, woman is the natural (and divinely ordained) equal of man. But in the relationships of family life God has ordained a certain order, and in this divine order the wife is to be subject to the husband. . . . This subordination does not imply inferiority.[18]

The wife may have a legitimate concern for equality in voting rights, or desire "equal pay for equal work." She does not have a right to demand the abolition of marriage, nor to assume leadership over the husband in the home. She is under divine obligation to submit first to the Lord as she yields her body to the control of the Holy Spirit, and He will enable her to submit to a loving husband.

Some confusion exists in the minds of some Christians concerning the equality of believers since Paul states in Galatians 3:28, "There is neither Jew nor Greek, there is neither bond or free, there is neither male nor female; for ye are all one in Christ Jesus." Harry A. Ironside, the great expositor, says that this has reference to our new creation, but

17. Norman V. Williams, *The Christian Home* (Chicago: Moody Press, 1952), p. 31.
18. W. G. M. Martin, "Ephesians," *The New Bible Commentary*, ed. F. Davidson (Grand Rapids: Wm. B. Eerdman's Publishing Co., 1953), pp. 1027-1028. Used by permission.

> ... it is important to remember that our bodies belong to the old creation still, and it will not be until the redemption of the body at the coming of our Lord Jesus Christ ... that we shall be above the natural relationships in which we stand to one another as men and women here in the world. ... To say as some do that because there is neither male nor female in the new creation, we are to pay no attention to the divinely given order pertaining to the respective places of men and women in the Church of God on earth is not only to go beyond Scripture, but it is positive disobedience to the Word of God. As long as we are subject to human limitations so long must we recognize our human responsibilities, and seek to maintain these in a scriptural way in order that we may commend the Gospel of Christ.[19]

The parallel passages concerning the role of the wife are Colossians 3:18, "Wives, submit yourselves unto your own husbands, as it is fit in the Lord," and I Peter 3:1, "Likewise, ye wives, be in subjection to your own husbands." These verses reinforce the teaching of Ephesians 5. Tim LaHaye makes the interesting observation that the command in Colossians 3:18 is preceded by 3:16, "let the Word of Christ dwell in you richly in all wisdom." Here the wife is to be filled with the Word of God whereas in Ephesians 5:18 she is to be filled with the Spirit of God. The results in both cases are "a singing, thanksgiving heart and a submissive spirit, independent of circumstances ... so unnatural that they can only be ours through the filling of the Holy Spirit."[20]

In American culture, a Christian young lady may be reared in a Christian home with a domineering mother. It is only natural for the young lady to acquire the attitudes of her mother, and she may rebel at being submissive to her husband. She may find it very difficult to allow him to take the leadership in the home. The resources referred to in Ephesians 5:18 and Colossians 3:16, the power of the living Word of God and the blessed indwelling Holy Spirit will enable such a person to submit to her husband.[21] It is not the natural thing to do, but the Holy Spirit is given to the Christian wife to enable her to obey God and her husband in a supernatural manner. The world cannot understand such submission, for the "natural man receiveth not the things of the Spirit of God: for they

19. Harry A. Ironside, *Lectures on the Epistle to the Colossians* (New York: Loizeaux Bros., Inc., 1928), p. 155. Used by permission.
20. Tim LaHaye, *How to Be Happy Though Married* (Wheaton: Tyndale House Publishers, 1968), p. 131.
21. The question of the saved wife and her relationship to an unsaved husband on the basis of I Peter 3:1 is discussed in chapter 14, "The Christian and Mixed Marriages."

are foolishness unto him, neither can he know them, because they are spiritually discerned" (I Cor. 2:14).

There is also the possibility of a Christian girl marrying a Christian fellow who does not understand his role, or who may change after marriage into a worldly, carnal husband. Concerning such circumstances Ironside remarks, "For the Christian woman this relationship once entered into there is no other position in conformity to the will of God than that of godly submission to the husband whom she herself has chosen."[22] A wife in such a situation must turn to the resources of the Word and the indwelling Holy Spirit for victory in her daily life of submission.

Although in the conventional wedding ceremony the bride promises "to obey" her husband, there is no direct command of Scripture to this effect. In Ephesians 6:1, children are exhorted to "obey your parents," and in 6:5, servants are to be "obedient" to their masters. According to Martin, in the Greek the word used in these verses is different from the word in verse 22 and "has the sense of 'obeying orders,' with an emphasis of 'literal obedience to command' that has no place in the phrase of verse 22, 'submit yourselves' which has the sense of 'arranging in order.'"[23] The idea in verse 22 is a ranking in order with the superior highest and subordinates below him. Thus Williams translates verse 22, "You married women must continue to live in subordination to your husbands." In like manner he renders Titus 2:5, "subordinate to their husbands" whereas the King James Version reads "obedient to their own husbands."

This does not mean that the wife is not to obey her husband, for the word subordinate according to Webster means to be "under the power or authority of another." A person under the authority of another is obligated to carry out the wishes of the superior and is guilty of insubordination if he does not. The husband who has a proper Scriptural role concept will not be guilty of giving commands or barking orders to his wife, but will treat her kindly as Christ treats His bride, the church.

The couple with good communication between themselves experience little difficulty in this area, for the wife is attuned to the needs and desires of her husband. Since he loves her as Christ loved the church, the wife's desire is to please her husband so that orders or commands are not necessary. In Titus 2:4, young women are asked "to love their own husbands," so that the submission of the wife is

22. Ironside, *Colossians*, p. 157.
23. Martin, "Ephesians," p. 1028.

based on reciprocal love between husband and wife. The Christian wife is able to say with the bride in the Song of Solomon, "I am my beloved's, and his desire is toward me." (Song of Sol. 7:10). Where this mutual love exists as God intends it, the wife does not find it difficult to accept her husband as the head of the home.

SCRIPTURAL ROLE CONCEPTS FOR THE HUSBAND

A different command is given to the husband in reference to his role. He is to love his wife as "Christ also loved the church" (Eph. 5:25), and to love his wife as his own body (Eph. 5:28). He is to show the same selfish concern for her welfare that he exhibits toward his own person and is to "nourish and cherish" her just as he does his physical body. On the other hand, he is to have the same self-sacrificing love for his mate that Christ has for His bride, the church.

This selfish and self-sacrificing love seems somewhat contradictory until we realize that we cherish most that for which we sacrifice most. Consider the time and attention given by a fellow to his first auto, for which he worked and saved over a long period, or the young couple and the first home they buy after years of saving for the downpayment. In real mature love, each partner sacrifices himself and his interests in order to meet the needs of his spouse. The emphasis is not on "me" and "mine," but "you" and "yours."

It is readily seen that this kind of love spoken of in the Bible is the very antithesis of the popular conception of a selfish "love" that puts the gratification of one's own personal desires above satisfying the needs of the mate. When a man is in fellowship with God and loves his wife as Christ loved the church, he treats her in such a kind, considerate, thoughtful manner that she finds it easy to respect him and to submit to him as "unto the Lord." She knows that just as he responds to the needs of his own body and satisfies them for its best welfare, so he responds to her needs and seeks her best welfare, since he loves her "as his own body."

The spiritual dimension of the proper roles of husband and wife is emphasized in I Peter 3:1-7. The role of the wife delineated in this passage has been previously discussed, but Peter has some specific statements directed to the husband in verse 7: " . . . ye husbands, dwell with them according to knowledge, giving honour unto the wife, as unto the weaker vessel, and as being heirs together of the grace of life, that your prayers be not hindered." Kenneth S. Wuest, in commenting on this verse, writes:

The husband is to dwell with the wife remembering that she is an instrument of God . . . to be used by Him to His glory. The husband must ever keep in mind that she is the weaker instrument . . . not morally or intellectually, but physically. . . . This attitude toward the wife . . . includes loving consideration of the wife in view of the fact that she is not physically as strong as he is. . . . The husband is to pay her honor so that their prayers be not hindered. The word "hindered" in the Greek text means literally "to cut in, to interrupt." Failure to give due honor to the wife will result in a cutting in on the efficacy of their united prayer times.[24]

The spiritual life of a couple is definitely impoverished if the husband does not accept God's role for his life. Referring to I Peter 3:7, Raymond C. Stedman makes the following comment:

Prayer here is the symbol of dependence on God, from whom all the richness and glory of life must come. It is only God that can make human life rich. . . . If the husband's failure prevents oneness . . . then inevitably marriage . . . becomes routine, humdrum, lifeless, boring because the glory is gone. . . . The man learns that he cannot go ahead of his wife in this respect. . . . Life can only be full and satisfying when they move together in a deeper, day by day contact with an indwelling God. This is what makes for richness in a home.[25]

The fullness of blessing that God desires for the Christian home is reserved for the home where the husband manifests his love by obeying the exhortations of I Peter 3:7.

ROLES PERTAINING SPECIFICALLY TO THE CHRISTIAN COUPLE

The Christian husband and wife share many of the roles common to any marriage. They play the roles of breadwinner, housewife, parents, neighbors, just as the secular family next door. Yet some roles are characteristic of their Christian faith.

The husband is to be the head of the home. This means that he is responsible for making decisions concerning the happiness and welfare of the family. He enforces discipline in the home.

The head of the home sets the Christian standards by leading a consistent Christian life, which is an example before the wife and

24. Kenneth S. Wuest, *First Peter in the Greek New Testament* (Grand Rapids: Wm. B. Eerdmans Publishing Co., 1942), 83. Used by permission.
25. Raymond C. Stedman, "Man, the Initiator," *The Marriage Affair*, Ed. J. Allan Petersen (Wheaton: Tyndale House Publishers, 1971), pp. 81-82. Used by permission of *Eternity* magazine, copyright 1969 Evangelical Foundation.

children. He conducts the "family altar," sees that the family attends the services of the local church, and is active in Christian service. Stedman makes the serious statement, "Every husband is ultimately responsible to God for what his home becomes."[26]

The Christian wife has a primary obligation to maintain a home that is distinctively Christian. She gives loving support and submission to her loving husband. Her relationship to her children is marked by love and discipline. She cooperates with her husband in his efforts to provide spiritual leadership in the home. She assumes this responsibility when it is necessary for the husband to be absent. She also engages in Christian service as her time and strength permit. For example, it is often difficult for the young mother to have a role in the local church because of the demands of her motherhood role.

One of her roles is to see that good Christian literature and music are provided. She is "given to hospitality" and uses the home to entertain God's people, and as a means of witnessing to unsaved neighbors. Solomon in his description of the virtuous woman in Proverbs 31:28 says, "Her children arise up, and call her blessed; her husband also, and he praiseth her." This is part of the reward of a Christian wife for faithfully fulfilling her roles.

These roles of the Christian couple are reciprocal. Norman V. Williams, in discussing the origin of the words *husband* and *wife*, indicates that the

> word "husband" means "house-band." Thus, husband is the one who binds the home together. . . . When the band breaks, the spokes of the wheel fall apart; the flowers fall scattered to the earth; the marriage may fall apart. . . . The word wife . . . means "weaver." The husband in his spiritual ministry provides the wife with rich graces and blessings which she in turn weaves into the fabric of the marriage life to the joy and blessing of the whole family.[27]

ROLE CONFLICTS

The misinterpretation of Ephesians 5 has resulted in a warped view of the husband's role in the Christian family. Some Christians seem to read only parts of verses 22 and 23, and fail to read the remainder of the chapter. They feel that the husband as the "head" is to be an absolute monarch or dictator in the home, and that the wife is to submit herself to him as his willing slave under his complete domina-

26. Ibid., p. 78.
27. Williams, *Christian Home*, p. 14. Used by permission.

tion. As children come, they also are to bow to his sovereign majesty, and yield unquestioned obedience to his dictates.

It is apparent that such an interpretation misses the very heart of the passage, which teaches that the relationship between a husband and wife is based on a mutual love and concern; it is not a one-sided power structure. In the home where Christlike love prevails, where roles are rightly perceived, the husband will have authority and his wishes will be carried out as love is a much greater motivation to action than fear could ever be. In reference to this Henry Alford writes:

> I cannot refrain from citing Chrysostom's very beautiful remarks, . . . "You see the rule of obedience? Well, hear also the rule of love. Do you wish your wife to obey you, as the Church obeys Christ? Then take care for her, as Christ did for the Church; and even if you must give your life for her, or be cut in a thousand pieces, or whatever you must undergo and suffer, shrink not from it; and even if you suffer all this, you have not yet done anything that Christ did; for you do this being already joined in marriage to her, but He suffered for a Bride who rejected and hated Him. As then He brought to His feet her who rejected Him . . . with wonderful care and affection, not with terror, nor with threats . . . so do you toward your wife. . . . A slave a man may perhaps bind by terror . . . but the partner of your life, the mother of your children, the subject of all your joy, you ought to bind not by terror and threats, but by love and gentle considerations."[28]

The ideal concept of the husband-wife relationship is the one found in the Bible. In reality, there are many factors which affect the actual roles in daily living. As mentioned in chapter 2, the changing role of women in our society has made it more difficult for them to accept the traditional role of homemaker and mother. The average working wife feels that she is intelligent enough and contributes sufficiently to the family income to deserve a major part in decision making. If she is among the large number who earns more than her husband, she may feel she should make the decisions.

This should not be a problem for the Christian family, for the wife will play her role of submission to her husband, and he, because of his great love for her, will consider her desires in any decision he makes for the family. Brandt uses a most appropriate illustration of the complementary roles of husband and wife in the areas of submission and decision-making by comparing them to roles played by the president and vice-president of a bank who have worked together

---

28. Henry Alford, *The New Testament for English Readers* (Chicago: Moody Press, n.d.) p. 1244. Used by permission.

many years. The bankers interact on the basis of policies which they have mutually determined are in the best interest of their company. Their roles are clearly defined and when the president is absent, the vice-president directs the business. There are other banks where they could use their skills but they have chosen to work together in this particular bank to further its interests. They do not argue or feud over decisions that have to be made, but the best interest of the bank is the determining factor in any situation.[29]

The applications to the roles of husband and wife are evident. They have chosen to work together and the best interests of their marriage should be the major concern of each spouse. Brandt asks,

> Should not the role of the wife be similiar to that of the first vice-president? The husband is the head of the wife, but this should be on the basis of friendship, loyalty, goodwill. Family policies should be ones she has helped to make, is in accord with, is limited by. We believe it to be a reasonable thing for the wife to be consulted and her opinions seriously considered when there is a decision to be made. Selfish interest has no place in marriage . . . both . . . subject themselves to the best interest and objectives of the marriage.[30]

Brandt also points out that problems can arise when the couple disagree. He suggests that in case of serious disagreement the husband "carefully make the decision." He "assumes . . . loyalty, and respect, and dedication between a couple." He also sounds a word of warning, "When crises arise repeatedly that cause friction, we must consider that marriage sick and outside help would be indicated."[31] It is apparent that the Christian family can experience role conflict like their unsaved neighbors if the partners do not agree, or if either refuses to accept the Biblical norm for his or her role.

DOMINANCE-SUBMISSION PATTERNS

Many times role conflicts result because husband and wife are socialized in homes with contrasting dominance-submission patterns. Children ordinarily derive their role concepts from the home. A boy reared in a home where the father is dominant and the mother submissive usually internalizes a dominant role concept. Similarly, a girl reared in this type of home ordinarily wants to play the submis-

29. Brandt and Dowdy, *Building a Christian Home*, pp. 52-53.
30. Ibid., p. 53. Used by permission.
31. Ibid., pp. 53-54.

sive role. When the fellow from this home begins to date as part of the mate-selection process in our culture, he *subconsciously* seeks a girl who plays the submissive role, just as his mother does in the home. If he dates a girl from a home where the mother is dominant, he may have problems, because the girl usually repeats her mother's pattern and he feels the girl is "too bossy." Instead of permitting him to plan the dates and activities, she assumes this role, and conflict results and the relationship is broken. In our system, the male then can continue to date until he discovers a prospective mate such as the young lady who wrote the following:

> I want my husband to "wear the pants" in our home and to be the spiritual leader! As far as money matters and things of this nature, I feel we both should discuss such matters together since they are of great importance, and probably the first year I will also be working. Therefore, some of the money I will have earned. But I don't feel that I should have the final say in these matters. I am only saying that he should know how I feel about the particular situation.

If he does not find such a girl and marries a dominant type, there is very likely to be conflict.

Many young men are reared in homes where the mother is dominant and makes the decisions for the family. She may go so far as to pick out and buy the clothing for the husband and sons. Many times the mother is dominant because the father refuses to accept his role in the home. Stedman comments "I know it is popular to make jokes about bossy wives and henpecked husbands but, having observed the marriage scene for considerable time and having personal involvement in it, I would say the problem is not so much due to the demand of wives to assert leadership as it is the refusal of husbands to assume their responsibilities."[32] He also remarks that some men are very careful to provide good leadership in their economic role in order to provide well for the family, but then they expect the wife to assume all the responsibility for the home and children.[33]

When a young man socialized in this type of home begins to date, he subconsciously looks for a girl to dominate him and make decisions for him just as his mother did. He expects his date to plan the evening, and to inform him of her plans when he arrives for her. If she does not, he is disappointed, and after a few dates, or when the relationship becomes too unhappy because of their role conflict, he

32. Stedman, *Man, the Initiator*, pp. 78-79.
33. Ibid., p. 71.

"breaks up" with her and seeks another. He searches in his dating until he subconsciously finds a girl who likes to dominate her date. If he doesn't, he finally marries a girl from a home with a submissive mother, and they have problems because neither one wants to assume leadership in the home.

A student expressed his feelings about the problems in his home in this manner:

> *When I marry, I want my home to be different than the one I was reared in. There was continual conflict because neither of my parents wanted to make a decision. My mother expected my father to tell the children what to do, and my father expected my mother to do this. If I asked my mother if I could go someplace she would say, "Ask your father." When I asked him his reply was, "Do whatever your mother said." As a result, I often had to make my own decisions, and if it displeased either of my parents, they would blame the other for letting me go somewhere.*

Life in such a house is not pleasant for either the parents or the children.

A third type of conflict arises when a person is reared in an equalitarian home where the decision-making is shared by the mother and father on a democratic basis. Although democracy is widely used as the basis for family relationships, it is the source for many family problems. C. W. Scudder goes so far as to say, "Loss of distinctive status and individual worth of the husband and wife in the widely extolled 'fifty-fifty' marriage . . . is one of the largest contributors to the deterioration of marriage and the home."[34] He also cites David Mace: ". . . the West may have gone too far in the direction of the democratization of the home. . . . Evidence is accumulating that in practice it [democratic idea] will not work because differentiation of role is essential to good family functioning. . . . The wife cannot function in her feminine role if her husband's masculine role is taken from him. The family group cannot function as a family if its natural head is dethroned."[35]

The young man or woman reared in a "headless" or two-headed" family tries to find a prospective mate who wants to help make the decisions. If a fellow dates a girl who wants to dominate him, he will be unhappy in her company. If he dates a girl with a submissive role concept, who expects him to assume strong leader-

---

34. C. W. Scudder, *The Family in Christian Perspective* (Nashville: Broadman Press, 1962), p. 11. Used by permission.
35. Ibid., pp. 12-13.

ship, this also makes him uncomfortable and he probably will end the relationship. If he should marry either of these, there is likely to be role conflict. He will be happiest if he marries a girl who wants to share in making the decisions.

The following chart illustrates some of the possible marriage combinations based on the dominant-submissive role concept patterns, and the probability of conflict or nonconflict situations:

	Male	Female	Non-conflict	Conflict
Biblical →	Dominant	Submissive	X	
	Dominant	Dominant		X
	Dominant	Equalitarian *50-50?*		X
	Submissive	Dominant	X	
chaotic →	Submissive *Nobody in charge*	Submissive		X
	Submissive *No responsibility*	Equalitarian		X
	Equalitarian *50-50*	Equalitarian	X	
	Equalitarian	Dominant		X
	Equalitarian	Submissive		X

The opinions of several hundred Christian college students indicate that most of them accept the Biblical role concepts, with the fellows desiring to be dominant, and the girls wanting to be submissive.[36] The young women do not want an autocrat for a husband, but they do look for a mate who will assume his headship in the home and give due consideration to their opinions. Some young people have difficulties accepting the Scriptural position, for they have had the misfortune of being socialized in homes with one or both parents unsaved, or in homes where the Christian parents were not obedient to the Word of God. The confusion engendered in young people reared in such homes is evidenced in the following statement written by a college student:

> *My mother became a Christian after she married my father, but he never came to Christ. He is not only unsaved, but also very much against all religion and everything which has anything to do with the church. In this type of atmosphere, my two sisters, my brother and I grew up, looking mostly to my mother, perhaps mistakenly in some*

36. Survey made in Marriage and Family classes at Cedarville College during the years 1967-1970.

cases, but at other times, simply because of my father's irritation with and dislike of the things which related to Christianity. Neither my mother or father is outspoken, but each spoke for himself. Many times, as children, we simply did not refer to our father when a decision or plans were to be made. We went to our mother, who would therefore probably have had the dominant role, at least with the children. The situation would necessarily have been much different had my father been a Christian also. My mother and father handle the decisions about finances and the home equally, making this portion equalitarian. I do not know how to classify the role relationship in our family.

A fellow who grows up in a home where the father refuses to be the head of the household, or where the father has to submit to a domineering wife in order to have any peace in the home, will very often rebel against his parents and will consciously vow to be the leader in his family when he marries. The girl reared in a similar situation occasionally feels so sorry for her "hen-pecked" father, that she also revolts against the role concept of her mother, and will determine to look for a mate who will be strong enough to be the "man of the house." Even though these young people sincerely want to assume the roles that God desires them to play in the dating and family relationships, they find it difficult due to their socialization in homes without proper role models. However, roles are learned behavior and can be changed, although it usually requires much effort by the one desiring to change his role behavior. The fellow with a father who is submissive will have to consciously assume the leadership in a relationship. He will have to plan the date and activities beforehand, and although decision-making will be difficult at first, it will become easier as it is practiced. The young lady who is prone to imitate her domineering mother will have to learn to hold her tongue when she is tempted to make the decision that should rightly be made by her date. Undoubtedly, there will be mistakes, but the Christian who desires his conduct to conform to the Word of God has the help of the indwelling Holy Spirit to enable him to change in the proper direction.

The question may be asked, "If the dominance-submission pattern is so important for happiness in the marriage relationship, why do so many individuals seem to make the wrong choice, resulting in role conflict and unhappiness?" There are many factors involved, but one of the main answers is that many couples become too involved in their physical attraction to one another too early in the relationship. They do not continue the friendship phase of their dating long enough to really get to know one another as persons rather than lovers. Once the physical aspect of the interaction becomes predominant in the relationship, it is very easy to overlook detrimental factors since so much pleasurable emotion is received from the necking and petting. The fact that a fellow depends upon a girl to make decisions irritates her, or in another couple, that the girl is over-bearing and competes with the fellow for the authority, is discounted since they have such a "good relationship" when it comes to physical involvement. When these couples marry and the physical needs have been satisfied, they then must face the difficult task of reconciling the different role expectations that they brought to the marriage from their family backgrounds. Many more adjustments will have to be made, and much more unhappiness is experienced than if they had taken time before they became physically involved, to see if their personalities were compatible in regard to role concepts. If the adjustments cannot be made, then they run to the divorce court.

DIVISION OF LABOR IN THE HOME

The earning of a livelihood and the division of labor within the home are also involved in a person's role concepts. American culture traditionally has defined the masculine role as that of breadwinner, and the feminine role as that of homemaker. The preparation for these tasks begin very early in childhood. A little girl is usually given dolls and dishes as toys to help prepare her for her adult roles as mother and cook for the family. A little boy receives toy trucks and guns as preparation for his role of employee and soldier when he matures. If a child adopts the role of the opposite sex, he is termed a "sissy" and she becomes known as a "tomboy." Fortunately, most such children successfully make the change to their proper role during adolescence, but if for any reason they do not, they face real problems in their relationships with others. A young lady usually prefers a "masculine" man over an effeminate one, and usually young men do not enjoy a "tomboy" as a dating partner.

These traditional roles have been modified since it became popular for wives to work. A survey of several classes of Christian college students indicates about 50 percent of their mothers worked either full or part time. The female students (with one exception) felt it was all right for wives to work until the family came or after they left home. They agreed that the mother with children belonged in the home. They did recognize that it might be necessary for the wife to work in case the husband were ill and could not be the breadwinner. Actually many women college students are earning their degrees as a type of family insurance in case the husband were to become ill or to die. Occasionally a male student will manifest the traditional role that he does not want his wife to work outside the home under any circumstances. Most Christian fellows express role concepts similar to the girls in that they do not mind the wife working when there are no children involved, or when conditions make it necessary to maintain the home.

Concerning the division of labor within the home, the same survey indicated that about 50 percent of the fathers helped in the home with such feminine tasks as drying dishes, vacuuming, doing laundry, grocery shopping, and other chores. This is about the same percentage (although not necessarily the same households) of homes with working mothers.[37] It seems to indicate that in Christian homes the husbands are assuming some tasks that the wives used to perform. As someone said, "If the wife helps to bring home the bacon, then the husband can help fry it!" Since young people do hold differing opinions as to whether the wife should work, and whether the husband should help with housework, couples should have a firm understanding in this phase of role concepts in order to avoid problems in this area when they marry.

BALANCE IN NUMBER OF ROLES PLAYED

The multiplication of roles for both husband and wife has also contributed to the difficulties faced in many marriages. The husband is not only father and breadwinner, but at the same time, he may also be a Sunday school teacher, deacon, youth advisor, leader in the Boys' Brigade, volunteer fireman, and a member of the City Commission. If he is employed in a second job, the situation is even worse. The wife is not only mother and homemaker, but she also has numerous role demands. She may be a Sunday school teacher, church organist, choir member, leader of the junior youth group, leader of the Pioneer Girls, president of the Women's Missionary Society, secretary of the Band Mothers, member of the executive committee of the PTA, and chairman of the local Cancer Society Fund Drive. Some wives attempt to do all this besides having a full or part-time job.

Most individuals can play several roles outside the home fairly successfully, but difficulties in role performance arise when the individual attempts too many tasks, with some done poorly, including those within the home. Some people devote too much time

37. Ibid.

to a particular role, and this can be a problem. This is particularly true in the employment role when the father spends long hours at the office or business, and has little time for the family. Brandt warns the father who is tempted to neglect his family by favoring the economic role: "And if for no other reason than that your work is your income, the hours spent working can vault out of proportion to the value that money should have in your family. The love of money and the notion that the things money buys are all important have meant shipwreck for many families."[38]   Those in full-time Christian service need to be very careful not to make this mistake. Pastors have been accused of being so preoccupied with their service in the church, they do not have time for their families, and often their children are alienated from the church.

Howard G. Hendricks tells of an experience he had on a plane trip when he was rebuffed as he tried to witness to the person seated next to him. He asked the man why he was so antagonistic to Christianity. The man replied, "Christianity robbed me of my parents, and I'm not interested in anything that would do that." His father had been a Christian businessman that traveled around giving his testimony, and his mother was too busy teaching home Bible classes to have time for the children. As a result all four sons grew up without Christ.[39]

The question of the conflict between the missionaries' service and the responsibilities to teenage children is not easy to resolve. It is quite common now for the missionary couple to remain home with their children during the troublesome high school years. Others send their children to boarding high schools. Each missionary has to resolve the conflict as God directs, and no one should be critical of them, for they are responsible to God alone and not to anyone else.

Mission fields would not be so understaffed when a couple decides to remain home with their teen-agers if many more of those who answer the call to missionary service would follow through their commitment to God instead of getting sidetracked here at home. Although the primary interpretation of I Timothy 5:8, ". . . if any provide not for his own, and specially those of his own house, he hath denied the faith, and is worse than an infidel," refers to the provision for material needs, a secondary interpretation or logical extension is that a man must also provide the affection, guidance, and discipline needed by teen-age children, or else he comes under

38. Brandt and Dowdy, *Building a Christian Home*, p. 47.
39. Howard G. Hendricks, *Heaven Help the Home* (Wheaton: Victor Books, 1973), p. 21.

the condemnation of this verse. After all, Christians believe the things of the spirit to be more important than the material satisfactions of life. Many Christian homes would be different if the parents would only realize that the spiritual needs of their children are more important than the material benefits they work so hard to earn for them.

Husbands and wives must strive to achieve a balance in their roles. If an individual has too many tasks, and he cannot do them all well, then some must be eliminated. This means some people must learn to say *no* when they are approached and asked to take another job when they already have more than they can adequately do. This overloading of work on an individual occurs quite frequently in smaller churches. Someone with a willing spirit and leadership ability continually will be asked to do more and more until finally he has more jobs than he can do well. The remedy for the situation is for him to say *no* so someone else will be found for the job. It is amazing how much unused talent there is in even the smaller churches.

The masculine-feminine roles in American society are becoming more confused as the return of our Lord Jesus Christ draws nearer. The efforts of the Women's Liberation Movement, the influence of the radical professors and students, and the propaganda of the mass media all add to the confusion of roles in the minds of our youth. However, the Christian young person has definite guidelines in the Word of God, and he can avoid much of the heartache that many marriages suffer if he will heed the Word and choose a mate with compatible role concepts. For the already-married couple with basic differences in role concepts, there is the help of the indwelling Holy Spirit (Eph. 5:18-21) and the indwelling Word of God (Col. 3:16-17) to enable them to work out these differences to the glory of God.

PERSONALITY INVENTORY

WHAT IS YOUR ROLE CONCEPT?

Write a short paragraph in answer to each of the following statements or questions. Please be as introspective as possible in order to determine your true feelings about the roles of men and women in marriage.

1 Who is (was) dominant in families of your paternal and maternal grandparents? In what ways is (was) this dominance manifested?

2 Discuss the dominance-submission pattern of your parents' interaction? Do you approve of this pattern? Why or why not?

3 Is there a sharing of traditional male-female roles by your parents? Do you plan to repeat this type of interaction when you get married?

4 Analyze the statement, "The mother's place is in the home."

5 State your views on the Women's Liberation Movement.

6 Give Biblical evidence for your view of the Scriptural role of husband and wife in the home.

7 Do you think it is important for young people today to be flexible in their role concepts? Why?

QUESTIONS AND DISCUSSION AND REVIEW

1. What evidence is there in society at large to indicate that marital roles are not clearly defined?

2. Discuss the Scriptural role of a husband in the home.

3. How does the Scriptural role of a wife differ from that of a husband?

4. What evidence is there that the changing role of women in American society has affected the role of the Christian wife and mother?

5. Why are some roles characteristic of only a Christian husband or wife?

6. Why are dominance-submission patterns important in mate selection?

7. How do some young people change their role concepts to differ from that of their parents?

8. Analyze the influence of the multiplication of family roles upon the average Christian family.

9. How does the role of a missionary conflict with the parental role?

10. Why is a balance in roles important for the Christian?

5

DATING

. . . the way of a man with a maid.
Proverbs 30:19

DATING—AN AMERICAN CUSTOM

Dating as a medium by which boy meets girl is an American social invention. It is difficult for the average young person to realize that in many parts of the world the family of the bride or groom arranges the wedding. In Bangladesh, for example, the bridal couple in a Muslim wedding do not see each other until the day of the wedding.[1] In certain African tribes the prospective husband must work several years for his bride just as Jacob did several thousand years ago. In other tribes wives are bought for a price termed "bridewealth."[2] Marriage brokers still do a thriving business in Europe.[3] Although the American custom has been carried to many parts of the world by the members of the armed forces, nowhere in the world do young people have as much freedom in boy-girl relationships as in America.

DATING AND SOCIAL CLASS IN AMERICA

The development of dating as a part of the mate selection process is directly related to the American social class system. Robert O.

---

1. Donna Ahlgrim, "Let's Go to a Wedding in East Pakistan," *The Message* (Philadelphia: Assn. of Baptists for World Evangelism, October 1962), p. 7.
2. M. F. Nimkoff, *Comparative Family Systems* (Boston: Houghton, Mifflin Co., 1965), p. 16.
3. *Newsweek*, March 29, 1965, p. 34.

Blood writes, "The fact that Americans date more than any other people in the world is no accident. Our social circumstances demand it."[4] Ours is a highly stratified society with many levels of social classes. Except for the three large inclusive classes (lower, middle, and upper), the divisions between the various levels are not very well delineated. However, each stratum of society has its own style of life, patterns of speech and dress, cultural values, and child rearing methods.[5] Since there is not a single, standardized method of child rearing, the result is a great variety in the patterns of personality development in the children. Our dating system has evolved to allow young people with diverse backgrounds to test their psychological compatibility so that a young person can find a mate whose personality will be agreeable with his.[6]

DATING AS A SYSTEM FOR MATCHING PERSONALITIES

In an African tribe where women are not very highly esteemed, and any family problem is settled by the husband's dominance, then the matching of personalities is not very important. Similarly in the Bangladesh culture, where there is little husband-wife interaction, it is evident that less attention can be paid to how well the personalities complement each other.[7] In our culture, with the changes that have taken place in the family structure, there is great emphasis placed on the psychological satisfactions that each partner receives in the marriage. It is very necessary that young people have the opportunity to test their personalities with many different individuals so that they may find the one that promises to yield the greatest happiness to each partner. Our system of dating and mate selection is basically a trial and error method and can produce good results if properly used. James H. Jauncey states there are the "possibilities of finding happiness in marriage beyond our wildest dreams."[8]

4. Robert O. Blood, *Marriage* (New York: The Free Press of Glencoe, 1962), p. 19.
5. Thomas E. Lasswell, *Class and Stratum* (Boston: Houghton, Mifflin Co., 1965), p. 65.
6. Blood, *Marriage*, p. 20.
7. Hanna Papanek, "Purdah in Pakistan: Seclusion and Modern Occupations for Women," *Journal of Marriage and the Family* August 1971, p. 520. Council on Family Relations, August 1971), p. 520.
8. James H Jauncey, *Magic in Marriage* (Grand Rapids: Zondervan Publishing House, 1966), p. 8.

DATING—A LEARNING EXPERIENCE

Dating usually follows a logical progression, moving from random dating through steady dating to engagement which ends in marriage. In random dating partners are chosen without any thought of serious emotional involvement. The authors of *Dating, Mating and Marriage* state, "In a large proportion of cases, the only function served by dating is that of providing sheer play, fun, and good times. This is, perhaps, the simplest form that dating can take."[9] Such dating may begin in junior high school and is quite common in senior high school. This type of dating should be the norm for young people during senior high and the first two years of college.[10]

Since the very purpose of the system is to allow young people to meet different personalities of the opposite sex in order to test their compatibility, they should try to meet as many as possible in order to discover the type of person with which they feel most comfortable. During these dating experiences the young person comes to know and understand his own personality better. He discovers weaknesses that need to be corrected. He encounters strengths that should be capitalized on. He sees certain traits in young women that he wants to avoid when he decides to choose a mate.

Learning the social skills of dating is one of the more difficult tasks, especially if a fellow or girl is somewhat shy. How to ask for a date and how to respond when asked does not always come easily, but like other skills, they become easier with practice. He discovers it is easier to ask for a first date with someone that he has already met in a class, a club, or some other social activity. He learns that on a first date it is easier to take the girl to a party or concert where there are planned activities so that their conversational abilities are not strained. She learns to give him little clues that she is enjoying the evening and thus relieves some of the strain that accompanies a first date, since both are trying to make a good impression. He also learns to differentiate between a girl's "polite excuse" because she does not want to date him, and the "raincheck" she gives him when she would like to accept but has a bona fide reason for not being able to accept his invitation.

During these formative years of dating, the young person is seek-

9. Jessie Bernard, Helen E. Buchanan, and Wm. M. Smith, Jr., *Dating, Mating and Marriage* (Cleveland: Howard Allen, Inc., 1958), p. 46.
10. This is the author's suggestion based on twenty-eight years of experience in working with young people as pastor, missionary, and college professor.

ing God's will for his life in regard to a vocation, and realizes the necessity of finding a life partner who has the same desire to do the will of God.[11] He becomes more aware of the values he holds, and how he needs a mate who holds to similar values. A young lady related her experiences concerning values as follows:

> I dated a fellow when I was confused in the area of life's goals, and this hurt our relationship. This guy valued money, not in the sense that he would do anything to get it; but it was important to him. I have never cared much for money. It seems of little importance to me, probably because it matters greatly to my mother. We, my mother and I, have a tendency to go in opposite directions.

This girl recognized that their values concerning money differed greatly and would be a source of conflict if she continued dating him.

DATING AND PERSONAL STANDARDS OF CONDUCT

Whenever dating begins, the fellow or girl has to decide what his or her standards of conduct will be in relationships with the opposite sex. The Christian young person faces the temptations involved in necking, petting, and premarital relations because he lives in a "sex-suffused society" just the same as the unsaved individual. Necking is usually defined as contact above the neck; light petting as contact between the neck and waist, and heavy petting as contact below the waist.[12] Having been reared in a Christian home and good Bible-teaching church will not exempt him from the evils of the day, but this godly training should give him a strong foundation on which to stand, and to form the basis of Christian behavior which is honoring at all times to his Lord and Savior Jesus Christ.

The unsaved young person may subscribe to the so-called "new morality," and the "playboy" philosophy, but the Christian may not, since his life is lived with the consciousness that "Thou God seest me." Although the world may condone sin and even encourage sin, he realizes that sin is sin and is under the judgment of God. He knows that his body is the temple of the Holy Spirit (I Cor. 6:19) and is to be kept pure and chaste in order not to grieve the indwelling Holy Spirit.[13]

11. Jack Wyrtzen, *Sex Is Not Sinful* (Grand Rapids: Zondervan Publishing House, 1970), p. 44.
12. Walter Trobisch, *Love Is a Feeling to Be Learned* (Downer's Grove, IL: Inter-Varsity Press, 1971), pp. 28-37.
13. Wyrtzen, *Sex Is Not Sinful*, p. 35.

The manner in which the Christian young person responds to the God-given biological urges which are manifested at puberty will largely depend on the way in which sex was presented in the home and church. There are two main attitudes toward sex in the fundamental churches today. One teaches that sex is only for marriage but is sinful, dirty, and is not to be openly discussed.[14] This view may have arisen because the Bible so sternly warns against sexual sins. God knows that stable family life is essential to any orderly society, and He knows that nothing is more disturbing to the family than fornication and adultery. Consequently, He is very careful to instruct and to warn the human race to avoid such perils. Such a view which overemphasizes the negative influence of sex makes it difficult for the adolescent to recognize his sexual desires as God-given and holy, and he may have problems in adjusting to interaction with the opposite sex.[15]

The second major interpretation includes the prohibition against sexual sins, but the primary teaching is that sexual desires are divinely given, are holy, and are to be satisfied and enjoyed only in marriage. C. W. Scudder comments, "Any stigma which has been attached to sex must be removed. Sex is not in itself evil. It is a positive good when used as God intended."[16] Children and young people are taught the dignity of the human body as the temple of the Holy Spirit. The dangers and virtues of sex are openly discussed between parent and child, pastor and young people, so that healthy attitudes toward sex are developed.

In this view the submission of the body to the control of the Holy Spirit is stressed rather than mere self-control. Chastity of the body then becomes much more than the simple preservation of one's virginity for the prospective mate. Purity of mind and body takes on a divine dimension, for He said, "Be ye holy, for I am holy!" Stephen F. Olford writes, "We do not become more spiritual by seeking to disassociate ourselves from our bodies, but by making them the perfect instruments of the will of God. The true path is to accept frankly and without reserve all the God-given functions of the body, bringing the sum total of thoughts concerning them into captivity to Jesus Christ."[17] Those who approach dating with these attitudes will find it much easier to face the challenge which their values will encounter during the dating and courtship period.

14. Trobisch, *Love is a Feeling*, p. 29.
15. Stephen F. Olford and Frank A. Lawes, *The Sanctity of Sex* (Westwood, NJ: Fleming H. Revell Co., 1963), p. 15.
16. C. W. Scudder, *The Family in Christian Perspective* (Nashville: Broadman Press, 1962), p. 21.
17. Olford and Lawes, *Sanctity of Sex*, p. 22.

The greatest threat to Christian standards of sexual behavior comes from the so-called "new morality" which is nothing more than the old immorality with a new title. Basically, this philosophy teaches that there are no divine moral absolutes, but every act is judged by whether or not it is done under the guise of "love." Quite often Joseph Fletcher, who wrote *Situation Ethics*, is thought to be the author of this philosophy, but he merely stated what has been practiced for some time. His book was written in 1966, whereas *Newsweek* (April 6, 1964) in its article, "The Morals Revolution on the U.S. Campus," wrote, "In its simplest terms, the new campus morality permits 'sex with love' provided a boy or girl doesn't fall in love with two people at the same time."[18]

This report simply catalogued the practices that are the result of two generations of religious liberalism in our churches, and the teaching in the public schools of John Dewey's relativity of morals, i.e., there are no absolutes, since the majority practicing an act make it acceptable conduct. In an earlier day the hedonistic "Playboy" philosophy of Hugh Hefner would likewise have failed, but the moral climate has been altered by the failure of our churches ("God is dead") and the dissemination of the relativity of morals. Thus, the "new morality" was not a creation of the sixties but was merely the full manifestation of the secularistic tendency in American society.[19]

Since the Christian subculture is influenced by the national cultural pattern, the young people in Christian churches have been affected by the "new morality" practiced by their peers. Although the vast majority would hold to the Biblical standard prohibiting sexual relationships outside of marriage, there are many individuals who justify their petting on the basis that it is all right if the couple "love" one another. If they are not in "love," they do not have the social approval of their peer group and the girl is labeled as "promiscuous" in relationship to petting. This peer group approval, and the fact that the young woman remains a "technical" virgin in the sense that she has never had a sexual relationship, are definite aspects of the "petting complex." However, from the Christian viewpoint, such a young lady is guilty of breaking the spirit of the moral law even though she has kept the letter of the law.

One young lady with guilt feelings from such an experience wrote, "I engaged in some necking and light petting with a fellow I planned

18. *Newsweek*, April 6, 1964, p. 54.
19. The reader is again referred to *It All Depends* by Fritz Ridenour, G/L Publications, Glendale, California. This paperback is an excellent criticism of the "new morality" as espoused by situation ethics and the Playboy philosophy.

to marry. We then were separated for a semester. After we parted I felt guilty, and wondered how many others I might possibly 'love' before I married. I may still marry him, but I have made up my mind to refrain from such activities until I am married."

Unfortunately, some young couples who engage in petting cannot stop short of the sexual relationship, and pregnancy results. Quite often they turn to the "new morality" and attempt to justify such behavior on the fact that they are in "love." Walter Trobisch gives a penetrating answer to such a couple who asked:

> Isn't all that matters is that it was done in love? I answered, "Love? Love to the baby for whom no proper home is prepared? Love to your partner whose professional career is now messed up? Love to your parents to whom you caused embarrassment and shame? Maybe you solved one problem—you released the sexual tension. But you created new ones—wedding, home, support, profession . . . Love?"[20]

He proceeds to say, "Love is hurt when it is not protected by divine will. Sex can hurt love. Therefore God protects love by confining sex to marriage."[21]

Christian young people need to be very careful not to reject the "new morality" in one area and then by the same philosophy attempt to justify behavior that is displeasing to God.

PROBLEMS OF "GOING STEADY"

The increased intimacy engendered by steady dating exposes the couple to temptations to transgress their standards in this area, and is one of the big disadvantages of this type of dating. This is particularly true when couples date before they are mature enough to handle the emotional pressures of prolonged physical contact. In reference to this situation, Robert C. Williamson writes, "The question remains whether going steady at the high school level is a prelude to informal engagement or simply 'making time' since this type of relationship offers the male certain sexual advantages that might border on exploitation of the opposite sex."[22]

Many of the difficulties couples face could be averted if they

20. Trobisch, *Love Is a Feeling*, p. 30. Used by permission.
21. Ibid.
22. Robert C. Williamson, *Marriage and Family Relations* (New York: John Wiley & Sons, Inc., 1966), p. 175.

avoided the compromising situations such as the parked car, where they are tempted to engage in necking and petting. Most Christian couples do not intend to violate their standards in this area, but do so when their emotions get out of control when they are in some "compromised situation."[23]

Most couples do not know that there is, as Dwight H. Small states it, a "moral law of diminishing returns" in physical relationships. [24] A couple who has progressed from holding hands to kissing cannot return to the less intimate level and be satisfied. If they have started petting it becomes very difficult to regress to kissing as the only means of physical contact. As the petting continues, more and more intimacy is required for satisfaction and the couple faces increasing temptation even though they do not realize it. At this stage it is easy for the emotions to get out of control and the results are regretted, and many time affect their families and friends.

When faced with temptation, Joseph said, ". . . how can I do this great wickedness, and sin against God?" (Gen. 39:9). He knew that such sexual indulgence was sin against God and he did not want to displease Jehovah. This is still one of the best motives for purity of life. Young people also need to remember that many relationships are broken and they need to ask themselves, "Would we be ashamed of this act if we broke up, or will we be sorry for it once we are married?"

The desire to touch and caress the partner is a definite part of romantic love, but it should be kept in its proper perspective in the total relationship. If it becomes the dominant factor in a dating situation, then the more important function of dating to test the psychological compatibility may be glossed over. When the physical aspect is dominant in a relationship, and a couple cannot proceed to engagement or marriage because of youth or finances, the biological pressures may build up until they break a relationship which might have become a very happy marriage. Even if the relationship does not break up, the individuals are filled with guilt feelings because they know they are misusing their bodies, and they have taken that which God intends to be holy and sacred and lowered it to the level of the sinful indulgence of the flesh.

Many of the problems of necking and petting can be avoided if the couple plan their dates so that little time is available to spend alone in seclusion. The situation is helped by thoughtful parents who set

23. In one class of 32 Christian college students, 17 of them stated they had violated their standards of personal conduct in dating.
24. Dwight Hervey Small, *Design for Christian Marriage* (Westwood, NJ: Fleming H. Revell Co., 1959), p. 165.

realistic hours for their young people to be home. It is difficult to begin this if the young person is already accustomed to coming in whenever he pleases. It is much easier if parents assume this responsibility when the son or daughter begins to date so that from the very beginning they know they are to be home at a particular hour. This is particularly helpful for the young lady, for in our culture she is expected to "draw the line" in relationship to necking and petting. It is not fair to give her all this responsibility, for the Christian fellow ought to realize his obligation to the Lord to keep himself pure and holy. Many fellows do hold such a standard, one similar to that expressed by a college student:

> I like to neck, but I am strictly against petting. My girl and I have not talked about it and made any kind of agreement; I just assumed responsibility myself for drawing the line, or controlling the situation. We kiss and embrace, but each kiss and embrace is kept to a very short time (10-20 seconds?). I have not touched her (except for my hand on her neck or my arms around her shoulders or waist, of course) and I do not intend to. My aim is to keep us from getting passionately involved, or "turned on."

There are those whose conduct is not what it ought to be, and who will seek to exploit the dating partner for the selfish gratification of their own desires. The young lady who agrees to " park" whether it be in the "lover's lane" or the driveway at home is inviting difficulty that could easily be avoided, and society (including the church members) will hold her responsible if moral standards are transgressed.

DANGER OF DATING UNSAVED PERSONS

The old cliché, "every date is a prospective mate" contains much truth. Whether it be a junior high date or a college date, the first one can lead to the second. The many individuals who marry childhood sweethearts support this fact. Consequently it is best for Christian young people to date only born-again individuals. If there is no first date with an unsaved individual, there will be no opportunity for a mixed marriage to materialize.

This standard of dating only Christians poses a real problem for girls, particularly in small churches where they usually outnumber the fellows. Consequently, many girls are left with the choice of no dates or dating the unsaved. If they choose the former, they miss some of the learning experiences that dating provides, and if they choose the latter they run the risk of marrying outside the will of God.

AGE AND DATING

The age at which dating begins is important. There is a tendency for adolescents to begin dating earlier today. Robert K. Kelley reports on a survey of 443 community college students of which "49 percent reported that their first date occurred during the seventh, eighth, or ninth grades."[25] A survey of Christian college students show that some girls have their first date at the age of twelve, and most of those who date had their first date by the age of fourteen. There were some who indicated they had never had a date. Among the fellows, dating began a little later, with thirteen being the youngest age, while the largest number had their first date at fifteen.[26]

This trend toward dating at younger ages means that the time span for dating is longer now than in the past. The average girl who begins dating at age fourteen and who marries at age twenty has a six-year period of dating. If she begins earlier and marries later the time is extended. If the young man decides to wait until he has finished his professional education, there may be a ten-year period during which he must delay marriage until he reaches his goal. Very often he will marry and pursue his education at the same time. Consequently, in our culture there is a relatively long time during which young people must control their biological desires until the actual time of marriage.

Conflicts arise when adolescents and parents differ on when the young person is old enough to date. Many parents feel that since they did not date until they were seventeen or eighteen years old, their children should not date before that age. They fail to realize that dating begins much earlier today as indicated by our survey of Christian college students. Some parents do not consider that each child is different and that some mature earlier than others. One daughter may be perfectly willing to wait until seventeen to begin dating, but her sister may be mature enough to start dating at fifteen. The wise parent will maintain good communications with the children and work out a plan for each child rather than setting arbitrary age limits at which dating can begin.

25. Robert K. Kelley, *Courtship, Marriage and the Family* (New York: Harcourt, Brace & World, Inc., 1969), p. 41.
26. Survey of 46 students in a Marriage and Family class at Cedarville College, 1969.

PARENTAL ROLES AND DATING

It is also wise for parents to assume responsibility in regard to dating in areas other than age. Certain rules should be established concerning the use of the family car. It is very embarrassing for Junior to plan to use the car for a date on Friday night when Dad must use it to leave town on a business trip. This can be avoided if there is an understanding that Junior talk with Dad before he makes a date involving the use of the car. The use of the family living room by sister and her date may conflict with mother's entertaining unless there is good communication between them. Most parents enjoy having their children bring their friends home with them, but the parents also lead a social life that occasionally requires entertaining their friends.

Although some young people may disagree, the parents have an obligation to counsel with their children in reference to their choice of dating partners. If the young person makes an unwise choice, the parent has a moral obligation to try to get the young person to see the error of his way. The parent also must be aware of his own limitations and not project his preferences and desires upon the children. Just because Dad preferred redheads to brunettes does not mean that Junior will also prefer redheads.

Sometimes young people will be justified in rejecting the advice of the parents if there is no valid reason for objecting to the son's or daughter's choice. Paul exhorts children to obey their parents "in the Lord" (Eph. 6:1), but the time comes when the children reach maturity and must make their own decisions concerning the will of God for their lives. If disagreements arise between the parent and the young adult as to what constitutes the will of God, then the young person must prayerfully make the decision that he feels is God's will for him. As an adult, he is responsible before God, and God will not hold the parent responsible for the actions of an adult son or daughter. The case of Mary and John illustrate this fact:

> *Mary and John met during their freshman year of college. Mary was very pretty, a superior student and had received a full scholarship. John was handsome, an average student but had musical talent and played in one of the college trios. Both were sincere in their dedication to Christ. Their relationship developed and Mary took John to her home for vacation. It was an unhappy time as her parents rejected John and made it quite clear they did not like him. They intended for Mary to finish college and then acquire graduate training in her field, so from their viewpoint marriage was out of the question until her education was completed. Perhaps the parents were projecting their own unfulfilled ambitions upon their daughter*

*and expected her to achieve goals which they had not gained. John
was a fine Christian man and there was no rational reason for their
rejection. John and Mary were very much in love and tried for two
years to gain her parents approval. This had not been secured by the
end of her junior year in college, so they were of age and decided to
get married in John's home church. At this point her parents realized
that the couple were sincere and they changed their attitude so she
could be married in her home church. Eventually a good relationship
was established between the couple and Mary's parents. However,
John and Mary's courtship had many unhappy moments because of
the parental opposition to John.*

THE RAPID DEVELOPMENT
OF COLLEGE DATING RELATIONSHIPS

The case of John and Mary also illustrates another point concerning dating in college. In the average Christian college where young people are not limited to seeing each other at specific times, the couple may have much more interaction than they ordinarily would if they were living at home and following the usual dating pattern. This type of dating can be called "greenhouse" dating since the relationship grows so much more quickly due to the amount of interaction between the fellow and girl.

At college the couple can have morning devotions together, go to breakfast and prayerband, attend classes, eat lunch, study in the library, have dinner, attend a basketball game or other social function, and finally have devotions at the close of the day. This "togetherness" can be repeated day after day so that after three months they have had more testing of personal compatibility than the couple at home would have in a year or two of ordinary dating. Unless the couple are very careful to keep their emotions under tight control, they will be ready for marriage much sooner than they expect.

Parents are quite often disturbed when a college couple who has only been dating a year desire to be married. They feel they have not known each other long enough since they are unaware of the great amount of interaction the couple has enjoyed during the year. They are reluctant to grant permission for the marriage and the couple must point out that the fellow and girl see much more of each other in college dating than do couples at home.

Parents need to be aware it is only normal that a relationship between a couple will develop until a point where they are biologically and emotionally ready for marriage. If for some reason marriage is not possible, the couple then face the danger of biological pressures tempting them to transgress their moral standards, or else these pressures subconsciously cause conflict which may eventually destroy the relationship.

Another possibility exists: the couple sees each other too often so that interest is dulled, and the relationship is broken. Actually, a college couple who are in each other's company from morning until night can see each other more than the average husband and wife, since the husband is employed for eight or nine hours. College couples have often been counseled to limit their interaction to once a day, or every other day in order to recapture some of the vitality which their relationship has lost because they have been seeing each other too often.

WHY SOME COLLEGE STUDENTS DO NOT DATE

Many young people have no difficulty in boy-girl relationships and have many dates. Others are not able to get involved in the dating game. Many fellows and girls arrive at college without ever having had a date. Kelley observes,

> For one reason or another, the courtship system does not serve this group adequately, and their prospects for successful marriage may be severely hindred by their lack of dating experience. When a possible partner does appear on the horizon, the nondater may accept him (or her) without a discriminating view of basic personality traits or a realistic appraisal of the future. Such individuals will probably be unaware of what is required of them in such a relationship.[27]

Although Bible schools and Christian colleges are facetiously spoken of as "match" factories, the truth is that they do bring together marriageable young people who have many things in common. There is no better place for a young person to find a mate with similar beliefs, goals, and values; and a multitude of happy Christian marriages have resulted from courtships on Christian campuses. If a fellow or girl leaves the campus without a mate or prospective mate, they will never again have such a wide selection of possible mate choices. While there may be eligible bachelors and single girls back home in the local church, the opportunities will be much smaller than they are on the campus.

It is important then that young people learn to date, as it is the initial step in our mate selection system. Through the years the students of one Christian college have contributed reasons why fellows and girls on that particular campus do not date. Some of

27. Kelley, *Courtship, Marriage, Family*, p. 47. Used by permission.

these are valid, such as "dating someone back home," but others indicate personality inadequacies that the individual needs to remedy. The following reasons are not discussed in any order of importance because of the personal variables involved in any attempt to rank them as to importance.

Some students do not date because they do not have the time. They intend to get as much out of their expensive college education as possible. They realize that graduate education is very important in today's culture, so they want the best undergraduate grade point average possible, since this is such a big factor in gaining admittance to a graduate school. They do not date because they know this may lead to serious involvement and marriage.

The returning GIs of World War II demonstrated that marriage does not hinder a person's studies but may help them. Other surveys have also demonstrated that students do better after marriage.

Parents often contribute to this pressure by telling the student they will help them with college expenses only if they remain unmarried. This attitude might be proper if they send the son to a school attended only by men or the daughter to a college for women. It seems unfair for a parent to send the young person to a co-educational college where they will be surrounded by members of the opposite sex, and to expect the young person to refrain from dating and courtship. It also displays an ignorance on the part of the parent of the functional role of the college in mate selection in American culture. Fortunately, most parents are aware of this role and for the parents of daughters it is one of the prime motivations for sending the girls to college. Usually such parents are willing to help the young couple to complete their education.

A small percentage of students come to college already involved in a relationship with a fellow or girl back home. This is a legitimate reason for not dating if there is a mutual understanding they will not date others during the separation. The facts are that most of these relationships are broken by the separation, for although "absence makes the heart grow fonder," it usually makes it grow fonder for "someone closer at hand."

Many students come from small churches where the number of prospective Christian dating partners is limited, and when they arrive at college they are often pleasantly surprised at the large number of fellows or girls available for dates. The partner back home begins to seem less favorable in the light of all the young people nearby in the college setting, and many such relationships are broken during the first quarter or semester of college. Where such relationships do not dissolve, it is because the couple had a long period of dating before the partner left for college so that a very strong bond developed between them, one which separation could not break, or else the college is located close to home whereby the student can get home very often to have interaction with the friend left behind.

It is unfortunate that on some college campuses there is social pressure against random dating. There is a tendency for a fellow to look over the available girls to make it a goal to date a certain one that he has chosen on the basis of physical appearance and perhaps a few casual meetings in the dining hall. If he succeeds in dating her, he is elated, but if she rejects his invitation for a date, he is crushed and just doesn't date.

The opposite is true with the girls. A girl sees a particular fellow as "the only one" and if he doesn't ask her for a date, she doesn't care to date anyone else. If he does date her, the rest of the fellows consider her as his "steady" and will not think of also asking her for a date. Students on such campuses miss the opportunity for dating interaction with some very lovely personalities, and perhaps end up with less than the best as a choice for a mate. They are unaware of the values to themselves of such dating, and of the part it plays in the mate selection system.

On most college campuses there are students who do not date because they have no desire to do so. Even at college age they have not matured to the point where they have a normal, active interest in the opposite sex. Sometimes such individuals have been conditioned against marriage by the example of very unhappily married parents. Anyone who has counseled young people for a long period of time is aware of the large number of unhappy and miserable Christian homes, and it is not surprising that children reared in such circumstances will occasionally have such a negative reaction that they resolve never to get married. Thus, they have no interest in dating, since to them it may lead to an unhappy marriage.

Such a young person needs to realize that though his home was not happy, there are many homes that fulfill Christ's expectations for a Christian marriage. If he will look around his church he will find a family that is happy, and which he can adopt as the "model" for his own marriage. He will then substitute a positive view for his negative one, and will consciously strive to make the change in his own thinking. A young person is not responsible for the environment in which he was reared, but he is obligated to change unhealthy ideas and attitudes that are not pleasing to God. He has all the promises of the Word of God, and the strength imparted by the Holy Spirit so he can say with the apostle Paul, "I can do all things through Christ, who strengtheneth me" (Phil. 4:13).

Many students do not date in college because they are shy and lack self-confidence. Usually such a person did not date in high school for the same reasons. The shy individual has had certain unhappy and painful experiences in childhood that has caused him to withdraw within himself. He has learned not to reach out to other people, for in that way he cannot be hurt again. Consequently, he has as little contact with other people as possible. In reference to dating, the shy fellow does not ask a girl for a date because he is afraid she will refuse. This would be another hurt for an already bruised ego, so he avoids the situation.

If a fellow calls a bashful girl and asks for a date, she refuses because she also is afraid to interact with the opposite sex since she cannot carry a conversation. These individuals may be very intelligent and very capable in many areas, but they have not developed socially. They may have the normal desires to date, but are unable to break out of their shells.

Clyde M. Narramore has an excellent booklet, *Improving Your Self-Confidence*, in which he makes the following suggestions: A person must develop competence in order to have self-confidence. By becoming a well-groomed person and learning correct etiquette a person develops poise. An understanding of one's own feelings and attitudes, with an awareness of the feelings of others can help to overcome timidity. Conversational skills need to be developed in order for a person to reveal his true self. Most important is daily communion with Christ and the dependence on the indwelling Holy Spirit, which give inner strength and confidence to be radiated from the life. Professional counseling may be needed by some people with problems too deep to be overcome by the individual alone. The cost of such services is minor in comparison to the lifelong benefits received. His last statement is especially valuable: "Confidence is the outworking of an internal condition—the natural fruit of a mature personality. And it can be yours!"[28]   Every young person will profit by the reading of this helpful booklet, but it will be invaluable to those who need to improve their self-image.

Social skills in dating can only be learned by practice, and the shy individual who makes an attempt to improve his self-confidence should begin to date. It will be helpful if at first he dates individuals that he knows so that there are some common interests that can serve as a focus for conversation. The use of the telephone is especially helpful in asking for a date since it avoids the face to face

28. Clyde M. Narramore, *Improving Your Self-Confidence* (Grand Rapids: Zondervan Publishing House, 1961), pp. 28-29.

interaction which makes the shy individual nervous. The shy girl may have to develop some social skills by learning to converse with girls before she will be noticed and asked for a date by a fellow. Since shyness is a learned behavior, it can be unlearned if the individual makes a sincere effort to change himself with the help of the Holy Spirit.

Physical problems prevent many young people from dating. In our culture there is the extreme overemphasis on physical beauty. Individuals who, by accident of birth or some combination of genes, lack beauty as defined by the culture are at a serious disadvantage in our dating system. Whereas in one tribe in Africa, the young bride-to-be is placed in a "fattening room" for three months prior to the wedding, our culture stresses "thinness" as a most desirable physical trait. The young lady who tends to obesity because of hormonal imbalance or poor eating habits is rejected as a dating partner even though she may have a beautiful personality.

Likewise the young man on the heavy side will encounter difficulty getting dates with the more desirable "thin" young women. Since there is a shortage of young men, he will be able to find a marriage partner, but the young lady with a weight problem will experience greater difficulty in finding a mate. These individuals must put forth greater effort to lose weight and to develop very pleasing personalities to compete for mates. They need not be discouraged, for if they will look around they will see many obese young people who are happily married.

Acne is another problem that hinders some young people from dating. Much medical research is being carried on to find a cure for this scourge of teen-agers and young adults, and progress in treatment is being made. Certainly the young person should seek medical aid and take advantage of the new medications which have proven effective aids in treating acne. In addition, the self-consciousness often engendered by acne must be overcome. Earlier suggestions for improving self-confidence will be helpful here.

Compatible goals in life pose a problem for some young people who date. When the person has a well-defined goal, such as a calling to the mission field, ministry, or medicine, he realizes the necessity of finding a mate who will eagerly share such a lifework. These are important values, for many a man has had to leave the ministry because of a wife who could not accept her role. Many a man called to the mission field has been sidetracked into God's second best because of a wrong mate choice. If the person is not strong enough to date randomly without getting involved with a person with an incompatible goal, then perhaps it is best to limit his dating.

The "rating" system deters many from dating on some campuses. In every school there are always those students who because of beauty, masculinity, or personality are rated more highly as desirable dates. Some students are so ego-centered that they will not date at all if they cannot date the highly rated persons. A corollary of this is the social pressure exerted in some dormitories whereby a girl or fellow is ridiculed if they date someone who is not rated highly by the friends in the dorm. The tragedy of this is that many individuals with winsome personalities are passed over as prospective dates because they do not have the physical beauty of some campus "queen" or "BMOC" (Big Man on Campus). On the other hand, it is unfortunate that on some campuses there are individuals who deserve a low rating because of a lack of spiritual commitment, and should be avoided as dating partners if one desires a successful Christian marriage.

Some fellows do not date because they don't have the money or a car. It is true that higher education is very costly today and even where parents tried to plan a program of savings to help their sons through college, they never realized the havoc that inflation causes to the best-laid financial plans. On the average Christian college campus there are numerous opportunities for dates such as athletic games, concerts, and church activities, that do not require a car nor involve any expense other than buying a soft drink and a sandwich after the event. The fellow with a low budget can still date if he plans well and makes a sincere effort to do so.

There are also some fellows who are normal heterosexual individuals but prefer the company of other fellows. They find more enjoyment in playing a game of touch football with the fellows than in having a date with a girl friend. When they do date, the girl often finds herself playing "second fiddle" to his gang of buddies. Unless a girl enjoys being alone much of the time, she should never consider marrying this type of fellow, for even after marriage, he will still prefer his friends' company to that of his wife.

The chief reason girls do not date is that they are not asked. Except for a few special events such as a "Sadie Hawkins" day, girls in our culture are not permitted to ask the fellow for a date. This problem is compounded on some campuses where the girls outnumber the fellows. There is not too much a girl can do in this situation except be warm and outgoing in her casual relationships with fellows so that they will get to know her personality in this manner and perhaps they will then ask for a date. She should avoid always being with a group of girls, since most fellows have difficulty enough asking for a date and would be hesitant to ask her in front of a group of girls. She should never appear "too eager," as this turns the fellows off as quickly as being too shy.

A small number of girls have such a high ideal for their prospective mate that they never see a fellow that measures up to their standards. It is good to have an ideal, but it should be tested by actual dating and adjusted to reality as needed. Some women spend a lifetime looking for a perfect partner, never realizing their own imperfections.

Some college women do not date because of a psuedo-intellectual attitude. They are so busy studying in an attempt to make the highest honor roll that they have no time to date. It is difficult to determine if this is an attempt to avoid dating because they lack the necessary social skills, or whether they are not asked, since men prefer to date women who are less intellectual than they are themselves. The truly intelligent girl will be able to use her ability to make the fellow think he is more intelligent than she is!

USE OF COMPUTERS IN DATING

The use of computers in selecting dating partners is increasing. On large campuses where computers are available, a "computer date night" is held periodically. Some companies are organized solely for this purpose and advertise on a national basis. The person fills out a questionnaire and sends a fee with the completed form to the dating service. It is programmed, put through the computer, and the client is mailed a list of eligible dates that live in his area who have also applied for the service. The idea is to try to scientifically match individuals and to assure as much compatibility as possible before they meet. Many of the factors that help to make a marriage successful are known, and these elements are programmed into the computer to remove some of the "trial-and-error" testing of compatibility that takes place in ordinary dating.

The pioneer in this attempt to scientifically match marriage partners was Karl Miles Wallace of Los Angeles State College. However, after six and one-half years of researching six thousand club members, Wallace felt that people were too reluctant to give up the "folklore of romance" and was disappointed and disillusioned in his endeavor to mate people scientifically. It was his opinion that the average fellow puts more thought and research into buying a new car than he does in selecting a life partner.[29]

29. *Parade* (New York: Parade Publications, Inc., October 6, 1963), p. 6.

Another early attempt was the Scientific Introduction Service founded by Eric Riss, a clinical psychologist in New York City in 1956. He followed a system similar to that of Wallace and also used a punch card and sorting machine. In seven and one-half years he engineered 710 marriages of which only three had ended in divorce, a very good average.[30]

There are many firms advertising their services today. Leonard Benson indicates that ". . . computerized introduction services have sprouted all over the country"[31] They appeal more to the intellectual and educated segment of the population. Their aim is to avoid basing marriages on physical attraction alone, and to insure some mental, emotional, and cultural compatibility. Any effort to help reduce the unhappiness in marriage and the divorce rate is commendable. It is doubtful that such services can be helpful to the Christian since his background and requirements are different than those of the average citizen. However, the emphasis on matching compatibilities in scientific mate selection rather than basing marriage on mainly physical attraction has much to recommend it to Christian young people. If a Christian college has computer services available, a "computer date night" might prove to be an interesting event. However, the commercial "computer dating" services are under suspicion because of fraudulent operations in the field and a person should be alert to this fact.

INDICATIONS OF DATING INCOMPATIBILITY

A definite feature of a "trial-and-error" dating system is the dissolving of relationships. Most young people will go through one or more experiences of "breaking up." The emotional results will vary with the extent of the time the relationship has been in progress and the intensity of the emotional involvement of the partners. One couple may go together a short while, not feel too deeply toward each other, and break up one week and be dating someone else the next. Another couple may suffer a traumatic emotional experience when they dissolve the relationship after a long and intense period of dating. They may not recover from the "broken hearts" and date again for several months.

Many times there are warning signs that a relationship is in

30. Ibid.
31. Leonard Benson, *The Family Bond* (New York: Random House, 1971), p. 65.

difficulty, and young people need to be aware of these as they often indicate that the relationship is not the best one possible. Most dating couples will occasionally have a "lover's quarrel," after which they will experience great emotional satisfaction as they "make-up." These quarrels are a normal part of the adjustments that two people make in learning to interact closely with one another. However, if the disagreements and quarrels are numerous, and often intense, this is a warning that something is wrong in the relationship. The couple should analyze the situation and try to determine the cause of the friction. If they discover they have irreconcilable differences in the important areas such as goals and values, then it would be best if they parted company. It may be that one partner uses quarreling as a neurotic release, and of course one would not want to go through life married to such a person.

Couples that frequently "break up," then get back together, should be aware that such behavior indicates there is some serious incompatibility in the relationship. They should examine their interaction to discover the area or areas where disagreement occurs. They then should seek to modify their behavior in these areas to see if adjustments can be made. They must be careful not to sidestep disagreeable issues by thinking it will be different after they are married. For example, if they have strong differences over the use of money while dating, the conflict will be worse after marriage. Avoiding issues to avert dissension will only lead to greater frustration and conflict at a later date. Mature young people will closely examine their compatibilities, and if agreement cannot be reached, they will end the relationship once and forever. They will then be free to seek a more compatible dating partner.

A lack of interest and concern for the dating partner is always a sign that something is wrong in the relationship. Many relationships are continued long after one partner has lost interest. When a couple are separated for a period of time, and one person does not communicate with the other, it is a definite sign that love no longer exists between the two people. It is the very nature of a person in love to be concerned about the loved one, and to desire to communicate as frequently as possible with that person. Anyone who has experienced the frustration of placing a call to a college dormitory during the evening hours is familiar with this aspect of love. These young people in love get on the phone and can talk for an hour about their activities of the day.

It is absurd for a fellow who has been going with a girl for two years to tell her he loves her and then fail to communicate with her during the summer months between the school years. In like manner, a fellow who does not give a girl a gift on her birthday or some other special occasion evidences a lack of love for her, for it is also the nature of love to give. There may be extenuating circumstances whereby a fellow may not have the money, but if this is the case, he certainly will explain. If she is in love with him, she will understand. A repeated lack of concern is an indication that the relationship should be examined to see if it should be continued.

A relationship is also in trouble when one partner wants to go further in the area of necking or petting than the other partner. Since fellows have the stronger sex drive, it usually means that he will be the one who wants to transgress in these areas. Since they are "in love" there may be the tendency for the girl to lower her standards, but she needs to remember that this does not justify such behavior. If she does give in to his desires, he may lose respect for her and eventually the relationship will be broken anyway.

Another situation occurs very often on Christian college campuses where the individuals engage in very intense dating, from morning to night. If after a year of such dating, a person is not willing to commit himself or herself to the partner in some understanding about marriage, then it is doubtful if there is much to be gained in continuing such a relationship. Self-revelation takes place very rapidly under such dating intensity, so a couple ought to know after several months of such interaction whether they are compatible or not. They should have enough knowledge of each other to know if they should proceed toward marriage.

Breaking a relationship is usually a painful emotional experience, but young people should realize that dating is for testing psychological compatibilities, and when incompatibilities cannot be reconciled, it is proper to stop and to start over with another partner. This process can be repeated numerous times until in the will of God the best possible partner is found. "The name of the game is dating," and if played rationally and well, it can lead to happiness in marriage.

PERSONALITY INVENTORY

ARE YOU A GOOD DATING PARTNER?

1 How often do you date? How do you account for either your frequency of dates or lack of dates?

2 If given the opportunity, would you prefer to date randomly (many different individuals) or to date one person steadily? Why?

3 Do you lack self-confidence in dating? If so, what definite steps can you take to increase your self-confidence?

4 Why is it so necessary to follow the rules of etiquette on a first date?

5 Do you need to improve your physical appearance in order to be a better date? What are you doing to enhance the image you present to others?

6 Discuss your feelings about the statement, "It is the young lady's responsibility to 'draw the line' regarding physical contact."

7 Do you usually enjoy double dates? Why or why not?

8 What was the nicest date that you can remember? Analyze the situation to discuss the factors that made it such a great time.

QUESTIONS FOR DISCUSSION AND REVIEW

1. Compare and contrast mate selection in American society with the method used in some other country.

2. What is the relationship of the American system of dating to the American social class system?

3. Why is psychological compatibility more important than physical compatibility?

4. Discuss the advantages of random dating.

5. How does the "new morality" conflict with Biblical ethics?

6. What is the "moral law of diminishing returns?"

7. What are some parental obligations in relationship to the dating of their young people?

8. How does college dating differ from high school dating?

9. State some reasons why fellows and girls do not date. Which of these are legitimate and which are largely rationalizations?

10. How may a person improve his self-confidence?

11. Are there any advantages to computer dating?

12. What are some "warning signals" that young people need to be aware of in a relationship?

6

ROMANTIC LOVE
IN COURTSHIP

. . . love is strong as death. . .
Song of Solomon 8:6

DIFFERENT KINDS OF LOVE

Love is one of the most overworked words in the English language. Part of the usage arises from the fact that there are so many different kinds of love. There is Christian love, which includes our love of God, for fellow believers, and for the unsaved; parental love, filial love, love between brother and sister, puppy love, romantic love, conjugal love, patriotic love, platonic love, and love of friends and relatives. Many times the word *love* is used as a synonym for *like*, as in "I love pizza, baseball, tennis, white shirts, blue socks, Early American furniture, antique clocks, or antique cars."

At other times the word is commonly used in the entertainment world where *lust* would be a better word. The "hippie" movement of the sixties also often misused *love* in place of *lust* for their "love-ins" were selfish displays of lustful gratifications of the flesh. In the philosophy of the "new morality" and "situational ethics" the justification for immorality is "being in love," which usually amounts to lust on the part of one individual or the other or both. In the light of the various uses of the word, it is easy to understand why young people are confused about the meaning of *love* when they reach dating age.

DEFINITIONS OF *LOVE*
AS USED IN THE NEW TESTAMENT

In defining *love* it is necessary to note the usage of the word in the Greek language.

> . . . *Storgé* . . . love, referred to several times in the New Testament, is the kind of love shared by parents and children or brothers and sisters. . . . *Storgé* love in marriage meets the need we all have to belong, to be part of a close-knit circle where people care and give utmost loyalty to each other. When the world shows itself as a cold, hard place, *storgé* offers emotional refuge.[1]

The second word is *philia.* Trench in his great work, *Synonyms of the New Testament*, says, ". . .[*philia*] without being necessarily an unreasoning attachment . . . is more instinctive, is more of the feelings, implies more passion. . . . "[2] The meaning is love as human affection or friendship. It is found in John 11:3 in the message of Mary and Martha to Jesus concerning Lazarus, ". . . He whom thou lovest is sick."

Agape is another word which Trench defines; it ". . . expresses a more reasoning attachment, of choice and selection. . . from seeing in the object upon whom it is bestowed that which is worthy of regard. . . . It should never be forgotten that the substantive agape is purely a Christian word, no example of its use occurring in any heathen writer whatever. . . . "[3] This is the word used of the nature of God in I John 4:8, ". . . God is love." It is also used in John 3:16: "For God so loved the world that he gave his only begotten son." It is this love that is the "fruit of the Spirit" (Gal. 5:22) and "is shed abroad in the believer's heart by the Holy Ghost" (Rom. 5:5). Paul's beautiful description of love in I Corinthians 13 is of *agape* love.

Dwight H. Small aptly expresses the meaning of *agape* in these words:

> Agape is not love that is grounded in any external value. Agape is pure love, and as such it does not have its source in the loved object. Agape does not love because of the lovableness of the loved one. It is unmotivated by anything outside of itself. Its motives arise wholly from within its own nature as love. . . . Agape is thus not an act of self completion or self-satisfaction by means of another. It cannot be frustrated because it does not demand anything in return. It is pure

1. Ed Wheat, M.D., *Love-Life for Every Married Couple* (Grand Rapids: Zondervan Publishing House, 1980), p. 60. Also see pp. 84-95 for a different, but very helpful discussion of romantic love.
2. Richard Chenevix Trench, *Synonyms of the New Testament* (New York: Blakeman and Mason, 1859), p. 67.
3. Ibid., p. 66.

outgoing desire to care for another. In its absolute form it denotes God's love, not human love."[4]

The fourth word is *eros*, which " . . refers to love in a physical sense. The word is not found in the New Testament."[5] Trench says, ". . . that the truth of God abstained from the defiling contact with them [*eros* and its derivatives]; yea, found out a new word for itself [*agape*] rather than betake itself to one of these."[6]

Robert K. Kelly adds to this description of *eros*:

> Eros was the Greek god of love, (called Cupid by the Romans). Eros represents sensual love, the erotic side of our nature, with an emphasis on sexual need and satisfaction. The classical picture brings to mind the love affairs of the gods and the orgiastic rituals of the mystery religions. We might define eros as sensual desire that recognized no limits of propriety or custom. It may be more destructive than constructive in the long run.[7]

From these descriptions of *eros* it is easy to understand why the Holy Spirit did not use the word in the writing of the New Testament.

The English language is not as specific as the Greek; when the word *love* is used, it may refer to any one of the thoughts expressed by these four Greek words. It also may represent an idea combining the meaning of two or more of these words. In order to be more definite, some descriptive word must be used with *love*, such as sensual love (*eros*), brotherly love (*philia*) or divine love (*agape*).

Some terms represent a combination of qualities such as infatuation, where the element of *eros* is strongest. It is the writer's opinion that romantic love is composed of love represented by *eros* and *philia* with a small measure of *agape*. The love mature enough for marriage or conjugal love is dominated by the *agape* element with the *eros* factor declining with the increasing age of the couple.

> Such a love is a necessity if two persons are to maintain a permanent and harmonious relationship. In this kind of love, there is a willingness to give when the loved one is not able to reciprocate, whether it be because of illness, failure, or simply an hour of weakness. It is a love that can repair bonds severed by unfaithful-

4. Dwight Hervey Small, *Design for Christian Marriage* (Westwood NJ: Fleming H. Revell, 1959), pp. 62-63. Used by permission.

5. Williams, *Christian Home*, p. 8.

6. Trench, *Synonyms of N.T.*, p. 70.

7. Robert K. Kelley, *Courtship, Marriage and the Family* (New York: Harcourt, Brace Javanovich, Inc., 1974), p. 214. Used by permission. Dr. Kelley gives credit for this description of *eros* to Dr. Floyd M. Martinson, *Marriage and the American Ideal* (New York: Dodd, Mead, 1960), pp. 107-108.

ness, indifference or jealousy. This agape is the ingredient that makes marriage more than a fifty-fifty arrangement, but rather a sixty-sixty or seventy-seventy partnership—that is, a partnership in which both husband and wife go more than halfway in order to express their love and concern for each other. Such love does not do away with eros but rather transforms it into its highest and finest fulfillment.[8]

Agape love is divine love that God shares with those who accept His Son as Saviour and Lord. As the husband and wife are filled with His love, they find that giving love is more important in the relationship than receiving love. Their desire is not what they can "get" from the relationship but what they can "give." As Cecil Osborne expressed it, "Love is the ultimate in living and expresses itself best by giving, without thought of return."[9] Consequently, the highest, noblest, and happiest conjugal love should be found in the Christian home.

DEFINITIONS OF ROMANTIC LOVE

Some disagreement exists as to which term should be used in describing the type of love prominent in dating and courtship. C. W. Scudder prefers the term "true love" rather than the commonly used "romantic love." He writes, "True love, although properly including a romantic element, is much more than romantic love" and this is true.[10] However, his term refers to what some writers would call *agape* love or conjugal love for he defines true love as "love which is mature and adequate for a marriage."[11]

Other writers prefer the term *immature love* when referring to romantic love, and *mature love* to designate *conjugal love*. Herman R. Lantz and Eloise C. Snyder present a continuum ranging from "Extremely Immature" to "Extremely Mature," on which a relationship may be placed. [12] There is not a one-to-one correlation between mature love and conjugal love, for many married couples demonstrate very immature patterns of love. Since this text is oriented

8. Ibid., pp. 214-215.

9. Cecil Osborne, *The Art of Understanding Your Mate* (Grand Rapids, Zondervan Press, 1970), p. 192.

10. C. W. Scudder, *The Family in Christian Perspective* (Nashville: Broadman Press, 1962), p. 37.

11. Ibid.

12. Herman R. Lantz and Eloise C. Snyder, *Marriage* (New York: John Wiley & Sons, Inc., 1962), p. 75. On pp. 93-96 they have a helpful table, "A Comparison of Significant Characteristics which Engender Immature and Mature Love."

toward the young person who is not yet married, the historical term *romantic love* is used and discussed in the following pages.

Romantic love as it is known today had its beginnings "in the twelfth century, in a form called *courtly love* (and sometimes *distant love*)."[13] This was the love of noblemen and knights of medieval times. Leonard Benson traces the development of this type of love through the Renaissance and how it filtered down to the middle classes and the working classes of the twentieth century.[14]

Romantic love is difficult to define: " . . if you have been in love, you know what it is and there is no sense defining it; if you have not, a definition is not likely to convey very much."[15] Various definitions have been given but none is entirely satisfactory since romantic love is mainly an emotional experience. The following definition is an attempt to summarize the essential elements: Romantic love is a strong emotional attachment to a person of the opposite sex that involves a concern for the spiritual, intellectual, and physical well-being of that person. Thus, a couple are not "in love" until enough interaction and self-revelation have taken place for the couple to become "attached" to each other, and dependent on each other to satisfy their emotional, mental, and physical needs.[16]

COMPONENTS OF ROMANTIC LOVE

It is easier to identify some of the components of romantic love than it is to define it. A strong physical attraction is a major feature of romantic love, and quite often it is mistaken for love itself. On the other hand, romantic love cannot exist without a real sexual interest in the partner. God has so constituted human beings that the urge for biological nearness is part of His plan for the formation of new families and the propagation of mankind. This desire for physical nearness is expressed by the sense of touch.[17] After a couple starts to date, the first physical contact is usually holding hands. Then as the dating continues and as the relationship develops, the next move is to kissing, then to embracing.

13. Leonard Benson, *The Family Bond* (New York: Random House, 1971), pp. 112-115.
14. Ibid.
15. William M. Kephart, *The Family, Society, and the Individual* (Boston: Houghton Miflin Co., 1972), p. 346.
16. Robert O. Blood, Jr., *Marriage* (New York: The Free Press of Glencoe, 1962), p. 95.
17. Pat and Jill Williams with Jerry Jenkins, *Rekindled* (Old Tappan, NJ: Fleming H. Revell Co., 1985), p. 137.

In the plan of God, the end result of these very normal desires is to move the couple toward marriage so that a new family can be established. As indicated in chapter 5, these physical intimacies are subject to the moral law of diminishing returns. A couple must proceed very slowly in this area, for once they have proceeded to one level of intimacy it is difficult, if not impossible, to return to a lower level. If they start embracing each other, usually they are not satisfied to return to a simple "goodnight" kiss without an embrace.

It is important that the couple test their compatibilities in other areas before they become too involved in the physical aspect of the relationship. This is necessary because many young people are misled by the popular concept of romantic love—they think a strong physical attraction between a fellow and girl is all that is needed to "live happily ever after." Hollywood movies, television programs, and mass literature convey the impression that if a fellow and girl have a great physical attraction to each other, they can marry and live happily, for this is all that is needed in marriage. Many young people, Christian and non-Christian, enter into matrimony with this highly romanticized concept of marriage. The marriage fails when the physical desires have been satisfied and the couple discover they do not have the basis for a sound marriage.[18]

The intensity of the sexual attraction varies from couple to couple. In one relationship the partners have a very great physical attraction from the first date. Just the sight of the other person quickens the heart beat. Some young ladies have difficulty in eating and sleeping. Thoughts of the loved one so encompass the mind that study and work are difficult until an adjustment is made to the new status of being "in love." This is the maximum of intensity.[19]

Another couple meet and are friends for a long period of time before they have their first date. The relationship develops very slowly until it finally passes an unknown moment when friendship ceases and love begins. They cannot pinpoint any specific time when they became lovers, but their attraction to each other is very definite and unmistakeable. Robert C. Williamson goes so far as to say, "It is impossible to determine precisely where love and friendship begin and end."[20] Other couples may fall in between this maximum and minimum of intensity, but for real love to exist, there must be a sexual attraction between the two individuals.

18. Lawrence J. Crabb, Jr., *The Marriage Builder* (Grand Rapids: Zondervan Publishing House, 1982), p. 18.
19. Blood, *Marriage*, p. 101.
20. Robert C. Williamson, *Marriage and Family Relations* (New York: John Wiley & Sons, Inc., 1966), p. 238.

A second feature of romantic love is companionship or desire to be with the person. Robert O. Blood calls this the "social element in love."[21] Ordinarily people choose companions on the basis of similar likes and beliefs. They enjoy doing the same things together and receive emotional satisfaction from the interaction together. If for any reason, the interaction fails to produce the desired response, the companionship ceases. Since two young people who marry are going to spend a long time in each other's company, it is important that they choose dating partners who are good companions apart from any sexual interest. If a young lady loves good music, she should date a fellow who is interested in the same thing, and who can enjoy a concert with her. If a fellow enjoys engaging in athletic contests, he should seek a girl who can at least enjoy such games as a spectator.

Since church attendance and service in the local church are such a large part of the Christian life, the young person who loves the Lord will certainly seek a life companion who enjoys the work of Christ as much as he or she does. The Bible asks, "What part hath he that believeth with an infidel?" (II Cor. 6:15), and it is difficult to understand how a Christian young person can claim to be "in love" with an unsaved individual, or one who does not enjoy the things of Christ. A person should be mature enough to objectively assess a relationship to see if they are good companions apart from their common sexual attraction. If they are not, they are not really "in love" but merely physically infatuated with each other and the relationship should be broken in order to avoid greater heartbreak and difficulties in the future.[22]

A third component of love is care or concern for the well-being of the dating partner. As a fellow and girl continue dating, they become more interested in the needs and desires of each other. The person who "cares" for another individual is more concerned about meeting the needs of that individual than he is about caring for his own needs. Care "requires a willingness to sacrifice or do something not pleasing to ourselves, in order to give to the one we love."[23] The girl simply has to mention that red roses would look nice on her dress for the junior-senior banquet, and her lover will skip meals or whatever else is legitimately necessary in order to have the money to buy the corsage of red roses. She will stay up all night typing his term paper because he "needs" it the next day. The general attitude is, "Your slightest wish is my command." After the honeymoon this attitude

21. Blood, *Marriage*, p. 95.
22. Anderson, *Family Living*, p. 32.
23. Kelley, *Courtship, Marriage, Family*, p. 217.

changes, and her strongest command may not move him out of his easy chair when she wants the garbage taken out. This change is one of the big differences between romantic love and conjugal love. In courtship, however, true love does not exist in any relationship where one individual or the other fails to display this care for the other's welfare.

Another constituent element of love is idealization whereby the person projects attitudes and attributes toward the partner that he does not actually possess.[24] A student dated a very ordinary girl, not especially attractive, but when he returned, he stated to his room- mate, "She's a living doll!" He had enjoyed her lovely personality and he attributed qualities of beauty to her that his roommate knew she did not really possess. Quite often a person may ask about a certain couple, "What does she see in him?" or "What does he see in her?" The answer is that the idealization factor of love causes the individuals to see qualities in each other of which the outsider is unaware.

This is important, for it enables imperfect human beings to find mates! If everyone waited for the perfect individual to appear, there would be no marriages. As it is, people who have imperfections meet other such individuals, and love develops as idealization operates in the relationship. As a courtship continues, and the couple get to know each other better, much of the idealization will disappear but by this time they both realize that, although they are not perfect, or may not possess the previously attributed qualities, they do have a good relationship and are very compatible with each other.[25] There may be the opposite result in that as they get to know one another, they realize they are not compatible and will break the relationship.

A danger in idealization occurs when a couple do not have a courtship long enough to really get to know each other, and then enter marriage really thinking that the partner has the qualities they have attributed to him. If this happens, then a disillusionment takes place during the honeymoon when the real selves are revealed, and the individuals realize they really did not know each other very well. This may be part of the explanation why so many divorces occur within the first or second year of marriage. Idealization is a definite part of romantic love, but it must be tested in personal interaction so that the couple can learn to know each other as real persons before they enter into marriage.

24. Kephart, *Family, Society, Individual*, p. 347.
25. Williamson, *Marriage and Family Relations*, p. 241. This is a good discussion of "Deidealization" which takes place after marriage.

INFATUATION AND ROMANTIC LOVE

The various components of romantic love will vary in degree and in intensity from couple to couple, but they must be present to some degree if love is to exist. For some couples the physical attraction will be very strong, but unless the other elements of companionship, care, and idealization are present, the couple are merely infatuated and not really "in love." Webster defines *infatuation* as "unreasoned passion or attraction"; the root word means "to make a fool of." Many a young person has admitted after an infatuation that he simply made a "fool" of himself by such "unreasoned passion."

Henry R. Brandt writes of infatuation, "It is a physical attraction based on looks, fun to be with, even held together against their better judgment, not based on a state of respect and comradeship that develops when there are similar ideas, tastes and hopes."[26] A relationship may begin with an intense infatuation, but as dating continues, the other elements of love should appear and a well-rounded love should develop. This is why it is important for young people with a strong physical attraction to give themselves enough time to really know each other before getting married.

In other couples, the companionship element may predominate. They really enjoy doing things together and the physical attraction is minimal, but it must be there or else it is mere friendship. In another situation the element of care is foremost. This is frequently seen in a relationship where a healthy individual is attracted to a handicapped person. The thing that distinguishes love from pity is that there is a sexual attraction and a desire for companionship with each other. Love may be a "many-splendored" thing, but it can be reduced to some basic elements that are fairly easy to distinguish if young people are aware of their existence.

CAN A PERSON LOVE TWO
PEOPLE AT THE SAME TIME?

Young people often ask, "Is it possible to be in love with two people at the same time?" This is a problem faced by some of the more popular fellows and girls who have many opportunities for dating and courtship. William M. Kephart estimates that on the basis of his research "the average college student has around eight roman-

---

26. Henry R. Brandt & Homer E. Dowdy, *Building a Christian Home* (Wheaton, Scripture Press, 1960), p. 138.

tic experiences prior to marriage." He also discovered "that about half of the respondents stated that at some time in their lives they had been infatuated or in love with two persons at the same time."[27] For example, it is conceivable that a young lady, dating two young men at the same time, could be in love with both of them. She could be physically attracted to them, enjoy the companionship of both, be concerned and care for their welfare, and attributes some qualities to them they actually do not have. Similar backgrounds and other requirements for a successful Christian marriage may be possessed by both young men. In such a case, the young lady through prayer and leading of the Holy Spirit will have to choose one fellow and let that relationship develop into marriage.

WHEN IS A PERSON REALLY IN LOVE?

A more frequent problem is faced by the young person who has difficulty in determining whether he or she is really in love with a particular individual. Dating has occurred over a reasonable length of time, but there are doubts as to the future of the relationship. Sometimes the perplexed individual has not received the great emotional response that the popular culture has led them to expect. Since the dating partner doesn't arouse a great emotional response, he or she feels that it cannot be love.

The solution to the problem, in addition to sincere prayer for God to reveal His will in the matter, is to examine the total relationship. Are all of the elements of romantic love present in some degree? It is necessary to keep in mind that these vary in intensity from couple to couple. Sometimes there is a tendency to compare the present relationship with a former one, and if there is not the same emotional response in the present one, then it is felt it cannot be love. If the previous romance was an unhappy one, "Willard Walter and Reuben Hill (1951) suggest that there may be a certain loss of capacity for love after unhappy experiences. The person develops various protective devices and collects 'scar tissue' from romantic wounds, dulling his sensitivity. However, there is no strong evidence that this always or even usually happens."[28]

Many times lessons are learned in early romances about keeping the emotions in check so there may be a lesser degree of infatuation in a person's third romance than in the first. Benson remarks, ". . . it may be impossible to ever again reach the intensity of your very first

27. Kephart, *Family, Society, Individual* p. 347.
28. Benson, *Family Bond*, p. 117.

love affair."[29] He also relates the findings of his research on the question whether the "most intense love affair led to marriage." About one-third of the sample indicated that it did not.

Some degree of sexual attraction must be present if romantic love is genuine, but one must remember that the physical aspect of a relationship is not as important as the other elements, since in marital interaction the physical relationship diminishes as companionship and care increase in importance.

The Christian will certainly spend much more time in prayer seeking to know if it is real love or not. Also he must make an objective analysis of the relationship. There are certain questions the person can ask himself to help determine if the love is genuine: "Is our love more relationship-centered than egocentric?" "Is our love relationship characterized by mutual trust, feelings of confidence, and security in each other?" "Am I proud to be seen with this person?"[30] Wayne J. Anderson has compiled a list of twenty-one questions to help a young person to determine if he is in love or merely infatuated.[31] Marriage is for a long time, and a young person needs to be sure they have the best love relationship possible.

LOVE AT FIRST SIGHT

Many young people wonder whether "love at first sight" is possible. There are some couples who have had such an experience and are real believers in such a phenomenon. Where two individuals have in mind an "ideal" type of person they would like to marry, and these people meet under propitious circumstances, it is quite possible for them to be strongly attracted to each other immediately. Since they do represent each other's "ideal" mate, the attraction will grow and the relationship will develop into a very harmonious and happy one.[32] This is a very rare occurrence and young people should not date with the hope that this will be the manner in which they meet their prospective mates. Most marriages result from ordinary, routine dating and building a relationship without the glamour of "love at first sight."

Most cases of individuals "falling in love at first sight" do not stand the test of personal interaction. Many of these people have

29. Ibid.
30. Lantz & Snyder, *Marriage*, pp. 94-95.
31. Anderson, *Family Living*, pp. 90-91.
32. Judson T. Landis and Mary G. Landis, *Building a Successful Marriage* (Englewood Cliffs, NJ: Prentice-Hall, 1968), pp. 135-136.

emotional problems and regularly "fall in love" when undergoing stress. It is quite easy for such a person to become infatuated with a new dating partner, to feel that it is "love at first sight." The new love experience acts as a release for the emotional stress the person is experiencing. This type of relationship will probably be broken when the interaction between the two reveals incompatibilities that were masked by the infatuation. A young person who feels that his experience is "love at first sight" should note that there is a distinction between "infatuation" and "love," and that the former needs to be tested over a period of time by personal interaction to see if the other elements of love are present in the relationship.[33] It is not wise to think that it is "love at first sight" until a good, sound relationship has been established.

IS IT POSSIBLE TO "FALL IN LOVE"?

It is almost impossible to discuss "love" without some reference to the phrase *falling in love.* The idea conveyed is that of two people who are physically attracted to each other, who can do nothing to prevent their "falling in love." With such attraction, it doesn't matter if there is nothing else in their relationship that indicates their compatibility as mates. This is part of the false Hollywood type of romance with which most young people are familiar. One college student expressed it in the following words:

> When I was young, my concept of love was that it was something that couldn't be helped. And that when you "fell in love," nothing circumstantial ever came between you. As a girl I thought that love was something that makes you happy and never made you cry. I thought it was all good and nothing bad. I thought that all people in love got married. I thought love was based as much on outward appearance as personality traits. I suppose this was a rather selfish and one-sided concept of love. I blame television for many of the ideas I had about love. I think many young marriages are based, and wrecked by some of these same concepts that have infiltrated our minds since the day we were able to communicate and receive communication through the television set. I am thankful that the Lord has seen me through many deep waters that He used to correct my false ideas of love.

This young lady was fortunate to learn from the "deep waters" of her romantic experiences what true love is. The tragedy is that

33. Kelley, *Courtship, Marriage, Family,* p. 225.

many Christian young people do not realize that physical attractions do not equal "love," and they can choose the type of person they wish to love. Small expresses it in the following words:

> . . . love must be more than merely an emotion . . . purposeful willing is at its core. Love must be willing to be committed. But then only love can afford to be concerned enough to take and be faithful to the responsibilities of marriage. This precludes the possibility of just "falling in love." One does not simply fall into a definite willingness to assume responsibility and to sacrifice for another, especially over an indefinite period of time. . . . One cannot fall into intimate knowledge of anything or anyone. Responsibility and fidelity do not just happen. [34]

Rational thought and decision-making are just as much a part of "love" as "the indiscriminate longing of the glands." God created bodies with biological desires, but He also gave them minds to control these desires. He expects the Christian to use the mind as well as the body in determining God's will in this important task of choosing a life partner. Nearly every quarter at least one young person comes to the author and says that he or she has "broken" the love relationship after giving it some rational thought as suggested in the Marriage and Family course.

THE DIFFERENCE BETWEEN LOVE AND LUST

At the beginning of this chapter, mention was made of the fact that *love* is often misused for *lust* in the popular usage of the word. Confusion also exists in the Christian use of the term *lust*. The dictionary defines the word as "a desire to gratify the senses," but a secondary meaning of "excessive sexual desire" is more prominent in the connotation of the word today. The term is used by Paul in II Timothy 2:22: "Flee also youthful lusts," and Peter (I Peter 2:11) exhorts the Christian to "abstain from fleshly lusts, which war against the soul." In I John 2:16-17, John commands the Christian to "stop loving the world" and classifies the "lusts of the flesh" as part of that world-system dominated by Satan which is to pass away in God's plan of the ages. It is very clear that the obsession with sex which characterizes our society today is part of the satanic world-system, and the Christian is under divine commands to "flee" from it and to "abstain" from it. The Christian is to submit his body

34. Small, *Christian Marriage*, p. 45. Used by permission

to the control of the indwelling Holy Spirit so that the fruits of the Spirit are produced in his life.

Although these passages make clear the Christian's responsibility, there is a passage concerning lust in Matthew 5:27-28 which is a problem to many young people as they become aware of their biological desires toward the opposite sex. Jesus said, "Ye have heard it was said by them of old time, 'Thou shalt not commit adultery': But I say unto you, "That whosoever looketh on a woman to lust after her hath committed adultery already in his heart.'" Anyone who has worked in an office, shop, or factory with unsaved individuals knows by experience how much "lusting" goes on today. Men see a woman pass by and make lewd and lustful comments among themselves. Kephart states, ". . . many writers refer to sex without love as lust, and in this sense lust is much more characteristic of males than females."[35] Promiscuity and infidelity are so widespread that men (and some women) desire (lust) to "go to bed with anyone." These individuals are guilty of committing adultery "in the heart." It seems that society is approaching a state similar to that of Noah's day when "the wickedness of man was great in the earth, and that every imagination of the thoughts of his heart was only evil continually" (Gen. 6:5).

A Christian may be guilty of the same sin if he permits his lower nature to desire or lust after other women or men. Small cogently remarks, "It is a fine line that separates between the sexual expression of love and the sexual expression of contempt. Lust is not ever far from love in human experience."[36] Men are aroused sexually by visual stimuli much more easily than women, and are prone to mentally dwell on sex. The difference between men and women is described by Kephart:

> Women . . . are not likely to be sexually aroused by visual stimuli, nor are they prone to indulge in sexual fantasies or day dreams. It would be an exceptional case, indeed, where a woman assessed a man in terms of his potentiality as a sex partner. Within our cultural norms a young woman's romantic interest is more likely to be held by a man who embodies the *totality* of desired personal and social traits, including those of husband-lover.[37]

It is for this reason that Paul exhorts the Christian to take "captive every thought to make it obedient to Christ" (II Cor. 10:5, William's translation).

35. Kephart, *Family, Society, Individual*, p. 355.
36. Small, *Christian Marriage*, p. 10.
37. Kephart, *Family, Society, Individual*, p. 355. Used by permission.

It is necessary to remember there is a difference between temptation and sin. Jack Wyrtzen writes:

> Do you feel guilty because you have lustful desires? Don't misunder-
> stand. We are all tempted. . . . Even though you are a born again
> Christian the thoughts of lust still come to your mind . . . Don't
> forget, temptation was placed in front of Jesus, "He himself hath
> suffered being tempted. . . . " But you are to resist. . . . When lustful
> thoughts enter your mind, don't dwell on them. Make yourself think
> of something else. . . . We are tempted every day of our lives. But sin
> doesn't come when you are tempted: it comes when you yield to
> temptation. And no born-again Christian needs to yield.[38]

A fellow may not avoid seeing the girl in the bathing suit on a
television commercial, which is a temptation, but he can control his
mind so that he does not dwell on the stimulus, which would be sin.
Martin Luther said, "We can't prevent the birds from flying over our
heads, but we can prevent them from making a nest in our hair." [39]

In a day of bikinis and tight-fitting clothing, a fellow would
have to become a hermit to avoid temptation to evil thoughts.
Although the Christian is in the "world," he does not have to
conform to the world, but can have his mind renewed and guarded
by the Holy Spirit. He may live or work in such ungodly surround-
ings that he will have to cry out with Saint Augustine, "Give me thy
purity, O Christ," with the assurance that such a heart cry will be
answered.

This problem of determining what is lust also arises in dating.
Many young fellows confuse their natural, God-given desires to be
with the opposite sex with "lust" and are filled with regret and guilt
when they read Matthew 5:27-28. In that passage our Lord is
referring to intense sexual desire that leads to adultery. This is
different from desiring to be in the company of a girl friend. If
Matthew 5:27 were interpreted to include the normal desire to be
with a loved one, then no individual with a natural, divinely given sex
drive could enter into marriage without mentally committing adultery during the courtship process. The desire of a male to consummate marriage with the betrothed is far different from the desire to
go to bed with every woman he sees.

This does not mean that a Christian fellow or girl may not be
guilty of lust if they are promiscuous in their necking and petting
relationships with the opposite sex. God expects the young person to

38. Jack Wyrtzen, *Sex Is Not Sinful* (Grand Rapids: Zondervan Publishing Co.,
1970), pp. 37, 38. Used by permission.
39. Ibid., p. 38.

have high standards in these areas, and to maintain them with the aid of the Holy Spirit. It is most important for the person's spiritual life and testimony that he "abstain from all appearance of evil" and make every thought "obedient to Christ."

THE SYNTHESIS OF LOVE

The romantic love of Christian courtship that leads to marriage is a blend of the factors found in *eros*, *philia*, and *agape*. In the early stages of the relationship the erotic aspects may predominate. As the relationship deepens, the companionship features of *philia* and the altruistic characteristics of *agape* must control the relationship. For a couple to marry with anything less than a love governed by *agape* is to risk failure in the marriage.

The couple who marry on the basis of love centered in God who is love (agape) find their personal lives enriched and their marriage relationship fulfilled in a manner that the unsaved cannot understand. Christian young people who wish to have the "maximum" happiness in their home need to make sure their love consists of the right elements in the proper amount and relationship to each other.

LOVE OR INFATUATION—WHICH?

The following list of questions has been prepared to help you define your feelings about a possible love relationship. There are no right or wrong answers. Indicate your answer to each question by answering "Yes," or "No," or "?"

1 Do you feel a close companionship without having to touch or talk to each other?

2 Do you like to do things for each other?

3 Have you been able to resolve a disagreement to the complete satisfaction of both?

4 Do you look forward to sharing your new experiences or ideas with each other?

5 Are you planning to reform your companion after you are married?

6 Are you proud to introduce your companion to your friends?

7 Is your companion a source of intellectual stimulation and an inspiration to you?

8 Are you organizing your long-range plans around this person;?

9 Do you trust this person so that you do not feel uneasy or uncertain about your relationship?

10 Is your companion's mental and spiritual self as attractive to you as his or her sexual charms?

11 Do you find that you generally like the same type of people?

12 Do you enjoy the same kind of activities?

13 Are you sensitive to certain things that you must avoid saying or doing lest there be hurt feelings?

14 Can you list specific personality characteristics about your friend that you like?

15 Are you in accord in your attitudes toward having and bringing up children?

16 Are you in agreement concerning the roles each will play in marriage?

17 Do you have similar systems of values?

18 Do you feel it a pleasure to work together?

19 Are you united in your thinking as related to the purpose of life?

20 Do you feel relaxed and comfortable with each other?

21 Have you been pleased with each other in a variety of situations? For example: social, religious, and work activities—also in situations of stress and responsibility?

From *Design for Family Living* by Wayne J. Anderson, © 1964 by T. S. Denison & Co., Inc. Used by permission.

QUESTIONS FOR DISCUSSION AND REVIEW

1. How do *eros*, *philia*, and *agape* differ in meaning?

2. Why is it difficult to define *love*?

3. How does romantic love differ from conjugal love?

4. Discuss the various components of romantic love.

5. What elements of American culture contribute to the "romantic love" complex?

6. Why is idealization such an important factor in mate selection?

7. Define *infatuation*. How does it differ from *romantic love*?

8. How can a person tell whether or not he is in love?

9. Is there such a phenomenon as "love at first sight?"

10. What is the difference between love and lust?

7

MATURITY IN MATE SELECTION

... when I became a man, I put away childish things.
I Cor. 13:11

THE NECESSITY OF MATURITY IN MARRIAGE

The marriage of two young people who are spiritually and emotionally mature will be much more successful than that of a fellow and girl who have not matured. Quite commonly Christian young people assume that just because they are both Christians they can meet, grow to love one another, and live happily ever afterward. They assume that their common belief in Christ will automatically overcome a poor mate choice or any personality inadequacies brought to the marriage. "You do not become a new or different person the day you marry. You take into marriage all that you are," is the way one writer expresses this truth![1] It is true that a union in Christ adds much to the stability of a marriage, but the wise selection of a partner who is spiritually and emotionally mature will mean greater happiness for even the Christian couple. The Christian needs to be aware of the factors involved in maturity, and be able to assess his own level of spiritual and emotional maturation.

1. Marjory Bracher, *Love, Sex, and Life* (Philadelphia: Fortress Press, 1964), p. 24.

123

THE NEW BIRTH AND SPIRITUAL MATURITY

The Bible clearly indicates that a person begins the Christian life by means of the new birth. Jesus said in John 3:3, "Except a man be born again, he cannot see the kingdom of God," and in verse 7, ". . . Ye must be born again." The great expositor Albert Barnes comments on this verse:

> . . . the beginning of this new life, is called the *new birth* or *regeneration*. It is so called because in many respects it has a striking analogy to the natural birth. It is the beginning of spiritual life. It introduces us to the light of the Gospel. It is the moment when we really begin to live to any purpose. It is the moment when God reveals Himself to us as our reconciled Father. . . . And as every man is a sinner, it is necessary that each one should experience the change, or he cannot be happy or saved.[2]

A person experiences the new birth, or is born again, by accepting the sacrifice of Jesus Christ on the cross of Calvary, and receiving Him as a personal Savior: "But as many as received Him, to them gave he the power to become the sons of God even to them that believe on his name, which were born, not of blood, nor of the will of the flesh, nor of the will of man, but of God" (John 1:12-13). Jack Wyrtzen says, "It is not a matter of head belief. You may believe that Jesus Christ lived and was a great man, but *saving faith* is believing that Christ died on the cross for you, to save you."[3]

The new birth is only the beginning of the Christian life. The believer in Christ has the responsibility to grow into spiritual maturity. In Romans 8:16 Paul writes, "The Spirit itself beareth witness with our spirit, that we are the children of God," i.e. those who have experienced the new birth. In verse 14 of the same passage, he writes, "For as many as are led by the Spirit of God, they are the "[adult] sons of God" indicating that a person's position in Christ is that of adult sons and that it is his responsibility to be dominated by the Holy Spirit, so that his daily experience gives proof that he is accepting the responsibilities that accompany such a high and holy position. In Ephesians 4:12-15 gifts are given to godly men for "the perfecting [maturing] of the saints . . . till we all come in the unity of the faith, and of the knowledge of the Son of God unto a perfect [*mature*] man . . . that we henceforth be *no more* children . . . but

2. Albert Barnes, *Notes on the Gospels*, vol. 2 (New York: Harper & Bros., Publishers, 1868), p. 222.
3. Jack Wyrtzen, *Sex Is Not Sinful* (Grand Rapids: Zondervan Publishing Co., 1970), pp. 60-61.

speaking the truth in love, may *grow up* into him in all things, which is the head, even Christ" (italics added).

The writer of Hebrews expresses the same truth in 5:12—6:1, "For when for the time ye ought to be teachers, ye have need that one teach you again which be the first principles of the oracles of God: and are become such as have need of milk, and not of strong meat. For every one that useth milk is unskillful in the word of righteousness; for he is a *babe*. But strong meat belongeth to them that are of *full age*, even those who by reason of use have their senses exercised to discern both good and evil. Therefore, leaving the principles of the doctrine of Christ, let us go unto perfection [maturity] . . . "(italics added).

In his Epistles Peter also emphasizes the necessity of growth for the Christian. In I Peter 1:23 he writes, "Being born again . . . by the word of God, which liveth and abideth for ever." A few verses later, in 2:2, he exhorts, "As newborn babies, desire the sincere milk of the word, that ye may grow thereby." His final benediction in II Peter 3:18 is an admonition, "But grow in grace, and in the knowledge of our Lord and Saviour Jesus Christ."

It is apparent from these, and other Bible passages, that the Christian is born into the family of God and is to grow in spiritual knowledge and experience. Consequently, spiritual maturity is not synonymous with physical maturity. A person may be thirty years old physically but only three months old spiritually. The Christian behavior expected from such an individual will be less than that expected from a person who is thirty years old spiritually. The individual who has only been saved three months will not be expected to know as much about the Bible and Christian living as the person saved for thirty years. However, God expects both to continue to grow so that daily they become more like the Lord Jesus. According to Romans 8:29, God has predestined each believer "to be conformed to the image of his Son," and it is the Christian's responsibility to live each day with the desire to be more like Jesus. Warren Wiersbe writes, "When you were born again through faith in Christ, you became a part of the New Creation. Just as the first Adam was created in the image of God, so those who belong to the last Adam are being 'recreated' to the image of Christ."[4] The hymnwriter aptly expressed this truth, "Be like Jesus, this my song, in the home and in the throng. Be like Jesus all day long, I would be like Jesus."

4. Warren W. Wiersbe, *Creative Christian Living* (Westwood, NJ: Fleming H. Revell Co., 1967). p. 22

The process of spiritual growth requires four elements analagous to those necessary for physical growth. A normal, healthy body requires food and water, air, exercise, and rest for its proper development. In like manner a healthy Christian life needs a daily portion of the Word of God, submission to the Holy Spirit, some service for Christ, and worship before His throne. It is impossible to develop spiritual maturity without these factors being present each day. This means that the young person must develop the practice of private devotions before the Lord, where he reads the Word, prays, and worships the Triune God. This daily experience then motivates him to submit his body to the indwelling Holy Spirit, to be used as an instrument in the service of Christ.

CHARACTERISTICS OF THE SPIRITUALLY MATURE PERSON

Spiritual growth is manifested in many areas of the yielded believer's life. "But . . . the fruit of the Spirit is love, joy, peace, longsuffering, gentleness, goodness, faith, meekness, temperance: against such there is no law (Gal. 5:22-23). These are produced in his life. According to Dwight H. Small, the nine different elements mentioned in this passage produce one "fruit": love. He quotes Donald G. Barnhouse's elucidation of these fruits of the Spirit:

Joy is love singing
Peace is love resting
Longsuffering is love enduring
Gentleness is love's true touch
Goodness is love's character
Faithfulness is love's habit
Meekness is love's self-forgetfulness
Self-control is love holding the reins[5]

All of these are not "fruits" but the "fruit" of love. Wiersbe writes, "Love is not something that we manufacture; it grows out of our lives as we are united to Christ, the Vine. When something is manufactured, there is noise and effort and dirt; but when fruit grows it is effortless, quiet, and beautiful."[6]

The love shed abroad in the believer's heart by the Holy Spirit (Rom. 5:5) manifests itself vertically in love for God, and horizon-

5. Dwight Hervey Small, *Design for Christian Marriage* (Westwood, NJ: Fleming H. Revell Co., 1959), p. 67.
6. Wiersbe, *Creative Christian Living*, p. 124.

tally in love for the Christian brethren, and for those who are lost and dying without Christ. The truth of Romans 6 and Galatians 2:20 of the self-life crucified with Christ, is experienced daily. A consistent prayer life in obedience to Philippians 4:6-7 results in a life filled with the "peace of God that passeth all understanding," so that the individuals who observe the life of a mature Christian marvel at the equanimity displayed in difficult circumstances.

One of the characteristics of the mature Christian is his definite separation from the world. Strict obedience is given to the exhortation of I John 2:15, "Love not the world, neither the things that are in the world. If any man love the world, the love of the Father is not in him." The body is presented as a living sacrifice according to Romans 12:1, and the transformation and renewing of the mind of verse 2 is experienced in the life.

What constitutes worldliness today is debated by many Christians. However, if one remembers that there are just two forces at work in the universe today—those energized by God and those under the direction of Satan—usually it is not hard to determine whether an event, attitude, or amusement relates to God or Satan. The writer of Hebrews, in the passage previously quoted (5:14), stated that maturity is marked by the ability to discern between good and evil. In Galatians 6:14, Paul indicated that a definite mark of a life crucified with Christ is being dead to the allurements of the world: "But God forbid that I should glory, save in the cross of our Lord Jesus, by whom the world is crucified unto me, and I unto the world."

Unfortunately, the idea has been propagated in the Bible-believing churches that God has one standard of spiritual maturity for laymen, and a higher standard for full-time Christian workers. This is a false concept, for the Bible presents one level, that of likeness to Christ, and God expects every Christian to strive toward that goal. It is easy to see why a spiritually mature young person who has established the habit of daily private devotions, is yielded to the Holy Spirit, is crucified with Christ, who manifests the fruits of the Spirit, including love for the brethren and the lost, whose life is filled with the peace of God and who lives a life separated from the world will make a much better mate than a less mature Christian.

MEASURING EMOTIONAL MATURITY

Intelligence tests, routinely given in elementary and secondary education, provide the means to measure the mental age of a student. In determining the mental age of a student, his chronological age is always taken into consideration. Measuring emotional maturity is much more difficult. Society links emotional maturity to physical development, chronological age, and mental age. For example, it is permissible for a child to cry when his wishes are blocked at age four, but it is not appropriate behavior for a young person eighteen years of age. A child of twelve years may change his goals in life each week without any censure, but a young man of twenty-four is expected to have a goal in life and be working toward its attainment.[7]

Although there is no one-to-one relationship between emotional maturity and chronological age, it is a fact that it "takes time to grow up." Some young people mature more rapidly than others. They are found in circumstances which are favorable for rapid emotional development. Others, such as those in a home with over-protective parents, mature more slowly. Maturation occurs more rapidly in some areas of an individual's personality than in others.[8] For example, a student may be very able in his relationships with the opposite sex, but be very childish in his inability to handle his money. A young lady may exercise leadership in a group, but be so ineffective in her relationships with young men that she never has had a date. Even the most mature individual has a few areas in his emotional structure that are underdeveloped.

CHARACTERISTICS OF THE EMOTIONALLY MATURE PERSON

Many factors must be considered when determining the emotional maturity of an individual. Primarily, his behavior should correspond to the societal expectations for a person of his chronological age. The actions of a college freshman are usually more immature than those of a college senior. A freshman may have difficulty adjusting to college dorm life, and this may cause him to fail a course and be placed on academic probation the following quarter. However, for a senior to fail a course is much more serious and may prevent his graduation with his class. A freshman without much dating experience may be forgiven some breach of etiquette, but the young woman will expect a senior fellow to know how to act in her presence. The mature young person will discharge his responsibilities as they arise, whether they be in the area of study, work, or dating. He may fail occasionally to meet an obligation, but his pattern is one

7. Mollie Smart and Russell Smart, *An Introduction to Family Relationships* (Philadelphia: W. B. Saunders Co., 1953), p. 229.

8. Floyd L. Ruch, *Psychology and Life* (Glenview, IL: Scott, Foresman & Co., 1967), p. 449.

that indicates he is a person able to assume responsibility. When failure does occur, it is used as a learning experience rather than accepted as an agonizing personal defeat. This capacity to assume responsibility is one of the most-needed aspects of maturity that is required for success in marriage. Bruce Larson writes,

> That is why so many marriages fail today—the partners are so immature, so selfish, so unschooled in real living that they cannot take spiritual responsibility for each other or for their children. . . . God in your life means maturity. Maturity is the basis for responsibility. Willingness and the capacity to take spiritual responsiblity for the other person are parts of the test of a thoroughly happy and unselfish marriage.[9]

One mark of the mature person is the ability to look objectively at himself and his relationships with others. He is able to examine his own personality and pinpoint his own strengths and weaknesses. He does not attempt to extend himself beyond his limits, and he tries to improve those areas wherein he is weak. Robert O. Blood says, "One characteristic of maturity is to accept the inevitable."[10] For example, if he is of average mental ability, he does not become discouraged if he does not make the Dean's Honor List. If he is of average physical appearance, he is not too disappointed if the "campus queen" turns down his invitation for a date even though he thought it was worth a try. If his athletic ability is mediocre, he recognizes his inability to make the varsity basketball team, and enjoys playing on an intramural team. If he has difficulty in math courses, he chooses a major in a subject area in which he has more ability even though he may enjoy math very much.

This same type of objectivity is applied when he encounters a problem. His reason rather than his emotions will motivate his actions. When a mature person meets a problem, he tries to place himself outside of it so that he can look at the different aspects of the situation in order to find a solution. He learns to separate the facts from his feelings, and tries to base his decisions concerning the problem on the facts involved rather than on his feelings in the matter. In order to seek a solution based on reason, he must be able to control his own emotions, and not become angry, upset, discouraged, or defeated when a problem arises. This does not mean that the mature person has no feelings, nor ever manifests an emotional reaction to a problem. He may manifest a reaction, but it is a

9. Bruce Larson, *Marriage Is for Living* (Grand Rapids: Zondervan Publishing House, 1968), p. 30. Used by permission.
10. Robert O. Blood, *Marriage* (New York: Free Press of Glencoe, 1962).

controlled one rather than an emotional outburst. The mature individual may be temporarily upset by some happening, but he quickly regains his composure and makes rational decisions based on the objective facts of the situation rather than on his feelings.

In reference to controlling one's emotions, a distinction needs to be made between "controlled" emotions, and "repressed" emotions. It is possible for a person to "repress" certain emotions and deny them expression until such behavior results in psychosomatic illness. The individual has been taught never to express overtly his anger, jealousy, hatred, or other anti-social feelings, and he keeps them "bottled up" inside until he develops a stomach ulcer, migraine headaches, or some other physical symptom of the inward stresses. [11] Such a person is emotionally immature, and needs to learn to recognize his feelings as being anti-social and seek to relieve them in a socially acceptable manner..

When little boys are angry with one another, they may express it in physical aggression by hitting one another. When grown men, in middle-class society, are angry with one another, they are expected to control their feelings. They may not hit each other with their fists, but they do have ways to express their frustrations such as hitting a little white ball on the golf course or driving range, or they may take the hoe and really dig up the garden. The mature individual learns that society expects him to "control" his emotions, and to release them in a manner approved by the social group. He knows that to repress them is not good for himself nor for those with whom he associates. Ralph Heynen suggests,

> To overcome anger we must first of all admit that we are angry. Many angry people are very good at denying their anger. A next step is for a person to ask himself why he is so angry. It may be well to look in a mirror at his own angry face. . . . It may be well to be angry, but it is never good to lose our temper. Jesus became angry, but He never threw a temper tantrum.[12]

The mature person is not only aware of his own emotions and able to control them, but he is able to understand and respond to the feelings of others. Most people are able to sympathize or to "feel with" another person in a time of loss or tragedy. However, only the mature individual is able to "empathize" with a person, that is to "feel in" a particular situation the same way that the person undergoing the situation feels. He is able to project himself into the

11. Larson, *Marriage Is for Living*, p. 13.
12. Ralph Heynen, *Where Are You Growing?* (Grand Rapids: Baker Book House, 1972), p. 14.

situation and experience the same emotions that the other person feels. Robert C. Williamson remarks:

> Some individuals seem devoid of the capacity to project themselves into the feelings of others or may be too insensitive to the emotional needs or values of others to be a responsive partner in any serious undertaking. They succeed in marriage only by a learning capacity that enables them to reeducate their own perceptual and emotional responses.[13]

The young person who has suffered a "broken heart" in a love affair knows how a person undergoing such an experience feels and is able to enter into the emotions much better than the young person who has never suffered a broken romance. When tempted to make a "cutting" remark that would hurt another person, the mature individual controls his tongue, for he is able to put himself in that person's place and knows how it will hurt. Needless to say, the empathetic person is able to get along well with other persons; he has the ability to discern their feelings and is able to identify with them. The individual who is always saying something that he later regrets, because of the hurt feelings engendered, lacks the quality of empathy and certainly needs to cultivate it.

The mature young person is one who is becoming independent from family and friends. Evelyn Duvall indicates that this is a phase in the development of the family when it serves as a "launching center" to push the young "from the home base and to sail off into a life for themselves. . . . The process of cutting apron strings characterizes the teen years and sets the stage for the son's or daughter's emergence as an emancipated young adult."[14] Two classic examples of failure in this area are the young person who leaves college the first week because of homesickness, and the young bride who "runs home to mother" whenever she has a quarrel with her husband.

In some families the members are very close to one another, and the young person has greater difficulty in achieving independence than the young person from a family where the members are not as dependent upon one another. It is easier for the young person to become economically independent in a family where he has learned to work and earn his own money, than it is where the young person has always lived on an allowance from the family.

Problems may arise between parents and young people in at least

---

13. Robert C. Williamson, *Marriage and Family Relations* (New York: John Wiley & Sons, Inc., 1966), p. 245. Used by permission.

14. Evelyn Millis Duvall, *Family Development* (Philadelphia: J. B. Lippincott Co., 1962), pp. 335-336.

two areas in this matter of becoming independent. Very often the young person tries to assert his independence before he is old enough, or mature enough to become independent. For example, the high school couple who announce they plan to be married even though the fellow has only a part-time job encounter resistance from their parents, for they believe the couple are not facing reality as mature young people should. The parents point out the difficulties such a marriage faces in the areas of finances or personal adjustments, with the hope that the couple will reconsider and postpone the marriage until they have completed their high school education or perhaps a year of college. Conflict arises if the couple do not accept the counsel of the parents. Much of the rebellion of many young people today is occasioned by this desire for independence while the parents feel the young people are not ready for it.

Problems may also arise if the parents refuse to relinquish control over the young person when he is old enough and mature enough to become independent. Consider the case of Jane, a college senior:

> My mother and I are having problems because she wants me to come live at home when I graduate, and she wants me to get a teaching position in the local school system which I attended. However, my roommate and I want to get positions in a Western state, and we want to live together in our own apartment. I appreciate what my parents have done in helping to pay my college expenses, but I am twenty-two years old now and feel that I should begin to make my own decisions in reference to employment and housing.

Jane's parents and particularly her mother are unwilling to accept the fact that their daughter is now a mature young adult who desires to make her own way in life. The wise parent encourages such aspirations of their children. Young married couples may face the same type of problem if they accept financial subsidies from their in-laws. The couple is not truly independent financially and there may be a tendency for the parental family to attempt to make decisions for their still dependent, though married, children. This is one of the difficulties faced by a couple who accepts a parental subsidy.

Attending college away from home is a maturing experience for many young people because it affords them an opportunity to make decisions by themselves and to meet new friends. Most students benefit by their newly gained freedom from immediate parental supervision, and gradually learn to do many things for themselves that they formerly expected their parents to do for them, such as writing their own checks to pay bills or doing their own laundry. Unfortunately, some students merely transfer their dependency from their parents to their roommates and then expect these newly acquired friends at college to help them make their decisions.

A small number of students are not able to adjust to the freedom of college life and use it as an occasion to rebel against parental standards and values that they have submitted to but have not genuinely accepted. They eventually become discipline problems and an embarrassment to their families and to the Christian institution where they attend. With appropriate discipline they often mature sufficiently to handle their freedom and become self-respecting members of the college group. A few persist in their rebellion and become a reproach to the name of Christ.

Another essential mark exhibited by the mature Christian young person is his commitment to Christ. He has thought through the Christian philosophy of life and has reached the settled conviction that salvation is only through faith in the atoning blood of Jesus Christ. For him "there is none other name under heaven given among men, whereby we must be saved" (Acts 4:12). The average high school student encounters enough opposition to his Christian faith so that by the time he reaches college he has faced such foes of the Christian faith as evolution, scientism, liberalism, communism, and various other "isms." In facing such encounters, he discovers that the Word of God is true and trustworthy, and that it contains the answer to all the devil's "isms." He comes to realize that the faith received at his mother's knee as a child is real and genuine, and it is able to strengthen him in the hour of testing and temptation. When difficulties come, he has learned to accept them as part of God's will for His life, and he claims the promise of Romans 8:28.[15] Even if God's will includes a lifelong physical handicap, this also is received as from His hand. It is refreshing to the spirit and a challenge to the soul to hear the testimony of these mature Christian young people with handicaps whose philosophy of life centers in the Lord Jesus Christ.

Deferred gratification is practiced by the mature young person, that is, he is willing to postpone immediate gratification of some desire so that he may achieve a greater satisfaction in the future. A child comes into the kitchen and asks his mother for a cookie. When asked to wait a minute until mother finishes her task, he throws a temper tantrum because he can only think of his immediate desire for a cookie. Some young people never mature beyond this stage.

15. In the writer's classes most students state that Romans 8:28 is the basis for their philosophy of life as a Christian. See Henry R. Brandt and Homer E. Dowdy, *Building a Christian Home*, pp. 73-74 for a case history illustrating this verse.

Whenever they want something, they must have it now. The young man "drops out" of high school because he has such a good paying summer job in the factory that he cannot give it up to return to school in September. He fails to realize that he may be laid off in February, or that it is a "blind alley" job with no future.

The mature young man is willing to sacrifice the money he might be earning in order to get some higher education or some technical training that will prepare him for a rewarding occupation in the future. He is willing to drive the old car in order to be able to go to college, even though some of his high school classmates have gone heavily in debt in order to purchase new super sports models. In these and many other areas, the mature young person will sacrifice present gratification for increased satisfaction in the future. "The mature person does not deny his desires and wants, but he is willing to plan and to wait, and, if necessary, to make sacrifices today in order to carry out plans that he has decided will mean greater over-all satisfaction in the long run."[16]

A responsible attitude toward sex is also characteristic of the mature young person. He cannot have the proper attitude if he does not have the correct information about sex. If the home has failed to give this knowledge, he will read factual books and pamphlets on the subject so that his understanding of sex is not based on the misinformation which is often gained from the peer group. He recognizes sex as God-given and holy, and if the home or church has presented sex as "dirty" and "unclean," he is able to make the distinction between the use of sex as God intended, and the misuse of sex, which is often "dirty" and "unclean" in the sense of promiscuity, fornication, and adultery.

If a young person has been reared in a home where affection was shown between husband and wife, and between parents and children, he is able to demonstrate affection toward the opposite sex. Henry R. Brandt, a psychologist, says, "Tender, considerate, unselfish, kind, mutual consideration for one another in the family will contribute to developing right attitudes in the child toward the opposite sex. The child must see a display of affection in the home—not merely hugs and kisses, but mutual consideration in a loving spirit."[17] The young person is aware of the emotional needs of the other person, and is able to meet those needs within the bounds of Christian love. He

---

16. Judson T. Landis and Mary G. Landis, *Building a Successful Marriage* (Englewood Cliffs: Prentice-Hall, Inc., 1968), p. 118.
17. Henry R. Brandt & Homer E. Dowdy, *Building a Christian Home* (Wheaton, IL: Scripture Press, 1960), p. 120.

never seeks to exploit the opposite sex in order to gratify his own physical desires.

This is one area where young people often manifest their immaturity, since they have not learned to submit their bodies to the control of the indwelling Holy Spirit. Small writes,

> The Scriptures say ". . . know ye not that your body is the temple of the Holy Ghost which is in you, which ye have of God, and ye are not your own? For ye are bought with a price; therefore glorify God in your body . . . " (I Cor. 6:19-20). Whatever the standard of the non-Christian, the standard for the Christian is clear. His body is a sacred trust from God, its functions meant to be restricted to and preserved for the ends designed by God. Jeremy Taylor prayed: "Let my body be servant of my spirit, and both body and spirit servants of Jesus."[18]

As young people are able to surrender their bodies to His holy dominion, they are able to distinguish between mere physical attraction and genuine romantic love. The mature young person is aware that much of what the world terms "love" is merely sexual attraction, and maintains the Biblical standards of purity and chastity in his relationships with the other sex.

He knows that sex is for marriage, and will be much more rewarding if he enters into the marriage relationship free from the guilt and remorse of premarital experiences. One individual, who learned by sad experience, stated, "Post-marital guilt is one of the best arguments for premarital chastity." However, the mature young couple prepare themselves for marriage during the engagement period by reading one or more marriage manuals so that they are informed as to their roles in consummating the marriage relationship.

One result of the maturation process is the development of a good self-image by the maturing young person.[19] Wayne Anderson suggests that a male student who needs a model to identify with to improve his self-image should consider some of the great men of history, or some contemporary political or athletic figure, or his own father.[20] Since the young person is learning to look at himself objectively, he sees his strengths and weaknesses. As he builds on his strengths, his self-confidence increases. With increasing spiritual maturity, he has an expanded view of himself as precious to God, and as

18. Small, *Christian Marriage*, pp. 174-175.
19. Bruce Narramore, *Parenting Within Love Limits* (Grand Rapids: Zondervan Publishing House, 1979), p. 114.
20. Wayne J. Anderson, *How To Understand Sex*, Guidelines for Students (Minneapolis: T. S. Denison & Co., Inc. 1966), pp. 131-132.

having an important part to play in serving the cause of Christ. He is "inner-directed" by the values which he holds, and though he is concerned about the needs of people, he is not conformed to the world around him.

All of these characteristics of maturity rarely are found in one young person. In reference to mate selection, the young person should attempt to find as mature an individual as possible. Just as a person may mature more rapidly in some spiritual areas than in others, so emotional maturity may progress faster in some aspects than others. If a young person is immature in some area, the important thing is that he should be aware of it, and he should be attempting to improve in that area. The ability to recognize the area of immaturity is itself a sign of increasing maturity, and is a plus factor in assessing the personality.[21]

MATURITY FOR MARRIAGE AND CHRONOLOGICAL AGE

It is evident that the spiritual and emotional maturity of a person are more important than the chronological age at the time of marriage. Most states have a legal minimum age of sixteen for girls and eighteen for boys—with their parent's permission[22] Based on 1970 census figures, the average bride is 20.8 years old, and the average groom is 23.2.[23] Since these are averages it indicates that many marry at younger and older ages.

However, those who marry later have far less risk of divorce. Paul C. Glick and Arthur J. Norton conclude:

> . . . the men with the smallest probability of divorce were those who married between 25 and 30 years of age, who were college graduates, or whose incomes were in the upper one-third—these groups had only about one-third as many chances of divorce during the first five years of marriage as men who married in their teens, who did not graduate from high school, or who were poor.[24]

Stated more positively, the men who marry between 15 and 19 years

21. Ralph Heynen, *The Secret of Christian Family Living* (Grand Rapids: Baker Book House, 1965), pp. 95-96.
22. Landis & Landis, *Successful Marriage*, p. 257.
23. Dan Golenpaul, ed., Yearbook, *Information Please Almanac* (New York, Simon & Schuster, 1974, p. 716.
24. Paul C. Glick and Arthur J. Norton, "Frequency, Duration, and Probability of Marriage and Divorce," in *Journal of Marriage and the Family*, May 1971, p. 317.

of age have three times as much chance of divorce as those who marry between 25 and 30 years of age. In an earlier study of actual divorce rates, Glick and Hugh Carter came to the same conclusion, "The 'worst' age for men to marry (in terms of the rate of dissolution) was between 14 and 19 years of age, and the 'best' (by the same criterion) was 25 to 29 years of age followed closely by the next older age group, 30 to 34 years."[25] Anderson states that "Brides under 20 and grooms under 21 account for 60 percent of the nation's divorces."[26] It is evident from these figures that many of the young people who marry in their teens are not mature enough to assume the responsibilities of marriage.

The average bride who is a college graduate is about twenty-four years old, and the average college-educated groom is about twenty-six years old.[27] Couples who graduate from college have happier marriages than couples who have only finished high school, but it cannot be determined whether it is the college experience that contributes to the happiness, or whether it is simply the fact that they are chronologically at least four years older, which gives them that much more time to mature.

Men usually marry women who are two or three years younger than themselves. The theory is that young women mature faster than the young men. Consequently, many young women are reluctant to date a fellow who is younger than she is. However, some studies have shown that the groom being a few years younger or a few years older does not affect the happiness of the marriage. A. Donald Bell mentions one study which found "that the largest percentage of happy husbands had married women who were three to four years older than they were."[28] The important factor is the emotional maturity of the individuals. Thus, a young lady should not hesitate to date a fellow who is slightly younger if he demonstrates sufficient maturity for his age level.

There is the danger of incompatibility in the "May-December" type of marriage where there is a large age difference between the two spouses. Twenty years difference may not appear too great at ages twenty-five and forty-five, but the physiological difference

25. Paul C. Glick and Hugh Carter, *Marriage & Divorce: A Social and Economic Study* (Cambridge, MA: Harvard University Press, 1970), p. 236.

26. Wayne J. Anderson, *Design for Family Living* (Minneapolis: T. S. Denison & Co., Inc., 1964), p. 35.

27. Ibid.

28. A. Donald Bell, *The Family in Dialogue* (Grand Rapids, Zondervan Publishing House, 1965), p. 155.

becomes greater after a decade or two as the older partner ages faster.

Age and emotional maturity are also very important for young adults who have passed the prime-marrying years of the early twenties. The stereotype is that the bachelor or bachelor girl in the early thirties cannot marry and make the needed adjustments in married living. Studies have proven this stereotype to be false, for most such couples are able to adjust and to live very happily together. One reason is that they have lived longer and are more emotionally and spiritually mature than those who marry in their early twenties. Also, when they do marry, they are strongly motivated to make the marriage a success, as they realize that a second opportunity at their ages is not very possible, whereas some young people enter marriage with the idea that if it does not succeed, they can try it again. [29] Emotional maturity is the important factor for it is possible for people in their early thirties to be emotionally immature and incapable of making the adjustments necessary for happiness in marriage.

MATURITY AND COLLEGE MARRIAGES

Maturity is especially important in two other marital situations. The first is marriage while attending college. Before World War II, a marriage of college students was a rare occurrence, and it was customary for young people to wait until graduation to get married. The influx of married veterans destroyed the idea that married students could not do as well as single students. Subsequent studies have shown that married students achieve better grades than they did as single students. [30] Many college and universities now provide housing facilities for their married students. Students contemplating marriage while in college need to realize they sacrifice much of the social life that is ordinarily associated with a college career. Most adult social activities in society at large are for married couples, but college social life is oriented around dating couples; activities for married couples are not as frequent. Unless a couple have had sufficient dating experience, and are reasonably sure they will not miss the social activities, they should not consider marriage while in college. [31]

The problem of financing both a college education and a marriage is a very real one for students considering matrimony while still in

29. Landis & Landis, *Successful Marriage*, pp. 124-125.
30. Williamson, *Marriage and Family Relationships*, p. 87.
31. Ibid., p. 86.

school. The cost of higher education climbs each year, as does the cost of living. If room and board were the only consideration, it is true that two can live together as cheaply in an apartment as two can live separately in the average college dormitories. However, there are other expenses involved, such as automobile costs and insurance, which are usually cared for by the parents.

Many couples solve the problem by letting the wife drop out of school and take a full-time job to help pay expenses. The husband goes to school, works part-time, and takes out loans to help pay the tuition costs. Other couples have their marriage subsidized by the parents either for all or part of their expenses.[32] Some parents feel the tuition cost is their obligation whether the student is single or married, and agree to pay this expense for the young married couple. Other parents are able to subsidize all the expenses so that both the husband and wife can finish their courses and receive their degrees.

Some parents help the young people on a loan basis, particularly if they have younger children who also will need financial aid for college. Some couples insist on paying their own way by only taking as many hours of college work as they can afford even though it extends the time they are in college to five or six years. Serious thought should be given to the financial considerations by a couple planning to marry while still in college.

MATURITY AND MILITARY MARRIAGES

Another type of marriage that requires considerable maturity for success is one when the husband is scheduled to leave for the armed forces. The couple must decide if they should marry before or after the service experience. Assuming they have had a courtship sufficient to test their compatibilities, the deciding factor is the amount of time they have as a married couple before the separation takes place. Many critical adjustments must be made during the first year of marriage, so the couple should have at least a year together before the separation takes place. This gives them time to work out any problems that may arise between them as a married couple.

A separation is difficult for any relationship to withstand, for the two persons are undergoing personality changes without the opportunity to adjust to each other. Even though letters are written each day, these are a poor form to communicate changes in feeling and attitudes. It is better for the couple to remain engaged and to wait

32. Blood, *Marriage*, pp. 163-165.

for marriage until the service obligation is fulfilled. If for some reason the relationship is broken, there is no necessity for a divorce with its legal and religious difficulties. Sometimes after the basic training, a serviceman may be assigned to a base in the United States and is allowed to live off the base. Marriage under these circumstances is not too different than when the groom holds a civilian job. If the couple are separated during his military service, it is wise to treat the reunion as a second honeymoon where they can have a few days together alone before returning to the routine of everyday life.[33]

MATURITY AND SUCCESSFUL MARRIAGE

The importance of a young person striving to attain spiritual and emotional maturity cannot be overemphasized. His success or failure in marriage is determined to a large extent by the level of maturity attained. Small expresses it so well:

... spiritual roots are important and cannot be ignored. Emotional maturity will engender emotional unity between a married couple, and in precisely the same way spiritual maturity will engender spiritual unity.... Christian marriage offers the way to real oneness by pointing to a unifying center and power outside of the couple themselves. This oneness is not a mere elusive idealism. It is rather the exciting possibility before every couple that is committed to the Lordship of Christ over all of their life together.[34]

Spiritual and emotional growth continue throughout life. This is what Paul had in mind when he wrote to the Philippians, "Not as though I had already attained, either were already perfect [mature] ... forgetting those things which are behind, and reaching forth unto those things which are before, I press toward the mark for the prize of the high calling of God in Christ Jesus." (3:12-14) "So let us all who are mature have this attitude" (4:15, Williams translation).

33. Landis & Landis, *Successful Marriage*, pp. 155-159.
34. Small, *Christian Marriage*, p. 9. Used by permission.

PERSONALITY INVENTORY

ARE YOU READY FOR MARRIAGE?

Write a short paragraph in answer to each of the following statements or questions. Please be as introspective as possible in order to gain some insights concerning your level of spiritual and emotional maturity.

1 Have you established the practice of a daily "quiet-time" with God? If not, why not?

2 Have you learned to daily yield your life to the control of the Holy Spirit?

3 How important to you is regular attendance at the services of the local church?

4 What forms of Christian service or witness are you involved in?

5 Explain your method of solving problems as they arise in your life.

6 How do you relieve frustrations? Do you need to make any improvements in this area?

7 What do you think is the will of God for your life work? If uncertain, why can't you decide?

8 How well do you know your own personality needs? Which areas need definite improvement?

9 Do you feel that you have had sufficient dating experience to know what kind of marriage partner would be compatible with your personality?

10 Are you still economically or emotionally dependent on your parents or siblings? Will this dependence, if any, create problems if you marry?

QUESTIONS FOR DISCUSSION AND REVIEW

1. Define *spiritual maturity*.

2. In what manner is spiritual growth similar to physical growth?

3. Is it possible for a spiritually mature Christian to consistently engage in "worldly" practices? Give Scriptural evidence for your answer.

4. What is the relationship between spiritual maturity and emotional maturity? Is it possible to have one without the other?

5. How is chronological age related to emotional and spiritual maturity?

6. What are some characteristics of the emotionally mature person?

7. How may parents hinder a young person from becoming an independent adult? How may they help him to achieve that status?

8. Analyze the statement, "The groom should be two or three years older than the bride."

9. Discuss the advantages and disadvantages of a couple marrying while both are in college.

10. What are some issues to be considered by a couple contemplating marriage just prior to the man entering military service?

8

THE ENGAGEMENT, WEDDING, AND HONEYMOON

*Whoso findeth a wife findeth a good
thing, and obtaineth favour of the Lord.*
Proverbs 18:22

ENGAGEMENT IN THE BIBLE

Engagement has been a part of the marriage custom in many countries for many centuries. Most Christians are familiar with the Genesis record where Jacob agreed to work for Laban seven years in return for the hand of Rachel in marriage, and those seven years "seemed unto him but a few days, for the love he had to her" (Gen. 29:20). He was deceived by Laban on the wedding night, and had to serve another seven years for his beloved Rachel.

The New Testament story of the engagement of Joseph and Mary is well known (Matt. 1:18-25). According to the custom of the time, a written contract of engagement was signed under oath, and then the bride returned to her home for a few months before the actual wedding. In this interval she received instructions in the home on the duties of a good Jewish wife. Thus, the engagement period aided the Jewish girl to prepare for her responsibilities as a Jewish wife and mother. If unfaithfulness on her part occurred during this time, the husband-to-be had the choice of either having her stoned to death, or he could give her a bill of divorce.[1] Joseph decided on the latter course of action, and that is when the angel appeared to him with the announcement that Mary was to be the mother of the Messiah.

1. Henry Alford, *The New Testament for English Readers* (Chicago: Moody Press, n.d.), p. 4.

ENGAGEMENT AS A SOCIAL RITUAL

Many Christians have heard missionaries from various countries tell about the "puberty rites" which the adolescents of various cultures pass through in making the transition to adult status. This is what sociologists speak of as "rites of passage." The society has a "ritual" of some kind to help the person to move from one status to another, particularly when the second status involves more responsibility than the first.[2]

American society has rituals in high school and college graduation ceremonies, and in rituals associated with marriage, birth, and death. Engagement in our culture is different from that of the New Testament Jewish culture in that it is not as permanent or binding, but it does perform the same function of a rite of passage to help prepare the young person for the responsibilities of married life.

The fellow giving the girl a ring, the announcement of the engagement in the newspapers, and the various "showers" given for the bride-to-be are all a part of the ritual associated with engagement. It is not necessary for a ring to be given for the couple to be engaged, and many couples are informally engaged for some time before a ring is given. "The ring is in most instances a diamond, however any ring or pin will do."[3] Although a ring is not absolutely essential, the ring is so important to the engagement ritual that a young lady feels "more engaged" if she has one.

FUNCTIONS OF AN ENGAGEMENT

A very important function of engagement in our courtship system is to give the couple a final opportunity to test their psychological compatibility in a more intimate relationship. In the dating process, young people reveal their true selves very gradually. In random dating very little of the self is revealed. However, as a couple continue to date, and become seriously interested in one another, more self-revelation takes place.

When the relationship develops to the point where the young man asks the girl to marry him, and they become engaged, they enter into a much more intimate phase of courtship with a large increase in

2. Joan P. Mencher, "The Nayers of South Malabar," M. F. Nimkoff, ed., *Comparative Family Systems* (Boston: Houghton–Mifflin Co., 1965), pp. 185-186. These pages describe the "rites of passage" in the Nayar culture.
3. Robert C. Williamson, *Marriage and Family Relations* (New York: John Wiley & Sons, Inc., 1966), p. 305.

self-revelation.[4] C. W. Scudder states that this "is a period of growing 'toward each other,' of growing toward oneness. It is a period designed to test the satisfaction derived from being devoted solely to each other."[5] During this time most couples adjust to this increased knowledge of each other and the relationship is solidified. For others, the increased intimacy reveals facets of personality that were unknown before and to which the partners cannot adjust, and the engagement is broken.

If the maladjustments result in conflict, the engagement should be broken, for it would be difficult to build a happy marriage from such a relationship. Although for the parties concerned broken engagements, with the "broken hearts" that accompany them, are difficult to endure, they are accepted by the church and society without reproach. Robert Williamson remarks that "among the middle class, approximately one-third of the men and one-half the women break their engagements."[6] Couples should give themselves enough time during engagement to really get to know each other well. If their compatibility passes this final test, they should not be afraid to consummate the engagement in marriage.

Another purpose of engagement is to give time to prepare for the wedding. The type of wedding determines the amount of time needed. A large, formal church wedding with several attendants, followed by a lavish reception, necessarily takes more time to plan than a simple wedding in the home or church with just two attendants. It is unfortunate that the wedding ceremony in many churches becomes a "status symbol." Each family tries to surpass the size and cost of the last wedding in order to display their financial ability, and much of the money spent for "conspicuous consumption" might better be given to the newlyweds to help them establish their household. Nevertheless, even a simple wedding ceremony can be quite involved, and the engagement period should allow sufficient time to prepare for a well-planned wedding day.

The engagement period also provides time for the couple to attempt to reconcile any differences they may have with their future in-laws. If one set of in-laws is against the marriage of the couple, the announcement of the engagement may serve notice that the young people are really serious in their desire to marry, and the in-laws will intensify their attempts to destroy the relationship between the

4. Mollie Smart and Russell Smart, *An Introduction to Family Relationships* (Philadelphia: W. B. Saunders Co., 1953), p. 250.

5. C. W. Scudder, *The Family in Christian Perspective* (Nashville: Broadman Press, 1962), p. 57.

6. Williamson, *Marriage and Family Relations*, p. 311.

couple. This opposition should serve as a warning signal to the couple that someone very close to the situation does not think it is the best relationship, and they should reexamine it in a mature, objective, and prayerful manner to see if there are deficiencies of which they are not aware. It is possible for young people to be so emotionally involved with each other that they cannot see the problems that may be perfectly obvious to their friends and relatives.

Where there is strong opposition to a marriage by one set of the future in-laws, or if other relatives and friends are opposed to the relationship, it may prove very helpful for the couple to seek the counsel of a godly Sunday school teacher, pastor, youth leader, or another Christian leader who will be able to give them unbiased, objective appraisal of their relationship. If the counselor has available some of the marriage prediction tests, it would be helpful to see if there are areas of possible incompatibility. The counselor can then alert the couple to areas in their relationship which need extra attention in order to make a good adjustment. Although the prediction tests are no longer used to forecast "success or failure in marriage," they do have value "when used by skilled counselors to pinpoint probable trouble areas."[7]

The will of God for the particular couple is the important matter. If after much prayer and godly counsel, the couple feel they should proceed with the wedding, they should make every reasonable overture to the objecting in-laws for a reconciliation prior to the wedding. If this is still impossible, they are duty-bound to do what they conscientiously feel is the will of God for their lives.

There are some situations where it is most difficult for a Christian parent to give their consent and blessing to the proposed marriage of a son or daughter. Since the union of a believer with an unbeliever is in clear violation of II Corinthians 6:14-18, a Christian parent cannot be expected to sanction such a marriage, for it is contrary to the Word and will of God.

A similar situation exists where the Christian parents have strong convictions against divorce, and the son or daughter wishes to marry an individual who has been divorced. Christian parents in such circumstances cannot approve of the desired marriage because of their own convictions concerning the will of God. Certainly the

---

7. Leonard Benson, *The Family Bond* (New York: Random House, 1971), p. 146. Also see William M. Kephart, *The Family, Society, and the Individual,* (Boston: Houghton-Mifflin Co., 1972), pp. 471-475, for a discussion and criticisms of marriage prediction studies.

parents will counsel the son or daughter to be obedient to the Word of God in such cases.

If the individual still insists on marrying outside the will of God, the parents have done their duty and there is little purpose in the parents opposing the wedding. The task then is to seek to establish some relationship with the couple in order to try to win the unsaved person to Christ in the future.

Parental opposition may be faced by the Christian young person who plans to marry a person with a different ethnic or socio-economic background. Even though both young people are Christians, the parents may feel that the cultural differences are too great for the couple to overcome and that a happy marriage cannot be achieved. They may also be exhibiting their prejudice against the nationality or social class of the intended spouse. In this case the couple must reassess their relationship, seek counsel, and then do the will of God in spite of parental objection. The engagement period provides time for making these reconciliations, for the couple who has the blessing of both sets of in-laws has a greater chance for happiness in their marriage. Leonard Benson makes the point that parental approval is one of the premarital conditions "linked to marital success."[8]

The engagement period also gives the couple time to really communicate with each other about many aspects of their future married life. Important decisions that will affect the future of the relationship need to be made during this period. The couple should discuss and come to a mutual agreement about such things as the roles they expect to play in marriage, their financial goals in life and the method of handling the money, the number of children and how they are to be spaced, and their spiritual goals in life and how they expect to attain them.[9]

Inability to talk about important issues should be considered a warning signal that the area is a potential source of incompatibility. If the individuals cannot agree on the use of money during engagement, they will not be in harmony after the wedding ceremony. If they cannot solve the problem of family planning before marriage, they can temporarily get by without really facing the issue. However, once they start on the honeymoon trip, it will have to be faced in a realistic manner.

8. Ibid., p. 144.
9. Robert O. Blood, Jr., *Marriage* (New York: Free Press of Glencoe, 1962), p. 173.

CONFLICTS IN AN ENGAGEMENT

Most problems young people face in engagement have a solution unless they involve a clash of incompatible values or goals. For example, if a young man feels called to full-time Christian service, and the partner feels she could never fulfill the role expectations of a pastor's or missionary's wife, then the best solution is to break the relationship and look for a future spouse that shares the same goal in life. On the other hand, a conflict over the use of money can be solved if the individuals are adaptable enough to compromise their views in order to reach a settlement that is mutually agreeable. If such an agreement cannot be reached, it indicates the individuals are not flexible enough to each give in to the other, and therefore it may be wise to dissolve the relationship.

Hopefully, two Christian young people who have the inspiration and help of prayer and the Word of God will be able to reach satisfactory agreements much easier than the unsaved couple who lack such aids for daily living. In either case, the couple must be able to communicate with each other during engagement if they expect this interaction to be characteristic of their married life. If they are successful in establishing communication, their engagement will be successful, and their marriage should be successful, for Burgess and Wallen "have contended that *engagement success* ranks among the best predictors of marital success."[10]

CONFESSING THE SINS OF THE PAST LIFE

Engaged couples who establish good communications often face the problem of how much of their past life to reveal to each other. Sometimes there are "skeletons in the family closet" that the partner needs to know about, since they may have an influence on the marriage itself. In this day of permissiveness and "going steady," young people quite often transgress their moral standards concerning necking, petting, and premarital sex and often feel the need to tell the engaged partner of their failures.

In Christian youth these experiences usually leave the person with a burden of guilt, and in an attempt to be honest with the present partner, they feel they should tell the person about their previous experience. Usually it is best not to tell unless the individual has been so promiscuous that it is common knowledge, or if there has been

10. Benson, *Family Bond*, p. 140.

some consequence such as contracting venereal disease or the birth of an illegitimate child which certainly should be told to the partner. However, sexual sins, if confessed and forsaken, are forgiven like other sins (I John 1:9), and should be forgotten, for God forgets them: ". . . for I will forgive their iniquity, and I will remember their sin no more" (Jer. 31:34).

If a young person has been guilty of such sins, and cannot find release from the burden of guilt even though he has confessed the sin to God, he should seek out a counselor, such as a pastor or teacher, and talk to that person rather than confessing his past to his loved one, who may be terribly hurt and disillusioned by such a revelation. A counselor is used to such confessions and can be objective in his viewpoint, but to confess such sins to a loved one may be too much strain for the relationship to bear. The engagement may survive such a revelation, but the memory may prove to be a real deterrent to a good sex adjustment in marriage. In other words, there is little to be gained and much to be lost through such a confession. The case of Rose and Eric illustrates this fact very well:

> *Rose met Eric at the beginning of their junior year in a Christian college. They seemed to be very compatible from the beginning. Their personalities fit each other, and in many areas they comple-mented each other. The romance developed and Eric gave Rose a ring in the summer preceding their senior year.*
>
> *When they returned that fall the relationship continued to grow. By mutual agreement their physical intimacy was limited to light necking. However, Eric's conscience began to bother him concerning an experience he had with a girl during his freshman year. It seems that his relationship with her had been very much on a physical plane with a lot of "making out" with light petting. On one of these occasions, their emotions got out of control and they engaged in heavy petting but did not go all the way. They were filled with regret which resulted in the breaking of the relationship.*
>
> *Eric felt that in honesty to Rose he must confess it to her. The revelation was more than she could bear, for Eric was such a fine Christian she could not conceive of his indulging in such behavior. Rose wanted to break the engagement, but Eric persuaded her to see a counselor. Over a period of weeks the counselor worked with Eric and Rose until she was able to see that God had forgiven Eric. She was able to forgive Eric and accept him for the fine person he really was. The romance culminated in marriage and they made a good adjustment to each other.*

If God has forgiven and forgotten the sin, then the young person should also.

In view of God's attitude, it is not proper for young people to pry into each other's past romantic life. One phase of love is accepting a person as he is, and if the partner is acceptable, what value is there to be gained from probing into the past? Paul's exhortation in Philippians 3:13 is applicable here: ". . forgetting those things which are behind, and reaching forth unto those things which are before. . . . "

PREMARITAL COUNSELING

The engagement period also provides time for the couple to seek premarital counseling and medical examinations. If the couple have had the advantage of a good high school or college course in Marriage and Family Living, then counseling will not be necessary unless there are problems in the relationship. Such individuals will be aware of the many adjustments they will have to make during the honeymoon and first few months of married life. Other couples who have not had the benefit of a Marriage and Family Living course will usually gain new information and attitudes from a trained counselor who can help prepare them for their new roles as husband and wife.

There are some individuals who have become disillusioned with premarital counseling. They believe engaged couples are so much in love that the reality of what they face in marriage cannot be comprehended. Cecil Osborne writes,

> I long ago abandoned as futile the effort to instruct young couples in these matters before marriage. They tended to look at me through star dust, with amused tolerance. . . . Finally I have come to the point where I ask only one thing of them: a solemn agreement that they will seek a competent marriage counselor or minister at the first sign that they are not communicating well.[11]

He proceeds to say that the husband is most reluctant to seek help.

Each partner should visit a physician for a premarital examination. Before the visit, the couple should read a good marriage manual so that they may ask the doctor any questions that need clarifying concerning the marital relationship.[12] The visit should be made sufficiently in advance of the wedding to provide time for any minor surgery that may be necessary. The doctor will also discuss the various methods of family planning, and will make a recommendation if asked to do so. Most states require a medical statement from a

11. Cecil G. Osborne, *The Art of Understanding Your Mate* (Grand Rapids: Zondervan Publishing House, 1970), p. 13. Used by permission.

12. Tim and Beverly LaHaye, *The Act of Marriage* (Grand Rapids: Zondervan Publishing House, 1976) is an excellent marriage manual written from a Christian viewpoint.

licensed physician, indicating the couple are free from veneral disease, before the marriage license can be issued. This may necessitate another visit to the doctor's office within the time limit specified by the law. Although most physicians in America are very busy men, they will usually take the time to counsel and help young people get a good start in their matrimonial life.

THE LENGTH OF THE ENGAGEMENT

The length of the engagement varies from couple to couple. Many young people have a private understanding that they are engaged to be married and may interact on this basis for many months prior to making a public announcement. During this time many of the purposes of engagement are realized as they test their compatibility. For such a couple, a long public engagement is not necessary as it is for a couple who have known each other for three months. Knowing each other such a short time does not give sufficient opportunity for the two persons involved to really get to know each other very well. Judson T. and Mary G. Landis remark, "Research studies show that longer engagements are among the factors predictive of happiness in marriage. All studies indicate that short engagements are more likely to be followed by poor adjustment in marriage and that the lowest percentages of very happy marriages are among couples who have not been engaged at all."[13]

Young people are better prepared for marriage if they have an engagement of at least one year or more. However, it is most important that the partners have much interaction during the engagement to really test their compatibility. It is possible for a couple to be engaged for a year and to be separated from each other so that they only see each other a few times during the year on special occasions. Very little self-revelation takes place at such times and the engagement function of a final testing of the relationship does not occur. In spite of being engaged for a year, the couple have no great advantage in compatibility testing over the couple with only a short engagement.[14]

It is also possible for a couple to have a lengthy engagement and still miss the benefits that should result from such a period. A couple may continue to see each other through the idealization of romantic

13. Judson T. Landis and Mary G. Landis, *Building a Successful Marriage* (Englewood Cliffs, NJ: Prentice-Hall, Inc., 1968), p. 133.
14. Ibid., p. 234.

love, and subconsciously refuse to bring their real attitudes and feelings to the surface, but after marriage time will eventually permit real feelings to manifest themselves. These real attitudes and feelings may be a source of incompatibility if they concern basic values or goals in life. Ordinarily the passing of time in the engagement permits additional self-revelation to take place so that potential areas of conflict are discovered and the necessary adjustments made. If these cannot be made, the engagement is usually broken. Unless the engagement period is used for self-revelation, a long engagement may not be any more useful than a short one.

Usually a couple should not announce their engagement until they are able to set an approximate date for the wedding ceremony. An engagement that is too long can be as detrimental to the relationship as one that is too short. However, studies have shown that of the two choices, lengthy engagements more often result in happier marriages. "Burgess and Cottrell found that the ratio of couples with 'poor' adjustment declined from 50 percent for engagements of less than three months to 11 percent for those of twenty-four or more in duration."[16] This may be partly explained by the fact that the added time allows the couple to make many of the adjustments to each other during the courtship period. When they finally do get married after an engagement of two or three years, they are so well adjusted to each other they do not have many of the conflicts which characterize most marriages which follow a short engagement. Those who marry after a shorter period of engagement may rate their marriage as less happy since they experience many conflicts early in the marriage.

There are two major perils to a relationship in a long engagement. The first is the possibility that the long waiting period may cause the relationship to "stagnate," that is, the partners lose interest in each other. This loss of interest may be mutual, but most often one partner grows weary of waiting, and breaks the relationship. Dwight H. Small describes such a situation: "Lovers get on each other's nerves when there is exclusive preoccupation with themselves yet with no workable goals to demand their thought and ingenuity."[17]

The second danger is the possiblity of becoming too intimate physically. By its nature, the engagement period is one of greater

---

15. Ibid.

16. Willaimson, *Marriage and Family Relations*, p. 307.

17. Dwight Hervey Small, *Design for Christian Marriage* (Westwood, NJ: Fleming H. Revell Co., 1959), p. 210.

intimacy than merely going steady. The normal God-given biological desires that find their fulfillment in marriage increase during this time. If this period is too long, the couple faces the possibility of transgressing their standards in the matter of necking and petting.

Sometimes there is the insidious temptation for the couple to reason, "We are going to be married soon, why should we wait?" There are several good reasons. The most important is that such behavior before marriage is sin in the sight of God and the Holy Spirit will bring conviction of sin and guilt to the heart. The act may cause the loss of respect for the partner and destroy the love between the couple. It certainly robs the couple of the joy that should be theirs on the honeymoon, and the guilt carried over into marriage could hinder the sex adjustment of the couple.

The large number of broken engagements indicate that the couple may never marry even though they engage in sexual relationships. Henry Brandt gives several illustrations where this happened. In one case the fellow was accidently killed a week before the wedding. In another situation the couple broke up, the girl met another man but was in a dilemma whether to tell him or not for fear that he might learn through gossip about her previous transgression. In a third case the fellow was drafted and the couple "became very suspicious and distrustful of each other."[18]

Small makes the point that some couples engage in premarital sex thinking that it will strengthen the relationship, but it may lead to a broken engagement. "Because of the low quality of such experience, and in the sense of guilt and frustration, disappointment may so cloud the whole relationship as to cause a broken engagement."[19] The possibility of pregnancy and the resulting shame of a baby arriving "too early" certainly make it worthwhile to wait. In the secular world much of the shame of having a baby arrive "too early" or illegitimately has been removed.[20] In most, if not all, Bible believing churches, there is still a stigma attached to an illegitimate birth, or the too early arrival of a baby. Someone has said that there has been no improvement in contraceptive devices as far as engaged couples are concerned, for so often they do not plan to engage in premarital sex but get carried away with their emotions. The result is an unplanned pregnancy. These are some of the valid reasons for saving physical intimacies until after the wedding ceremony.

18. Henry R. Brandt and Homer E. Dowdy, *Building a Christian Home*, (Wheaton, IL: Scripture Press, 1960), pp. 136-137.
19. Small, *Christian Marriage*, pp. 212-213.
20. "Single Motherhood," *Time*, September 6, 1971, p. 48.

BREAKING AN ENGAGEMENT

Since engagement is a final testing of a relationship, it is only reasonable to expect some to fail the test. There are no reliable statistics, but estimates for young people in general indicate that from one-third to one-half of all engagements are broken.[21] Benson makes the following comment:

> Apparently engagement is a very brittle relationship, but one which, once broken, does not ordinarily cause prolonged sorrow or any deep sense of bereavement. The nation is full of people who have survived broken engagements.[22]

The high divorce rate suggests that it might be better if more relationships were broken during engagement rather than going on into a marriage doomed to failure. The functions of an engagement for the Christian are the same as those for the non-Christian, but hopefully Christian young people will prayerfully discern the will of God before committing themselves to an engagement. "This commitment to engagement should not be made while there are evident areas of the relationship as yet unevaluated or unrevealed."[23] In another place Small suggests, "Much that is usually relegated to the engagement period should properly be incorporated into courtship preceding engagement."[24]

Many young women experience "premarriage" jitters or doubts about the relationship as the wedding day approaches. "For some individuals the feeling of mental and physical distress as the wedding day approaches generally signifies to the individual the momentous step he is taking."[25] Since marriage ia a lifelong commitment for the Christian, it is easy to understand why a young lady might have doubts. The only way to determine whether the doubts have a legitimate basis or not is to objectively reexamine the entire relationship. An examination of this type should demonstrate whether or not there are basic incompatibilities that threaten the future marriage. If the overall relationship is judged a good one, the doubts should be put out of the mind and be replaced by a positive attitude

21. Williamson, *Marriage and Family Relations*, p. 305.
22. Benson, *Family Bond*, p.140.
23. Small, *Christian Marriage*, p. 208.
24. Ibid., p. 198.
25. Williamson, *Marriage and Family Relations*, p. 306.

toward the impending ceremony. If the appraisal indicates there are serious incompatibilities, and if the couple cannot resolve the difficulties, then it is better to break the engagement.

A couple may hesitate to take this step if showers have been held and numerous gifts received. It is much better to suffer the embarrassment of returning the gifts than to enter into a relationship that is less than the best for the two individuals concerned. Life is too short to spend it in an unhappy marriage simply because the bride-elect is afraid to send back some gifts.

Occasionally one hears of a bride or groom who does not show up for the wedding. Even this embarrassment, as crushing as it is to the ego, is better than consummating a union that results in unhappiness. Such an experience indicates that the couple had unresolved problems and it should not occur to couples who have established a good relationship before committing themselves to an engagement.

Frequently young people have doubts about their engagement if they feel a physical attraction to someone other than the partner. Many young people and older ones as well, do not understand that it is possible for a person to be physically attracted to a person of the opposite sex without becoming involved or at times, even acquainted with that person. When this attraction comes to a mature person, it is put out of the mind as simply a passing fancy. This type of problem is very common on the college campus where young people through propinquity are daily in close contact with many other attractive persons of the opposite sex. Consider the case of John and Mary:

John and Mary began going steady during their sophomore year in college. The relationship developed and they became engaged at the end of the junior year, planning to be married soon after graduation. During the last semester, John worked in a small group on a class project. Another member of the group was Jane, a very attractive student with a nice personality and a strong spiritual commitment. After several weeks John became strongly attracted to Jane, and wondered if he had really made the right choice when he became engaged to Mary. The frustration became so severe that he sought out a counselor. The entire relationship with Mary was thoroughly examined, and it was established that they were well suited to each other. The counselor was able to explain to John that throughout a lifetime of Christian service (he felt called to the ministry), he would be thrown into contact with many very attractive persons of the opposite sex, but that it was his responsibility to keep his thoughts and emotions under control realizing that his love was pledged to Mary. With this help, John was able to stabilize his feelings, and he and Mary married soon after graduation as they had originally planned.

Not all such experiences have a happy ending, for many engagements are broken because one of the partners becomes interested in someone else. The fact that there is no cultural bias against breaking an engagement serves to help young people decide to sever an incompatible relationship. Usually they have the encouragement of relatives and friends, particularly if the courtship has been noticeably unhappy. Some individuals resort to "Dear John" letters, but this is not in good taste if a personal confrontation is possible. Since the individuals have spent much time together, the least they owe one another is a personal meeting to explain why they want to break the engagement. Certainly a person wants to do the will of God, but it is not proper to blame Him for the breaking of a relationship without some very valid reasons for doing so. Marilyn had an unhappy experience of this type:

> *Jim and Marilyn met during his sophomore year while she was a junior. They had many things in common such as their aim to become teachers. At the end of the year they had reached a "private understanding" of engagement, but early in the summer Jim was drafted into the army. He corresponded and telephoned regularly while in basic training. Near the end of his first leave he purchased a ring and gave it to Marilyn with a pledge of undying love. The next day he left for an army base in a neighboring state. A week went by and Marilyn did not hear from Jim. This was very upsetting as Jim had been such a good correspondent during the basic training. After two weeks she telephoned him and he was very apologetic and promised to write. The promise was not kept and she phoned again. This time he told her he was not sure it was God's will for them to be married and did not want his ring back, but could give no logical reason for his indecision. Eventually, Marilyn sent the ring to him. It later developed that Jim had met a girl in the local church, and had wanted Marilyn to keep the ring until he solidified his relationship with the new girl whom he married two months after receiving the ring back. He attempted to blame the will of God for his own infatuation.*

"Honesty is the best policy" is a good maxim in breaking a relationship. It is much better to break an engagement which should be broken than to enter into a marriage which might eventuate in a broken home.

The Christian couple can make the engagement period a time of great spiritual blessing and growth. The practice of reading the Word of God and praying together accentuates their growth toward spiritual oneness in Christ, and lays a firm foundation for continued spiritual growth in their marriage. Problems arising due to the increased self-revelation of engagement are prayed about, and worked through to a mutual adjustment. The favor of God is invoked upon all the plans for their life together. His guidance is sought in daily activities, and for their lives in the future. During engagement the Christian couple can begin to appreciate the truth oft repeated, "Each for the other, and both for the Lord."

THE MARRIAGE CEREMONY

The successful engagement usually culminates in a wedding.

> It marks both the end of one way of life and the beginning of another. It is the point at which society recognizes the establishment of a new family. It establishes new social and legal responsibilities as well as approving new social privileges and opportunities. It is an event of great significance. . . . Because of its significance, it should be carefully planned.[26]

Occasionally a couple elopes and avoids the planning and expense of a wedding, but most Christian couples have their marriage solemnized in a church wedding ceremony.

James Jauncey makes some interesting observations about the religious nature of the wedding ceremony. He writes:

> The purpose of the religious service is to bring out in bold relief the spiritual side of marriage. Of course, the spiritual factor is there anyway, whether the marriage is performed by a justice of the peace or by a clergyman. The ceremony does not put it there. It simply recognizes the spiritual aspect and ministers to it. . . . Although the religious service of marriage does not guarantee anything it does give the spiritual side of marriage a head start. For this reason it is tremendously important.[27]

Some parents may object to the expense involved in a lovely church wedding, but it is interesting to note that a higher percentage of happily married couples were married in a church than those who were not married in a church. Undoubtedly there are other factors which may account for the higher happiness rating, such as the religious commitment of those having church weddings. On the other hand, it does help to give a good beginning to a marriage when the blessing of God is invoked upon it.

26. Scudder, *Family in Christian Perspective*, pp. 58-59.
27. James H. Jauncey, *Magic in Marriage* (Grand Rapids: Zondervan Publishing House, 1966), pp. 26-27. Used by permission.

Traditionally the bride and her family plan and pay for the wedding, and the groom assumes the responsibility of the honeymoon. Although the bride often chooses to have the ceremony in the parsonage, or in her home, or on the lawn or in the garden of the home, the majority prefer the traditional service in the church sanctuary. The families of the bride and groom may make suggestions, but it is the bride's "day" and her wishes must override the desires of all other individuals connected with the wedding.

There are numerous etiquette books which treat the details of the actual wedding, so it is not necessary to repeat them. The wedding should be carefully planned within the budget of the family, and should not be a display of "conspicuous consumption" or used as a "status symbol."[28]

The actual ceremony will be largely determined by the pastor who officiates, although most men will be considerate of the wishes of the bride. The selection of the music and the vows to be spoken can be mutually agreed on by the pastor and the bride and groom.

Referring to the ceremony, Scudder writes that it "should be a sacred and meaningful religious experience for the bride and groom." He quotes Theodore Adams as saying, "When all is said and done, there is no higher or finer hour in the life of a young man and young woman than when they stand before God and their loved ones and, before a minister of Jesus Christ, pledge themselves to the high adventure of sharing life with each other in marriage forever after."[29] Many dedicated Christian couples desire that the ceremony contain some gospel witness to the unsaved who are present, many of whom only attend a church for a wedding or funeral. Often the pastor can weave the plan of salvation into his remarks to the congregation or to the couple; however, the pastor must use tact and wisdom, remembering that it is a wedding and not an evangelistic service. Some couples use a printed bulletin which includes the testimonies of the bride and groom, and an invitation for the reader to recognize his own need of the Savior if he does not know Him.

The value of retaining some parts of the typical ceremony may be questioned. For example, the sentence, "If any man can show just cause why they may not lawfully be joined together, let him speak now, or forever hold his peace," may be superfluous when a young couple reared in the church are married, but it is a safeguard for the minister when one of the individuals has been married before.

28. Williamson, *Marriage and Family Relations*, p. 315.
29. Scudder, *Family in Christian Perspective*, p. 60.

Wyman Ritchie relates that on one occasion he halted the ceremony because of a valid objection to the wedding. The event occurred when a woman, whose husband had disappeared and had been legally declared dead, was to be married to a second husband. When the invitation "to speak now or forever hold your peace" was given, the woman's first husband stood to his feet and declared his identity. He explained how he had endured marriage with the woman for several years, but in order to save his sanity, had deserted her but had lived close enough to know what she was doing. He explained that he did not want any other man to have her even though he could not live with her himself and keep his sanity.[30] So there are occasions when this seemingly outdated exhortation is very worthwhile.

Marriage is "until death do us part" for the Christian couple, and the wedding ceremony should be one happily recalled on the "golden" wedding anniversary.

THE RECEPTION

Most weddings are followed by a reception which provides an opportunity for the guests to personally congratulate the bride and groom. If it is a church wedding, the reception may be held in a church facility or a rented hall if the church does not have a place. If it is a home wedding, the affair naturally is held in the home, or on the lawn, or in the garden, depending on the location of the ceremony.

Photographs of the bridal party are often taken before the ceremony, which avoids a delay between the wedding ceremony and the beginning of the reception. If taken after the ceremony, then music is provided to fill the interval. Others utilize this period by having a person open the gifts so they can be admired by the guests.

The food served at the reception may range from simply serving the wedding cake with a beverage to a full meal served at tables or to an elaborate buffet. This is often the most costly part of the wedding, but it should be within the budget of the family.[31] The cutting of the wedding cake by the bride and groom is the high point of the reception. After greeting the guests, the newly married couple are free to prepare to leave on their honeymoon.

30. Related in the Marriage and Family Class, Cedarville College, Fall Quarter, 1970.
31. Blood, *Marriage*, p. 182.

THE HONEYMOON

The final ritual of the wedding as a rite of passage is the honeymoon. "These are the days when the bud of romance blossoms into . . . married love. . . . This time together ought to be the mountain-top of delectable experiences. . . . "[32] Floyd Martinson remarks, "The honeymoon is a part of our romantic tradition. . . . Though there have been romantic misconceptions about the honeymoon, such as that there will be no period in life before or after to compare with it, it nevertheless serves a very useful function and can be all that the couple had hoped and dreamed it would be."[33]

In American culture the honeymoon is a necessity. It has developed to enable the newlywed couple to begin their new roles as husband and wife in privacy. A great amount of self-revelation takes place at this time as there are many facets of personality that can only be discovered in the intimacy of marriage itself. Consequently, there are many adjustments to be made in the first few days of marriage. These include "a whole set of practices—sharing the same bed and bathroom, dressing and undressing, ordering or preparing breakfast—and introduce flexibility in roles and habit alterations so necessary to marriage."[34] The couple can make these adjustments easier if they are apart from relatives and friends. A pleasant honeymoon experience does not just happen but requires careful planning and preparation on the part of the couple.

The honeymoon should be planned to fit within the budget. Many couples feel this is a once-in-a-lifetime experience, so they should really live it up! They borrow money and go into debt for an expensive honeymoon trip, and begin their married life with economic problems. They return home without money to pay the first month's rent on their apartment, and may have to borrow money from their parents for groceries. This is evidence of immaturity, but it happens more often than it should. The mature couple will use the engagement period to plan their honeymoon and save enough money to pay for it. If necessary they will change their plans to fit their budget.

The location where the honeymoon is to be spent should be a place that is acceptable to both partners. There are some areas, such

---

32. Jauncey, *Magic in Marriage*, p. 35.
33. Floyd M. Martinson, *Marriage and the American Ideal* (New York: Dodd, Mead & Co., 1960), p. 259.
34. Williamson, *Marriage and Family Relations*, p. 318.

as the Pocono Mountains in Pennsylvania where hotels specialize in providing accommodations for newlyweds. Upper-class and upper-middle-class couples often choose the Bahama Islands. Most couples choose a hotel or motel not too distant from the place of the wedding. The couple should not plan to spend much of their time traveling, as this is tiring. "When a couple plans to spend their honeymoon 200 or more miles away, they should only travel 40 or 50 miles the first night, then travel leisurely the rest of the way the next day."[35]

It is better to select some one place where they can spend most of their time getting to know each other better. This does not prohibit some local sightseeing which is far different than trying to spend a two-week honeymoon traveling by car from New York to California and back! Most couples like to keep the location secret to avoid the practical jokes that some people like to play, or to avoid an overprotective parent such as the mother who called her son three times on his wedding night! However, the parents or other close relatives should be informed so they can locate the couple in case of an emergency such as serious illness or death of a relative or close friends.

The length of the honeymoon will depend on several factors such as the amount of time off from employment and the budget limitations. An ideal period might be one week, with an absolute minimum of three days. This gives the couple time enough to adjust to each other before returning to the routine of daily life. If the honeymoon is too long, the couple may get anxious to be in their new home, and this anxiety may have a dampening effect on them. Regardless of the length, the important thing is that the honeymoon be taken immediately after the wedding, for if it is delayed even for a few days, it is no longer a honeymoon but simply another trip, for the functions provided by the honeymoon have already been accomplished. Martinson states, "It is better to have a honeymoon of three days . . . than a postponed trip of three weeks."[36] If circumstances prevent an extended honeymoon, it is imperative that the couple leave for at least a day or two so that they have some time together in privacy.

A central feature of the honeymoon is the self-revelation involved in completing the marriage through physical intimacy. In most states the marriage is not considered a bona fide marriage if the couple do

35. Herbert J. Miles, *Sexual Happiness in Marriage* (Grand Rapids: Zondervan Publishing House, 1967), pp. 82-83.
36. Martinson, *Marriage and American Ideal*, p. 260.

not or cannot enter into a sexual relationship, and the union can be annulled by a court of law.[37] If the couple has planned well, and are considerate of each other, the first sexual relationship need not be the traumatic experience that one often reads about in the case histories of the marriage counselor's file. A couple that have read a good marriage manual, or who have had good premarital counseling, should encounter no great difficulty if they do not expect too much from the first experience.[38] They will also understand that the area of sex adjustment is one which often requires varying periods of time to reach a mutually satisfying adjustment.[39] If they are mature, they will have a realistic view of the sexual relationship, and will not be greatly disappointed if the act does not produce all the thrills and sensations that the "romantic love" complex of our culture leads many young people to expect from a sexual relationship. In one study, "about three-fourths" of the married women surveyed "looked back on their honeymoons with great satisfaction," and some others "considered their honeymoons highly successful anyway," even though they experienced some problems at that time. [40] However, many couples have little or no problem and the honeymoon for them is the peak of sexual enjoyment for the entire marriage cycle.

Mature Christian young people seek to use the engagement period wisely as a final "pretest" of the marriage. They plan the marriage ceremony and honeymoon carefully so that they enter into their life together enjoying the blessing of God upon their union. When they return from the honeymoon they have a good foundation on which to build their marital relationships.

37. Landis and Landis, *Successful Marriage*, p. 267.

38. Several marriage manuals are now available for Christian couples. The oldest is *Sexual Happiness in Marriage* by Herbert J. Miles (Grand Rapids: Zondervan Publishing House, 1967; rev. ed., 1976). Ed Wheat, M.D., produced two 90 minute cassettes entitled, "Sex Technique and Sex Problems in Marriage" (Bible Believers Cassettes, Inc., Springdale, Ark., 1975). Dr. Wheat and his wife, Gaye, have also written *Intended for Pleasure* (Old Tappan, N.J.: Fleming H. Revell Co., 1977). Tim and Beverly LaHaye authored *The Act of Marriage* (Grand Rapids: Zondervan Publishing House, 1976). Any one of these books will prepare an engaged couple for their honeymoon and a lifetime of marital bedroom bliss if the instructions for living and loving are put into practice.

39. Benson, *Family Bond*, p. 178.

40. Ibid., p. 177.

ANALYZING AN ENGAGEMENT

The following questions should prove helpful in assessing either an informal or formal engagement. The mature young person should examine objectively a relationship and determine whether it has the potential for a successful Christian marriage.

1 How long have you gone together? How long do you expect your engagement to last before you are married?

2 Have you been separated for any length of time? What effect, if any, did the separation have on the relationship?

3 Have you ever given serious thought to breaking the engagement? If so, why?

4 Are you able to communicate freely on all subjects, or are there areas that you avoid discussing because you disagree?

5 List the factors in your background that will contribute to compatibility in your marriage.

6 What areas in your background are potential sources of incompatibility? What adjustments are you making in these areas?

7 Discuss the values and goals that you have in common. Any areas of disagreement or conflict? If you have disagreements, how do you intend to reconcile them?

8 Do you consider your knowledge of sex adequate for marriage? Do you have any attitudes toward sex that might prove a hindrance in your marriage? Have you read a marriage manual?

9 Have you discussed and reached agreement on such important subjects as the use and handling of money; the number, spacing, and discipline of children; the family altar, etc.?

10 Do your families and friends approve of your engagement? If not, how valid are their objections? Have you discussed these objections with a counselor who was impartial in his appraisal of the situation?

11 If you have arrived at the time where you are making wedding plans, do both partners agree on the details?

12 Are your plans for a honeymoon realistic according to the time and money that you have available?

QUESTIONS FOR DISCUSSION AND REVIEW

1. How may engagement be considered a "rite of passage"?

2. Discuss the functions of an engagement in American society.

3. Why is psychological compatibility more important than physical compatibility?

4. Discuss the following statement made by a young lady: "We don't care what our parents think about our getting married since we are going to establish our own home."

5. Why is communication especially important during the engagement period?

6. Should a person reveal his past erotic involvements to his partner? If so, how much or what type of information should be revealed?

7. What is the relationship between the length of engagement and happiness in marriage?

8. What are some typical reasons that might lead a couple to break their engagement?

9. Why is it important to have a church wedding?

10. Why is it important for a couple to have a honeymoon? What are some factors to be considered when planning the honeymoon?

9

ADJUSTMENT IN
CHRISTIAN MARRIAGE

*. . . I beseech you . . . that ye be perfectly
joined together in the same mind. . . .*
I Corinthians 1:10

NECESSITY OF ADJUSTMENT

A pastor once advised a couple about to be married that there were two little "bears" that would help to make their marriage a successful one: *bear* and *forbear.* If they would bear with each other's personality differences, and forbear saying or doing things that would hurt or hinder the relationship, they would probably have a successful marriage. The pastor was using common-sense terms to tell the young couple that many adjustments are to be made in any marital relationship.

Some young people are unaware of the many varied changes that have to take place when they are married. Each partner comes from a different family, different background, is of a different sex subculture, and has a different personality structure. The more diverse the couple are in these respects, the greater the number of adjustments that will be needed. Even though the partners are well mated, they still have individual personalities that need to be harmonized so they can function and experience growth as a family unit as well as individuals.

Because marriage provides the opportunity for the most intimate, personal relationship in life, it can, if properly experienced, become the best means for the growth of two persons into real personhood. In a happy marriage blessed by Christ's presence, two people discover with joy that they can meet each other's need for love, affection, sympathy, and community, and in so doing fulfill themselves as beings created in God's image, the man becoming more of a real man and the woman more of a real woman.[1]

Most young people are not only unaware of the adjustments that are needed, but they also lack preparation to make these adjustments. This

> ... ignorance of marital processes for the unmarried is sociologically quite understandable; as a child one interacts with parents within a parent-child relationship. There is little interaction which gives a child much insight into the husband-wife relationship from which he is excluded. . . . Much of the most important husband-wife interaction is deliberately excluded from children's observation. . . .[2]

As someone has stated, "The only course in 'Marriage and the Family' most young people ever receive is in the parental home, and very often it is not a very good course."[3]

The average young person receives very little preparation in high school or college for the interaction involved in marriage.

> With all our enthusiasm to protect and educate the "whole personality" so that the individual will be ready to meet various problems in life and to play all roles effectively, one would assume that everything possible is also being done to prepare him for marriage. Indeed, since so much more is required of two individuals to be successful in marriage today, one would expect preparation for this role in life to be given top rank importance. Unfortunately, relatively little is being done at present to inform, train and prepare youth for one of the most significant roles of their lives.[4]

Consequently, many couples have very little knowledge of how to make the many adjustments they face after the ceremony is over.

1. E. L. Hebden Taylor, *The Reformational Understanding of Family and Marriage* (Nutley, NJ: The Craig Press, 1970), p. 34.

2. J. Richard Udry, *The Social Context of Marriage* (Philadelphia: J. B. Lippincott Co., 1966), p. 269.

3. Remark made at the Annual Conference of the National Council on Family Relations, Portland, Oregon, October 31—November 4, 1972. The writer cannot recall the name of the speaker making the statement.

4. J. L. Hirning and Alma L. Hirning, *Marriage Adjustment* (New York: American Book Co., 1956), p. 13. Used by permission.

MALE AND FEMALE SUBCULTURES

E. E. LeMasters in his book, *Modern Courtship and Marriage*, says that many of the adjustments are necessary because marriage marks the first real intimate union of two persons reared in separate male and female subcultures. He indicates that fellows and girls are socialized according to their sex, which creates a subculture for each sex. It is possible for a fellow to be reared in a home without sisters, and without even a mother, if the father is divorced or widowed. A young man reared in such a home is at a disadvantage in relating to young women in comparison to a fellow reared with one or more sisters. The latter is somewhat acquainted with girls and some aspects of their subculture, such as their emotions or their emphasis on clothing.[5]

In a similar manner a young woman may be reared in a home without a father or brothers. A survey of classes in a Marriage and Family course at a Christian college indicates that approximately one-fourth of the fellows and girls are reared in homes where there are no siblings of the opposite sex.[6] Thus, when she marries, a young lady without brothers comes into intimate interaction with a fellow from the male subculture for the first time. She may not be aware or fully realize the importance of sports and autos to the average American male, and this can create conflict situations in the marriage.[7]

The male and female subcultures are noticeable in areas other than the home. They are also evident in the school system. Leonard Benson writes,

> With the decline of same-sex bonding, we find it necessary to define ourselves to a much greater extent in terms of relationships with the opposite sex. Since elementary school children and adolescents now spend more time in heterosexual relationships, the average boy learns to think about himself partly in terms of the way girls react to him, certainly more so than in the past. But he still gets his main sense of *male* identity before reaching adolescence in interaction with other boys.[8]

5. E. E. LeMasters, *Modern Courtship and Marriage* (New York: McMillan Co., 1957), p. 488. Used by permission.

6. Marriage and Family Classes, Cedarville College, 1970. In the Fall quarter 20 percent did not have siblings, and in the Winter and Spring quarters 25 percent lacked siblings. The survey is taken each quarter, and the percentages may vary up or down 5 to 10 percent but close to the 25 percent figure.

7. LeMasters, *Modern Courtship and Marriage*, p. 487.

8. Leonard Benson, *The Family Bond* (New York: Random House, Inc. 1971), p. 58. Used by permission.

The same observation may be made of girls, i.e., most of their interaction is with other girls, and women function as role models for self-identification purposes.

It is important that young people be informed as to some characteristics of the subculture of the opposite sex. This is especially true if they do not have siblings of the opposite sex. The male subculture, for example, is characterized by an extreme interest in athletics, either as a participant or spectator. The television programming for a recent New Year's Day carried eleven hours of football.[9] One lady became so disgusted with her husband for his excessive watching of football games on television that she offered the television set and her husband for sale in the classified ads. Some women are regularly termed "golf" widows. Athletics, according to LeMasters, function as a "symbol of adult manhood" in high school and college, which helps to explain the inordinate emphasis given to these activities by these organizations. This interest does not cease on leaving school and is perpetuated by adult leagues in the various sports.[10] Young women need to be ready to adjust to this interest in athletics, or else look for a mate who is not typical in this respect.

The male interest in automobiles and racing events of various categories is also difficult for some young women to understand. Unfortunately, in many areas the automobile functions as a status symbol even at the high school level, and girls are sometimes more interested in a fellow's car than in his qualities as a person. Consequently, a fellow cannot wait to buy his own car even though it may impose severe financial problems for him or his family. This interest in cars does not cease when the young man enters marriage. If he marries a girl unfamiliar with the expense necessary to buy and maintain a late-model auto, she may be shocked at the large percentage of the family income consumed by such auto expenses. The potential for conflict over money spent on cars is tremendous, but it is lessened if the wife is fully aware of the part autos play in the male subculture, and it is minimized if the husband outgrows the immature need for the auto as a status symbol to bolster his ego. [11]

One feature of the female subculture that the average fellow finds difficult to understand is the different clothing needs of women. This is the subject of many cartoons which picture a woman looking into a closet filled with dresses, who says to her husband, "I don't have a

9. The Sugar Bowl, Cotton Bowl, Rose Bowl, and Orange Bowl were televised January 1, 1985.
10. LeMasters, Modern Courtship and Marriage, p. 491.
11. This is the writer's opinion.

thing to wear!" Although males are giving more attention to their dress than formerly, they still do not have the same needs women do. Before they are married, girls have to dress well in order to compete for husbands, and after they marry, they have to dress to reflect their husband's social position. They also have to dress for different seasons, whereas men now wear the "year-round" suit. Women like to have ensembles that match, but many men do not mind wearing brown shoes with a blue suit. LeMasters points out that a fellow can avoid many problems in this area by marrying an unkempt girl who is unconcerned about her wardrobe, or by marrying a rich girl who can afford to buy her own clothing.[12] Another suggestion would be to find a girl who has learned to sew well, thereby keeping the clothing bills down.

Certain biological differences also make adjustment difficult. Women are weaker than men in relation to brute strength, but women live longer than men.[13] Because the man is stronger, the woman learns to use other means to adjust to him since she cannot compete on a basis of physical strength. Men are more susceptible to certain illnesses such as ulcers, whereas women are more likely to have thyroid gland difficulties.[14] Heart disease is much more common among men than women.[15]

After marriage, men must adjust to certain aspects of the female physiology such as menstruation and pregnancy. Most fellows do not realize how complicated the female reproductive system really is. They have a vague understanding that there are changes in moods and feelings at a certain period, but in marriage they face the reality of the situation.[16] Pregnancy also requires many adjustments. Some young women have no problems at all, while most experience some "morning sickness." In a few cases the wife may be sick the entire term of pregnancy. During this experience the husband needs to extend an extra measure of kindness and consideration to the wife.

The male and female subcultures are also manifested in marriage by the manner in which men and women spend money. In American culture men like to spend money to buy cars and to support hobbies.

12. LeMasters, *Modern Courtship and Marriage*, p. 501.

13. Judson T. Landis and Mary G. Landis, *Building a Successful Marriage* (Englewood Cliffs, NJ: Prentice-Hall, 1968), p. 19.

14. Wayne J. Anderson, *Design for Family Living* (Minneapolis: T. S. Denison & Co., Inc., 1964), pp. 135-136.

15. Sophia P. Derbyshire and Robert L. Hoeppner, *Study Guide for Landis' Making the Most of Marriage* (New York: Appleton-Century-Crofts, 1970), p. 25.

16. LeMasters, *Modern Courtship and Marriage*, p. 503.

Women like to use money to purchase clothes and home furnishings. If the husband wants to buy a new car or travel trailer, and the wife wants to buy new carpeting instead, then there is likely to be conflict.[17]

The couple need to be aware of each other's ego needs in these areas, for a man often receives his status from the car he drives and the wife hers from the way she furnishes and keeps up her home. A man should not have such a weak ego that he must have a new car every year, nor should a wife have to "keep up with the Joneses" by purchasing new furniture every other year or so. Many of the material things that a family "needs" may be merely "wants" when the motivations are closely examined. A mature couple ought to realistically assess their transportation and home furnishing needs, and then plan ahead so that the family has a decent car and furniture.

A man may think that he will never really understand women, and this is true to some extent, but he should be familiar with some of the difficulties in relation to the female subculture. Certainly a woman will never fully understand men, but the effort must be made to comprehend how the culture operates to mold them into American males. A mutual attempt to understand the opposite sex should make it easier to adjust to each other in marriage.[18]

PSYCHOLOGICAL ADJUSTMENTS

The partners in a marriage may be well mated but they still have individual personalities that need to be harmonized so they can function as a family unit as well as individuals. "Each partner needs to provide a new anchor for the other—an anchor of intimate associations to replace the parental anchor. If the partners can do this, they become the *primary resource persons* for satisfying each other's personality hungers."[19] As indicated in chapter 8, in a long courtship many of the adjustments between the personalities are made so that the couple experience less unhappiness after the wedding.

Regardless of the length of courtship, marriage adds a new and much more intimate dimension to the relationship.

17. Ibid.
18. Ibid.
19. Howard J. Clinebell, Jr., and Charlotte Clinebell, *The Intimate Marriage* (New York: Harper & Row, Publishers, 1970), p. 110.

No matter how adequate a couple's engagement experiences were, there are many problems to be met in the early post-wedding years. Most of the problems of marriage aren't really problems until after marriage actually begins. They have little reality for the couple until an existential collision with the problems occurs in the actual business of living together.[20]

Living together twenty-four hours a day is far more demanding on the personalities involved than merely seeing each other for a few hours at various times during the week. Many marriages fail because the individuals have not tested their psychological compatibility sufficiently, and they cannot adjust to the demands of living together in such an intimate relationship. Mature young people recognize that changes must take place and are willing and able to alter their habits and behavior so that their personalities begin to harmonize rather than clash with one another. Conflicts are inevitable but they should be fewer and more constructive in nature.

Men and women also differ in their emotional lives. A fellow who grows up with sisters has some understanding of female psychology, but the man reared without sisters is a definite disadvantage. In our culture, girls are permitted to cry whenever the occasion or their pent-up emotions demand it. A boy or man is not allowed to cry other than for physical pain, or in a time of bereavement. Since men have little experience in crying, it is difficult for them to understand why some women shed tears so easily. In reality, it is well that women can find emotional release in tears, for it avoids the buildup of emotional pressures that lead to nervous breakdowns.[21] A husband soon learns to let his wife relieve her emotions by crying. At first he may feel that some act of his may be the cause of tears, but he soon discovers that usually her tears have no relationship to his actions.

Men and women have the same overall level of intelligence, but they do think differently, which often causes adjustment problems. In discussing this matter of sex differences in intelligence, Floyd L. Ruch concludes:

> Putting together the results of these studies, it seems reasonably safe to conclude that boys excel girls in *spatial intelligence* and most kinds of problem solving, whereas girls excel boys in *memory, reasoning, word fluency* and *numerical ability*. Since boys are better in some primary abilities and girls in others, these differences cancel

---

20. Ibid., p. 111.
21. Anderson, *Family Living*, p. 137.

each other out when general tests are used, with the result that no difference between the sexes is found in overall intelligence.[22]

In actual life the husband takes a more direct approach to solving a problem, whereas the wife with her "word fluency" is more likely to follow the indirect approach. Thus, it is not unusual for them to have difficulty in understanding each other's viewpoint. Since many differences exist between the average bride and groom, it is remarkable that they are able to work through differences and achieve as good an adjustment as they do. Wayne J. Anderson says, "They should seek to understand and adjust to the different characteristics that can be attributed to sex. A better marital adjustment will take place if each spouse will accept the other's differences and profit from the special abilities which each brings to the marriage partnership."[23]

TIME REQUIRED FOR ADJUSTMENT

These adjustments between two personalities, and other necessary changes, take time and will not be accomplished on the honeymoon. Christian newlyweds may think they do not have to make many adjustments because of their common faith in Christ, but they, too, bring different personalities to the marriage and have to work at achieving adjustment between them. Louis H. Evans writes, "The most practical and thrilling therapeutic characteristics in any home is our willingness and desire to see ourselves as we are in the mirror of God, to desire to change, and in submitting ourselves to Him, allowing that change to take place."[24] The Christian couple do have an advantage over the unsaved couple since they have spiritual resources to help them make the adjustments. Many authorities feel that many of these adjustments are made during the first year, making it a critical period in the life of a marriage.

It is significant that approximately 40 percent of all marriages which occur in any one year end in separation or divorce by the end of the first five years. The causes of these broken marriages usually have their basis, first, in bad mating and, second, in the inability of

22. Floyd L. Ruch, *Psychology and Life* (Glenview, IL: Scott, Foresman & Co., n.d.), p. 169.
23. Anderson, *Family Living*, pp. 137-138.
24. Louis H. Evans, *Your Marriage, Duel or Duet*, (Old Tappan, NJ: Fleming H. Revell, 1972), p. 61.

the individuals to establish a satisfactory basis for meeting life's problems during the first year.[25]

God recognized the importance of this stage in marriage, for in Deuteronomy 24:5 we read, "When a man hath taken a new wife, he shall not go out to war, neither shall he be charged with any business: but he shall be free at home one year, and shall cheer up his wife which he hath taken." The newlyweds were not to be separated, nor was the husband to have any extra responsibility so that the couple could make the necessary adjustments in their marriage.

Newlyweds enter marriage to assume the new roles of husband and wife for which they have received little or no specific education, and many times they have been reared in Christian homes where the parents have been poor models of what a Christian husband or wife should be. Consequently, they must learn these new roles as they interact with each other after the wedding. Howard J. Clinebell, Jr., and Charlotte Clinebell say it this way:

> Becoming a need-satisfying and adequate husband or wife—what Jolesch calls learning appropriate spouse roles—is the developmental task of the first years of marriage. Mates can support each other in the struggle with understanding and acceptance of the feelings of inadequacy and inevitable anger which accompany it.[26]

If the partners have established good communication with each other during engagement, and have discussed the type of roles each expects to play, then the adjustments should be easier. They can be patient and understanding (bear and forbear) with each other when mistakes are made since they realize that both are learning roles that are new to them. Since it is difficult enough to learn to play these roles well, it is wise if the couple postpone the coming of the first child for a time so they do not have to assume the roles of mother and father before they are accustomed to the roles of husband and wife.[27]

In the critical first year some couples have the problem of adjusting to the basal metabolism of the partner. Some people are "cold-blooded" and others are "warm-blooded" and require different room temperatures in order to be comfortable. When two people such as

25. R. G. Foster, *Marriage and Family Relationships* (New York: The MacMillan Co., 1950), p. 107.
26. Clinebell and Clinebell, *Intimate Marriage*, p. 111. Used by Permission.
27. Ibid.

this marry, one is always too hot and the other too cold at a given temperature. In the winter, the warm-blooded person feels the furnace thermostat is set too high, and in the summer, the cold-blooded spouse feels the air conditioner thermostat is too low. An adjustment has to be made, and it usually means the cold-blooded individual will wear a sweater the year round! A similar situation exists when a man whose metabolism is slow in the morning has difficulty arising, then stays up late at night, but is married to a woman who likes to rise early and go to bed early. These habits are not only learned behavior but are linked to the body's metabolism, so it is not easy to change them. Henry R. Brandt and Homer E. Dowdy give a case history of a young couple who had problems similar to this, with the additional difficulty of the young wife snoring, which kept the husband awake![28] The couple with these kinds of problems must reach some accommodation if they are to live together happily.

SEXUAL ADJUSTMENT

Another area of adjustment which is critical in the first year is the attainment of a satisfactory sexual relationship. A good marriage manual will help engaged couples prepare for their sexual life together. Some couples are fortunate in that they achieve a fairly happy adjustment in the relationship during the honeymoon. Others require many years to arrive at a mutually satisfying experience. Most couples need more time than that allowed by the honeymoon, but they adjust to each other's needs during the first year.

In his excellent marriage manual for Christians titled, *Sexual Happiness in Marriage*, Herbert J. Miles compares learning to swim with learning to have intercourse to illustrate what a "complex procedure" the latter behavior is. In effect he says that a person may read a book on swimming and may even have a teacher tell him how to swim. This does not mean that the first time he jumps into the water he is able to swim. He fails many times and has to keep jumping in until he finally masters the skill of manipulating his arms and body so that he draws himself through the water. In a similar manner, a couple may read a marriage manual and receive good premarital counseling, but this does not guarantee that the initial

28. Henry R. Brandt, and Homer E. Dowdy, *Building a Christian Home* (Wheaton, IL: Scripture Press, 1960), p. 8.

sexual experience will be a success. They have to keep trying until they are successful.[29]

Miles also made a study of 151 Christian couples who had received premarital counseling. These couples filled out questionnaires on their sexual relationships after they had been married from six months to two years. Over 80 percent indicated they enjoyed their first sexual relationship during the honeymoon.[30] When asked to rate their "personal sexual satisfaction up to now," 58.5 percent of the husbands and 44.9 percent of the wives checked "excellent," and 32.6 percent of the husbands and 36.8 percent of the wives checked "good." None of the husbands rated the adjustment "poor" and only 0.7 percent of the wives did so.[31] These figures indicate that in a relatively short period of time over 90 percent of the husbands and 80 percent of the wives had reached what they considered either an "excellent" or "good" adjustment. The figures might be lower for those who had not received premarital counseling.

The Bible teaches in I Corinthians 7:2-5 that one of the reasons for marriage is to enable the partners to fulfill each other's sexual needs, and a good relationship in this area is helpful to the entire marriage:

> The husband must always give his wife what is due her, and the wife too must do so for her husband. The wife does not have the right to do as she pleases with her own body; the husband has his right to it. In the same way the husband does not have the right to do as he pleases with his own body; the wife has right to it. You husbands and wives must stop refusing each other what is due, unless you agree to do so just for awhile, so as to have plenty of time for prayer, and then to be together again, so as to keep Satan from tempting you because of your lack of self-control. (Charles B. William's Translation), Copyright, Moody Press, used by permission.)

James H. Jauncey comments, "What it means is that the wife, *from her point of view*, should consider her body as belonging to her husband. That is, she allows his need, not her own inclinations, to be the factor which determines whether she will give herself. The same principle holds for the man."[32] If couples in a secular marriage seek

29. Herbert J. Miles, *Sexual Happiness in Marriage* (Grand Rapids: Zondervan Publishing House, 1967), p. 91. Used by permission.

30. Ibid., p. 136.

31. Ibid., p. 148.

32. James H. Jauncey, *Magic in Marriage* (Grand Rapids: Zondervan Publishing House, 1966), p. 40.

to meet each other's needs, how much more concerned should the Christian spouse be about meeting the needs of his or her mate. The couple must see that in meeting each other's sexual needs they do not fall into a routine of fulfilling their desires a certain number of times a week or only on certain days of the week. Spontaneous reaction to the partner is one of the keys to successful sex adjustment. Although sex does not play the most important role in marriage (as the Hollywood romantic love image presents it), the sexual relationship is still very important in the total relationship between husband and wife.

There is much written in the popular press about what constitutes good sex adjustment in marriage. A danger in all this public discussion is that couples are led to believe they do not have a good adjustment unless they experience the ideal results described in the marriage manuals and press articles. It is important to emphasize that there are many good, satisfying relationships that never reach the ideal. Jauncey, a clinical psychologist, after thirty years of marriage counseling reinforces this point:

> There is little doubt that the most satisfying fulfillment comes when both achieve orgasm at the same time. . . . But adjustment will come through experience and understanding. . . . But do not assume that the climax is always essential, especially in the woman. . . . In fact, many women seldom or never experience an orgasm at all. I have had women who have confessed to me that after twenty or thirty years of *happy sexual life* (italics mine) that they didn't know what a climax was. . . . The important thing is that people be themselves and not attempt to fit into externally determined molds, sexual or otherwise.[33]

The couple must be frank in discussing their sexual experience, and if both are satisfied, they should not be disturbed by what they read.

PROBLEM AREAS IN SEXUAL ADJUSTMENT

If one partner is unhappy with the sexual adjustment, the spouse should strive to meet the needs of that partner. Most often it is the wife who encounters problems, and the husband must remember that the wife has been conditioned since childhood by society against having sexual relationships outside of marriage. Judson T. and Mary G. Landis state, "Girls are likely to be impressed more than boys with sexual taboos. . . . Many parents solve the practical problem of

33. Ibid., p. 45. Used by permission

protecting a daughter by overimpressing her with the dangerous aspects of sex activity. All such policies may create emotional attitudes that later handicap sex adjustment."[34] Consequently, many young wives find it difficult on the wedding night and the following weeks to discard the inhibitions built into their psychic superstructure over the years. The wife must be aware of the cause of her attitude, and the husband needs to be patient and prayerful, and, given a little time, the problem can be solved. However, if the problem is too great, or if it is not solved over a period of time, the couple should seek professional counseling.

The informed young couple also realizes that the sexual relationship, the most intimate of their marriage, reflects the attitudes and moods of the total relationship. Ignorance of this fact has caused some to blame poor sexual adjustment for the dissolution of many marriages, whereas in fact the inadequate sexual relationship was simply a mirror of disharmony between the spouses.[35] For example, a couple cannot expect to be quarreling all day about money matters and expect everything to be harmonious when they retire for the night. In discussing this subject, William Kephart says, ". . . if the day-to-day congeniality of the spouses is at a low level, it is probable that their sexual adjustment would be hampered even assuming an otherwise equality of interest in sex relations."[36] Jauncey remarks, "It is important for a husband to realize that a wife's sexual ardor is highly sensitive to psychological factors. If he has been criticizing her or has been unpleasant to her in any way she will be cold as ice. Generally he will have to put these matters right first before she will consent to his arms."[37] It is evident that a couple with a problem in sexual adjustment must first of all examine their total marital interaction patterns to make sure their relationship is free of differences in other areas before concluding that it is a problem in sexual adjustment.

Some couples may encounter problems of frigidity in the wife or impotence in the husband. Authorities do not agree on the definition of frigidity, for they range from the inability to have an orgasm to a "complete lack of sex desire with a resulting inability to respond to stimulation and arousal."[38] If either spouse has a severe problem

34. Landis and Landis, *Successful Marriage*, pp. 311-312.
35. William M. Kephart, *The Family, Society, and the Individual* (New York: Houghton-Mifflin Co., 1972), p. 450.
36. Ibid.
37. Jauncey, *Magic in Marriage*, p. 42.
38. Robert O. Blood, *Marriage* (New York: Free Press of Glencoe, 1962), p. 375.

that the couple cannot solve with earnest effort, they must seek professional help from a physician, psychiatrist, or professional marriage counselor.[39]

If the wife is not experiencing a good sexual response, it sometimes may be caused by failing to use the pelvic muscle named the pubococcygeus. This muscle is located beneath the vaginal passage about one to two inches from the opening and has pressure sensitive nerve endings. " . . William H. Masters and Virginia E. Johnson of Washington University. . . . have shown that contraction of these muscles is the first, and probably foremost, physical reaction of feminine response."[40] Arnold Kegel of the Kegel Clinic at Los Angeles County General Hospital discovered that the tone of the pubococcygeus muscle is directly related to feminine response in sexual intercourse. He also indicated that the tone could be improved by simple exercises each day for a period of two or three months. Once in tone, it retains its tone. The result is that many women enjoy their marriage relationship after doing the exercises and learning to use the muscle during intercourse.

Paul Popenoe of the American Institute of Family Relations who cooperated with Kegel in the research wrote, "We found that in a series of over 1000 patients who received such help, some 65 percent of sexually unsatisfied women gained relief. The remaining 35 percent had serious emotional or physical problems."[41] The research has been publicized by an article in the October 1968, *Reader's Digest*, and in a book by Ronald M. Deutsch, *The Key to Feminine Response in Marriage*, published by Random House.

It is evident that every wife (not just those experiencing difficulties) should learn to use the pubococcygeus muscle since it is "the key to feminine response." Tim LaHaye writes:

> Since the muscles of the vagina, like other muscles of the human body, can be developed by exercise, a wife should attempt to tighten these muscles daily, both during intercourse and when lying in bed. Five to ten minutes of daily flexing and tightening these muscles strengthens them and increases the capacity for sexual stimulation, thus assisting her ability to reach an orgasm.[42]

As indicated above, after two or three months of such exercise, the

39. Jauncey, *Magic in Marriage*, p. 43.

40. Ronald M. Deutsch, "A Key to Feminine Response in Marriage," *The Reader's Digest*, October 1968, pp. 114-118. This article is used as a basis for these paragraphs.

41. Ibid.

42. Tim LaHaye, *How to Be Happy Though Married* (Wheaton, IL: Tyndale House, 1968), p. 70. Used by permission.

muscles seem to stay in tone without further exercise and contribute greatly to enjoyment of the relationship by both husband and wife. Difficulties in sex adjustment are caused by many other factors. Privacy must be assured for the greatest enjoyment. A wife may not be able to relax if she is afraid of interruptions, or afraid that others will hear noises.

Fatigue of one or both partners may interfere with sexual adjustment. Young couples who both work and study often have several roles to play that do not leave much energy for the sexual relationship. The young mother is often exhausted after caring for the children all day, particularly when they are small and need so much time and attention. The thoughtful couple is considerate of each other and endeavor to find a time such as early morning when both are refreshed. It is better to wait a few hours than to risk a frustrating experience because of fatigue. As sex is an integral part of marriage, time must be made for it. Dwight H. Small remarks, "Many Christian couples are guilty of being so occupied with living as to leave no time for loving."[43]

Until after the menopause, when the possibility of pregnancy is over, the fear of conception prevents some wives from readily responding and enjoying sex in marriage. Each couple needs to prayerfully consider the will of God in family planning. Most couples choose some form of contraception to aid them in this planning. If a wife still has fears while using one type, the couple may consider using two types at the same time to see if it will help the wife to conquer her anxieties so she can respond adequately in the relationship.

Another difficulty is faced by some couples when the wife has a subconscious hostility toward her husband. This usually is caused by the wife's attitude toward her father, which is projected onto her husband when she marries. This problem can often be recognized if she will review her feelings toward her father as she grew up. If she harbored a hostile attitude toward him, then she is likely to do so toward her husband. Other cases may require the services of a professional counselor to help the wife discover her real attitude toward men, including her husband.

When a Christian couple encounter a problem in sexual adjustment, they should take advantage of every available means of medical and other professional help to enable them to reach a satisfying sex relationship. The husband and wife can aid each other by maintaining an attitude of love, concern, and tenderness. The

43. Dwight Hervey Small, *Design for Christian Marriage* (Westwood, NJ: Fleming H. Revell, 1959), p. 89.

Christian philosophy that it is more blessed to give than to receive applies to every phase of a couple's marriage and includes their sex life.

SEXUAL ADJUSTMENT AND HAPPINESS IN MARRIAGE

The sexual natures of the husband and wife are received from God. Since the sexual relationship in marriage is also of God, it is logical that the Christian couple who seeks to live in harmony with God's will for their lives should enjoy better adjustment and greater happiness in their marriage. Modern research proves the truth of this statement. Landis and Landis report that where students came from a "devout or very devout" religious home, 43 percent of them rated their parents' marriages as "very happy," 30 percent as "happy," and 27 percent as "average or unhappy." The percentages are almost reversed when the students came from homes that were "indifferent or antagonistic" to religions: 25 percent rated their parents' marriages "very happy," 30 percent as "happy" and 45 percent as "average or unhappy."[44]

Allan Snider, pastor of an Assembly of God Church studied the marital adjustment of 208 couples for his doctoral dissertation at the University of Southern California. He indicated that 48 percent of the fundamentalists achieved "highest marital adjustment," but only 31 percent of the evangelical denominational Protestants, 30 percent of the Catholics and 22 percent of the liberal Protestants.[45] He also discovered that "the more puritanical—and rigid—a couple's view of sex, the greater likelihood they would rank among the 'highly adjusted' couples."[46] Thus, adjustment is aided if a couple have a "puritan" or a Biblical view of sex, for such a view means they also have a high regard for their respective needs. Small writes,

A Christian view of sexual relationship implies an interrelatedness of persons in their total being in such a way that both function and being are preserved and honored together. . . . Sexual intercourse is more than a physical act; it is the symbol of a spiritual relationship, and the expression of the complete oneness of two persons in married love.[47]

44. Landis and Landis, *Successful Marriage*, p. 349.
45. *Dayton Journal Herald*, August, 1971.
46. Ibid. See LaHaye, *The Act of Marriage*, pp. 195-217 for a sex survey of 3,377 persons. His conclusion is that born-again Christians achieve better sexual adjustment than non-Christians.
47. Small, *Christian Marriage*, p. 82. Used by permission.

In the early years of marriage, the sexual relationship assumes more importance than later in the marriage cycle, yet it is important throughout the life of the couple. Most couples enjoy intercourse until their drives diminish with old age.[48] A couple should be willing to make every effort in the first few months to achieve adjustment and lay the foundation for a lifetime of rewarding sexual enjoyment.

Small points out that sex and marriage are interdependent. He says, "Sex enhances marriage by giving it a meaning and value it would not otherwise have. Marriage likewise gives sex a meaning and stability it would not otherwise have."[49] Landis and Landis state, "Although the place of sex in marriage is often exaggerated, it does make a major contribution in successful marriage . . . Studies among happily married couples all agree that couples who have achieved the highest degree of mutuality in their sex relations are among the most happily married."[50] Since a good sexual adjustment helps to make a happy marriage, it is worth all the prayer, time, effort, and professional help necessary to achieve a satisfactory adjustment.

A final note of warning is necessary to remind young people that a marriage cannot be built on a good sex adjustment alone. Miles states, "In order to have happiness in marriage, all the phases of total life experience (the spiritual, the mental, the social, the emotional, the moral, the physical, and the sexual) must work as a cooperative unit."[51] The challenge facing every young couple taking the marriage vows is to blend their separate lives into one in many different areas. They must keep a balance between these areas so that one element is not emphasized to the detriment of another. The spiritual factor operates as an integrating factor binding all the areas into one harmonious unit.

METHODS OF ADJUSTING DIFFERENCES

There are several ways in which couples come to an agreement over differences that arise between them. The most important means is simple compromise. The couple who have established good communication between themselves are able to talk over their problem intelligently. The Christian couple desires the will of God in every phase of their marriage and prays for God's guidance in the situation.

48. Blood, *Marriage*, pp. 371-372.
49. Small, *Christian Marriage*, p. 82.
50. Landis & Landis, *Successful Marriage*, p. 306.
51. Miles, *Sexual Happiness*, p. 123. Used by permission.

Each gives in to the other so that both are satisfied and happy with the solution. Neither partner gets his or her own way, but each person benefits since now they function as a unit rather than as individuals with separate viewpoints.[52] For example, one spouse may prefer to buy a two-story house, whereas the other has a strong preference for a one-story ranch-style house. After much prayer and discussion a typical compromise might be a split level which is neither a two-story nor a one-story but has some of the advantages of both types. Robert O. Blood suggests that compromise is not always possible. If a man has a choice between a new job in a distant town or his present one, no compromise is possible. He must choose one or the other.[53] Compromise as a method of settling differences is necessary in all human relationships and is indispensable in the intimacy of marriage if it is to be a successful one.

In some marriages there are some areas where the couple cannot agree to compromise. In this case they "agree to disagree" and each holds to his own viewpoint even though the other partner is unhappy or may even harbor some resentment against the mate for refusing to compromise.[54] They reach a state of accommodation similar to labor and management who cooperate with one another to achieve production although neither organization trusts the other. Needless to say, in matrimony such a method of resolving differences is not a very happy one. Christians should be able to pray about such matters and seek the mind of God, and then follow His leading. Some people take a position and then refuse to change regardless of prayer or the will of God.

A similar situation occurs when the couple have a difference between them and they "agree to disagree" but genuinely respect each other's viewpoint. There is no desire to change the other person. In the realm of politics, one spouse may be a Republican, the other an independent and each allows the other the privilege of retaining their views in marriage. This toleration of each other's views does not hinder the happiness of the relationship in any way since they respect each other as genuine persons.[55] Toleration is different from accommodation in that it is a positive solution whereas accommodation has a negative effect, since each partner desires the other to change.

Differences also may be adjusted by assimilation when one partner

52. Blood, *Marriage*, p. 253.
53. Ibid.
54. Francis E. Merrill, *Society and Culture* (Englewood Cliffs, NJ: Prentice-Hall, Inc., 1965), p. 37.
55. Hirning & Hirning, *Marriage Adjustment*, p. 267.

accepts the view of the other. This usually follows prayer and discussion of the issues involved. One spouse changes and accepts the position of the other. Often one individual so respects and admires the partner that it is easy to accept the opinions and judgments of that person. Where such a condition prevails, there will be little disharmony and much happiness.

AIDS TO MARITAL ADJUSTMENT

Couples who develop the habit of daily devotions together establish one of the best methods to help in adjusting to each other. The Christian is to live the Christian life at all times, and the place where this is most important is in the home. It is just as necessary to manifest the fruits of the Spirit (Gal. 5:22-23) in a gracious Christian life in the home as it is in the office or factory.[56] The husband and wife who desire to please the Lord at all times will also find it easier to please one another. When differences or disagreements arise between them it will be easier to pray and seek the Lord's will in the matter. Since they each have experienced the forgiving grace of Christ (Eph. 4:32), it will be easier to forgive each other when a mistake has been made. This forgiveness must take place before they can pray, for they cannot approach the throne of grace while harboring resentment or ill-will against each other (Matt. 5:23-24), I Peter 3:7).

The home is where the husband and wife are called upon to display the "*agape*" love described in I Corinthians 13. It is amazing how many Christians think of this love in reference to those outside the home, but fail to acknowledge that it has an application to those within the family. This love is described as "suffering long . . . not puffed up . . . not easily provoked . . . bears all things, believes all things, hopes all things, endures all things." (I Cor. 13:4-8). The couple who are filled with the love of God, and with love for one another should find it easy to be longsuffering or patient with one another.[57] During courtship individuals are not "easily provoked," but after the honeymoon period (first year) is over, often it does not take very much to "provoke" one another. This will not be true of the couple who daily read the Word of God together and are reminded of His great love for them, and who bring each other before the throne of grace petitioning the heavenly Father for aid in

56. LaHaye, *Happy Though Married*, p. 130.
57. Brandt, *Building a Christian Home*, p. 10.

resolving any differences between them. Such individuals will know the fullness of blessing in a successful Christian marriage.

The old cliché, "the family that prays together stays together," has real truth in it. Charlie W. Shedd in his excellent book, *Letters to Karen*, cites statistics he heard that "one marriage in four ends in divorce." However, for those families that are regular in church attendance, "the ratio is one to fifty-four," and for those "who pray together, the ratio is one to five hundred." After hearing these figures Shedd began to analyze his own counseling records, and made the amazing discovery that out of two thousand cases covering twenty years he had *"never had one couple or one member of a marriage come to me with their troubles if they prayed together* (italics his). There were a few, perhaps a dozen, who said, 'We used to!'"[58] This testimony should encourage every young couple to begin the habit of having devotions together during courtship so that it becomes an important part of their relationship. It will be natural for them to continue this fellowship with God when they become husband and wife. This devotional life together will become the basis of the family altar when children come. The importance of this altar in molding the lives of the children will be discussed in chapter 13.

Another factor which aids newlyweds to adjust to each other is commonly referred to as the "honeymoon attitude." Although the actual honeymoon may only last a few days, the chief concern of each partner is to please the other, and the primary interest is to meet each other's needs. This attitude does not end with the honeymoon, and is particularly strong during the important first year of marriage when the couple has so many changes to make in themselves and in their relationship.[59] In a really good marriage this attitude will be the prevailing one throughout the years. However, in many marriages a state of accommodation is reached and the partners refuse to make any more important changes, and expect to be accepted as they are. In the large number of marriages that end in early divorce, the "honeymoon attitude" apparently is not strong enough to help the couples in their adjustment problems.

A very important aid in solving the problems of adjustment is good communication between the spouses. The couple should begin the habit of objectively talking over their problems during courtship, and this pattern should be continued into marriage. "Studies show that 'satisfying talk' relieves emotional tensions, helps avoid

---

58. Charlie W. Shedd, *Letters To Karen* (Nashville: Abingdon Press, 1965), p. 154.

59. Hirning and Hirning, *Marriage Adjustment*, p. 267.

quarrels, clarifies thinking, and helps hold a marriage together."[60] The calm discussion of differences as they arise enables the individuals to seek solutions that are mutually agreeable, and helps to avoid the emotional tension that occurs when these differences accumulate without consideration. The couple must agree that every aspect of the relationship is to be open to discussion at any reasonable time, and that they will discuss grievances as they arise rather than let them collect until they create a problem.[61]

The necessity of open and frank communication in marriage cannot be overemphasized. Brandt recites the experience of a New York Domestic Relations Court judge who reported on 250,000 cases of marital failure. The judge concluded that "bottled up resentments constitute one of the greatest dangers to marriage."[62] Brandt also quotes a marriage counselor who claims that " . . the inability of husbands and wives to talk to each other is our 'Number 1' marriage problem."[63] It is most important that young people learn to talk to each other.

Unfortunately, young people in our culture are not taught to communicate with each other on a person-to-person basis. Cecil G. Osborn makes the following interesting statement:

> The art of communication is much more complex than learning to drive an automobile, or to type, yet we expect young people in their late teens or early twenties to be able to establish a happy marriage and know how to communicate without the slightest preparation. The human personality is much more complex than an electronic computer, yet we would not dream of turning a totally inexperienced person loose in a room with a battery of computers, suggesting that he would learn to operate one successfully by trial and error! Society has failed miserably in preparing us for marriage.[64]

Thus, the young person must learn to talk to his partner about most of the issues that face them in marriage.

It is not wise to talk about all the issues one faces because there are some things better left unsaid. J. Richard Udry says, "Probably *selective* communication is the key to successful marriage."[65] He then

60. Anderson, *Family Living*, p. 138.
61. A. Donald Bell, *The Family in Dialogue* (Grand Rapids: Zondervan Publishing House, 1970), p. 36. The need for good communication in marriage is the thesis of this book.
62. Brandt, *Building a Christian Home*, p. 65.
63. Ibid., p. 66.
64. Cecil G. Osborne, *The Art of Understanding Your Mate* (Grand Rapids: Zondervan Publishing House, 1970), p. 63. Used by permission.
65. Udry, *Social Context of Marriage*, p. 280.

illustrates this point: "A wife who continues to communicate to her husband her disappointment that he is not more affectionate when she has seen that he is incapable of changing [is communicating a fact that is] not going to do anything but hurt the relationship." The couple will discuss this problem a great deal but will turn to more fruitful conversation when they realize they cannot solve the problem. Udry emphasizes ". . . that it is the fruitful control and direction of the communication process which distinguishes satisfying marriages, not the volume of material communicated or the amount of time spent communicating it."[66]

However, some times are more appropriate than others for discussing problems. Differences between the husband and wife must never be discussed when other people are present. It is not wise to bring up some problem for communication when either spouse is tired or hungry. It is better to wait until both are well fed and rested.[67] Some couples set aside a particular hour each week for a "family conference" when they discuss any aspect of their relationship or the family which needs attention. Others find this too "mechanical" and prefer to discuss matters in the normal course of events during the week. The most important factor is for the couple to keep the communication channels open at all times, and make an honest attempt to solve problems as they arise.

A well-developed sense of humor is a great asset in any human relationship, and it particularly helps partners in getting accustomed to living with one another. Marriage is a very serious matter, but there are many little incidents that take place each day that have their humorous aspects. If the couple learns to look for these and laugh over them, they avoid many tense situations. Solomon said there is a "time to laugh" (Eccles. 3:4), so a couple needs to look for those times and enjoy life together as much as possible. A home where laughter is often heard is usually a happy home.

MANAGING QUARRELS IN MARRIAGE

Understanding the nature of quarrels and how to handle them helps many couples in their adjustment. Occasionally a couple who have been married fifty years state that they have never had a quarrel. It is possible to live this long together without one, but it is more probable that after fifty years they have forgotten many things

---

66. Ibid.
67. Landis and Landis, *Successful Marriage*, p. 292.

that took place in their early years together. A couple may establish a good adjustment and get along very well, and yet be faced occasionally with a problem that resists their usual attempts at solution, and creates a great deal of tension between them. Perhaps even a little hostility may be generated. It is this difficulty of solution and intensity of feeling that distinguishes a quarrel from an ordinary discussion.[68] For a couple with poor communication, quarrels may serve a useful purpose in that they are forced to face problems that they otherwise would avoid. It would be much better if the couple would establish open lines of communication so they could discuss their problems rather than quarreling about them.

Certain guidelines for conducting a quarrel may be helpful to some couples, but as in many areas of conduct, it is easier to make rules than to follow them. A quarrel is indicative of some underlying difficulty in a relationship, and the first task is to discover what is the real basic issue.[69] For example, a wife is accused by the husband of spending too much money on clothing. This couple must determine what is normal for a wife in her social stratum to spend in order to dress appropriately. It may be that due to the differences between the male and female subculture in relationship to clothing that the wife is not overspending. It is merely the case of a husband not understanding the wardrobe problems of a woman.

If it is established that she is spending too much, then they must determine her motivation.[70] Does she have subconscious ego needs that are satisfied in this manner and that she needs to deal with? She could have an inferiority complex and overspend on clothes to compensate for this inferior feeling. If the husband handles the money, and the wife buys clothing on charge accounts, perhaps she is subconsciously "striking back" at his exclusive control of the family money, and this becomes an attempt to control part of it, for he must legally pay her bills. Only after the basic problem has been isolated can the couple take real constructive steps to settle the difficulty once for all. If they do not seek the source of the difficulty, they will continue to argue about symptoms rather than settling the basic problem. It may take much prayer, soul-searching, or even professional counseling to find the source of problem, but the Christian couple have all the resources of their faith in Christ to help discover a solution.

68. Anderson, *Family Living*, p. 141.
69. Blood, *Marriage*, p. 246. A good discussion on "recognizing that an issue exists."
70. Norman M. Lobsenz and Clark W. Blackburn, "Hidden Meanings of Money in Marriage," *The Reader's Digest*, March 1969, pp. 141-144.

Once a basic issue has been discovered and discussed and a solution found, then it should be permanently settled. It should not be brought up again. It is unfortunate that some couples are unable to settle issues, and each time they have a quarrel they exhume the same old problems to add to the new one. Such couples obviously experience a great deal of unhappiness. It is imperative that young couples establish the habit of finding solutions to their differences so they do not go through life arguing about the same old issues.

In discussing an issue that is the basis of a quarrel, the couple should not attack each other's personalities.[71] As a couple live together, they learn each other's weak spots, and it becomes very easy to hurt the partner during an argument. For example, he knows she bitterly resents being compared to her mother, so in the heat of a quarrel, it is easy for him to say, "You are just like your mother!" She knows he is very sensitive about his inability to handle money so it is easy for her to say, "You never have a dime in your pocket!" The couple should learn to leave personalities out of the discussion and to concentrate their time and energy on solving the fundamental issue.

Each partner has certain basic personality traits and habits which may become a source of quarrels. Many of these are really not very important, but may be given more attention than they deserve. Blood calls these irritants "tremendous trifles." He says, "Any problem that is tremendously significant to the injured party but merely a trifle to the 'innocent' one is a 'tremendous trifle.'" He indicates that they arise because of the "intimacy of marriage." "In living together under the same roof, the partners are exposed to the seamier aspects of each other's lives."[72]

The classic illustration is the couple who quarrels about squeezing the toothpaste tube. He likes to carefully roll up the tube and she just grabs it in the middle and squeezes it. Every time he brushes his teeth he resents her squeezing the tube and it becomes a source of friction. In reality, it does not matter how the toothpaste is pressured out of the tube so long as all of it is used up! There are several solutions to such a problem such as "his" and "her" tubes with each using his own method of extracting the toothpaste. For the Christian, the grace of God (II Cor. 12:9) is sufficient for such little trifles, but often the couple forget to apply their Christianity to the practical aspects of adjusting to everyday married life.

71. Anderson, *Family Living*, p. 142.
72. Blood, *Marriage*, p. 224.

CONCLUSION

The adjustments that newlyweds make are many and varied, but the Christian couple have the special resources of the Word of God and prayer, of faith and love. Consequently, the adjustments should be made easier, resulting in a happier Christian home. Ralph Heynen writes:

> We must learn to accept our mate in wedded life for what he or she is, not just what we would like to have them be. But with this attitude, neither the husband, nor his wife need to be afraid to admit that he has failings and sins, for there is always the feeling that we are willing to forgive in the same way that we seek forgiveness from our Father in heaven. This leads to true Christian acceptance of each other.[73]

Words of Clyde M. Narramore are a fitting conclusion to this chapter on adjustment, ". . . if you're expecting perfection in your marriage, you are bound to meet with some disappointment. But if you enter marriage desirous of making the necessary adjustments even though there are differences, you will undoubtedly be happy."[74]

73. Ralph Heynen, *The Secret of Christian Family Living* (Grand Rapids: Baker Book House, 1965), p. 15.
74. Clyde M. Narramore, *Life and Love* (Grand Rapids: Zondervan Publishing House, 1956), p. 73.

QUESTIONS FOR DISCUSSION AND REVIEW

1. Why is it necessary to understand the differences between the male and female subcultures in order to achieve a good adjustment in marriage?

2. List and discuss some of the chief characteristics of the male subculture.

3. List and discuss some of the chief characteristics of the female subculture.

4. What are some psychological differences between the sexes?

5. Why is the first year so important for marriage adjustment? What are some typical problems faced by a couple during this period?

6. In what ways is sex adjustment related to the total marital relationship?

7. Why doesn't premarital counseling guarantee a good sex adjustment during the honeymoon?

8. What are some problem areas in sex adjustment? How may these be dealt with?

9. Discuss several methods which couples may use to achieve adjustment in areas where they have differences.

10. How may a knowledge of the nature of quarrels help a couple achieve good adjustment in marriage?

10

ADJUSTMENT
TO IN-LAWS

Therefore shall a man leave his father and his mother. . . .
                                                    Genesis 2:24

MARRIAGE AND THE KINSHIP GROUP

When God instituted marriage and before there were children from the union, He ordained that the newly married couple were to separate from the parental family. God in His infinite wisdom knew this method was best for the happiness of all the families concerned. C. W. Scudder writes, "Carlyle Marney speaks of marriage as separation. 'That is to say, marriage is a separation from the place of sonship in order that there might be the creation of a new place as husband and father.' . . . No human relationship is to have priority over the marriage relationship. In this sense marriage is separation from all other relationships."[1] Although there have been many changes in family life, it is still best for the newlyweds to start their own home separated from the parental families.[2]

This does not mean that the parental relationships are severed completely. Some couples who experience difficulties with their prospective in-laws think that at marriage they can ignore their parents and forget them completely. This is virtually impossible because of emotional and legal ties that no marriage ceremony can

1. C. W. Scudder, *The Family in Christian Perspective* (Nashville: Broadman Press, 1962), p. 23.
2. Tim LaHaye, *How to Be Happy Though Married* (Wheaton, IL: Tyndale House, 1968), p. 33.

sever. David R. Mace writes, "When John says, 'I'm marrying Mary, not her family,' he has the wrong point of view. He is in fact marrying into Mary's family, and it's worth a great effort, for Mary's sake, to make himself pleasing to her parents and other relatives."[3]

In American culture, marriage is into the family system, with a network of kinship within the respective in-law families. It is true that with the mobility of American society the kin-group in urban areas is much weaker than it is in rural areas. Some children are reared hundreds or thousands of miles from their nearest relatives. However, most couples maintain rather close ties with the parental family even though they may not have too much contact with other relatives such as aunts and uncles.

Marvin B. Sussman states; "Since 1950 there has been a plethora of studies undertaken in a variety of disciplines which support the notion that a viable kin network exists and that it has numerous functions supportive of the goals of other social systems."[4] Sussman and Burchinal summarize some of the findings of this research, one of which is, "The exchange of aid among families flows in several directions, from parents to children and vise versa, among siblings, and less frequently, from more distant relatives. However, financial assistance generally appears to flow from parents to children."[5] Thus, the kingroup is still a very definite part of the American family system.

J. L. Hirning and Alma L. Hirning point out that marriage enlarges the social contacts for some people:

> The social life of a young person often is expanded when he marries a mate who has brothers and sisters. Under favorable circumstances, the newcomer is welcomed and, in turn, the mate's siblings are accepted as friends. In such cases, the union between husband and wife becomes closer, is strengthened, and made secure. . . . To the extent that the parents, the young married couple, their brothers and sisters, and the latters' wives and husbands are forged and shaped into one large family, there emerges a greater sense of power for each of them.[6]

This extension of social contacts can be harmful to the couple if they do not establish good relationships with all the siblings and their

3. David R. Mace, *Success in Marriage* (Nashville: Abingdon Press, 1958), p. 68.
4. Marvin B. Sussman, "Relationships of Adult Children with Their Parents in the U.S.," in *Social Structure and the Family*, ed. Ethel Shanas and Gordon F. Streib (Englewood Cliffs, NJ: Prentice-Hall, Inc., 1965), p. 68. Used by permission.
5. Ibid.
6. J. L. Hirning and Alma L. Hirning, *Marriage Adjustment* (New York: American Book Co., (1956), p. 413. Used by permission.

mates. This may be true in a large kin-group that stresses unity in the family. If one sibling and his mate do not get along with a set of in-laws, then the harmony of the family gatherings is marred. "It is an irony that stresses and strains that occur in the larger circle of family relationships often create insecurity in what is normally a stable husband-wife relationship. And unfortunately, this often shows up at times when the whole family is together."[7] The happiness of the newlyweds can be helped or hindered by their ability to relate to the many sets of in-laws in a kin-group.

The basic problem in in-law adjustment is how to separate from the parental families and yet maintain harmonious relationships. If the couple do not break away sufficiently, there may be difficulties. If they go to the other extreme and ignore the parental families, then serious problems arise. The problems are compounded if a partner in either the parental family or the young new family is neurotically attached to a child or parent and refuses to give the other individual freedom to play the necessary role. For example, a mother may cling to her daughter and interfere with her married life. A daughter may cling to the mother and refuse to leave the hometown, and create very difficult situations in her marriage. Examples of such attachments are numerous.

IN-LAW PROBLEMS CAUSED BY PARENTS

The mother-in-law is blamed for many in-law difficulties. "No kinship role has been the butt of more jokes than that of mother-in-law. . . . Even though the mother-in-law stereotype is well entrenched in our culture, Duvall reports a definite trend toward rejection of the stereotype by young urban couples. Over one-half had no mother-in-law complaints."[8] Henry R. Brandt asks a pointed question:

> Is it unreasonable to extend Paul's statement, "he that loveth his wife loveth himself" to include also the person his wife loves? . . . to love God rightly is to love others, too, and that includes your own parents and your in-laws. Any couple rightly related to God and each other must come to mutual agreement in this matter. Relationships with your families will not be settled once and for all, but must be revised according to their changing need and yours.[9]

7. Gordon Jaeck, and Dorothea Jaeck, "Ins and Outs of In-laws," in *The Marriage Affair*, ed. J. Allan Petersen (Wheaton, IL: Tyndale House Publishers, 1971), p. 307.
8. Floyd M. Martinson, *Marriage and the American Ideal* (New York: Dodd, Mead & Co., 1960), p. 453.
9. Henry R. Brandt and Homer E. Dowdy, *Building a Christian Home* (Wheaton, IL: Scripture Press, 1960), p. 48. Used by permission.

Although the mother-in-law is involved in in-law difficulties more often than other family members, there are different conditions where either in-law can create real obstacles to happiness for their children.[10]

A very common situation occurs when the parents think so much of their child that they feel no one is good enough to marry that child. Whenever the young person is dating, they continually find some reason for rejecting the suitor, and they endeavor to break the relationship. Even if a young lady of such parents were to find Prince Charming himself, such parents would find some fault in him and advise their daughter against such a person.

The opposite case occurs when the parents have rejected a child. For those young people reared in good Christian homes where they have been the recipients of much affection, it is hard to realize there are thousands of children and young people whose births were not planned by their parents and who were rejected by their parents when they were born. One young mother of two small children became pregnant and gave births to twins. Since their birth occurred only ten months after the second child, she was burdened down with caring for three infants at once. She totally rejected the twins, and their personalities were warped by such treatment.

The mother who rejects a daughter may also refuse to accept the fellow she marries, and this creates hardships. Psychologists say that in extreme cases the mother may actually try to win over the affection of the daughter's suitor, divorce her husband, and marry the young man.[11] It is difficult enough to understand this kind of behavior in an unbeliever, but it becomes almost incomprehensible when a Christian mother does this.

Unfortunately, some Christian parents are unhappily married and adopt the attitude that no one else can be happily married. Such parents are continually examining the relationship of the young couple, looking for any situation they can exploit to prove to the young people that they are not really happily married. They tend to blow up out of proportion any little thing that happens between the young couple in order to prove their point. The solution for such in-law difficulties is for the young couple to move a thousand miles away where the in-laws cannot interfere![12] Where this is impossible, the young couple must recognize this type of behavior when it

---

10. Gerald R. Leslie, *The Family in Social Context* (New York: Oxford University Press, 1973), p. 315.

11. Hirning and Hirning, *Marriage Adjustment*, p. 414.

12. Robert C. Williamson, *Marriage and Family Relations* (New York: John Wiley & Son, 1966), p. 503.

occurs, and agree to carefully examine the motivation of any comments made by the in-laws to prevent them from destroying their happiness together.

There are occasions where in-laws reject a son or daughter-in-law because they do not like some facet of his or her background. Such is the case when only one child in a family is a believer and marries another Christian. Quite often the unsaved family rejects the young Christian family because of their stand for Christ. Although it is difficult to find someone to take the place of the real mother and father, yet the Christian couple can find a wonderful fellowship in the local church with the people of God. The psalmist said, "When my father and my mother forsake me, then the Lord will take me up" (Ps. 27:10).

A similar situation may exist when the child marries someone from a lower social class level. Social class distinctions are very much a part of American culture, and many people are not aware of the great influence that social class pressures exert in their lives. Consider Jim and Mary:

> Mary was from an upper-middle class professional home. She met Jim at the Christian college which they both attended. He was reared in a fine Christian home. His father was a factory worker and not able to help Jim with his college expenses, so he had to work to pay all his college expenses. Mary and Jim were very compatible and deeply interested in spiritual things. When Mary wrote home of her growing friendship with Jim, and asked permission to bring him home to meet her parents, they refused on the simple basis of his working-class background. They had higher aspirations for their daughter. Mary and Jim finally married against her parent's wishes, and several years after the marriage, the parents still had not accepted Jim nor the grandchildren.

Domineering parents can create great problems for their married children. Such parents desire to continue their domination after the child marries, and this is resented by the mate. A mother who has always made decisions for her daughter may attempt to make them for her after marriage.[13] She tells her what kind of drapes to hang, or what style of furniture to purchase. A father may insist that the son purchase a home in a particular neighborhood.

In either case, the spouse may object to such advice, and demand that his or her voice be heard before a decision is made on drapes, furniture, or neighborhood.

The couple must recognize that advice from parents, if solic-

---

13. Mirra Komarovsky, *Blue Collar Marriage* (New York: Random House, 1964), p. 269.

ited, may be helpful, but it is not binding upon them. They must learn to make their own decisions.[14] This type of parent is easily recognized before marriage, and an individual should avoid marrying a person dominated by his or her parents unless they can live comfortably with such domination, or unless the couple plan to live a great distance from the in-laws.

Overattachment of a parent for a child can be just as damaging to a marriage as domination is. It is possible for both parents to be overly protective and neurotically attached to a child, but more frequent is the case of a widowed or divorced mother who rears a child without a father.[15] She bestows upon the child the affection which would ordinarily be given to a husband. The same can be true of an unhappily married wife who gives all her affection to the children instead of the husband.[16]

The child reared in such a home has great difficulty in breaking the ties because the mother will make her son feel guilty whenever he shares his affection with a girl friend or when her daughter shares her affection with a boyfriend. Some mothers try to prevent their son or daughter from marrying so they can continue to enjoy their company.[17] Some cling to the children for "social security" in that they expect the single son or daughter to care for them in their old age. They attempt to make life so easy and enjoyable at home for the child that it becomes difficult for the person to think of giving up such a delightful existence for the weighty responsibilities of married life. In reality, such a mother is being very selfish, for she fails to realize that the son or daughter will be left to a life of loneliness after her death.

Young people who marry mates from such homes should be prepared to share the spouse's affection with his or her parent. One such mother inveigled herself into accompanying her son and his bride on their honeymoon trip![18] In these types of cases the symptoms of in-law difficulty are experienced during the courtship stage, and should be considered a "warning signal" in the relationship. Marriage should be entered only after the greatest consideration of the possible effect the overattachment of the in-law will have on the couple's happiness.

14. Mace, *Success in Marriage*, p. 65.
15. Hirning and Hirning, *Marriage Adjustment*, p. 414.
16. Mace, *Success in Marriage*, p. 67.
17. Richard H. Klemer, *Marriage and Family Relationships* (New York: Harper & Row, 1970), p. 278.
18. Hirning and Hirning, *Marriage Adjustment*, p. 414.

There are some in-law situations caused by the rejection of the parents by the spouse, or of the spouse by the parents for no ascertainable reason other than incompatible personalities.[19] They may be good Christians, of the same social class level, belong to the same political party, but yet they will express an open dislike for each other. Social interaction between the parental family and the young family is virtually impossible because of these attitudes. This situation is sometimes helped by the birth of grandchildren, but the grandchildren may be rejected also. The spouse of the rejected in-law needs to be sympathetic and understanding with the mate. To condemn the mate does not help the matter. If attempts to change the situation fail, the couple must accept the situation, and draw closer to one another to compensate for the failure of the in-laws concerned to play their role effectively.

IN-LAW PROBLEMS CAUSED BY MARRIED CHILDREN

The exploitation of parents by young couples is the cause of many in-law problems. Many times the couple get themselves into financial difficulty and expect the parental family to come forth with a gift to help save them from financial disaster.[20] Couples who get into such financial straits do not know how to handle their money, and when the in-laws come to their rescue, they do not help the basic cause of the problem. The young couple are wise enough to know that no loving father is going to stand by and see his children or grandchildren go without food, or be evicted from their home for failure to pay the rent, or go without needed medical care. Part of the problem may be due to failure on the part of the parents to teach their child how to manage money when they were growing up in the home. Some parents may subconsciously enjoy helping their child because it keeps the child in a status of dependence upon the parent.

The problem can only be solved by the young couple learning financial responsibility. A first step in this direction would be for the couple to learn how to make a budget, and then learn how to live on it. The older family may have some pressure to exert by refusing further financial help until a real effort is made by the couple to learn to live within their means. This may result in some temporary hardship for the young family, but it may have permanent results if they make a sincere effort to manage their funds wisely.

19. Ibid., p. 415.
20. Klemer, *Marriage and Family Relationships*, pp. 283-284.

Another source of difficulty occurs whenever the young family tries to take advantage of the grandparents by asking them to babysit for the grandchildren.[21] Most grandparents do not mind, and actually enjoy caring for the children on occasions. However, if the mother is inconsiderate and expects the grandparents to babysit the children several times a week, they usually object to such expectations. One daughter regularly took her children to her mother every afternoon, and then came for them just before dinnertime. This did not give the grandmother any afternoons for herself. Finally she had to tell her daughter she would only babysit one afternoon or evening a week since there were many things she would like to do herself. This awkward circumstance could have been avoided had the mother made such a statement when the daughter first began imposing on her. If the grandparents reside close enough to become involved with babysitting, it is wise from the very beginning to have an understanding in this matter.

MAJOR PERIODS OF ADJUSTMENT

There are two periods in the marriage cycle when in-law adjustments are particularly necessary. The first is in the early years of the marriage when the young couple are becoming independent of the parental family.[22] This is a difficult time, for in American culture the young family is expected to emancipate itself from the families of orientation, yet society does not lay down any guidelines for the families to follow.

The changes in the American family life also are affecting the in-law relationships since many young families are fully or partially subsidized while the young husband and wife complete their educations. "High rates of parental support are probably associated with marriages of children while they are still in a dependency status; those among high school or college students are examples."[23] This complicates the emancipation process, for the young family does not assume a fully separate and independent status. The same difficulty faces the many teen-age couples in high school who are forced into marriage by premarital pregnancy, and must live with one of the in-law families while they complete their secondary education. Cou-

21. Robert O. Blood, *Marriage* (New York: Free Press of Glencoe, 1962), p. 323.
22. Judson T. Landis and Mary G. Landis, *Building a Successful Marriage* (Englewood Cliffs, NJ: Prentice-Hall, 1968), p. 328.
23. Sussman, "Relationships of Children with Parents," p. 69.

ples in these circumstances will encounter many more adjustment problems than will the couples who are financially independent and able to separate from the parental families.

One maxim of good in-law adjustment is that the newlyweds must never live in the home of an in-law.[24] There are enough adjustments to be made between themselves as they learn their new roles of husband and wife, so they must not be encumbered with learning each hour the role of son or daughter-in-law. They must be free to adjust to each other without the interference of any third party. If necessary, it is better for the couple with limited means to live in a one-room furnished apartment, and to accept a lower standard of living than to move in with the in-laws.

If during the courtship, there are indications that there may be difficulties with the in-laws, it is wise for the newlyweds to move to another town to establish their home. A long distance between the two families may be a great aid to good in-law relationships! Landis and Landis suggest the following: "The young person who is still immature may have a better chance to grow up if he is away from his family during the first adjustment period of marriage. The too-interested mother may also find interests other than the lives of her children, if the children are not living near her during the first months after they marry." They also indicate that as the young couple mature, they may reach the point where they enjoy good relationships with the in-laws and be able to live near them in a satisfactory manner.[25]

Many of the difficulties can be avoided in the first years of marriage if both the parental and young family recognize that a change of status and role takes place at marriage. Prior to the wedding, the bride and groom were dependent children in their respective families. At the wedding a new family is established, and the bride and groom take a new status of husband and wife in a new family that is on a par Scripturally, legally and morally with the parental families. They are no longer dependent children but now have the roles of husband and wife that are equal to those of their parents.

Although the parents still have the role of parents, the relationship is changed and it is helpful for the young family to think of their parents also in the role of good friends.[26] As such they are free to

24. Mace, *Success in Marriage*, p. 69.

25. Landis and Landis, *Successful Marriage*, p. 341.

26. Reuben Hill, "Decision Making and the Family Life Cycle," in *Social Structure and the Family*, ed. Ethel Shanas and Gordon F. Steib (Englewood Cliffs, NJ: Prentice-Hall, Inc. 1965), p. 115.

seek the advice of their parents, but like the advice of other friends, they are not duty bound to accept it. Such advice should be carefully weighed, as the parents have twenty-five or thirty years more experience, and it should be considered in any decision made. "Parents have a wisdom and maturity from which younger couples can well profit."[27] The parental family must avoid giving advice unless it is asked for. Simply because they have more years of experience does not give them the right to impose their views on the younger couple. They should let the newlyweds know that they are available for advice and help if needed, but should wait until it is asked for before it is given.

Difficulty may also be caused if the new family is too sensitive to suggestions or advice from the parents. In their desire to become independent, the couple may interpret any offer from the parental family as an attempt to retain some control over them. Now, it is true that some parents use monetary gifts and loans in an effort to influence and perhaps even control the direction of the young family.[28] Thus, if they want the son to live in the same area they may offer the gift of a lot on which to build a new house only if the couple buys near the parents. This is clearly an unfair interference in the decision-making process of the couple. Many couples appreciate parental help in purchasing a home, but the wise couple refuse such offers if unfairly restricted. On the other hand, the offer of a gift or low interest loan to purchase a home can be a real blessing to the couple, for it may help them to begin acquiring equity in a home much sooner than they could if they had to first save for a down payment.

Financial aid to complete a person's education is also very helpful if unrestricted:

> The current clarion call for young people to stay in high school, and if at all possible, to go to college . . . is an indication of extended parental financial support for children. . . . Today approximately 25 percent of college undergraduates are married . . . Conditions are such that parents expect to support their children . . . until the children are properly launched into careers.[29]

27. Jaeck and Jaeck, "Ins and Outs of In-laws," p. 308.
28. Gail Putney Fullerton, *Survival in Marriage* (New York: Holt, Rinehart & Winston, Inc., 1972), pp. 175-182. A case history is presented of a young couple whose parents tried to influence them by helping to purchase a home.The couple rebelled and "dropped out" of middle class society and chose to live in poverty.
29. Sussman, "Relationships of Children with Parents," p. 79. Used by permission.

It is certainly unfair and unwise for a parent to offer to help only if the young husband agrees to follow the career chosen by the parent. Parents who wish to help their married children can do so by making wise and unrestricted gifts at appropriate times such as birthdays, anniversaries, and Christmas.[30] It is customary to give gifts on such occasions, and the couple should not be embarrassed by gifts at such times. Conversely, they should recognize these are "gifts" and should not come to expect them on every occasion, nor be too disappointed if an event passes without such a gift. Many parents do help the couple get established in one way or another, the amount depending upon the financial status of the parents.[31] Even though the parents may make mistakes from time to time, the young couple need to remember that the parents do have the best welfare of the couple at heart, and thus be forgiving and understanding in their attitudes toward the parents. Gordon and Dorothea Jaeck ask the young couple to accept their "parents as people who have an understandable stake in your marriage and who desire, above all, its success and your happiness."[32]

Most problems are with the parental in-laws but another difficulty of the early years involves adjustment to the brothers or sisters-in-law. Many times a mate resents the favored treatment by the spouse's parents of a sibling. For example, a parent with two married daughters may be more generous toward one of them, and such partiality may be resented by the husband of the less-favored daughter. [33] Similarly one daughter may exploit her parents for financial reasons, and this type of conduct causes resentment by the other girl and her husband who manage their money very well. The actions and attitudes of unmarried siblings still at home may also cause animosity toward them.

A great difference in personality, religion, or political views may make for incompatibility between brothers and sisters-in-law. This can cause real friction if the individuals are not mature enough to avoid the areas of conflicting views when they are together. Good adjustment in these cases may mean that the couple will have to forgo visiting each other until they are mature enough to visit without arguments and hurt feelings.

The second major period of in-law adjustment occurs when the

---

30. Klemer, *Marriage and Family Relationships*, p. 284.
31. Sussman, "Relationships of Children with Parents," p. 77.
32. Jaeck and Jaeck, "Ins and Outs of In-laws," p. 307.
33. Hirning and Hirning, *Marriage Adjustment*, p. 415.

parents become old, and often infirm, and the children must assume their care. "In American society with each passing year the prospects for survival and living into old age increase."[34] If the Lord Jesus tarries, the task of providing for parents should become less of a problem in the future since many more people are covered by private retirement plans as well as Social Security. However, many of the present generation who went through the Great Depression, are forced to live on Social Security benefits which are inadequate to meet all their needs. Consequently, the children find it necessary to help with the support of their parents:

> Alvin Schorr points out that money contributions for parents is the only gift that can actually be compelled by law from children but the money aid is relatively unimportant. . . . The recent findings by Shanas that married children are willing to assume responsibility for aged parents including financial aid, providing a home for them, and locating close to the residences of aged parents or vice versa suggest a change in attitude from the period of the 1940's (explored by Dinkel).[35]

This provides an opportunity for children to fulfill their Scriptural obligation to care for their parents, and also to help repay them for some of the care and help provided earlier in life. The apostle Paul wrote, "But if any widow have children or nephews, let them learn first to show piety at home, and to requite [pay back] their parents: for that is good and acceptable before God'" The problems arise between in-laws over such things as sharing equally in the support, where the parent or parents should live, failure to visit the parents and the domestic problems.

When the parents are well, gerontologists usually feel it is best for them to live in their own home when feasible and as long as it is wise. There are times when it is not wise: an aged couple living in a twelve-room house, or parents unable to care for their home or for themselves. When a move becomes necessary many couples go to warmer climates such as California, Arizona, or Florida. Some prefer the security of an apartment or condominium in a retirement colony where many services are provided. Others who are well prefer individual homes. Many find that mobile home living has much to offer. Some prefer an apartment near one of the children.

A real decision must be made when a parent becomes too ill to live

34. Sussman, "Relationships of Children with Parents," p. 80.
35. Ibid. Used by permission.

alone, and yet not ill enough to be hospitalized. One of the children must take the parent into the home and provide nursing care, or else the person must be placed in a nursing home. Taking the parent into the home is difficult and often impossible in a small home. Nursing homes are very expensive, and many are very dreary places for an ill person to live. Some church groups have homes for their aged, providing a wholesome environment for them. The Lord leads when such decisions must be made, and the Christian couple can depend upon his leading when faced with such a situation.

CONCLUSION

Good in-law relationships can add much happiness and be a help to a Christian marriage. The relationship of Ruth and Naomi is an example of this. The women of Israel gave expression to this fact when Obed was born: ". . . thy daughter-in-law, which loveth thee, which is better to thee than seven sons, hath born him" (Ruth 4:15). Many a Christian parent has experienced something of the same feeling when a son or daughter-in-law has become as precious to them as their own child. Mace says, "The goal to be aimed at was well expressed by the mother who said, 'When Tom married Peggy, I thought I lost a son. But what actually happened was that I gained a daughter.'"[36] Like Ruth, many an in-law has come to love the mother-in-law with the same affection they feel for their mother.

Young people must remember that when they marry, they marry into an established family, but that their new family is on an equal level with the parental families. When difficulties arise, they must always act as a family unit, realizing that loyalty and affection for the spouse takes precedence over that for the parents. The Jaeck's express it:

> The rewards are immeasurable for making the effort to establish a harmonious and loving relationship with parents-in-law. . . . Their continued interest in and emotional support of their married children can be a valued asset. . . . Letters . . . telephone calls . . . personal visits, whatever the means used, the message of love should get through to our in-laws.[37]

Happy is the couple who experiences pleasant relationships with their in-laws!

---

36. Mace, *Success in Marriage*, p. 70.
37. Jaeck and Jaeck, "Ins and Outs of In-laws," p. 36. Used by permission.

QUESTIONS FOR DISCUSSION AND REVIEW

1. What basic problem creates in-law difficulties in marriage?

2. Discuss the relationship between social contacts of sibling in-laws to the young couple.

3. Why do parents reject a child? How does this affect the parent's relationship to the person the child marries?

4. What are some "warning signals" of possible in-law difficulties that a person may look for during courtship?

5. How may "exploitation of the parents" cause in-law problems?

6. Why is it important for the newly married couple to establish their own home separate from the parental families?

7. Discuss the role changes that take place when a couple are married.

8. List several methods which can be used by the parental family to financially help the young family without creating in-law problems.

9. In what ways do aged parents cause in-law problems?

10. What basic principle should guide a young family faced with an in-law difficulty?

11

CHRISTIAN STEWARDSHIP
AND BUDGETING

. . . it is required in stewards, that a man be found faithful.

I Corinthians 4:2

THE MAJOR SOURCE OF CONFLICT IN MARRIAGE

The chief cause of conflict in American families, Christian or non-Christian, is the use of money.[1] Since there is not enough money left over after the bills are paid in the average family to supply the desires of both husband and wife, differences arise which often lead to argument and conflict.[2] In our economy most often the husband earns the money and the wife pays the bills and keeps the books. Since the husband is not aware of all the demands on his paycheck, he may wonder what happens to it and why it is so quickly exhausted.[3] This can cause real arguments.

Money problems are not confined to any one period in the marriage cycle. Robert O. Blood and Donald M. Wolfe indicate that only 10 percent of couples have disagreements over money during the honeymoon. In the stage of the family-life cycle with preschool children, the percentage jumps to 28 percent. During preadolescent

1. Robert O. Blood and Donald M. Wolfe, *Husbands and Wives* (New York: The Free Press of Glencoe, 1960), p. 245.
2. Richard H. Klemer, *Marriage and Family Relationships* (New York: Harper & Row, 1970), pp. 266-267.
3. Robert O. Blood, *Marriage* (New York: Free Press of Glencoe, 1962), pp. 291-292.

stage it is 24 percent, during the adolescent stage it is 23 percent, and in the postparental and retired stage it is still 21 percent.[4] One retired couple had problems because the husband wanted to use some of their ample savings for a trip abroad, and the wife refused to go.

Unfortunately, some mates use or misuse money in order to punish each other. The husband buys a new hunting rifle without consulting his wife. She retaliates by buying an expensive sewing machine, or something equally expensive. Norman M. Lobsenz and Clark W. Blackburn point out that "the handling of finances is, in fact, one of the major emotional battlegrounds of marriage. Half of the couples who come to Family Service agencies for counseling report severe problems with money. Yet only a tiny proportion—six percent to be exact—are in difficulty because of inadequate or unusual financial need."[5] They proceed to say that the two main reasons why these couples have such problems are that they either have immature or unrealistic attitudes concerning money, or they use money as "a weapon or as a compensation for inadequacies."[6]

Money is often used to compensate for personality weaknesses. Each person brings to the marriage a personality with certain attitudes toward money that affect the total relationship. One spouse may come from a home where money is highly valued because it can buy status symbols for conspicuous consumption. The mate may come from a home where thrift and saving money are practiced. It is evident that it will take real effort for these two to adjust in their use of money.[7]

Some young people overspend, purchasing expensive items such as stereos and cameras to "shore up their egos."[8] Many times the motivation of these individuals is to "keep up with the Joneses." Their ego needs are such that they require something newer or bigger than the neighbors in order to reassure themselves that they are important. Such a person must examine himself and discover that such an attitude reflects immaturity, for only "children depend upon others for their self-regard. Those who reach adulthood and still depend upon others for their feelings about themselves have never grown up."[9]

4. Blood and Wolfe, *Husbands and Wives*, p. 247.
5. Norman M. Lobsenz and Clark W. Blackburn, "Hidden Meanings of Money in Marriage," in *Reader's Digest*, March 1969, p. 142.
6. Ibid.
7. Klemer, *Marriage and Family Relationships*, p. 264.
8. Lobsenz and Blackburn, " Hidden Meanings of Money," pp. 142-143.
9. W. Clark Ellzey, "Money, Marriage and Romance," in *The Marriage Affair*, ed. J. Allan Petersen (Wheaton, IL: Tyndale House Publishers, 1971), p. 353.

Other people compensate for earlier deprivations in their lives by "oversaving," even to the extent that they find it almost impossible to spend money for necessities. One wife from such a deprived background could not buy herself a dress even when the husband took her to a store and encouraged her to buy one.[10] Such individuals need professional counseling to help them "understand the basis for their money habits" if they are going to solve the conflict in the family over money.[11]

A husband who is not very sure of his masculinity is threatened if he permits the wife to handle any of the money. He insists on controlling the money and only gives the wife what he thinks she needs to run the household. James H. Jauncey tells of a man who, after he had doled out the grocery money to his wife, insisted on telling her what to do with it! The solution was for the husband to realize that the spending of the housekeeping money was the wife's role.[12] Even if the wife works, a husband may insist that she turn over her paycheck to him so that he can have complete control of the finances. Conflict in such a situation can only be solved as the husband gains insight into the relationship between money and his personality.

The Christian couple who have conflicts over money that they cannot solve themselves should seek outside help for the problem. Jauncey suggests that such problems are "solvable by an astute combination of love and skill: love that gets through to a person's heart; skill that penetrates to the reluctant mind. It take perserverance, faith, and courage. Prayer, too."[13] The combination of professional help, spiritual power, and the proper attitude of love and concern for each other can solve most, if not all, financial conflicts.

BASIC PRINCIPLES OF STEWARDSHIP

Much of the unhappiness caused by conflict over money can be avoided by a Christian couple if they have a correct understanding of Christian stewardship, of their responsibility before God to wisely use for His glory the material benefits which He entrusts to their care. Many Christians do not realize that their use of money is determined by their yieldedness to the Lord. Some Christians permit

10. Klemer, *Marriage and Family Relationships*, p. 266.
11. Lobsenz and Blackburn, "Hidden Meanings of Money," p. 143.
12. James H. Jauncey, *Magic in Marriage* (Grand Rapids: Zondervan Publishing House, 1966), p. 122.
13. Ibid., pp. 123-124.

money to dominate them rather than using money well and wisely as stewards of God. Wayne J. Anderson states:

> Money itself is of *no* importance. It is *what is done* with money that counts [italics his]. Money is really nothing more than a medium of exchange which we use to obtain something we need. If we use it wisely, it becomes our servant. If we acquire money simply to look at it, and delight in its possession, it becomes our master.[14]

The Bible gives us examples of both those who were dominated by money and those who used money as a trust from God. The parable of the rich fool warns against the danger of being dominated by material things without regard for spiritual values. The rich fool said to himself, "Soul, thou hast much goods laid up for many years; take thine ease, eat, drink, and be merry." But God said unto him, "Thou fool, this night thy soul shall be required of thee; then whose shall those things be, which thou hast provided?" The Lord then warns, "So is he that layeth up treasure for himself, and is not rich toward God." (Luke 12:16-21) The lesson is clear: material things must be used for the glory of God.

The Macedonian believers, however, are good examples of those who use wisely and well the resources God permits them to possess. Paul writes in II Corinthians 8:2-5:

> How that in a great trial of affliction the abundance of their joy and their deep poverty abounded unto the riches of their liberality.
> For to their power, I bear record, yea, and beyond their power they were willing of themselves.
> Praying us with much intreaty that we would receive the gift, and take upon us the fellowship of the ministering to the saints.
> And this they did, not as we hoped, but first gave their own selves to the Lord, and unto us by the will of God.

The Macedonians had accepted the most important principle of stewardship: yielding up the self and will to do the will of God. George M. Bowman writes, "The success you have with money will be determined by the degree in which you give yourself to Jesus Christ.... To be faithful stewards is not a question of giving our gifts to God, but of yielding ourselves to Christ."[15]

Stewardship and consecration are invariably linked together. A Christian cannot be conscientious in his use of money until he

14. Wayne J. Anderson, *Design for Family Living* (Minneapolis: T. S. Denison & Co., Inc., 1964), p. 116.
15. George M. Bowman, *Here's How to Succeed with Your Money* (Chicago: Moody Press, 1960), p. 14.

realizes that all that he is, and all that he possesses, belongs to Christ and must be yielded to Him. In I Corinthians 6:19-20, Paul writes, "What? know ye not that your body is the temple of the Holy Ghost . . . and ye are not your own? For ye are bought with a price: therefore glorify God in your body, and in your spirit, which are God's." The believer has been redeemed "with the precious blood of Christ" (I Peter 1:19), and as such is to present his body as a living sacrifice to do the will of God, (Rom. 12:1-2).

This will of God should determine what the individual does with his life, and how he uses the material resources which God bestows upon him. He is merely a steward (or in modern terminology, a manager) of these resources which are to be used to bring glory to God. A. T. Pierson once wrote, "Not only money, but every gift of God is received in trust for his use. Man is not an owner, but a trustee, managing another's goods and estates, God being the one original and inalienable owner of all."[16] God expects each Christian steward to be faithful (I Cor. 4:2) in his employment of his money, and will hold him accountable for its use: "For we must all appear before the judgment-bar of Christ, that each may get his pay for what he has done, whether it be good or bad" (II Cor. 5:10, Williams' Translation).

In American culture today the prevailing philosophy is materialism. The Bible teaches in Luke 12:15 that a "man's life consisteth not in the abundance of the things which he possesseth," a teaching directly opposed to materialism. The Christian is surrounded by a culture that continually emphasizes the acquisition of new homes, new furniture, new cars, new boats, new campers, ad infinitum. He is encouraged to use "easy credit," until he, like those in the world surrounding him, is only "one pay check from bankruptcy." Louis H. Evans says:

> How to curb this god of inordinate and uncontrolled desire is a problem. We must control our "wanting" as well as our acting. This craving to "get," this uncontrolled sense of "gimme" within brings about this idolatry. . . . But this god never satisfies. . . . The wanting loses itself in infinity and the worshiper loses himself in frustrated despair. But how easily can this worship of things creep into the temple of the heart and of the home![17]

The Christian must always be on guard against the intrusion of

16. A. T. Pierson, "Giving Is Living." in *The Marriage Affair*, ed. J. Alan Petersen (Wheaton, IL: Tyndale House Publishers, 1971), p. 345.
17. Louis H. Evans, *Your Marriage, Duel or Duet* (Old Tappan, NJ: Fleming H. Revell Co., 1962), pp. 106-107. Used by permission.

materialism into his life. Jesus warned against the danger of this materialism and gave the promise, "But seek ye first the kingdom of God, and his righteousness; and all these things shall be added unto you" (Matt. 6:33).

Improper teaching of tithing rather than Christian stewardship may have contributed to materialism in our churches, for many Christians have the mistaken belief that if they give a tenth of their income to the Lord, they are free to use the remaining nine-tenths for their own selfish gratification. It never occurs to them that the Lord might want them to give two-tenths or three-tenths of their income to His work. In a day of great affluence, with many Christian homes having two incomes, the churches, Christian schools, and missions continue to suffer great needs because the vision of giving is limited to a mere tithe. Pierson once remarked, "Never will the work of missions, or any other form of service to God and man, receive the help it ought until there is a new conscience and a new consecration in the matter of money. The worldly spirit blinds us to the fact of obligation, and devises flimsy pretexts for diverting the Lord's money to carnal ends."[18]

This does not mean that tithing is wrong. Millions of Christians, including the writer, can give testimony of the financial blessing of God because of practicing tithing. Tim LaHaye observes, "You can literally accomplish more financially with God's blessing on the expenditure of the 90 percent than you can the 100 percent without God's blessing. I have never known a couple that was not blessed by tithing."[19] The point is that most Christians do not get beyond giving the 10 percent because they believe that is all that belongs to God. The Bible teaches that all we have belongs to God and in this affluent society many Christians ought to be giving much more than merely 10 percent.

It is perfectly Scriptural for a young couple to decide on a tithe or 10 percent as the basis for their Christian stewardship early in their marriage. Jauncey concurs with such a suggestion:

> The ten percent of our income that we give to the kingdom of God is the *token of our recognition* that everything is His. (Italics mine) This is the Scriptural way. The tithe has great wisdom wrapped up in it. It is big enough to involve us in real sacrifice. . . . It shows that your heart is not wrapped up in your money. Yet it is not so big that it impoverishes.[20]

18. Pierson, "Giving Is Living," p. 349.
19. Tim LaHaye, *How to Be Happy Though Married* (Wheaton, IL: Tyndale House Publishers, 1968), pp. 30-31.
20. Jauncey, *Magic in Marriage*, p. 123. Used by permission.

However, it must be emphasized that the tithe is only the beginning of real Christian stewardship and should *not* be considered the norm for Christian giving as is often taught in our churches. William Goetz says the question should be, "How much of God's money may I keep for myself?"[21] Many examples could be given of individuals who have increased the proportion of their income given to God with resultant blessings. The stewardship of R. G. LeTorneau is an example well known to many Christians.

Sometimes Christian couples are given the idea that if they tithe they will experience very little conflict over money, and that they will be relatively free from financial problems.[22] This is not necessarily true, for it is possible for a family to tithe and be conscientious about giving but still make poor financial decisions. For example, the car of a couple already heavily in debt needs repairs costing two or three hundred dollars. They can either have it fixed or buy a different one, incurring additional debt of several thousand dollars and large monthly payments. For a family already overburdened with debt, the latter decision probably would not be a wise one, and would create additional strain on an overloaded budget. The fact that a couple tithe generously does not necessarily mean they will always make good, sound financial decisions. If they do not use good judgment, they can suffer the results of such poor judgment the same as the person who does not tithe or have a vision of Christian stewardship. The Christian couple must learn how to use the limited resources that God entrusts to their care in the wisest possible manner.

There are, however, many fine Christians who have a real burden to give to the cause of Christ. It is the purpose of this and the following chapter to encourage this generation of young people to increase the number of those who are dedicated to Christian stewardship of all they are and possess rather than to be bound by an inadequate view of tithing.

Another basic principle of Christian stewardship is that in order to give more, one must have more. In the parable of the talents in Matthew 25:14-30, there was an unequal division of the talents by the master. The servants were judged on the basis of their faithfulness in the use of the talents, but the servants who had more to begin with were able to gain more than the one with just one talent. The master condemned the unfaithful servant for not giving the money to "the exchangers" so that it would have at least earned some interest.

21. William Goetz, "Teenagers—and Their Money," in *The Alliance Weekly*, April 28, 1965, p. 14.
22. Jauncey, *Magic in Marriage*, p. 123.

This passage clearly teaches the use of money to increase the amount of money.

One of the problems in evangelical Christianity today is that there are so few individuals able to give substantial gifts to sustain and enlarge Christian organizations. One of the problems in the early church at Jerusalem was that the members sold their houses and lands (their capital assets) and spent the proceeds. Then the apostle Paul had to take up collections from the churches in Asia Minor to send to the "poor saints . . . at Jerusalem" (Rom. 15:26). It is necessary for the believer to accumulate capital in order to increase his ability to give more funds for the work of the Lord.

In this accumulation he must be careful to follow the will of God for his life, to maintain his devotion to Christ in the midst of a materialistic generation. This is very difficult to do and many sincere Christians have backslidden because they could not stand prosperity. Henry R. Brandt writes that over the years different men came to him with plans to acquire wealth and thus aid the cause of Christ. He says:

> Two who outlined their plans have made good progress, but have become so absorbed in the task and so attached to their possessions that they have lost sight of their goal and become absorbed in using their wealth to acquire more wealth. Some day, they say, their capital will not be tied up and there will be some available for Christian causes.[23]

The young person should not be discouraged by these examples of men who failed the Lord. Many successful businessmen are faithful stewards and give generously to the work of Christ, which indicates that financial success and spiritual growth are compatible goals in life. God does not expect every Christian to become wealthy, but each person must be faithful in the use of money entrusted to him. God will judge each one on the basis of how faithfully he uses what is given to him. The words of the Lord of the servants in the parable of the talents was, "Well done, thou good and faithful servant; thou hast been faithful over a few things, I will make thee ruler over many things: enter thou into the joy of thy Lord" (Matt. 25:21).

WHO SHOULD HANDLE THE MONEY?

This is a question that should be settled during the engagement period so the couple will be able to plan effectively for the honey-

23. Henry R. Brandt and Homer E. Dowdy, *Building a Christian Home* (Wheaton, IL: Scripture Press, 1960), p. 36. Used by permission.

moon and the first few weeks of marriage. In the final analysis it does not make much difference whether the husband or wife handles the money so long as the most capable person does it and the arrangement is agreeable to both partners.[24] Some men believe it is part of the male role to care for the finances, and their masculinity is threatened if the wife does it. The husband may be the one to do it if this is mutually agreeable, but if he is a compulsive spender, it would be unwise for him to assume the role of money manager. In like manner, if the wife is an impulsive buyer, better for the husband to take the job even though he may not like to do so. One wife had spent her husband into bankruptcy once, and was well on the way again when the creditors suggested she see a counselor. Some couples decide on a division of labor whereby the husband pays for the major items as taxes, insurance, car and house payments, and the wife buys the minor items as clothing, groceries, sundries, etc. There must be unanimity in this area if the couple are going to be successful in their stewardship for Christ.

David Mace, out of his extensive experience, lists four "basic principles for the management of family finances."[25] These may be summarized by saying that all money is to be regarded as "family" money, with each partner fully informed as to its source and destination. Money is used only after mutual discussion and agreement, and each partner receives a small amount for his own personal use without any strings attached. The couple with good communication have no difficulty following such principles, for they desire to inform each other about such matters.

SHOULD THE WIFE WORK?

The Scriptural and traditional role is for the wife to be a mother and homemaker. When polled, most Christian young women indicate a preference for this role, but they also are desirous of working for a year or two before the children come. Almost without exception they want to be home when they have children.[26] Again, the couple should be in firm agreement as to the specific role the wife is to play. Most fellows do not object to the wife working for a while, but there are some who believe she should not work unless the male breadwinner is ill.[27]

24. Anderson, *Family Living*, p. 118.
25. David R. Mace, *Success in Marriage* (Nashville: Abingdon Press, 1958), pp. 55-58.
26. Survey taken in Marriage and Family classes, Fall and Winter quarters, 1969.
27. Ibid.

The number of married women who work outside the home has been increasing since World War II. A study made in 1984 indicated that six out of ten mothers with preschool or school age children were working. This is an increase of twenty percent from 1970 when only four out of ten mothers were employed. The mothers of children under three accounted for most of the increase.[28] It is apparent that an increasing number of women feel they can play the role of employee in addition to those of wife and mother.

It may be necessary for some college-educated wives to work in order to pay off loans owed for college expenses. Due to the high cost of a college education today these can be substantial. Other wives believe they should utilize the expensive education they received, and they desire to teach or nurse for a year or two after marriage. Later in the life of the marriage the wife may go back to work to help pay for the children's college expenses. Some wives also return to work as therapy during the menopause.

If the wife works before children are born and there are no educational loans to pay off, the couple should save the wife's income after tithing and offerings. They should discipline themselves to live on the husband's salary from the very beginning. There are two reasons for this. The first is that the couple will be oriented to living on one salary if the wife becomes pregnant and cannot work. Many couples get accustomed to living on two salaries and face real hardship when the wife cannot work. Evelyn Duvall remarks, "The husband and wife who have been living up all their joint income while both were working get a shock, when suddenly, with the coming of the first baby, they must live on one set of earnings at the very time that they face big increases in expenditures."[29]

The second reason is that the saving of the wife's income can provide the basis of financial security for the family, and for increased Christian giving throughout the life of the marriage. A substantial downpayment can be made on a home, which will lower the monthly payments and allow more of the current income for family needs and Christian stewardship. Some of the savings can provide an emergency fund so that future savings can be invested in such forms as mutual fund or common stocks which will provide for capital gains as well as interest on the savings.

There are also some disadvantages to the wife working. Often the

28. *Information Please Almanac* (New York: Houghton-Mifflin Co., 1985), p. 537.
29. Evelyn Millis Duvall, *Family Development* (Philadelphia: J. B. Lippincott Co., 1962), pp. 162-163.

husband must help with the traditional feminine tasks of cooking and housekeeping—and some men do not enjoy this.[30] If both salaries are used for living expenses, the birth of children may be postponed entirely, or else the couple may become parents when they should be grandparents.[31] One very real danger is "propinquity," whereby the wife may become involved with another man at the store or office. This should not happen to Christians, but they are still "in the flesh."

If the wife continues working after the children come, the disadvantage of children being raised by babysitters must be discussed. Many studies have been made concerning the effect of maternal employment and its effect on the children. Gerald Leslie summarizes the research on this subject:

> . . . it may be repeated that research generally contradicts the idea of there being generally significant differences between the children of working and non-working mothers. Maternal employment operates in interaction with too many other variables to be studied alone. Scattered pieces of research that have utilized adequate controls indicate that there may be some relationships with juvenile delinquency at middle-class levels, that part-time maternal employment has a favorable effect upon the adjustment of adolescent children, and that the effects upon younger children may vary by sex. Any general conclusion to the effect that maternal employment is undesirable seems unwarranted.[32]

The fact still remains that Scripturally the role of the Christian wife and mother is to be played in the home and not in the world of work. Paul wrote in I Timothy 5:14, "I will therefore that the younger women marry, bear children, rule the house, give none occasion to the adversary to speak reproachfully." There may be times because of illness of the breadwinner or some other unusual circumstances when it may be necessary for a Christian mother to work outside the home, but ordinarily the children prefer the mother to be in the home to care for them herself. In the same manner the wife with a Scriptural role concept finds her greatest fulfillment and happiness in being with her children rather than in employment outside the home.

There are times when wives work to provide "extras" for the family that they cannot afford on the husband's salary. In many

30. *Dayton Journal Herald*, Jan. 14, 1979.

31. C. W. Scudder, *The Family in Christian Perspective* (Nashville: Broadman Press, 1962), p. 14.

32. Leslie, *Family in Social Context*, p. 566. Used by permission.

cases more careful budgeting may provide some of these extras and the mother must weigh the possible results of her absence from the home against the worth of the other "extras" her employment provides. Very often working mothers in such a situation attempt to assuage guilt feelings by giving lavish presents to the children to compensate for failing to give them more time and attention.

Other mothers feel they cannot stand the routine of homemaking, so they go to work and hire a babysitter to care for the children and some of the housework. Henry R. Brandt makes a cogent comment concerning this matter:

> There is routine work in homemaking as in any profession. Think of the number of throats, ears and nostrils that a doctor looks into every day. . . . We do not feel sorry for the doctor, because he does not feel sorry for himself. . . . The wife, like the doctor, will become a contented person as she sees beyond the routine to the satisfaction gained from effective service . . . to husband and children. Self-interest is incompatible with effective service, marriage or parenthood.[33]

Women bored with housework often fail to realize that they are substituting the routine of a job for the routine of homemaking. Clyde M. Narramore writes:

> When a mother leaves her children and spends her time with other people during the day, she is usually saying by her actions, "I value other people's presence more than I do yours." As a married woman, you can do many things during your lifetime. But there is nothing which you can do that will be more important than developing and maintaining a spiritual home for your husband and children.[34]

There may even be an economic disadvantage if the wife's income places the couple in a higher income bracket. After the work-incurred expenses and the added tax are calculated, it may not be economically advantageous. Having an independent income may also produce an independent spirit in the wife, one that could harm the relationship. Tim LaHaye says, "I am convinced that one of the reasons young married couples divorce so readily today is because the wife is not economically dependent upon her husband; whenever difficulties and pressures arise she can say, as a young lady said to me, "I don't have to take this kind of thing; I can live by myself.""[35]

33. Brandt and Dowdy, *Building a Christian Home*, p. 56. Used by permission.
34. Clyde M. Narramore, *A Woman's World* (Grand Rapids: Zondervan Publishing House, 1963), p. 63. Used by permission.
35. La Haye, *Happy Though Married*, p. 29. Used by permission.

The disadvantage most often cited by working wives and mothers is lack of enough time and energy to devote to their husbands and children. Although the Women's Liberation Movement desires "a redefinition of marital roles that would assign equal responsibility to husbands and wives for performance of household duties and cares,"[36] this is not yet a reality.

Most wives and mothers still expect to play their traditional roles of caring for husbands and children, and they feel guilty when they cannot live up to their own expectations or those expectations of the spouse and children. Narramore quotes a working mother:

> "What bothers me is that I always give my best hours, my best disposition to someone other than my husband and children. They always see me at my worst. I go to work feeling fine. By the time I get home, I'm like a dishrag, and I'm afraid I'm as cranky as a witch. If I didn't have to go to work everyday, I could be giving my best to the ones I love most."[37]

Working outside the home may also limit the spiritual growth of the mother and of the family. She does not have time for periods of devotion with the Lord. "Starved spiritually, they have little time to read and meditate on the Word, little time for a mature prayer life . . . too busy to lead souls to Christ. In addition, their associates on the job may be a detrimental influence. When these same women go home to be with the Lord, they will be strangers to their own Savior."[38] However, some mothers who are well organized do find time to develop their spiritual lives and are capable witnesses for the Lord.

If the wife feels she should work, then she should seek to find some kind of work she can do in the home. Perhaps she can do babysitting for others and remain with her children while earning extra income for the family. Those with art and musical skills often give lessons in the home. The creative mother can usually find some work she can do in the home if she feels she must supplement the family income.

Some professional women, such as teachers and nurses with school-age children, find employment where working hours coincide with the school hours of the children. This enables them to be home when the children are. She still must face the problem of having sufficient energy to play her roles of wife and mother well when she does arrive home.

36. Leslie, *Family in Social Context*, p. 567.
37. Narramore, *A Woman's World*, p. 57. Used by permission
38. Ibid., pp. 57-58.

If a young couple enters marriage without large educational debts, and can save all that the wife earns until the children come, their financial situation should not require that the mother work, assuming, of course, that they learned to budget the husband's income and make wise financial decisions. Any mother with small children facing a decision to return to work outside the home needs to ponder well the words of Narramore:

> There is a place in the home which only a wife or mother can fill. A child doesn't especially need wall-to-wall carpeting and beautiful drapes or a car with the latest lines. But he *does* need his parents [italics his]. Many women who have made these choices now wish that they could go back and change their vote. Only after it was too late did they see what they and their children missed.[39]

THE NEED FOR A FAMILY BUDGET

Arch W. Troelstrup points out that the "three most important areas in family finance are budgeting, buymanship, and credit."[40] Good money management requires a budget, a plan for spending a limited income. The income of the average family is limited, so the money needs to be divided in order to supply the needs and wants of the family in the most satisfactory manner.

The Christian family needs to make sound financial decisions in order to have a strong testimony for the Lord before the secular families which surround it. John Bass has suggested that a good testimony includes financial responsibility.[41] A family that is forever in debt or which does not provide adequately for the needs of the children usually does not command the respect of the unsaved people. Occasionally, in the providence of God, a family may suffer financial reverses or chronic and expensive illness that result in poverty and distress, but still maintain a good testimony for the Lord.[42] Usually, the blessing of God implies the ability to meet the financial needs of the family according to the particular social level of the family in the community. A budget is one device that will help the family manage its income in a way that pleases the Lord.

39. Ibid., p. 59. Used by permission.
40. Arch W. Troelstrup, *Consumer Problems and Personal Finance* (New York: McGraw-Hill Book Co., 1965), p. 29.
41. John Bass, "Ten Ways to Stretch a Paycheck," *Moody Monthly*, December 1964, p. 23.
42. "Letters" to the editors, *Moody Monthly*, February 1973. Page 6 has an example of a family who ended up living in poverty due to unusual circumstances.

Careful budgeting has other advantages. David Schoenfeld and Arthur A. Natella list some of the more important ones:

1. A plan for spending enables a person to satisfy his short and long-term objectives.
2. A budget helps you to manage your money efficiently.
3. A budget forces the individual to place each single expenditure in proper focus.
4. A budget leads to better understanding of the power inherent in money.
5. A budget provides valuable economic education for the entire family.
6. A definite plan for handling your income gives you a feeling of well-being and security.[43]

The first step in preparing a budget is to determine short-term and long-term financial goals of the family.[44] The short-term goals will consist of certain expenses that are relatively fixed each month, such as tithes and offerings, rent or mortgage payments, insurance premiums, and certain installment payments. Long-term goals will include a fund for emergencies, savings, a vacation, college education for the children, and retirement. The fixed expenses and long-term expenses are added up for a month and subtracted from the monthly income. What is left is available for the day-to-day expenses such as groceries, clothing, recreation, and hobbies. This will provide a guideline for the distribution of the income each month.

A successful budget is also a flexible one.[45] The partners must agree to it, but it should be flexible enough to take care of unexpected needs such as a dress on sale, or emergency repairs for the auto. The emergency fund is built up over a period of time and may serve to meet such small items as a dress or auto repairs. However, the major purpose of the fund is to take care of larger items such as loss of income due to temporary unemployment or illness of the breadwinner, or unusually large medical bills.

There are several systems of handling money in a budget. Some couples prefer the "envelope" system whereby the money for each item is deposited in an envelope after the payday, then used as needed during the month. This system makes it fairly easy to determine how much money is available in any category at any time.

Other couples prefer to use a bookkeeping journal to list the

43. David Schoenfeld and Arthur A. Natella, *The Consumer and His Dollars* (Dobbs Ferry, NY: Oceana Publications, Inc., 1970), p. 150. Used with permission.

45. Jauncey, *Magic in Marriage*, p. 123.

disbursements each day and these are totaled at the end of the period to see how the money was spent and if it conformed to the budget. Office supply companies and stationery departments of larger stores carry reasonably priced home budget records that provide for the average budget. Printed columns for each month of the year, plus several pages for financial records, simplify budget keeping for the average couple. The disadvantage of this method is the obvious bookkeeping involved, and the necessity of each partner to keep track of money paid out.

The third method widely used is the checking account system. The money is deposited each payday into a checking account. Then the partners pay all bills and make all purchases by check. A check is written for the savings account. One check is cashed to provide spending money for the couple. The check stubs provide a record of the spending for the period. The disadvantage here is that the couple must be sure to carry a checkbook with them at all times, as very little cash is used in this system.

The couple should remember the purpose of a budget is to help them manage their money more efficiently to the glory of God. Whenever spending habits have been established over a period of time, it may be possible to dispense with a formal budget. In like manner, if the techniques of keeping a budget become a source of friction between the spouses, it would be better to give up the budget system. However, the couple must have some kind of spending plan or else they may encounter financial problems. "Financial success does not depend upon a wishbone—it must be planned."[46]

Bowman has written an excellent book for Christians entitled, *How to Succeed with Your Money*. It is very practical and should be read by every young couple before establishing a budget. He makes the suggestion that the amount of income left after taxes and tithe are paid should be divided according to the "10-70-20" plan.[47] The first 10 percent left should be devoted to savings and investments, the next 70 percent to living expenses, and the last 20 percent to be used for debts and as a buffer fund. He writes that the 10 percent of a net income of $350 or $35 invested in a cross section of securities earning an average of 6 percent compounded yearly will amount to $33,205.20 in thirty years or a gain of $20,605.20 on the $12,600 invested.

He points out that people who make it a habit to save 10 percent never miss it. Some just assume they have received a 10 percent cut in pay and live on the rest. This same principle applies to living on 70

46. Bowman, *Succeed with Your Money*, p. 46.
47. Ibid., pp. 129-135. Used with permission.

percent of the disposable income. A family lives on whatever their income is whether $300 a month or $3000 a month. Thus, a couple can live on 70 percent of their income if they determine to do so. The final 20 percent can be used to pay debts if necessary. When not used for debt requirement, this amount can also be saved and invested. Such a view requires self-discipline, but the couple who will practice some self-discipline and self-denial will be pleasantly surprised at how much they have to give to the Lord's work.

CONSUMER ORGANIZATIONS

Much information is available to the consumer. Wise Christian stewardship and good budgeting require that the individual or the family be informed consumers. The government is giving more attention to the needs of the consumer.[48]

> The establishment of the many departments of consumer affairs and consumer protection bureaus as official agencies of our City, State, and Federal government and the enactment of truth in lending and truth in advertising legislation is proof, if there need be any, of the recognition of the need to protect consumers, even against their own improvidence.[49]

The Office of Consumer Affairs has replaced the President's Committee on Consumer Interests established in 1964. This gave, "for the first time, American consumers . . . a top level representative in the executive branch, with White House status and access to the national news media that this carries."[50]

Several organizations have existed for many years to aid the consumer, "focusing a spotlite of publicity on fraudulent [business] operations and by providing information and protection which in the long run will benefit the ethical members of the business community."[51]   A Better Business Bureau exists in all large cities. They receive complaints from dissatisfied customers and discourage illegitimate or unethical business practices.[52]   They also publish pamphlets that are very informative to the consumer.

48. Troelstrup, *Consumer Problems*, p. 18.
49. Michael G. West, "Desclaimer of Warranties—Its Curse and Possible Cure," ed. Gordon E. Bivens, *The Journal of Consumer Affairs*, Winter 1971, p. 169.
50. Troelstrup, *Consumer Problems*, p. 18.
51. Schoenfeld and Natella, *Consumer and Dollars*, p. 51. Chapter 2, pages 17-35 of this book lists governmental agencies of interest to the consumer.
52. Sidney Margolius, *The Innocent Consumer vs. The Exploiters* (New York: Trident Press, 1967), pp. 156-157. Margolius says that "home improvements are the latest single problem area for the Better Business Bureau and have continued to be year after year in most cities."

Two large independent agencies buy products on the open market, test them, and then report the results in a magazine. Consumers Union publishes *Consumer Reports*, and Consumers' Research publishes *Consumers' Research Magazine* (formerly *Consumers' Bulletin*).[53] The Consumers Union also studies other areas of great interest such as life insurance and family planning and publishes their findings in separate volumes. Each December they issue a *Buying Guide* of nearly five hundred pages covering items tested in prior years and includes an excellent chapter on "Consumer Information." Many times the magazines recommend products that cost much less than some name brands and yet are of a better quality. These magazines are in public libraries, but the information is so valuable it is recommended that the family subscribe to one in order to have it available in the home. The regular use of such a magazine will help fortify the buyer against high-pressure advertising, and enable him to save considerable sums on large items. One person wanted to purchase a color television set. He consulted the *Consumer Reports* on color television sets and noticed one brand had the lowest frequency-of-repair record. He was able to purchase a year-old model for half the price of a new one at a household auction, and in three years it only required the replacement of two small tubes.

Some magazines also test articles advertised in their pages and then guarantee them to be as advertised. *Good Housekeeping* and *Parents* magazines feature this service for the consumer. *Good Housekeeping* also features a special section of consumer information. *Better Homes and Gardens* regularly has features that are very helpful to consumers. Some of the magazines such as *Popular Mechanics* and *Mechanics Illustrated* often test autos and give the results in their pages. Any public library has numerous magazines and books to help the consumer make intelligent purchases, but the buyer must read and be informed in order to take advantage of these sources.

THE USE OF CREDIT

The American economic system is based on the widespread use of credit, and wise Christian stewardship necessitates a proper understanding of credit and how to use it.

Some individuals prefer to save their money and pay cash for everything they buy except a home. This has the advantages of enabling the person to buy when things are on sale, or where he can

---

53. Ibid., pp. 41-47. Pages 53-56 lists industrial and professional associations of concern to consumers.

get the best price. Such a person never has to be concerned about debts since he never incurs any. The disadvantage is that the cash buyer does not have a credit rating which he may need at sometime. For example, a family with six children were able to rent a home in Pennsylvania, but when the husband was transferred to Ohio, it was necessary to buy a home, since it was impossible to find a landlord who would rent to a family with six children. The husband had great difficulty in securing a loan for a mortgage as he had no credit rating in Pennsylvania since he had always paid cash for everything.

If a couple prefers to follow a "cash only" buying policy, they should establish credit by taking a "passbook loan" at their local bank, or by buying some items on a "ninety-days same as cash" basis. Each community has a credit bureau, and when a person moves to a new community, the credit bureau in that town can get a reference from the office in the place of previous residence. It is very important for the couple who always pay cash to establish a good credit rating in case it is needed.

Most major items in the budget such as an auto or furniture are bought by many couples on the installment plan. A down payment is made and monthly payments are then paid until the principal amount plus interest is paid. This form of credit has helped to create the high standard of living that Americans enjoy, for it enables many people to own products that would be impossible if they had to save and pay cash for the total amount. One wonders how many new cars would be sold if the buyers had to pay cash.

Easy credit has been a disadvantage for many families with low sales resistance. They tend to purchase too many items on the installment plan, so that the payments consume too much of their income. They are unable to meet their payments or to save some money for emergencies such as illness of the breadwinner or temporary unemployment. Instead of enjoying life, it becomes one long struggle to make ends meet.[54] Some authorities in the consumer education field estimate that one-third of the young families in America are only one paycheck away from bankruptcy.

One suggestion to avoid such financial stringency is to buy only one major item on the installment plan at a time. A person paying for a car on a monthly basis should avoid buying a new color television set until the car is paid off. If the black and white set needs repairs, it should be fixed. This type of financial plan requires discipline and self-denial for success, but this is true for success in any area of life. God is not pleased with Christians who are unable to

---

54. Schoenfeld and Natella, *Consumer and Dollars*, pp. 176-177. An example is given of a young couple who filed for bankruptcy with debts of $3,160.

meet their financial obligations, or with those who are so hard
pressed financially that they cannot give generously to His work.

Each family must face the question of using credit cards, either
those from companies such as Sears or Penneys or from banks such
as Visa or Master Charge. Credit cards are easy to use and the bank
cards present a record of all transactions during the month, an aid to
budget keeping. The bank cards also have the advantage that if one is
lost or stolen, there is only one company to notify, whereas if a
person were to lose his wallet with several company cards, it would
mean several companies would need to be notified. However, these
cards make it easy for individuals to buy things they don't need or
can't afford. Impulsive buyers certainly should avoid the use of
credit cards.

Whenever it is necessary to borrow money, the individual *should
shop for the lowest net interest cost.* The Truth in Lending Act
requires the lender to state the true annual rate and the total interest
cost for any loan made.[55] If a family has a savings account in a bank
or savings and loan institution, it is possible to take out a "passbook
loan." The bank loans the money with the individual's savings as
security and the passbook to the account is kept by the bank. There
are two advantages to this type of loan. The savings are not spent and
continue to earn interest. This results in the second advantage of a
low net interest cost. If a person borrows $1000 at 6 percent for one
year, the interest cost is $60. His savings earn 5 percent interest or
$50. Thus, the net cost for borrowing the $1000 is $10 or 1 percent
interest. The loan is usually limited to 90 percent of the account, and
may be paid back in one lump sum or in monthly installments.

If an individual does not have a savings account on which to
borrow, he might have cash value in a life insurance policy on which
a loan can be made. These loans usually carry a lower annual interest
rate, but they do not have to be repaid since the loan can be taken
out of the policy proceeds on the death of the policy holder. An
individual may pay interest on a loan for years and years, which is
not good money management.

Another source of credit is a credit union, if one is a member. The
interest rate may be lower, but it should be compared with the other
sources of credit.

It is usually unwise to borrow from a small loan company. These
companies cater primarily to people with poor credit ratings. Consequently, the state which charters these companies permits them to
charge higher interest rates than those charged by other lending

55. Ibid., p. 189.

institutions. A typical rate is 1½ percent per month on the unpaid balance or approximately 18 percent per year. Any unpaid interest on a missed monthly installment is added to the amount, and interest must be paid on the interest also the following month. If an individual cannot secure a loan from any other source, it is a good sign he should not borrow the money.

Occasionally it is possible to borrow from relatives and friends. This may result in a lower interest cost, but it also may cause hard feelings if payments are missed. There are times, such as borrowing for a down payment on a home, when an individual may lack sufficient collateral for a loan and the only source may be a relative or friend who has confidence in the individual's ability to repay the loan. However, as a general rule, it is best for personal relationships to avoid borrowing from friends and relatives unless it is absolutely necessary.

Buying on credit is a part of American family life, but it must be used intelligently. George Bowman says, "Uncontrolled credit buying is the best proof I know to support the statement that dollars and *sense* [italics his] do not always go together. Credit buying can be a blessing or a curse. It becomes a curse when we fail to control it." [56] In another place he warns, "Never agree to pay a monthly payment that will eat into your savings, hurt your family's standard of living, or send you into heavy debt. Surely one does not need very much intelligence to realize that to make such sacrifices in order to buy on credit is wrong." [57] A proper understanding of Christian stewardship should enable the young couple to limit the use of credit and avoid stress in their marriage caused by financial problems.

MAKING A WILL

Many couples neglect to make a will, but good stewardship involves the making of a will immediately after marriage, since a couple will have some assets at that time. As the financial worth of the family improves, it becomes even more important to have a will. If a person dies without a will, the state will dispose of the property according to state laws. This may impose real restrictions and even hardship on the wife and children. [58]

56. Bowman, *Succeed with Your Money*, p. 51. Used by permission.
57. Ibid., p. 53.
58. D. G. Kehl, "Keep Your Money Alive," ed. J. Allan Petersen, *The Marriage Affair* (Wheaton, IL: Tyndale House Publishers, 1971), p. 356.

Most Christian organizations today have a stewardship department that will help a family plan a will that realizes tax savings where possible, and that enables the couple to exercise their Christian stewardship toward Christian organizations. The actual writing of a will is done by a lawyer for a very nominal fee. D. G. Kehl makes the following remarks:

> The only thing worse than having no will at all is having a defective one. . . . Consequently, preparing a will is not a do-it-yourself proposition. Lawyers charge as little as $20 for drawing up a will, and even a detailed one rarely costs more than $50. E. N. Harrison disposed of an 80 million dollar railroad empire with a will of ninety-nine words, possibly costing as little as $10.[59]

Whenever there are minor children, it is necessary for the parents to designate a person to serve as their guardian in case something happens to both parents.[60] This may be made part of the will. Usually state law requires the guardian to be a resident of the state where the children live. If no guardian is designated, the court is at liberty to appoint one of its choosing, and this may not be in the best interest of the Christian family. Certainly the children of Christian parents should be reared in a Christian atmosphere, so it is incumbent upon parents to see that a Christian guardian is designated for their children.

In the parable of the unjust steward, Jesus said, ". . . the children of this world are in their generation wiser than the children of light" (Luke 16:8). It is disappointing to see Christians who do not manage the money God entrusts to them as well as their unsaved neighbors. Christians should discipline themselves in their spending habits and hold to a savings and investment plan that will enable them to give more to God. In view of the "pay day" at the judgment seat of Christ (II Cor. 5:10, Williams' Translation), it is important that the money received each "pay day" here be used wisely for the glory of God.

---

59. Ibid., p. 358.
60. The new law giving young people the right to vote at eighteen does not give them full legal rights. Some states are making this change, but the age for legal maturity continues to be twenty-one in some states.

QUESTIONS FOR DISCUSSION AND REVIEW

1. Why is there so much conflict over money in American marriages?

2. How does the concept of "Christian stewardship" differ from the concept of "tithing"?

3. Is it true that "one must have more in order to give more?"

4. Is it always necessary for the husband to handle the money?

5. Discuss the question, "Should the wife work outside the home?"

6. What factors need to be considered when designing a family budget?

7. Explain George M. Bowman's "10-70-20" plan.

8. In what ways are magazines such as *Consumer Reports* and *Consumers' Research* helpful?

9. Discuss the proper role of credit in a Christian family.

10. Why should a Christian make a will?

12

MAJOR PURCHASES
AND INVESTMENT

. . . lay up for yourselves treasures in heaven. . .
Matthew 6:20

Every family has certain major purchases to make that will consume a large share of the family income. The ability to buy these items wisely largely determines how much of the disposable family income is left for savings and investments. If young couples take the suggestion of George M. Bowman and determine to save at least 10 percent of their income before spending any for living expenses, and if they learn to manage well these major items in the budget, they should not have any great difficulty with their Christian stewardship.[1]

THE PURCHASE OF A HOME

Most young families start married life in a rented apartment or home. An increasing number are discovering that a mobile home provides good housing at a reasonable cost, particularly if the couple buys a used one that has depreciated in value. A new mobile home decreases about 20 percent the first year and about 7 percent annually in following years.[2] It is not good stewardship to buy a new mobile

1. George M. Bowman, *Here's How to Succeed with Your Money*, (Chicago: Moody Press, 1960), pp. 126-135.
2. Sylvia Porter, "Basic Economics of Mobile Homes," *Xenia Daily Gazette*, January 18, 1971, p. 10.

home due to the depreciation loss, but one that is two or three years old may be a wise purchase if it meets the needs of the couple.

There are times when it is better for a family to rent rather than to buy a home. If a family intends to be in an area for only two or three years, the costs associated with buying and selling a home may make it economically undesireable for the family to buy a home, and it would be better to rent. Many retired families or individuals find the upkeep and maintenance of a home are too great, and prefer to sell the home and buy a condominium where a fee is paid for maintenance, or else rent an apartment.[3] Many such retired individuals are also discovering that mobile home living, particularly in parks that cater to adults only, has many advantages, especially in warm climates such as Florida and California.

Whenever a family intends to be settled in an area for a long period of time, it is best from a financial viewpoint to buy a home. The person who pays rent does not build up any equity or value in a home. "In other words, if you live for ten years in an apartment that has a monthly rental of $175, you will spend $21,000 over the ten-year period, assuming that the rental is always the same. This money will have been spent and no part of it can ever be recovered by the tenant."[4] For the person who buys a home, a part of each mortgage payment is credited to the principal of the loan, and month by month the homeowner's equity is increased. For the past two decades inflation has also contributed about 2 percent per year to the value of real estate so that the homeowner has gained added value. Both interest costs and real estate taxes are deductible from the federal income tax. The person who rents forfeits these economic advantages.

The advantage of buying a home over renting one is well illustrated in a study done by the editors of *Better Homes and Gardens*. They projected the cost of a $20,000 home over a twenty-year period and compared this to a renter paying a rental of 13 percent of the value of the house each year. The results are clearly in favor of buying after two years. If the house inflates in value at 2 percent annually, after twenty years the owner would be $40,000 better off than the renter. If the value of the house remains unchanged, in twenty years the gain over renting is $21,000. Even if the house

3. David Schoenfeld and Arthur A. Natella, *The Consumer and His Dollars*, (Dobbs Ferry, NY: Oceana Publications, Inc., 1970), pp. 201-203.
4. Ibid., p. 202.

depreciates 2 percent annually for twenty years, the buyer is still $11,000 ahead of the renter.[5] With increased inflation, the same type of study on a $60,000 home would show a much greater disparity between buying and renting.

After a decision has been made to buy rather than rent, the family is faced with yet another important question. Should they buy or build? Before this decision is made, the couple should visit the library and do some extensive reading. In view of the large amount of money involved, it would certainly be worth investing in the helpful book, *Building or Buying the High-Quality House at Lowest Cost* by A. M. Watkins.[6] He indicates the items to check in buying an old house, and tells how to determine good construction in a new home. The closing chapter is a checklist of 175 items that need to be considered in either building or buying a house.[7] Also discussed are the role of the real estate broker, methods of financing, and other related matters. No family should build or buy until they have read widely enough to become an informed consumer in this area. The advice of parents and friends, especially those involved in the construction industry, are of great value in making this important decision.

When the family has resolved to buy or build their own home, they must decide how much to pay for one and how to finance it. A family should buy a home that fits their income and budget. Some suggest that a house should not cost more than "2½ times one's annual income. Preferably, to be on the safe side, the price should be no more than twice one's annual earnings. . . . Total monthly costs should be no more than one week's take-home pay. One week's take-home pay should equal 1 percent of the purchase price of the house."[8]

After the amount that the family can afford to pay has been decided upon, they usually need to secure a mortgage to help buy or build the house. There are two major types of mortgages—the conventional loan or a government insured loan such as V.A. or F.H.A.[9] A conventional loan may be either a fixed rate or an adjustable rate (ARM). A young family usually pays 10 percent down on a conven-

5. Peter Lindberg, "Is a Home Still a Good Investment?" *Better Homes and Gardens*, September 1969, pp. 46-54.
6. A. M. Watkins, *Building or Buying the High-Quality House at Lowest Cost*, (New York: Dolphin Books, Doubleday & Co., Inc., 1962).
7. Ibid., pp. 249-259. See also George Huffman, *How to Inspect a House* (Reading, MA: Addison-Wesley Publishing Co., 1985.)
8. Schoenfeld and Natella, *Consumer and Dollars*, p. 206.
9. Watkins, *Building or Buying*, pp. 208-215.

tional mortgage. To purchase a $50,000 home requires a down payment of $5,000 in order to secure a $45,000 conventional mortgage. A similar home could be purchased with an F.H.A. loan for $48,000 and a down payment of only $2,000. The reason for the smaller down payment is that the government guarantees the loan, and agrees to assume the mortgage if the borrower defaults on his payments. Both loans also require payment of closing costs.

Sometimes it is possible for a couple to assume a loan granted to the prior owner. The big advantage is that in a time of rising interest rates, the mortgage is assumed at a lower interest rate. This can mean a considerable savings over the life of the loan. This type of procedure usually requires a larger down payment, for the buyer has to pay the seller for his equity in the house.[11]

Interest rates may vary and in most communities some financial institutions have better reputations than others, so it is very important for the prospective homeowner to shop for the lowest interest rates. The best financial planning requires as large a down payment as possible and the lowest interest rate available. To illustrate, the interest cost of a $45,000 mortgage over twenty years at 10 percent is $59,222.20. The same mortgage over twenty years at 12 percent has an interest cost of $73,917.60, or an additional $14,695.20 for the same mortgage.

A similar savings in interest cost can be achieved by making the mortgage for as short a term as possible. The $45,000 at 12 percent paid off in 20 years with monthly payments of $495.49 has a total interest cost of $73,917.60. If the period is extended to thirty years with monthly payments of $462.88, the interest cost almost doubles to $121,636.80. If the newlyweds save the wife's salary for several years, a sizeable amount can be paid down on a home, and it can be paid off in a much shorter period of time. The interest rates vary with the economy, but it will pay for the couple to shop for the best possible interest rates.

The importance of having a lawyer care for the legal details for the buyer of real estate cannot be overemphasized.[12] His costs are very

10. According to John Pohlman, a Vice-President of Home Federal Savings and Loan, Xenia, Ohio, there is a trend for many families to take out fixed rate mortgages with 20 percent down and for shorter terms such as 15 years. cent, which is included in the closing costs.
11. Watkins, *Building or Buying*, p. 217.
12. Arch W. Troelstrup, *Consumer Problems and Personal Finance* (New York: McGraw-Hill Book Co., 1965), p. 275. Chapter 10, "A Home for Your Family," is a very thorough presentation.

nominal in relationship to the total cost of a home. He can check to see that the title to the property is clear and free from all claims. He can advise concerning the signing of a contract to buy.

It is also important to have the property surveyed if the property lines are not clearly indicated by surveyor's pins. Stories abound of people buying a home and discovering that half their garage is on the neighbor's property. Again, the cost of surveying is small compared to the possible cost of moving a garage.

If a young family is willing to practice what the sociologists term "deferred gratification" in buying a new home, and make their first real estate purchase an income-producing property, they can enjoy a better home later. The idea is that the person defers present gratification in order to enjoy greater pleasure in the future. If a couple buys a duplex or small apartment building first, and live in one apartment until they have a good equity in it, then they can use this equity and the income from the apartments to afford a nicer home at a later date.[13] This implies that they be willing to assume the obligations of a landlord in exchange for the added income. It also means for the Christian that he will have additional income to use for the work of Christ.

Buying a mobile home may also be deferred gratification. When the couple are ready to buy a regular home, they rent the mobile home, which will give them a good return on their investment and increase the amount of income available for their needs and for giving to the Lord's work. The "children of this world" (Luke 16:8) use every legitimate means to increase their assets and wealth for selfish gratification, and it is incumbent upon the Christian steward to see that his assets are put to their best advantage for the glory of God. Many times this involves his assuming the role of landlord in order to make the best use of money available for housing.

After the home is bought, the lender requires that it be insured. Most companies issue a "homeowners policy" that covers losses by wind, hail, fire, and vandalism. Most policies also provide personal liability coverage which protects the homeowner from law suits arising from a person who injures himself on the property. Some also protect against losses from burglary. These policies are usually written for a three-year term which saves paperwork for the company, but it also protects the owner against a rise in premium during that period, a good feature in a time of inflation.[14] The homeowner must

13. The new home can be purchased by using the equity in the apartment building to secure a "blanket mortgage" covering both the apartments and the new home.
14. Troelstrup, *Consumer Problems*, p. 288.

shop for the best buy in insurance coverage, as the price for identical coverage varies from company to company. If possible, the policy should have an "inflation clause" which automatically increases coverage to keep pace with inflation.

THE PURCHASE OF AN AUTOMOBILE

The largest single purchase a family ever makes is that of a home, but they spend many more dollars over the life of the marriage for automobiles.[15] The American economy is largely based on the production and sale of new autos. It provides a livelihood to one American out of seven.[16] The credit business thrives on the financing of autos as most are bought on the installment plan with monthly payments.[17] Autos have become so important as status symbols to so many Americans that it is not difficult for the industry to sell eight to ten million new cars annually. Consequently, the money spent for payments, gas and oil, and maintenance consume a good percentage of the average American family's budget. Social pressure to "keep up with the Joneses" motivates many people to buy new or expensive autos as status symbols even though they cannot afford them.

Since Christians are influenced by these same cultural pressures, many of them have had their values warped by society and have joined in the race to achieve social status. They have forgotten that the *major purpose* of an auto should be to provide transportation rather than to function as a status symbol. Consequently, they spend money for expensive autos, funds that should have been used in the Lord's work or saved for their children's education, their retirement, or some other financial goal of the family.

A Christian family must decide whether their auto is going to serve as transportation or as a status symbol. Since a new car depreciates roughly one-third in value for each of the first three years, it is impossible to justify the purchase of a new car for transportation. An ad for Volvo cars once showed a man putting a "For Sale" sign in the window of his old car. The ad read, "You don't buy a new car. The bank buys a new car. By the time you buy your car back from the

15. Schoenfeld and Natella, *Consumer and Dollars*, p. 125.
16. "Detroit's Gamble to Get Rolling Again," *Time*, February 10, 1975, p. 69. Consumer Finances Association, 1971), p. 47.
17. Unfortunately, many families accept these payments as a way of life and are never able to pay cash and avoid the high interest costs.

bank, it's old!"[18] The only thing the buyer receives for the $2000 or more in depreciation the first year is the status feeling of owning a new car. Today new cars are usually financed on a 48- to 60-month basis while the trade-in cycle is from 42 to 48 months. When a new car is bought to replace the worn-out one, the unpaid balance of the old loan is added to the new loan.[19] Christian stewardship demands that this money be more wisely used as savings, investments, or as a contribution to the Lord's work.[20]

Some years ago people justified buying a new car by saying they were getting rid of problems or avoiding prospective problems. New cars were supposed to be, and usually were, relatively free from problems for many thousands of miles. However, in recent years the quality control exercised in the manufacture of new cars has been so poor that many of them arrive from the factory with mechanical or body defects commonly referred to as "bugs." Consequently, today a person may have fewer problems buying a slightly used car that has had the "bugs" corrected by the first owner. The following is the experience with a "new" car related by Thurman Moore, a student in a Marriage & Family class.

Feb. 28, 1972 I purchased a new Ford LTD wagon. The sticker price was $5183. I traded in a 1969 LTD wagon in perfect condition. In fact, I had just replaced the brake shoes and run it through a diagnostic check the week before. The new wagon however was a different story; it really took me for a ride.

We drove our new wagon home that evening and parked it in the garage. The next morning we stared at the garage floor, all covered with slick new transmission fluid. With less than 100 miles on our new auto we faced repair #1. Result: the loss of eight hours work and the transmission only temporarily fixed.

Problem #2 concerned the brakes. I tried to explain to the service department that the pedal should not extend to within two inches of the floor but they told us that it was a new car and it would adjust. We then called Cincinnati, and the representative found that the wrong linkage had been installed on the production line. Result: the loss of eight hours work, phone bill, upset nerves, etc.

Problem #3 wasn't so bad. The window on the driver's side, when

---

18. *Newsweek*, October 23, 1967, p. 13.

19. Many families are leasing cars because monthly payments are cheaper, but it is better to buy, for in the end, the buyer has his car free and clear.

20. It is always distressing to hear students whose families drive new cars tell of their difficulty in working their way through college when the depreciation on their parents' auto would pay a sizeable amount of their college education. One student did relate how his family drove the same car for twelve years in order to completely finance his education!

rolled up, had an air space of ¾ of an inch. Result: After an argument with the service department, it was fixed.

Problem #4 was the real one. At the grand old age of 400 miles the differential began to clang and grind. Naturally the service department said there was nothing wrong and to drive it that way until it went out. Another phone call to Cincinnati and then two weeks without our new car while it was being repaired.

Then one day the parts finally came in for the transmission. Result: the loss of eight hours work and a two-mile hike home.

There were other problems. For example, the front end needed alignment. Cost: $8.00. And the motor missed. By this time I was tired of arguing with them so I fixed it. Result: the cost of points, plugs, etc.

However, we finally got our new wagon patched up. . . .well, almost. . . .the transmission will now change gears beautifully if you lift your foot from the accelerator and allow it to change.

Our neighbors purchased our wagon from the dealer. Know what? That's right, he hasn't missed one day's work.

If the family decides that basically the auto should serve as transportation and not as a status symbol, then they need to study carefully how they can best spend their money for transportation. *"For the average one-car family use, the best used-car buy is a recent model of a subcompact, compact, intermediate, or lower priced full-sized line [Italics his].*"[21] The size of the family and the daily use of the car are the major factors in making this choice. If the car is used for long trips, consideration should be given to an intermediate or full-sized car. Many families find that a subcompact or compact model is adequate when most of the driving is for relatively short distances.[22]

Subcompacts such as Spirit, Pinto, and Omni enable American manufacturers to compete with the economy foreign cars. The gas mileage may not be as good as some of the imported cars, but parts availability and the lower cost of repairs give them a decided advantage over the imports.

A good used foreign car such as a Volkswagen, Renault, Toyota, or Datsun may give good economical transportation. Some makes such as the Volkswagen hold their resale value well, but some models depreciate greatly in the first couple of years. Japanese cars such as Toyota and Datsun have improved in quality and may make good used car buys. Tires on the small foreign car can get two to three times the mileage of tires on bigger American cars. However, many

21. "Buying Guide," *Consumer Reports*, (Mt. Vernon, NY: Consumers Union of United States, Inc., December 1972), p. 395.
22. Ibid., p. 389.

owners of imported cars get discouraged with the high cost of mechanical repairs, a factor which often cancels out the savings on gasoline bills.

The buyer should read and become informed on how to buy a good used car. The December issue of *Buying Guide of Consumer Reports*, and the April issue of each year feature excellent articles on the subject.[23] The April issue is devoted to cars and lists the frequency of repair record of various makes. This informs the buyer as to which models would make good used car buys and which models should be avoided. Some models develop a reputation for certain mechanical troubles, particularly when a new model is introduced, and it is wise not to buy one of them.

One should follow some basic principles in seeking to get the best used car buy. One is that the mileage the car has been driven is more important than its age. As far as basic transportation is concerned, a three-year-old car with 80,000 miles for $4000 does not have as many miles of transportation left as a five-year-old car with 35,000 miles for $2000. The latter is a much better bargain than the former and only half the price, assuming, of course, that both have equally good bodies and interiors.

It is also wise to shop for a low-mileage car at the dealers of prestige cars such as Cadillac, Oldsmobile, Lincoln, or Chrysler. Here the informed buyer can take advantage of social status, for many people who drive the more expensive autos may drive lower priced cars as a second car. In order to keep up with their neighbors they have to trade their cars in even though they do not have many miles on them.[24] Thus, the prospects of finding even a Ford or Chevrolet with low mileage is better at the prestige dealers. The individual who trades a Ford or Chevrolet in to a dealer of that make is more likely to own only one car which will be driven by all members of the family and is more likely to have high mileage.

It is also wise to buy only from a franchised dealer. Although there are exceptions, the franchised dealers will sell their less desirable used cars to the independent dealers either directly or through a dealer's auction. Ordinarily the best used cars are kept by the franchised dealers.

In some areas where there are plants owned by the auto manufacturers, the executives are allowed to buy cars at a reduced price each

---

23. Ibid., p. 395-417. Good suggestions for "Buying a Used Car."
24. The author once found a five year-old car with 17,000 miles which had only been driven in the summer by the wife of a wealthy real estate broker. Such cars are to be found but it takes time to locate them.

year. The executives then sell them at the end of a model year. Many times it is possible to buy such a late-model car on which some of the depreciation has already taken place. Since a dealer allows only the wholesale price to the person trading in a car, which is usually $500 to $600 less than the retail price, many individuals will try to sell their cars privately and hope to realize more for their auto than the dealer will allow. This is a good way to buy a car, particularly where the seller bought the car new. Many times a service record may be available, and some cars carry a guarantee that is transferable. There is a charge connected with this transfer and the buyer has to decide if the benefits promised are worth the $25 to $50 which it costs to transfer the warranty.

Diagnostic centers are a new development which can be very helpful to the prospective buyer of a used car. These centers will run up to two hundred different tests on the car at the cost of only $30 to $60. If the diagnostic center is connected with a garage, the prospective buyer must make it plain that he does not own the car and does not intend to have any repairs made by the center. This is important, because Ralph Nader's Center for Auto Safety discovered that the diagnostic centers connected with repair garages are not as impartial as those which do not make repairs.   Margaret B. Carlson, formerly associated with the Center for Auto Safety and Ronald G. Shafer have written a book entitled, *How to Get Your Car Repaired Without Getting Gypped.* Every car owner who has little knowledge of auto mechanics should have a copy.

If a diagnostic center is not available, and if the prospective buyer does not feel competent to judge the mechanical aspects of the car selected for purchase, then he should hire a trusted mechanic to inspect it to see if it will soon need major repairs.

If a car passes these tests without indicating the need for expensive repairs, the prospective buyer can feel much safer in purchasing the used car. If extensive repairs are needed, then the car should not be bought unless the seller will make the repairs indicated.

Another principle in buying any used car is to plan to spend at least $200 for a tune-up and minor repairs. If tires are needed, this amount will need to be increased. It is better to plan on an occasional repair bill on a good used car, than to be burdened down with

25. Margaret B. Carlson and Ronald G. Shafer, *How to Get Your Car Repaired Without Getting Gypped*, (New York: Harper & Row, 1973), pp. 36-40. One individual ran a used car through such a diagnostic center and it indicated that it needed new spark plugs and a ball joint on the front wheel. Since the car was priced under the prevailing market price, he felt safe in buying it. Thousands of miles of trouble-free driving vindicated his judgment.

large monthly payments on a new car which hardly match the monthly depreciation. Tires can be bought very reasonably if the buyer looks for sales on factory blemished tires, tires with discontinued tread designs or new car "take-offs." Some new car buyers like a particular brand of tire so much that when they buy a new car, they go to a tire dealer and buy a set of the brand they like. The tire dealer then sells the take-offs at a discount of up to 50 percent. These types of tires are not always available, so it pays to begin shopping for them a month or two before they are actually needed.

If a person cannot pay cash for a car, he must secure a loan. Here he must shop for credit to find the lowest net interest cost for the loan. The dealer often tries to influence the buyer to secure a loan from the auto manufacturer's loan company, but it is not necessary to get the loan through the dealer, and it will probably be cheaper somewhere else.[26] The usual sources of credit such as a credit union or a bank should be explored, and the loan secured from the institution with the *lowest net interest cost.*

When the car is purchased, it must be insured. Most states require the auto owner to carry personal liability and property damage liability. This will usually be a minimum figure but higher coverage such as $50,000-$100,000 costs only a few dollars more per year and is recommended.[27] The lending institution will require the auto purchaser to carry protection against collision. This is usually a "deductible" policy whereby the owner pays the first $50 or $100 and the insurance company the remainder of the damage bill. The higher deductible ($100) is recommended. When a car gets old and its value decreases, collision insurance can be dropped, as it is no longer feasible. The lending institution also requires comprehensive coverage which takes care of loss by fire, theft, or vandalism. This is not very expensive and should be continued after the loan is paid off.

Optional coverages include medical payments which are inexpensive and worthwhile in view of the high cost of medical services. Some states which do not require all auto owners to have insurance, give the buyer of insurance the option to take out coverage for the "uninsured motorist." If the policyholder has a claim against an uninsured motorist for personal injury, the policyholder's own insur-

26. S. Lees Booth, *1971 Finance Facts*, p. 48. Of the $35.5 billion on car loans, about $10.0 billion is owed to finance companies "most of which was financed by the subsidiaries of the manufacturers, that is GMAC, Ford Credit, and Chrysler Credit. "

27. "Buying Guide," December 1972, p. 436. A good presentation of auto insurance including "Ratings" of twenty-four different auto insurance companies.

ance company reimburses him for his loss. When the coverages needed have been determined, the *buyer must shop* to get the best rate, as rates may vary as much as $150 between different companies for the same coverage. A car dealer may try to sell the buyer insurance, or maybe the company making the loan also sells insurance, but the buyer is under no obligation to either. He should contact various companies and *get the best price* for the coverage he needs.

"No-fault" auto insurance, whereby each motorist involved in an accident would be paid by his own insurance company for any loss up to a specified amount, is becoming more common. Each state that has enacted no-fault auto insurance legislation has its own peculiar regulations, so you should become familiar with the provisions in your state.

Just as a person seeks out a good doctor and lawyer when he moves into a community, he should also look for a good, honest mechanic. These people are discovered by asking friends and associates who performs these services for them. Once a good mechanic that can be trusted is discovered, he should be given your business whenever possible, for such men need to be encouraged.[28] A dependable mechanic is fairly accurate in diagnosing problems and stands behind his work. However, do not expect perfection, for an auto is a complicated piece of equipment, and at times it is very difficult for even the best mechanic to pinpoint the source of some problems.

Much of the routine maintenance on a car can be performed by the average person who is willing to learn by reading an auto repair manual. A *Motors Repair Manual* costs approximately $15 to $20 and is filled with information which the care owner can use.[29] Many people live near vocational or technical high schools that offer evening courses in auto mechanics such as tune-up and engine rebuilding. Such courses are very inexpensive. A few evenings spent in such a course can save hundreds of dollars on tune-ups alone over a period of years.

28. Charles Bresnihan, "Confessions of an Auto Mechanic," *Parade*, March 22, 1970, pp. 6-9. The writer presents some of the "tricks of the trade" used to defraud customers, and also presents suggestions on how to find a good mechanic.

29. Auto repair manuals can sometimes be borrowed from the public library, or they can be purchased in bookstores or through the mail order catalogs. If a person plans to keep a car several years, he can usually buy a "factory manual" through the dealer for his particular make or model. See *Better Homes and Gardens*, March 1972, page 29 for an article on do-it-yourself car repairs and a suggested list of tools needed.

Where the source of difficulty is known, such as a faulty carburetor, it is usually cheaper to buy a rebuilt one from a mail order house such as Sears or Wards and replace the entire assembly. It usually costs more to have a mechanic work on it and there is no assurance he can correct the problem. Washing and waxing a car are also jobs that the owner can do to help preserve the appearance of the car.

For the individuals whose status-needs are so great they can only be fulfilled by driving a car newer than the "Joneses," the expense of buying and maintaining such a car takes a good percentage of the family budget. For those who are satisfied with good, safe, dependable transportation rather than a status symbol, the auto is not a burden but a blessing, allowing the owner to have more and give more to God.

THE PURCHASE OF INSURANCE

Insurance for the home and auto have been discussed in the preceding pages, but there are other types of insurance that the family should have. Most families in the United States today are covered by Social Security. This government program provides for benefits in case the covered worker is totally disabled for six months or longer; for benefits to the widow and children on the death of the worker, income and medicare benefits for the worker and spouse at his retirement, and provides a small sum to aid with burial expenses.[30] The benefits depend on the length of time the worker has been covered and the amount of taxes paid into the Social Security fund. The taxes and benefits are relatively small and are designed to be supplemented by the worker with additional insurance. Any Social Security office has pamphlets available explaining the various coverages.

Two areas that the family must provide for are hospital and physician fees, and for sickness or a disabling accident to the breadwinner. Many companies provide group plans for hospitalization and physician fees. One of the best and most widely used hospitalization plans is "Blue Cross." This plan pays all hospital costs for the number of days provided for in the policy.

The "Blue Shield" plan pays for doctors' surgical fees, but the

---

30. *Social Security Information for Young Families*, U.S. Dept. of Health, Education and Welfare, Social Security Administration, U. S. Government Printing Office, February 1970, pp. 1-3.

benefits do not always pay what doctors or anesthesiologists charge. This can be supplemented by a major medical policy which usually has a deductible amount and pays for charges not covered by a hospitalization or physicians' plan. Hospitalization plans are expensive and the family may be tempted not to carry a policy, but with the rapid increase in the cost of medical care, it would be most unwise not to be covered.

Some companies have employee coverage that pays benefits when a person is disabled by accident or sickness, but most people are not covered. This coverage is not very expensive and can be bought from private insurance companies. The policy usually has a waiting period of seven or fourteen days before benefits begin, and then it pays so much per day until the person is able to return to work. The breadwinner should not be without sickness and accident coverage. [31]

The family should also be protected by life insurance on the breadwinner, with only enough on the wife and children to pay for burial expenses. There are four basic types of life insurance policies, with many variations of each type. The first is "term" life insurance, which is pure protection. A policy is bought for a specific number of years or "term" and expires when the time limit of the policy is reached. Auto and home insurance policies are "term insurance." A variation of this is "decreasing term" or "reducing term" whereby a policy is taken out for a term of several years but the coverage decreases each year although the premium remains the same. This form is commonly used to insure a mortgage. Term life insurance is the cheapest form since the policyholder is only buying protection, and not using his life insurance as a vehicle for savings. [32]

The second major form is called "ordinary" or "whole" life insurance, which is a combination of decreasing term insurance and a savings plan. As the value of the life insurance decreases each year, the insurance company uses the policyholder's savings to make up the difference between the term insurance and the face amount of the policy. For example, John Doe has a $10,000 policy with a cash value of $3,780 after paying the policy for twenty years. If John Doe were to die, his widow would not receive the face amount plus the cash value or $13,780. She would only receive $10,000, which would be his savings of $3,780 plus the term insurance of $6,220. The longer John Doe lives the less insurance he has and the more savings he has. If he lived to be 100 years old, the cash value would probably

31. For those preparing for a full-time Christian ministry or who are actively engaged in a Christian ministry, the Minister's Life and Casualty Union, Minister's Life Building, Minneapolis, Minnesota 55416 has these types of coverage available.

32. Troelstrup, *Consumer Problems*, p. 356.

equal the amount of the policy.[33] This is the type of policy most frequently sold because the salesman gets more commission for selling this kind of insurance.

Endowment policies place the emphasis on savings rather than protection and are therefore more costly than term or ordinary life. They are usually written for a given number of years such as twenty or thirty. This type of policy was once widely sold to help provide money for college expenses. Whenever a child was born, the salesman would sell a policy on the child's life. The difficulty here was that if the breadwinner died there was no one to pay the premium for the child.[34] Any insurance for such a purpose must be on the breadwinner!

A fourth type of policy widely sold today is the annuity which serves as a supplement to retirement income. Many Christian institutions offer annuities to their constituents. The principal of the gift provides income for the person during his lifetime, and on his death, it becomes a gift to the institution. Some of the old, well-established institutions can boast of having never missed a monthly annuity payment, which is very commendable.

There are two little paperback books concerning life insurance which each family should own. *Life Insurance: How to Get Your Money's Worth* by Arnold Geier is published by Collier Books and is very informative.[35] The other is *The Consumers Union Report on Life Insurance* by the editors of *Consumer Reports*.[36] These two books, and especially the *Consumers Union Report*, contain information that will enable the family to establish a sound insurance program.

Writers in the field of Family Life Education have for years recommended that young families buy life insurance for protection only, and to invest their savings in other areas which provide for a good return and also serve as a hedge against inflation.[37] The savings in an insurance policy do not have such a hedge, and are eroded by inflation.

The *Consumer Reports* magazine periodically carries special articles on life insurance designed primarily for those who are buying

33. Editors of *Consumer Reports, The Consumers Union Report on Life Insurance*, (Mt. Vernon, NY: Consumers Union, 1972), p. 23. Material used by permission.

34. Arnold Gier, *Life Insurance, How to Get Your Money's Worth* (New York: Collier Books, 1965), pp. 72-73.

35. Ibid.

36. *The Consumers Union Report on Life Insurance* was first published in 1967 and was revised in 1972.

37. Judson T. Landis and Mary G. Landis, *Building a Successful Marriage* (Englewood Cliffs, NJ: Prentice-Hall, 1968), p. 397.

insurance for the first time or for those who need to acquire additional coverage. These articles discuss such subjects as "estimating how much coverage you need," how to "decide what type of insurance you want," how to "shop for the best price." They also list and rate the major term and cash value policies, and give illustrations of the cost at different ages by the various companies.[38]

Most workers today are covered by Social Security insurance whose benefits are a major factor to be considered in determining the life insurance needs of a young family. A family can receive up to $200,000 in benefits from Social Security depending on the circumstances. It provides for disability payments for total disability. Survivor benefits are paid to the widow and children until the youngest child reaches age eighteen. The widow may begin receiving benefits at age 60 if she so chooses. The benefits are calculated on the basis of the number of years worked and the amount of taxes paid.[39]

One important section of the *Consumer Reports* article teaches a young family how to figure its insurance needs and uses the illustration of a typical young family with two children. If a husband has a $30,000 group life insurance policy and $33,500 in other assets, he would need $168,300 more insurance to provide $1400 living expenses for the family, to educate the two children, and to provide $840 a month retirement income for the widow (including all Social Security benefits at each stage of the family cycle). In 1980, the husband could buy $100,000 of five year renewable term insurance for $210.00 a year.[40] A family can afford this amount for insurance, but not $1800 for $100,000 of ordinary life. If the widow needed an additional $420 per month while working during the "blackout" period when there are no Social Security benefits available from the time the youngest child is eighteen until she retires at 62, she could be covered if the husband bought an additional $50,000 term policy which the family can afford at this time.[41]

Renewable term insurance should always be renewable without medical examination, and it should be convertible to permanent life insurance in case the policyholder so desires. A policy should *never* be bought without these two features. The premium goes up at each renewal, but some units can be dropped as insurance needs decline with the passing years so that the actual amount paid at renewal may be less. This makes it a very flexible type of policy.[42]

38. *Consumer Reports*, March 1980, p. 169.
39. *Consumer Reports*, Feb. 1980, pp. 82, 83.
40. Ibid., pp. 80-102.
41. Ibid., p. 80.
42. Troelstrup, *Consumer Problems*, p. 358.

The oldest insurance company in America is the Presbyterian Minister's Fund founded in 1759 before the Revolutionary War.[43] It insures people engaged in full-time Protestant ministry. For such individuals it provides life insurance, including term insurance, at low rates and also pays generous dividends. There are about eighteen hundred other life insurance companies in America, so a person must shop and choose wisely when buying life insurance.[44]

The public and the insurance companies have become aware that life insurance as a form of savings cannot compete with other forms of investments such as mutual funds. *The Wall Street Journal* in an article on Tuesday, November 28, 1967, stated that an increasing number of people were buying term insurance rather than ordinary life, and investing the difference in mutual funds. The article indicated that many of the insurance companies were starting their own mutual funds so that their salesmen could sell term insurance and also mutual fund shares to the same customer.[45] An article on mutual funds in *U.S. News and World Report*, April 26, 1971, stated that over two hundred insurance companies then had their own mutual fund companies.[46] The idea is to buy the necessary protection for the family by means of term insurance, and to invest the savings dollars in mutual funds where they are able to increase rather than be eroded by inflation. The Presbyterian Minister's Fund has now created their own mutual fund for the benefit of its policyholders who wish to invest in a fund.

One area of Christian stewardship that has not been fully utilized is the naming of a Christian institution as the beneficiary of a life insurance policy. Under many circumstances, the premiums for such a policy are deductible from the federal income tax. If a term policy were used, a sizeable amount of insurance could be purchased for a modest premium, and the Christian steward will be a real benefactor to the institution of his choice.[47]

There are many insurance companies and many different types of policies, and these may be confusing to the young family. However, it is important for them to know that adequate protection for all the

43. Schoenfeld and Natella, *Consumer and Dollars*, p. 225.
44. Ibid.
45. William M. Corley, "Top Insurers Plan to Start Mutual Funds to Halt Decline in Share of Savers Dollars," *The Wall Street Journal*, August 28, 1967, p. 32.
46. "What You Should Know About Mutual Funds," *U.S. News and World Report*, April 26, 1971, p. 48.
47. The Stewardship Department of the Christian Institution of your choice will be glad to give more information in this area.

needs of the family, in case of the father's death, *can be bought reasonably if renewable term insurance is purchased.* Insurance salesmen can present many reasons for buying other types of policies containing a savings feature, but these should never be bought until the needs of the family are adequately provided for. It is wise for the family to keep their protection and their savings separate, and not combine the two. Chapter 6 of the *Consumers Union Report* indicates that the individual will be money ahead to invest the difference between the price of a term policy and an ordinary life policy. [48] Bowman in his book, *Here's How to Succeed with Your Money*, recommends term insurance and also the separation of insurance for protection from the money to be saved. He writes, "I am acquainted with a large number of financial men. I do not know one of them who has anything else but term insurance on his life. There must be a reason for this."[49] The family must buy insurance for protection only, and invest their savings where they will increase the most.

MAKING WISE INVESTMENTS

The Lord Jesus taught that God expects an increase whether it is in the spiritual realm (parable of the sower—Matt. 13:1-23), or in the material realm (parable of the talents—Matt. 25:14-30). He asks the question in the parable of the unjust steward, "And if ye have not been faithful in that which is another man's, who shall give you that which is your own?" (Luke 16:12). The Christian steward is under divine obligation and has a divine purpose in saving money and investing it, i.e., he wants to see it increase in order to bring glory to God.

As indicated earlier, at least 10 percent of the family's disposable income should be saved. A savings account is basic to financial security. The money should be put in a bank, credit union, or savings and loan association where it will earn the most interest and be readily available if needed. The financial institution should be covered by a federal insurance program so that the saver's account is insured up to 100,000. The savings account provides a fund for emergencies, for the children's education, for special family goals, and for a supplement to retirement income. Few people realize how

48. *The Consumers Union Report on Life Insurance*, pp. 69-84.
49. Bowman, *Succeed with Your Money*, p. 31. Mr. Bowman suggests reducing or decreasing term insurance to provide protection. This is a little cheaper to buy initially, but it is not as flexible as five year renewable term insurance in units of $10,000 or $25,000 each whereby units can be dropped as the need for insurance decreases.

money doubles at compound interest, so the higher the interest rate, the sooner it doubles. At 4 percent it doubles in eighteen years; at 5 percent in fourteen years; at 6 percent in twelve years, and at 7 percent it doubles in ten years. In like manner it is amazing how quickly a sum saved regularly each month grows to a sizeable sum. If a family were to save in a savings and loan association 10 percent of $500 income or $50 per month at 5 percent compounded quarterly, it would amount to $3,412.65 in only five years. In ten years it would amount to $7,787.80; in twenty years it would total $20,507.97.[50]

If the couple accepts the suggestion given previously and saves the wife's entire income for two or three years, they will have a fund that can undergird their complete marriage cycle. Just $5000 at 5 percent interest compounded quarterly will increase to $8218.10 in ten years, and to $13,507.42 in twenty years. Ten thousand dollars in ten years will grow to $16,436.19 and to $27,014.85 in twenty years.[51] With such a nest egg and a regular savings plan the family will be able to give more to the Lord.

After the savings account reaches an amount that equals at least six times the family's total monthly income, they should begin to invest their savings in a manner which brings a higher return.[52] Many Christian institutions and churches offer bonds that pay higher interest rates than a bank pays on savings accounts. If money is invested in such bonds, it will provide a good profit and also aid the cause of Christ. Some government and high-grade corporate bonds also pay a high rate of interest. Bonds are usually a safe investment, but they do not have any hedge against inflation.

Some individuals may wish to purchase stocks on the American or New York exchanges. Any library has numerous books explaining the techniques of buying and selling stocks. For a small sum a paperback may be purchased called, *How to Buy Stocks* by Louis Engel.[53] A cardinal rule of stock investing is that the family have a good savings account before investing in stocks. Money cannot be lost on the stock market unless a company goes bankrupt (which seldom happens to "Blue Chip" companies), for if a stock is down in price, it may always go up. People only lose money when they are

50. See appendix for table showing how various sums per month will multiply at 5 percent interest compounded daily.
51. See appendix for a table illustrating how various sums increase over varying periods of time.
52. Harold M. Finley, *Everybody's Guide to the Stock Market* (Chicago: Henry Regnery Co., 1971), p. 228.
53. Louis Engel and Brendan Wood, *How to Buy Stocks* (New York: Bantam Books, 7th Rev. ed. 1983).

forced by some financial emergency to sell while the market is down. If a family has a fund for emergencies, it will never have to sell its stock at a loss, and it cannot lose if it holds good stock.

A fairly recent development that can greatly affect the finances of the family is the availability of Individual Retirement Accounts (IRA's). An employed husband and wife can invest up to $4000 in IRA's ($2250 if the wife is not working), and they do not have to pay federal income tax on this amount. The money can be deposited anytime between January 1 through the April 15 tax-filing deadline in the next year. The earlier the funds are deposited, the more interest will be earned over a period of years. These funds compound tax-free until they are withdrawn, preferably at retirement. Merely saving $9.60 per week amounts to $500 a year which compounded for 30 years will make a nest egg for retirement. If funds are withdrawn before 59½ years of age, there is a ten percent penalty for early withdrawal. An IRA can be opened at any bank, savings and loan, mutual fund, insurance company, or brokerage house. There is usually a small start-up fee and also an annual maintenance fee. A person may have several accounts to diversify his investments, but the fees will hinder the growth of the accounts. Since an IRA is a long-term investment, a mutual fund is an excellent avenue to achieve growth.[54]

Investing surplus savings funds in a good mutual fund has several advantages. The fund is diversified in its holdings, which gives it opportunity to share the gains of different stocks. The fund has professional management, supposedly having greater know-how than the average small investor does. Most mutual funds have done very well over a period of years. It must be remembered that a mutual fund investment is a *long term investment*—for at least five years and preferably ten years or longer. The fund also enables the small investor to share in the splits and dividend distributions of more stocks than he could invest in alone. There is less paperwork and record keeping in owning mutual fund shares than in stock ownership.[55]

---

54. *Money*, 1985, "Your IRA, How to Open it, Invest it, and Build it into a Fortune," pp. 7-12.

55. Murray Teigh Bloom, "Are Mutual Funds for You?" *Reader's Digest*, February 1972, pp. 19-23. More information about mutual funds may be secured by writing to the Investment Company Institute, 1775 K St. N.W., Washington DC 20006; or to the No-Load Mutual Fund Association, 375 Park Ave., New York, NY 10022.

There are hundreds of funds, some of which have specific objectives, such as growth funds, income funds, and balanced funds (growth and income). Some charge commissions to sell the buyer shares (load funds), others do not (no-load funds). The investor must read and be informed about mutual funds. Public libraries and broker's offices have books which list the past performance of all mutual funds. Two of the best known are *Johnson's Investment Company Charts* and Arthur Wisenberger's *Investment Companies.* The past performance is a good indicator of the value of a fund but is not infallible! After doing his research and deciding what the family's objectives are, he should consult a broker in a brokerage firm for additional information. Only then should he invest in a fund. However, a good fund can be a good investment. The top twenty-five mutual funds over a recent ten-year period registered gains from 402 1522 percent, with ten of them gaining over 600 percent.[56]

The Christian family can be as wise as "the children of this world" and use and increase their money for the cause of Christ. It takes dedication, information, and self-discipline, but Christians can manage money well and increase the number of faithful stewards able and willing to help the cause of Christ here at home and abroad. Pierson wrote, ". . . what I thus surrender for the sake of others comes back to me in larger blessing. It is like the moisture which the spring gives out in streams and evaporation, returning in showers to supply the very channels which filled the spring itself. 'It is more blessed to give than to receive' " (Acts 20:35).[57]

56. "The Money Rankings of Mutual Funds," *Money*, October, 1985, pp. 173-208. The above figures are for "Long Term Growth Funds." The top "Maximum Capital Gains Fund" achieved a 948 percent gain.
57. A. T. Pierson, "Giving Is Living," ed. J. Allan Petersen, *The Marriage Affair* (Wheaton, IL: Tyndale House Publishers, 1971), p 347.

PERSONALITY INVENTORY

WHAT ARE YOUR VALUES CONCERNING MONEY

1 What is your view of Christian stewardship?

2 Have you established the habit of systematically giving a portion of your income to the Lord?

3 Do you approve of George M. Bowman's "10-70-20" plan? Why or why not?

4 Who do you feel should manage the family income? Why?

5 If you received a legacy of $1000, how would you use it?

6 If a wife works either full or part-time, how much control over her income should she have?

7 If you had a choice of buying a so-called "new car" and not saving any money, or of buying a slightly used car and saving $50 per month, which car would you buy?

8 Which type of budget plan do you think the young family should follow? Why?

9 In what ways would you handle your income differently from your parents?

10 In what ways do you feel you need to "keep up with the Jones family"?

QUESTIONS FOR DISCUSSION AND REVIEW

1. Discuss the advantages and liabilities of buying a mobile home.

2. When should a family consider renting rather than buying a home?

3. What are the different methods of financing a home?

4. How may "deferred gratification" be practiced in relation to home ownership?

5. What two basic purposes are served by the automobile in American society?

6. Discuss some of the basic principles to be followed in buying a used car.

7. What types of insurance coverage are needed by the average family?

8. Explain why an "ordinary" life policy is in reality a "decreasing" term policy.

9. Why should the young family buy term insurance for protection only? Why should it be renewable without medical examination and be convertible?

10. Discuss the advantages and disadvantages of the various methods which the family can use to invest its surplus funds.

13

CHRISTIAN PARENTHOOD

Train up a child in the way he should go:
and when he is old, he will not depart from it.
Proverbs 22:6

DIFFICULTIES IN ACHIEVING PARENTHOOD

Christian marriage carries with it the responsibility of planning a family and rearing children. Occasionally a person is found who does not desire to become a parent, but this individual is an exception because many young people are motivated to marry by a desire to have a family of their own. "Where there is commitment to have and to care properly for children, marriage has fuller meaning and life is immeasurably enriched."[1] The method of family planning and the number and spacing of children are subjects that the engaged couple should thoroughly discuss so there are no misunderstandings to mar their harmony when they do marry. A person who wishes to have children should never marry an individual who does not want them, for only heartache and unhappiness can result.

The ability to beget and to bear children are considered to be very essential roles in the American family system just as it was in the days of Abraham and Sarah. In Pennsylvania and Tennessee, the inability to have children constitute grounds for divorce.[2] The failure to perform these roles because of sterility creates a great

1. C. W. Scudder, *The Family in Christian Perspective* (Nashville: Broadman Press, 1962), p. 32.
2. Judson T. Landis and Mary G. Landis, *Building a Successful Marriage* (Englewood Cliffs, NJ: Prentice-Hall, 1968), p. 444.

253

amount of stress in many families.[3] Wives who want to bear children but who are unable to conceive, often become very frustrated because of this failure, and may suffer emotional and psychosomatic illness. Intensive research is being carried on into the causes of sterility, and much progress is being made.[4] The taking of fertility pills to increase the possibility of pregnancy has had the side effect sometimes of causing multiple births.[5] The couple experiencing difficulty in conception should not resign themselves to adoption until they have exhausted the medical resources that are available to help them today.[6]

NECESSITY FOR FAMILY PLANNING

The psalmist wrote, "Lo, children are an heritage of the Lord . . . happy is the man that hath his quiver full of them" (Ps. 127:3, 5). In a rural economy children were an asset because of the labor they could provide, but they may become an economic liability in our industrialized society. The apostle Paul stated, "But if any provide not for his own, and specially for those of his own house, he hath denied the faith, and is worse than an infidel" (I Tim. 5:8).

A Christian couple should plan and pray for the number of children they will be able to provide for adequately. They must remember that in American society this includes more than just food, clothing, and shelter, for the parent is also responsible to provide an "education, preventative medical care, leisure time activities, and cultural opportunities."[7] This also includes some form of higher education, which is very expensive.

Many sincere Christians today desire to limit the number of children, not because of economic reasons, but because of over-

3. Wayne J. Anderson, *Design for Family Living* (Minneapolis: T. S. Denison & Co., Inc., 1964), p. 167.
4. The oral contraceptives were a development of sterility research. See "Birth Control: The Pill and the Church," in *Newsweek*, July 6, 1964, pp. 54-55, and "Contraception," in *Time*, April 7, 1967, p. 78 for some historical background on how the fertility pills became oral contraceptives.
5. *Time*, April 7, 1967, p. 79.
6. Recent research claims it is possible for a family to have a child of the sex they desire. See the article, "How to Choose Your Baby's Sex." *Look*, April 21, 1970.
7. Evelyn Millis Duvall, *Family Development* (Philadelphia: J. B. Lippincott Co., 1962), p. 129.

population.[8] The pressure of population upon our land and natural resources is acknowledged as a serious problem. A corollary of this is the pollution caused by too many people. Some couples, instead of having children of their own, are adopting children. Others, after having one or two children of their own, adopt additional children when they desire to increase their family.

The area of family planning is one where Christian liberty prevails, for there are no clear statements of Scripture delineating it. Each couple must arrive at their own convictions as to which method of family planning they wish to use. Even with the best methods of family planning, there are unwanted pregnancies. Nevertheless, if a couple communicate well and are conscientious in the use of the chosen method of contraception, they can achieve great control over the number and spacing of children.

A newlywed couple has a number of optional methods of family planning available. Some of the more commonly used are the oral contraceptives (the "pill"), the diaphragm with vaginal jelly, the vaginal foams, condoms, intrauterine devices, and the "rhythm" method.[9] The couple should discuss the type of family planning with a doctor during the engagement period, for some methods are available only through a physician. After a couple have the desired number of children, many fathers are using vasectomy (male sterilization) as a means of permanent contraception.[10] This is a relatively simple, inexpensive operation that is 100 percent effective.[11]

Some individuals refuse to plan their families by adopting a fatalistic attitude: if children come, then it is God's will, and if perchance, a pregnancy doesn't occur each year, that also is God's will. The individuals absolve themselves of any concern for bringing more children into the world than they can support. The exhortation of Paul, in Ephesians 5:17 seems appropriate in this type of situation, "Wherefore be ye not unwise, but understanding what the will of the Lord is." God desires the Christian to seek His will in *all* matters of life, and this certainly applies to the number of children,

8. Leonard Broom and Philip Selznick, *Sociology* (New York: Harper and Row, 1973), p. 271.
9. See Henry L. Miles, *Sexual Happiness in Marriage* (Grand Rapids: Zondervan Publishing House, 1967; rev. ed., 1976) for a fuller description of the various methods of contraception. See also LaHaye, *The Act of Marriage*, pp. 182-194.
10. Gerald R. Leslie, *The Family in Social Context* (New York: Oxford University Press, 1973), p. 511.
11. Tim and Beverly LaHaye, *The Act of Marriage* (Grand Rapids: Zondervan Publishing House, 1976), p. 193 indicate that vasectomy is usually done in a physician's office. Tying of the wife's fallopian tubes is often done while she is in the hospital recovering from the birth of the last child, but this is much more expensive.

and the spacing of time between their arrivals. It is not only the bearing of children, but the caring for them that must be considered.

PARENTHOOD FOR THE FIRST TIME

A couple who waits for some time before having the first baby has time to learn the roles of husband and wife before assuming the new roles of mother and father. Studies show that the average couple become parents within two years after marriage.[12] They must then learn the role of parents before they are thoroughly familiar with their roles as husband and wife. If the wife is pregnant at the time of marriage, the situation is even more complicated.

Charlie W. Shedd in *Letters to Karen* advances another reason for a young couple to delay parenthood. He makes the following suggestion:

> Most young men come into marriage with a large reservoir of sexual frustration which has accumulated through their growing years. This is one reason it is important for you to keep from having babies too soon . . . it is good for you both if you can thoroughly clear your systems of the things you had to backlog before it was legal. . . . But the child will have a better mother and father if they have spent plenty of time learning each other and pouring out their love to each other with no competition for the first few years.[13]

Evelyn Duvall calls the period of the wife's first pregnancy the "expectant phase" of the family life cycle.[14] She indicates that some of the tasks facing the couple at this time include the arrangements for the physical care of the new baby, for reallocating the income, sexual relationship during pregnancy, communication with relatives and friends, and providing for the maintenance of "morale and a workable philosophy of life."[15]

It is evident that the announcement of the pregnancy initiates a series of changes in the young family that may stimulate stress in the best adjusted relationship. The couple may read books on becoming parents and eagerly anticipate the role, yet may be unprepared for the changes that are necessary when the pregnancy becomes a reality.

12. Henry R. Brandt and Homer E. Dowdy, *Building a Christian Home*, (Wheaton, IL: Scripture Press, 1960), p. 76.
13. Charlie W. Shedd, *Letters To Karen*, (Nashville: Abingdon Press, 1965), p. 106. Used by permission.
14. Evelyn Millis Duvall, *Family Development*, pp. 157-183.
15. Ibid.

"Considering the powerful physical and emotional changes involved—chiefly for the wife, but also for the husband—it's no wonder that marital attitudes and relationships are strongly affected. . . . Both must make major adjustments that are often taxing, even for those who are stable and mature."[16]

The couple will now have to share their time and affection with the newcomer. The father is apt to feel slighted and hurt, and may become jealous of the child. If the husband is immature or suffers from low self-esteem, "he may regard his wife's first pregnancy as an impending disaster . . . may try to ignore the unborn child and treat the pregnancy as if it were an illness. . . . To him—and perhaps to her—the baby seems an interloper who will alter the interlocking roles that form the structure of their lives."[17] However, the mature father realizes "he has a new status as father which brings sobering responsibility, a feeling of authority, and increased respect from relatives and friends."[18]

The new mother usually enjoys her role as mother. The danger is that she may become so concerned with this role that she neglects her husband and thereby creates problems. He then becomes a rival of the baby for her attention and affection. "The young wife makes the mistake of becoming closer to her baby than to her husband. The baby becomes the center of her life which makes the husband feel like an outsider."[19] The mature young mother recognizes that some time and energy must be reserved for her husband. She still is a "wife," even though the duties of motherhood now consume so much of her time.

Many difficulties are avoidable if, before the baby is born, the couple discuss some of the changes they expect to take place and how they hope to react to them. Most couples make extensive preparations for the arrival of the baby by preparing a nursery, buying clothing and furniture, but do very little to prepare themselves psychologically for the infant's birth. Such preparation can avert much unhappiness over an occasion that should bring a couple closer together rather than create tensions in their marital relationship. John F. Rogers affirms that "when prospective parents under-

---

16. John F. Rodgers, "That Eternal Triangle: You, Your Husband, Your Baby-to-come," in *Family Circle*, January 1965, p. 80.

17. Gail Putney Fullerton, *Survival in Marriage*, (New York: Holt, Rinehart & Winston, Inc., 1972), p. 390.

18. Katherine Whiteside Taylor, "The Opportunities of Parenthood," in *Family, Marriage, and Parenthood*, ed. Howard Becker and Reuben Hill (Boston: D. C. Heath & Co., 1948,) p. 460.

19. Walter Trobisch, *I Married You* (New York: Harper & Row, 1971), p. 16.

stand and anticipate the changes that occur during the prenatal period, they are able to cope with the family relationship both during and after the pregnancy."[20]

PREGNANCY—PROBLEMS AND PRECAUTIONS

When a couple decide it is the will of the Lord for them to start their family and the wife becomes pregnant, usually she experiences nausea or "morning sickness' the first few months.[21] After a month or two many enjoy good health until the baby arrives. Unfortunately, for a few women, they are sick the entire nine months, which makes the pregnancy an unhappy experience. Some wives have a problem with miscarriages. For various reasons they are unable to carry the fetus for the full term of the pregnancy. Some are forced to lie down most of the time in order to avoid the miscarriage.

Certain precautions should be taken by the pregnant wife to avoid difficulties. In the first few months it is wise to shun extensive travel by auto. Many a miscarriage has resulted from a sudden jolt from an unforeseen bump in the road. Tasks should not be undertaken that place undue strain on the body. Heavy housecleaning such as washing the kitchen walls should be left to the prospective father! The physician will advise the couple as to sexual relationships during the pregnancy. Ordinarily they can take place up to six weeks before the baby is expected and are prohibited for six weeks after the birth to avoid the danger of infection. The couple should be informed as to the signs of approaching birth, and allow sufficient time to reach the hospital. It is possible for a child to be born in the home, but the risks of complications to mother and child during the birth are too great to take. The birth of a healthy child brings great joy and blessing to the new mother and father.

ADOPTION—AN ALTERNATE ROUTE TO PARENTHOOD

The couple who cannot have children themselves should pray and seek the will of God concerning the adoption of children. Each year thousands of children are adopted with over half of them by unrelated persons.[22] The Christian couple can seek the services of an agency

20. Rogers, "That Eternal Triangle," p. 80.
21. Leslie, *Family in Social Context*, p. 521.
22. Robert F. Winch, *The Modern Family* (New York: Holt, Rinehart and Winston, Inc., 1971), p. 198.

supported by their church. If a child is not available through such an agency, there are Family Service agencies in most cities which offer adoptive services. Another source would be the local Child Welfare Department. On a nationwide basis, there are about ten times as many families wanting a child as there are children placed.[23] Occasionally a physician or lawyer may arrange an adoptive child for a fee, but this is more costly than securing a child through an agency. There are some organizations that specialize in international adoptions, particularly the unwanted children of American servicemen overseas.

The legal rights of an adopted child are well protected by the laws and courts of the land. Since adoption does have these legal complications, it is absolutely necessary that the couple have their own lawyer involved in the legal aspects of the case rather than depending entirely on the legal services of the agency.

The average adoptive parents desire to secure an infant. This gives the mother the joy of caring for a baby, but it also has the advantage of permitting the parents to rear the child in the manner which they deem most proper. Personality formation does begin very early in childhood, and it is better if an infant can be adopted. If a baby cannot be secured, it would be better to adopt an older child rather than miss the joy and privilege of being parents. Many couples are rising to the challenge and adopting children who are in their late childhood, and some are adopting children who are handicapped in some way. A childless couple should not be deterred from adopting a child for fear of possible problems in rearing the child, for many natural parents encounter problems in raising their own children. The grace of God is sufficient for these difficulties, whether they be with adopted or natural children.

PARENTS AND THE SOCIALIZATION OF CHILDREN

When children are born into the home, the parents have the great responsibility of rearing them for the honor and glory of the Lord. "The great business of the home is to develop sound persons for a useful and happy life."[24] It is a task for which little or no education is given to the parents, so that each young mother and father start out to rear their children by trial and error. Since lessons are learned

23. Ibid., p. 199.
24. Hazen G. Werner, *Christian Family Living* (Nashville: Abingdon Press, 1958), p. 33.

caring for the first child, parents are somewhat better prepared for the subsequent children.

At times every parent wishes that all children were born with a good nature that only needs to be educated for the infant to become a model child and adult, a liberal doctrine that has no basis in Scripture. Unfortunately for parents, the Biblical doctrine of total depravity is true, so they are faced with rearing a child born with a depraved nature prone to evil, and almost constantly in need of teaching and correction. Consequently, a large part of child rearing is concerned with these two tasks.

Sociologists and psychologists often debate the influence of heredity versus environment.[25] It is true that certain diseases are inherited such as "Huntington's chorea"—a degenerative disease of the nervous system.[26] Heredity certainly has a major influence as to what kind of an environment a child is born into, for after his birth he lives in the social class of his parents. The Christian also recognizes that when the new birth takes place in a person's life, he becomes a "partaker of the divine nature" (II Peter 1:4). Thus, any discussion among Christians of heredity versus environment must include the fact that a spiritual birth through faith in Jesus Christ can have influences in the life that cannot be accounted for either by heredity nor by environment alone.

In Ephesians 6:4 Paul exhorts, "Ye fathers, provoke not your children to wrath, but bring them up in the nurture [discipline] and admonition of the Lord." The Christian parent must strive to rear his child in such a manner that the child grows to love Jesus Christ and to serve Him in whatever walk of life he enters. This is a difficult task in view of the corrupt society in which the task must be accomplished, yet it is not an impossible task as evidenced by the multitudes of fine Christian young people who have had the wonderful experience of growing up in a home where the Lord Jesus was honored and exalted. It is imperative that parents be successful in this role, for there is no second chance. If they fail, a young life may be ruined and lost eternally. Many of the problems of young people in American society today can be blamed on parents who failed to give their children a set of values to guide them in their everyday lives. The words of Solomon in Proverbs 30:11 describe these young people: "There is a generation that curseth their father, and doth not

25. Paul Henry Mussen, John Janeway Conger, and Jerome Kagan, *Child Development and Personality* (New York: Harper & Row Publishers, 1963), p. 37-39. A good discussion of the "Nature-Nurture Controversy."
26. Ibid., p. 38.

bless their mother." Their parents failed them, and now they are failures and "drop-outs" from the mainstream of American society. These words may be true also of some Christian "drop-outs" whose lives are blighted because of the permissive attitude of their parents.[27]

Numerous books have been written on the subject of raising children, so the following ideas are only an introduction designed to stimulate the reader's interest. One of the best books for Christian parents is *The Child in the Christian Home* by Margaret Bailey Jacobsen.[28] The author describes each year of the child's development from infancy to preadolescence. She pays particular attention to the spiritual development of the child in each stage of his growth.

Parents have the responsibility of rearing the child to be an upright citizen in this life, and preparing him for the life to come. Carle C. Zimmerman states, "This nature of the family . . . makes the good domestic unit the fountainhead of citizenship."[29] This means that the job of teaching the child must begin at a very early age. He learns his most important lessons in the home, and these are reinforced by the Sunday school and church. He should be taught to love the Lord Jesus Christ, and be led to a saving knowledge of the cleansing blood of Christ.

The question may be asked as to what age a child should be led to Christ. It varies from child to child, but the maxim is that when they are old enough to love their parents, they are old enough to love the Lord Jesus, and to place their faith in Him as their personal Savior from sin. Jacobsen, in describing the four-year-old child, comments on this subject: "When a child is old enough to realize he has done wrong, he is old enough to understand and believe the gospel, 'how that Christ died for our sins' (I Cor. 15:3). Many Christians date their new life in Christ from this four-year-old period."[30]

However, this does not imply that all children are converted at such a young age. Jacobsen also warns, "It is useless, and could be dangerous, for a Sunday School teacher to press a child of this age for a decision."[31] Another author states, "To establish any pattern

---

27. Clyde M. Narramore, "Disqualified for Service?", *Psychology for Living*, February 1971, p. 15. A helpful article of encouragement to parents who have done their best and yet their children have rebelled.

28. Margaret Bailey Jacobsen, *The Child in the Christian Home* (Wheaton, IL: Scripture Press, 1959).

29. Carle C. Zimmerman, "The Future of the Family in America," *Journal of Marriage and the Family*, May 1972, p. 325.

30. Jacobsen, *Child in the Christian Home*, p. 83-84.

31. Ibid., p. 89.

of conversion age for all children of the church is dangerous. No two will grow alike spiritually."[32] Some children are saved at a very early age, and others take much longer to come to the point of decision for Christ. The parent needs to be sensitive to the working of the Holy Spirit in the child's life and be ready to help the child when he indicates a desire to be saved.

To teach a child to love the Lord is much more than just taking a child to Sunday school and church. It includes teaching him to pray as soon as he is able and then to read the Word when he is old enough. Many children are able to learn much about the Bible long before they are able to read. Jacobsen gives the illustration of a mother whose two children were saved at an early age and quotes her as saying,

> Also Catherine Vos's book, *Child's Story Bible* was read through to the children twice before Elizabeth, the elder, was able to read it for herself. It is safe to say that the children had more Bible doctrine in their minds by the time they were six years old than most young people who attend church have by the time they are sixteen.[33]

Children and young people should also be taught the doctrine of the indwelling Holy Spirit. One reason so many second-generation Christians are weak and powerless, and often defeated in their experience, is that they have been taught the norms of the Christian life, but have not been instructed concerning the necessity of yielding their bodies to the domination of the Holy Spirit. They attempt to live the Christian life in their own strength. They sincerely love the Lord Jesus, and do not understand why they fail in their attempts to please Him. Once they learn to submit their lives daily to the control of the blessed Holy Spirit, they come to know the joy of overcoming victory in their lives. Warren W. Wiersbe says, "Doing the will of God is not a burden, nor a battle to the believer whose will is yielded to the Spirit."[34] The parents cannot leave this important truth to be taught by the Sunday school teacher, or the pastor, but early in the child's experience they should instruct him in this wonderful doctrine.

32. Alta Mae Erb, *Christian Education in the Home* (Scottdale, PA: Herald Press, 1963), p. 38.

33. Jacobsen, *Child in the Christian Home*, p. 85. Used by permission.

34. Warren W. Wiersbe, *Creative Christian Living* (Westwood, NJ: Fleming H. Revell Co., 1967), p. 116.

ROLE MODELS FOR THE CHILD

The fact that the child comes to know the Lord Jesus as Savior at an early age will not make him a little saint or angel. He will still need to be taught the basic values such as honesty, purity, and gentleness, but the job should be much easier if the child is saved. The child also needs instruction in the rudiments of the roles that he or she is to play in life.

Roles are learned by children from their parents. Much of this learning takes place on the conscious level because parents want their boys to act like boys and will teach them accordingly. They buy toy cars, trucks, farm equipment, and athletic equipment for them since these are appropriate for the male role in adulthood. Parents permit more aggressive behavior from boys than girls, for men are to be aggressive in society. Talcott Parsons says that the male role is "achievement- and task-oriented."[35] The father is the "model" for the son as he learns his role.[36]

Little girls are taught roles that are characteristic of women. They are given dolls and dishes as toys since they become mothers and housekeepers in adulthood. The girl is expected to be gentle and tender, for these are female qualities in American culture. Parsons speaks of this as the "expressive role" and it includes "comfort-seeking, affiliation, tenderness, solicitude, and nurturance."[37] The mother is the "model" and the girl identifies with her as she grows up.[38]

By the time they are five years old, most children are aware of the proper behavior appropriate to their sex. When given a choice of toys they choose the toys that correspond to their sex.[39] If for any reason a child does not manifest the proper behavior, a boy is called a "sissy" and a girl a "tomboy." Parents pressure such children in an attempt to get them to conform to the roles society expects them to play. "Definite patterns of praise and punishment from both parents and playmates during the preschool and school years put pressure on the child to adopt sex-appropriate behaviors."[40]

35. Quoted by Boyd R. Mc Candless, "Childhood Socialization," ed. David A. Goslin, *Handbook of Socialization Theory and Research*, (Chicago: Rand Mc Nally Co., 1969), p. 806.
36. Mussen, Conger and Kagan, *Child Development*, p. 264.
37. McCandless,"Childhood Socialization", p. 806.
38. Mussen, Conger and Kagen, *Child Development*, p. 264.
39. Ibid., p. 263.
40. Ibid., p. 262.

It is apparent that both parents have responsibilities as role models. This is why it is most important for children to be reared in a home with both parents present. It also means that parents need to support each other in their roles. If a mother does not approve of the husband or

> . . . if there is chronic antagonism between husband and wife, the boy discovers that if he identifies with his father it is at the price of losing his mother's love and approval; if she is antagonistic toward and disapproving of the husband, she will feel scant enthusiasm for seeing her son become "just like him."[41]

The girl faces the same kind of dilemma.

Alice Hershey expressed the necessity of the wife supporting the husband in these words:

> If my husband is respected and loved by me, my child will acquire the same feeling for him. If he sees that what father says and wants counts with me, he cannot fail to be impressed and influenced. Young children need a hero. Why not Dad? It is an immeasurable boost to a father's ego to know that he is the most prominent person in his child's life. . . . A child needs experiences before he can learn. A child cannot verbally be told Dad's place in the home; he must be shown the practical outworking of this truth.[42]

The opposite is also true, for the way in which a husband treats the wife will have an influence on the daughter.

As a method of training for Christian stewardship, the children should be given a weekly allowance and be taught how to tithe it, how to save a percentage of it, and how to spend wisely what is left. Children cannot be expected to know the value of money if they are not given some opportunity and instruction in how to handle it. As they get older, they can be reimbursed for doing certain tasks around the home. A parent does his child a gross injustice if he just doles out money generously, so that the child never really comes to appreciate the value of money nor how to handle it wisely. Parents who are both employed are often subconsciously guilty of this, for they try to give the children money and gifts to substitute for their lack of time to spend with them.

41. Ibid., pp. 270-271.
42. Alice Patricia Hershey, "Put Him in His Place, Wife," ed. J. Allan Petersen, *The Marriage Affair* (Wheaton, IL: Tyndale House Publishers, 1971), p. 91. Used by permission of *Christian Life* magazine, July 1967, Christian Life, Inc.

THE FAMILY ALTAR

Some Christian parents believe that just taking or sending the child to the services of the church is sufficient for the religious education of the child.[43] The home must assume the leadership in this area or disaster may result. The church reinforces what has been taught in the home. The family altar is one of the great aids to help the parents achieve their goals in this area. Some families will meet at bedtime when the children are small, and then change to meeting around the dinner table as they grow older. It makes little difference when the family meets, as meeting consistently is more important than the time. The parents take turns reading the Bible and praying in some families, while in others the father reads the Word and prays. As children become old enough to pray and then to read, they participate also. This enables them to pronounce many of the more common proper names, and the Old English words in the King James Version. There are many ways of conducting the family altar and it should be varied so that it does not become a mere routine or ceremony.[44]

The family altar is a time when children are free to ask questions about the Bible or doctrine that they might be too shy to ask of a Sunday school teacher or youth worker.[45] It is also an excellent place for the children to learn how to pray and the value of prayer. They can pray about their daily needs such as school problems, and the salvation of their playmates. This helps the children see that Christianity has a very practical application to their daily lives, and is not merely the formality of attending so many church services a week. The reading of the Word can be interspersed with reading a short chapter from the biography of some missionary hero.[46] This serves the dual purpose of informing the children of missionary history, and also helping to create interest in missions. This interest can be increased by gleaning prayer requests from publications of

43. Jacobsen, *Child in the Christian Home*, p. VI.
44. There are many booklets on how to conduct a family altar. *How to Begin and Improve Family Devotions* by Dr. Clyde Narramore, (Grand Rapids: Zondervan Publishing House), is inexpensive yet contains many helpful suggestions.
45. A. Donald Bell, *The Family in Dialogue* (Grand Rapids: Zondervan Publishing House, 1970), pp. 102-112.
46. Moody Press publishes some excellent short biographies of the great missionaries such as *The Life of David Livingstone, Hudson Taylor, Adoniram Judson*, and *The Triumph of John and Betty Stam*.

mission boards, and making these a definite matter of prayer. One of the children can be the secretary to record the answers to prayer.

The family altar is also an excellent way for the family to memorize Scripture verses. The psalmist said, "Thy word have I hid in my heart, that I might not sin against thee" (Ps. 119:11). This is one way in which the parents can help to strengthen their children to live in the sinful world surrounding them. Verses should be learned on the subject of personal soul-winning so that the children can be effective witnesses to their playmates in the neighborhood and at school. Local churches often sponsor Scripture memorization programs such as those promoted by the Bible Memory Association. Occasionally the family could quote verses as a substitute for reading the Word.

The family altar can be one of the most effective aids in the religious education of the children. It can give the family a sense of unity and help to cement the family ties. When the children leave home, they are aware that the family is praying for them daily, an encouragement to them as they face the problems of college and employment. Having devotions together as a family takes time, effort, and planning, but it is worth it all since eternal dividends result. As Jacobsen states, "Though many American families have to fight to maintain daily family worship, they will find the benefit from such a time worth any sacrifice."[47]

PRINCIPLES OF DISCIPLINE

Since children are born with a sinful nature, they not only need to be taught what is right, but they also must be corrected when they do wrong. Some parents accepted the "permissive" child-rearing theories of modern psychology only to discover that it permitted their children to act like little monsters, and to see them grow up rebellious against any authority.[48] The child who is disciplined in the home and learns to obey and to respond to authority, will not have difficulty in being obedient to teachers when they go to school, nor to governmental authorities as they mature and come into contact with them. If the parents do not discipline their children,

47. Jacobsen, *Child in the Christian Home*, p. 187.
48. James Dobson, *Dare to Discipline* (Wheaton, IL: Tyndale House Publishers, 1970), p. 12. An excellent book for parents to own. Two pamphlets of value on this subject are *Christian Discipline*, Erwin J. Kolb, Concordia Publishing House, St. Louis, MO, and *Discipline in the Christian Home*, Clyde M. Narramore, Zondervan Publishing House, Grand Rapids, MI.

they cannot expect the school or the church to do it for them. Donald R. Cressey, a criminologist, writes, "Almost everyone agrees that the most important difference between the situation of delinquent and nondelinquent children is in 'home discipline.' "[49]

One of the major complaints of public school teachers is that they have to spend so much time disciplining the children they do not have enough time to teach them what they need to know. Rare is the Sunday school teacher or youth worker who does not have one or more undisciplined pupils who make the hour unpleasant for the others in the class.

Few modern parents would desire to return to the old-fashioned methods of the autocratic disciplinarian who reared children to be seen and not heard. There is a middle ground between the "permissive" and the "autocratic" methods whereby firm but gentle, loving correction is given to the child so that he responds positively, and internalizes into his personality the norms of the church and society.[50] Discipline is never an easy task, and it is often an unpleasant one even for the parent. There are some principles which, if followed consistently, will make the job somewhat easier, and hopefully, more successful.

The parents must love the child in such a way that he feels secure in the home even when disciplined. Showing affection is one means of demonstrating love, and small children particularly need to be cuddled often so that they are constantly reassured of the parent's love. One writer states, "It is impossible to overemphasize the importance of providing our children with the assurance that we love and understand them. . . . Even the adolescent, with all his apparent indifferences to his parents, desperately needs to feel the security of their love."[51]

When it is necessary to correct the child for some action, or for failing to do something he should, the parent must make clear that it is the misbehavior that is rejected and not the child. If Johnny continues to bounce the ball when he is told to stop, then the ball is taken away as punishment and Johnny is told, "We love you, Johnny, but we don't like you to bounce the ball at this time. You must obey when mother speaks." In this case Johnny does not have

49. Edwin H. Sutherland and Donald R. Cressey, *Criminology* (Philadelphia: J. B. Lippincott Co., 1970), p. 209.
50. William M. Kephart, *The Family, Society, the Individual* (Boston: Houghton and Mifflin Co., 1966), p. 532.
51. Donald M. Maynard, *Your Home Can Be Christian* (Nashville: Abingdon Press, 1952), pp. 36-37.

to wonder whether he is loved or not for he has been reassured verbally.[52]

Love is also demonstrated in the attitude that the parent exhibits toward a child. In one family of four children, the third child was always referred to as "the bad one." He was a little more active, and perhaps more mischievous than the others, and perchance even did some things to get his share of the parent's attention since the children were only a year or two apart. It is easy to see how this child could feel unloved and rejected because of the negative attitude expressed by the parents toward him. Soon he realized he was "a bad one" and played the role for he knew his parents expected him to be bad.

One truth of social psychology that parents must know and observe is that individuals try to live up to the role people expect them to play. Arthur Gordon has written, "The human being is a unique creature in that he will often make more effort to please someone else than he will to please himself. To recognize and use this principle in dealing with children is probably the most effective and subtle way to demand."[53]

If a child is continually told he is "bad," he eventually will adopt this role; this is attested to by thousands of juvenile delinquents. It is true a child is "bad" in the sense that all children have a sinful nature prone to evil, but the parent's job is to show him he is capable of doing much that is good. A child must never be referred to as bad; he is a "good" boy who is loved and accepted, but it is his bad behavior that is rejected and for which he is punished. For example, if Johnny strikes his little sister while playing with her, the mother should not say, "Johnny, you are a bad boy for hitting your little sister," but "Johnny, you are a good boy, and a good boy doesn't hit his little sister." She then may proceed to slap his hand to help him remember that "a good boy doesn't hit his little sister." From childhood through adolescence the parent must always strive to let the child know that the best behavior is always expected from him, and usually he will try to live up to the expectation. The child's love for the parent is always better motivation for good behavior than his fear of punishment by the parent.

A second principle is that the parents must be consistent in their discipline. If Jane is allowed to do one thing one day and nothing is

---

52. Dobson, *Dare to Discipline*, p. 36. He has a good discussion of the difference between "punishment" and "discipline."

53. Arthur Gordon, "Demand Their Best," ed. J. Allan Petersen, *The Marriage Affair* (Wheaton, IL: Tyndale House Publishers, 1971), p. 179. A good article concerning role expectations written from a layman's point of view rather than a sociologist's.

done about it, and then is punished for doing it the next day, she will be very confused. In like manner, if Jane misbehaves and is not punished, whereas Johnny is punished for the same misconduct, the children will be confused and resentful toward the parents. If the child is guilty of some misbehavior for which punishment is meted out, then the parent should be consistent in giving that punishment. A child is wise enough to take the chance if he feels the parent may not punish him for his misdeed.

Discipline should be given immediately upon the infraction of a rule or misbehavior of any kind. This is particularly true with small children. Some mothers make the mistake of having the children wait for hours until the father comes home to administer the punishment. Discipline of this type is not nearly as effective as that given immediately upon the committal of the forbidden act. "Effective punishment is prompt, not hasty. It brings the results of misbehavior close to the act, so that a child, especially a young one, remembers why he is being punished."[54]

Parents need to be fair in their administration of punishment. Oftentimes children are punished for behavior that is normal for a child of that age. Henry R. Brandt suggests that the responsibility of discipline "includes the necessity to comprehend the needs of children and to understand how youngsters develop and their processes of learning."[55] Another author writes, "There is no magic whereby a Christian parent comes to understand all about personality development and the emotional needs of children. They must work to discover the kind of parental reactions that make for normality and fullness of life."[56]

It is natural for a two-year-old child to wiggle and squirm and be very active. It is unfair for a parent to expect such a child to sit still for an hour during a church service that he does not comprehend, then take him out of the service and spank him for squirming. Often the parents cannot determine which child has been guilty of an act so they punish all the children just to be sure they get the right one. This is unfair to the innocent, and the children will resent such actions on the part of the parent.

It always is helpful to children to know what is acceptable and unacceptable behavior. The parents should agree on this, and inform the children where the limits are. "Specific limits ought to be as few as possible, reasonable, enforceable, withdrawn (or modified as the

54. Wayne J. Anderson, *Design for Family Living* (Minneapolis: T. S. Denison & Co., Inc., 1964), p. 245.
55. Brandt and Dowdy, *Building a Christian Home*, p. 108.
56. Werner, *Christian Family Living*, p. 39.

child grows older)."[57] This is especially necessary in Christian families since the norms or behavior are different than those of the surrounding culture. Parents should be able to give a good explanation when certain behavior is prohibited so that the children understand the reason for the prohibition. It is unfair to simply tell them it is a "no no" without some Scriptural or logical reason.

Some Christian parents have reared their children using the negative approach of "Thou shalt not" without adequate explanation, and without a corresponding emphasis on the positive aspects of Christianity, with the result that the children have rejected, and often rebelled against, the norms of the family and church. The negative is very necessary, but the positive must receive the emphasis for successful child rearing.

A couple should agree on the method of discipline before marriage because young people are raised in homes where different methods are employed. A girl reared in a home where corporal punishment was never used would find it very hard to accept her husband using corporal punishment on the children. The Bible indicates that corporal punishment is to be used, for we have verses such as Proverbs 13:24, "He that spareth his rod hateth his son: but he that loveth him chasteneth him betimes (as needed)," and Proverbs 19:18, "Chasten thy son while there is yet hope, and let not thy soul spare for his crying."

However, common sense needs to be used as to when to spank children.[58] It certainly does not make much sense for an irritated parent to spank a six-months-old baby when it is crying because it needs its diapers changed, or is hungry. Young children who are old enough to understand the reason for punishment can benefit greatly from a spanking. There comes a time when spanking is no longer necessary, and other forms of discipline may be more fruitful. Bruce Narramore remarks that "spankings should never be utilized when there is another effective method of discipline available. Spankings are usually more necessary in the first few years of life. After a child is old enough to communicate well and to profit from other measures, spanking should be ended."[59] Withholding privileges from an older child may be much more positive than a spanking.

Children are not to be physically aggressive toward children, but should be taught to settle their differences by verbal means rather

57. Brandt and Dowdy, *Building a Christian Home*, p. 111.

58. Dobson, *Dare to Discipline*, pp. 58-59.

59. Bruce Narramore, *A Guide to Child Rearing* (Grand Rapids: Zondervan Publishing House, 1972), p. 91. This is a manual for parents to accompany *Help! I'm a Parent*. Both are highly recommended to parents.

than by physical assault.[60] The parent should use the same approach in settling differences with the older children and adolescents. If a teen-ager does not respond positively to reason and logic, it is highly unlikely that corporal punishment can accomplish the goal the parent has in mind. It probably serves only to accentuate the rebellion of the teen-ager.

The principle to observe in disciplining adolescents is to treat them as young but immature adults. Teen-agers in America have a difficult time because the culture has no particular role for them to play. They are no longer children, and they are not yet adults. They are too old to play, and too young to work. The Minimum Wage Law has made it impossible for thousands of teen-agers to find part-time jobs. For several years (from about thirteen to eighteen) they have no productive role to play. Many do not enjoy the role of student, which adds to their difficulties. Long before they are adults they are exposed to temptations by the purveyors of pornography, illicit sex, drug pushers, and alcohol. Yet most teen-agers grow into responsible citizens, with only a small percentage becoming the "drop-outs" of society.

The Christian teen-ager is faced with the same problems and temptations as the unsaved fellow or girl. He has to make the transition from a dependent child to an independent adult.[61] If parents have established the habit of talking things over with their children, and talking things out when there are misunderstandings, then they should not encounter any "generation gap" when the children reach the teens. The "gap" is caused by a breakdown in communication between the parents and teen-agers. Very often this is caused by the parents' attempt to treat the teen-agers as children rather than maturing young adults. Parents need to help teen-agers make the transition to adult status by slowly giving them the right to make decisions that concern themselves and their future. *The aim is to achieve a balance* between giving them too much freedom too early, and dominating them too long.

There is a happy medium whereby little by little as the teen-ager matures, he is able to make more and more of the decisions affecting him, until he becomes thoroughly able to do so by age eighteen. If he goes off to college or to the service, he will be able to take care of himself. It is tragic to see a young man enter college unable to purchase his own clothing, or a young lady in the dorm who does not know how to operate an automatic washer! It is also tragic to see

60. Dobson, *Dare to Discipline*, p. 55.
61. Vera Channels, *The Layman Builds a Christian Home* (St. Louis: The Bethany Press, 1959), p. 79.

young people rebelling because they are forced to go to college by domineering parents. The parents of such young people have failed in the responsibility to help their children become mature young adults. However, such failure on the part of the parents does not excuse the young person from striving to overcome this failure by learning to make intelligent decisions as they have opportunity for such decisions.

There may be a child who is such a discipline problem that the parent should seek professional help for the child. Clyde M. Narramore remarks, "Strangely enough, parents who will rush their child to the doctor because of a slight temperature rise or a pain in his little finger, hesitate to consult a doctor or psychologist on behavior troubles. Extreme behavior may well be due to physical causes. But whatever the cause, there is help available for the emotionally unstable youngster."[62] He then gives an illustration of a ten-year old problem boy who had been given a physical that revealed he had suffered a brain injury. With medication and a change of attitude by the parents, the boy's behavior improved. If a family cannot afford psychological help, most communities have some agency such as the Child Guidance Clinic supported by the United Fund that provides counseling with fees based on the family's ability to pay.

The Christian parent must always remember that the aim of all discipline, regardless of the methods used, is to teach the child to discipline himself. Unless the child internalizes the norms that the family teaches him, then the child will not display the proper behavior outside the home. If the parent succeeds, the child's actions become more and more controlled by himself. He finally becomes "inner directed" rather than "other directed." He is sensitive not only to the principles taught by the parents, but also to the leading of the Holy Spirit in relation to his interaction with others. Such a young person is a joy to his parents and to those with whom he interacts. Such discipline requires firmness, faith, and patience, but the rewards are most gratifying!

SEX EDUCATION BY CHRISTIAN PARENTS

The problem of sex education of children in American culture is being widely discussed, and it is a subject of controversy in many areas where the public schools have assumed this role for them-

62. Clyde M. Narramore, *Discipline in the Christian Home* (Grand Rapids: Zondervan Publishing House, 1961), pp. 27-28.

selves.[63]   The need for children to be educated as to sex and reproduction is not debatable. The difficulty arises when the question is
raised regarding who is going to do the teaching. Until recently, it
was the parents' task to give children the necessary information in
these areas and to create the proper attitudes toward the opposite
sex. The church was to supplement and to reinforce the teaching
received in the home.

Many Christian families and churches fulfilled their role in an
acceptable manner. The many fine happy Christian homes are evidence of this success. However, in many families and churches, the
subject of sex was taboo. The children received their sex information
from the peer group and books.[64] Much knowledge gained in this
way was inaccurate and unreliable, and the prevailing attitude was
that sex is "sinful and dirty" rather than holy and God-given.

The failure on the part of some parents may be attributed to the
fact that they were reared in a generation where the discussion of sex
was not as free and open as it is now. Parents were not given
instructions on how to play their roles, and since individuals tend to
perform their roles as their parents did, they also did not know how
to teach their children about sex and reproduction.

The Bible severely condemns sexual sins, since morality and the
sanctity of the home are necessary for the existence of an orderly
society, and some churches have emphasized this negative aspect of
Scripture rather than the positive view. The Bible teaches that God
created man as a sexual being, and that the sexes were to complement each other (Gen. 2:18-25). Sex within marriage is to be
enjoyed (Heb. 13:4), and serves to prevent the misuse of the body
for sinful purposes (I Cor. 6:9—7:5). The body is to be presented to
God as a living sacrifice and used only for His glory (Rom. 12:1-2).
The church has an obligation to teach the whole counsel of God, and
this certainly includes the positive presentation of sex.

Many authorities in family living agree that the home is the best
place for sex instruction. If parents do their job well, there is no need
for the public school to become involved in this area. The parents are
with the child when he first begins to wonder why he is different
than the opposite sex. He begins to question where his existence
started long before he is ready for the first grade. Obviously, then,

63. See articles in *Moody Monthly*, December 1969, pp. 40-44, and *Christianity Today*, January 30, 1970, pp. 10-13 for information on sex education in the public schools.
64. Only 15 out of a class of 41 college students in a Marriage and Family class received their sex education from their parents. The others received theirs from the school health classes, peer groups, siblings, and books.

the home and its attitude toward sex should determine the child's attitude toward it.

Brandt quotes David B. Treat as saying, ". . . sex education is 20 percent education and 80 percent attitudes." He then makes the point that "tender, considerate, unselfish, kind, mutual consideration for one another in the family will contribute to developing right attitudes in the child toward the opposite sex. The child must see a display of affection in the home—not merely hugs and kisses, but mutual consideration in a loving spirit."[65]

Christian parents who correctly view sex as something holy and God-given are able to instill a proper attitude in their children long before the subject is discussed by the peer group. This means that the parents strive to maintain free and open communication with their children in all areas so questions that children naturally ask are frankly answered.[66] All children at sometime want to know where babies come from, and how they are made. The wise parent is able to give a simple explanation that satisfies the child's curiosity. Brandt lists a few "universal questions with simple answers":

> Where do we get a new baby? It lives and grows inside Mother.
>
> Where does the baby come out? Through a special opening in Mother's body.
>
> How does the baby grow? Mother's body gives it food and keeps it warm. Every day it gets bigger and stronger until it is born.
>
> When the baby kicks, won't it hurt Mother? Babies never kick hard enough to hurt their mothers.
>
> Why do you get so big before you have a baby? Because the baby is growing.[67]

If the parent answers questions about sex as the child raises them, the child feels free to come to the parents with other questions. Bruce Larson writes, ". . . it is terribly important for parents to be free to talk about sex with their children. . . . But if we cannot begin in early years to discuss this with our children, it will become increasingly difficult as they grow older."[68] It is necessary to begin communication with the small child, and as the child matures, the parents feel free to discuss such subjects as menstruation and reproduction with the child to give necessary information as needed. The

65. Brandt and Dowdy, *Building a Christian Home*, p. 120.
66. Bruce Narramore, *Parenting with Love & Limits* (Grand Rapids: Zondervan Publishing House, 1979) pp. 127-135.
67. Brandt and Dowdy, *Building a Christian Home*, p. 125. Used by permission.
68. Bruce Larson, *Marriage Is for Living* (Grand Rapids: Zondervan Publishing House, 1968), p. 40.

child or teen-ager has the proper information, and when the peer group confronts him with misinformation, he is able to discuss it with his parents.

The parents can best relate the facts of sex and reproduction to love, responsibility, and the will of God for the Christian child and teen-ager. Sexuality cannot be divorced from morality, and the child needs to learn the proper use of sex. The task of the church is to reinforce this view that the child has received in the home. In this "adulterous and sinful generation" (Mark 8:38) children and young people need all the help they can get to resist the temptations they meet. It is unfortunate that some liberal church groups have condoned premarital relations and "situation ethics." The church can teach young people the Biblical view of sex in Sunday school classes, the pulpit ministry, youth meetings, summer camp sessions, and special retreats.[69]

Since the area of sex is still taboo in some churches, youth leaders need to exercise wisdom and caution in meetings planned to help young people in the area of sex education. They should have the cooperation of the pastor and permission of the parents before attempting to have any kind of special effort that deals specifically with sex education.

Christian parents can impart the necessary information and the proper attitudes towards sexuality if they establish and maintain communication with their children and are frank and honest in their answers to questions that are asked. This is not something that is done at one time, but is a process that continues until the young person leaves the home. The attitude of husband and wife to each other has a subtle, but powerful, influence on the children and their view of how love operates between a man and woman. Young people reared in such an atmosphere of love, and who have been taught that their bodies are the temples of the indwelling Holy Spirit will be able to withstand any temptations to impurity they encounter.

Christian parenthood is the logical end of Christian marriage, and the rewards of rearing children to the glory of God far outweigh the testings and difficulties that are involved in such a task.

69. Herbert J. Miles, *Sexual Happiness*, pp. 149-151 contain helpful suggestions for pastors concerning sex education in the church.

QUESTIONS FOR DISCUSSION AND REVIEW

1. Give some reasons why it is necessary for the family to plan the birth of children.

2. What adjustments need to be made by the wife and husband before and after the birth of the first child?

3. Present arguments for and against the adoption of children into a family.

4. Why is it important that the parents fulfill their role faithfully?

5. When should a child be led to a saving knowledge of Christ?

6. Why is it important that the family have a "family altar"?

7. Discuss several principles to be followed by parents in disciplining their children.

8. How does the discipline of teen-agers differ from that of children?

9. Why is the home the best place for the sex education of children?

10. What are some of the responsibilities of the church in helping families in the area of sex education?

14

THE CHRISTIAN
AND MIXED MARRIAGES

Be ye not unequally yoked together
with unbelievers. . . .
II Corinthians 6:14

THE NATURE OF GROUPS AND MARRIAGE

Every society is composed of groups of various kinds which interact with each other according to norms which are mutually understood. Some groups are small and primary, such as a nuclear family, and others are large and secondary such as a major religious denomination. In order to survive, each of these groups develops attitudes and feelings in its members so that they identify each other as part of the "in-group" and those outside as members of the "out-group."

In American society there are many "in-groups," including such large classifications as religion, race, or social class. These large groups are then subdivided into a myriad of smaller groups. Each of these becomes an "in-group" for its members who are socialized in the group and whose values and goals are internalized in the personality structure of the person reared in the group.

Marriage is nearly always encouraged with members of the "in-group." The young person will find a greater similarity of background, beliefs, and values in a member of his own group, and these make for compatibility and success in American marriage. It is also encouraged, for the survival of the group may depend upon the families to perpetuate the beliefs or characteristics that help distinguish the "in-groups" from the "out-groups." Marriage within the group is termed "endogamy" and marriage outside is termed "exogamy."[1] The more common terms for exogamous marriages are "intermarriage" or "mixed marriage."

There are some types of intermarriage such as intergenerational or interclass that do not occur as frequently as others. They do not receive much attention in American society unless the persons involved are prominent public figures. The mass media gives much publicity to a wealthy heiress marrying a poor boy, or an older senator or supreme court justice marrying a girl young enough to be his granddaughter.

Two groups manifest great concern when intermarriage occurs. The marriage across religious or racial lines is almost universally discouraged because of the problems arising in these types of marriage outside the "in-group." These two kinds of exogamous marriages are discussed in this chapter.

MIXED MARRIAGES AND THE AMERICAN CULTURE

The heterogeneous society in which American young people are reared and the prevalent dating and courtship system make it fairly easy for young people with different ethnic, racial, or religious backgrounds to meet and to marry. ". . . Cities and suburbs are much more likely to have culturally mixed backgrounds. . . . People still tend to marry partners who are close in distance, but the closeness is more likely to be as of right now rather than as of their childhood homes."[2]

This diversity of background means that more and greater adjustments have to be made if the couple are going to be compatible according to the norms of American marriage. The ease with which divorces are secured makes it fairly simple for such couples who fail to make the adjustments to secure a divorce. Albert I. Gordon, a rabbi for thirty-five years and a social scientist for twenty years made a study of this subject in his book *Intermarriage*. He concludes, "The statistical evidence incorporated in this study makes it clear that the 'odds' do not favor intermarriages, in that almost two to four times as many intermarriages as intramarriages end in divorce, separation or

1. Gail Putney Fullerton, *Survival in Marriage* (New York: Holt, Rinehart and Winston, Inc., 1972), pp. 284-285. A good discussion on "The pool of eligibles."
2. Richard H. Klemer, *Marriage and Family Relationships* (New York: Harper and Row, Publishers, 1970), p. 86.

annulment. This is a highly significant fact. It is objective and utterly free from emotion-inducing factors."[3]

Broken marriages often result in broken homes. "More than 10 million children are now living with one parent, and 2 out of 3 of these are the product of divorce or separation."[4] Broken homes are involved in the increase in juvenile delinquency, for "research reports indicate that from 30 to 60 percent of delinquents come from broken homes, and the percentages tend to cluster around 40 percent."[5]

The rupture of the relationships in the home is often preceded by much unhappiness for both parents and children. When the home is broken, it is usually a traumatic experience for the children involved.[6] The mother usually receives custody of the children, and she is then left to rear them without the help of the father. If she cannot support them, the family may become one of the numerous families supported by the taxpayers. Thus society has a stake in mixed marriages, and the behavioral norms of the culture discourage any marriage where there are great differences in the cultural backgrounds of the individuals involved.

INTERFAITH MARRIAGES

The church also has a stake in mixed marriages since "every generation is only one generation from the eclipse of the Christian faith. Each generation must reach the next."[7] Parents bear much of this responsibility, for they must transmit the faith to their children. This is difficult, and often impossible in a mixed religious marriage. Each major religious body, whether Protestant, Roman Catholic, or Jewish, teaches that young people ought to marry within their own faith.[8]

3. Albert I. Gordon, *Intermarriage, Interfaith, Interracial, Interethnic* (Boston: Beacon Press, 1964), p. 372. Used by permission.
4. "Throwaway Marriages"—Threat to the American Family, *U.S. News and World Report*, Jan. 13, 1975, p. 43.
5. Edwin H. Sutherland and Donald R. Cressy, *Criminology*, (Philadelphia: J. B. Lippincott Co., 1974), p. 207.
6. For a heartrending story of the effects of divorce on one child, see *Scars of Divorce*, Narramore Christian Foundation, Rosemead, CA.
7. George Sweeting, message delivered at Moody Memorial Church, February 1970.
8. See Gordon, *Intermarriage*, chapters 5, 6, and 7 for a fuller discussion of the Protestant, Catholic, and Jewish views on interfaith marriages.

The Christian has two roles to play in his personal relationships to other people. He is first and foremost a Christian, a member of the family of God, and he interacts with other Christians as fellow believers. He is also a citizen of the world, and as such, he daily interacts with unbelievers. He is in the world, but is not to become worldly in his attitudes nor behavior. Jesus prayed in John 17:15, "I pray not that thou shouldest take them out of the world, but that thou should keep them from the evil." He is to be a witness and testimony for Christ to the unsaved around him, yet "hating even the garment spotted by the flesh" (Jude 23).

Christian young people, during their dating years have contact through propinquity with many unsaved fellows and girls. Many of these are very attractive physically, and they also have pleasant personalities. The Christian reasons that he can be a witness to such an unsaved person and is tempted to date the individual. He feels there is no harm in "just one date" with such a person. William W. Orr remarks, "Don't, however, ask God to guide you in relation to explicit principles which are taught in the pages of Scripture. For instance, don't ask whether you should allow yourself to become serious with a girl or fellow who's not a Christian. The answer to this has already been given (II Cor. 6:14-16) with clarion clarity in the Bible."[9] The young person must remember the rule, "Every date is a prospective mate." He may very well feel he can keep his emotions under control, forgetting the verse, " . . . the heart is deceitful above all things . . . " (Jer. 17:9) One date leads to another, and finally the Christian's emotions take precedence over his reason, and he goes into an interfaith marriage against the wishes of his parents and his fellow believers in the church.

The problem is especially difficult for the Christian girl. In the United States in 1982, there were approximately two million more single women than single men between the ages of 18-24.[10] The situation in the average church is more drastic, for usually there are many more Christian young women of dating age than there are fellows. The church seems to lose the fellows after they enter high school. Many cannot maintain their Christian testimony and resist the temptations that are present in the average high school.

Consequently, Christian girls are faced with dating unsaved fellows, or not dating at all. If they do date them, they run the risk of an interfaith marriage. If they don't date, they miss out on many of

9. William W. Orr, *Love, Courtship and Marriage for Christian Youth* (Wheaton: Scripture Press, n.d.), p. 20.
10. U.S. Bureau of the Census, *Statistical Abstract of the United States*, 1984, (104th edition), Washington, D.C., p. 44.

the school social activities. Although this latter course of action produces unhappiness, it is better than running the risk of greater and life-long unhappiness by dating contrary to the will of God.

It is not only Protestant churches that counsel against mixed religious marriages, but the Roman Catholic Church and the Jewish faith also warn of the difficulties confronting such a marriage. In the ecumenical spirit of this age, the Roman Catholic Church has softened its attitude towards mixed marriages since Vatican II.[11] It no longer requires the non-Catholic to sign an antenuptial agreement. It also permits its clergy to participate in non-Catholic ceremonies, and non-Catholic clergy may have a part in a Roman Catholic ceremony. The clergy, both Roman Catholic and non-Catholic, recognize the greater difficulties in adjustment that such marriages face and ordinarily recommend against such a union. John Kelley, a University of Dayton professor, "commenting on the dangers inherent in an interfaith marriage says, 'I think we never encourage them. I would repeat the universal opinion of ministers that whether it be interfaith, interracial, wherever there is a great disparity of backgrounds, it adds a dimension of stress to a marriage.' "[12]

WHY YOUNG PEOPLE ENTER INTO INTERFAITH MARRIAGES

It is not difficult to understand why a person would enter an interfaith marriage if he had received little or no religious education in the home and has little or no faith in God. It makes little difference to such a person if the spouse attends church or not as long as she is not too religious and does not give too generously to the church. He is not concerned enough for his children's spiritual welfare to see that they get to a Sunday school or to a church.

It is difficult to understand how a young person reared in a Christian home, who attended a church since he was four weeks old, who professed faith in Christ at an early age, could ignore this background and enter into a marriage with an unbeliever. Such a young person is usually counseled by parents and pastor against such a union, but still persists in marrying contrary to the will of God. A definite spiritual problem exists, for the Bible is clear in its teaching that believers in Christ are not to be unequally yoked together with

11. Judson T. Landis and Mary G. Landis, *Building a Successful Marriage* (Englewood Cliffs, NJ: Prentice-Hall, Inc., 1968), p. 186.

12. Anne Doll, "More Freedom now in 'mixed' wedding rites," in *Kettering-Oakwood Times*, October 17, 1968, p. 17.

unbelievers (II Cor. 6:14). In this same passage, the apostle Paul raises the logical question as to what fellowship a child of God can have with an unbeliever. Technically, they belong to two different worlds, their goals in life should be different, and their eternal destinies are different. Dwight H. Small expresses it well when he writes, "One's relationship to Christ is a whole way of life, not a matter of what church one attends and what creed one holds." [13] For a young person to enter into a mixed union indicates he is out of fellowship with God, for He never leads a child of His contrary to the teaching of His Word.

For some young people, a mixed marriage is the result of rebellion against the church and family that begins when they are teen-agers. The period of adolescent growth is a difficult one for many, and particularly for Christian young people. The attractions and allurements of the satanic world-system are stronger at this stage of life than at any other time.

If the young person does not have a good Sunday school class, youth group, or high school Bible club to serve as a reference group to reinforce the beliefs and norms of the home and church, he may very easily backslide. He rejects the beliefs and norms of the home and accepts those of the peer group.

He may have been taught these norms, which require a high standard of conduct, without having been taught about the ministry of the indwelling Holy Spirit, who gives power to live according to Biblical standards. When the young person is faced with temptations, he does not have the power of the Holy Spirit to help him resist. Eventually a pattern of rebellion against the family and church develops, and it may culminate in the person marrying outside the faith. If there is much conflict between the young person and his parents, he may subconsciously use such a marriage to hurt and embarrass the parents.

Other young people are not essentially rebellious, but unwittingly become involved in a romance that leads to a mixed marriage. A young lady may honestly date an unsaved person with the idea of witnessing to him, perhaps with the thought that there will not be any more dates. However, the first date leads to more, and little by little the young lady becomes so emotionally involved, she becomes motivated by emotion rather than reason. She enters into the marriage still with the hope that he will be converted, and she will eventually have a Christian home.

13. Dwight Hervey Small, *Design for Christian Marriage* (Westwood, NJ: Fleming H. Revell Co., 1959), p. 151. Used by permission.

If he does not accept Christ, this can become one of the most unhappy homes, because the wife is not rebellious and wants to attend church and rear her children in the Sunday school and church. If the husband objects, the unhappiness can lead to conflict and divorce, or else the wife gives up her church attendance in order to keep peace in the family.

Many a young person has entered into marriage thinking she was marrying a Christian mate only to discover that the spouse had never really been converted. Oftentimes a fellow professes to accept Christ and join a church in order to get a Christian girl to marry him or vice-versa. He attends church faithfully with her during the courtship.

Soon after the marriage he loses interest and the young wife must attend church by herself. She finds herself unequally yoked with an unconverted husband although she thought she was marrying a believer. She can pray that he will be genuinely saved, but if he isn't, she faces the unhappiness of such a marriage, and the difficult task of rearing children without a Christian father.

Some young people become involved in a mixed marriage because of physical attraction. The unsaved person is so appealing that the Christian fellow or girl is willing to sacrifice convictions and future happiness in order to satisfy physical desires. He becomes so infatuated with the dating partner that appeals to reason or Scripture fall on deaf ears. Needless to say, after a year or so of marriage, the physical desires having been fulfilled, the Christian realizes the marriage lacks many enjoyments that are found in a successful Christian marriage.

The desire for higher social status may motivate some Christian young women to marry outside the faith. In American culture, the wife usually assumes the social class position of her husband and this is one avenue of upward social mobility for women. It is possible for a young woman out of fellowship with God to desire the manner of living and the status symbols of a higher social class than that in which she was reared. If she has opportunities in college or in her employment to meet young men from those higher classes, she may very well choose a mixed marriage to achieve her goal of moving up the social ladder.[14]

Unfortunately, some young women enter into an interfaith marriage for fear they are not going to be married otherwise. American culture places great stress on the necessity for marriage in order

14. See Appendix I for a case study of a mixed marriage where the Christian girl enjoyed the status symbols and life-style of an unsaved dating partner.

to find "happiness." David H. Olsen says a major limitation of our present dating system is that it is so effective that many people get married who should not get married. Parents and friends encourage people to get married so they can avoid the stigma of society placed on those who remain single.[15]

When a Christian young lady reaches the late twenties, she may feel that she is not going to find a Christian mate. For fear of becoming an "old maid" she may settle for an unsaved partner in order to find "happiness." The young lady who makes such a decision does not understand that happiness is found in the will of God and not in marriage. She usually lives to regret such a decision and to discover that an unhappy marriage outside the will of God does not bring the happiness that many single women know in the will of God.

PROBLEMS OF INTERFAITH MARRIAGES

There are difficulties in every marriage, but the Christian who consummates a union with an unbeliever can expect to encounter problems that are not found in the intrafaith marriage. One of the great blessings of the truly Christian home is the spiritual fellowship that the husband and wife enjoy together. This element is missing in the mixed marriage. The couple cannot pray together over decisions that need to be made, nor do they have the help and strength of the Holy Spirit when the "woes of life overtake them."

In II Corinthians 6:14, Paul asks, ". . . what communion [fellowship] hath light with darkness?" Obviously the couple in a mixed marriage cannot have fellowship together in the most important area of the Christian's life. They may have many common interests which give great satisfaction, but a gulf will exist between the believing and the unbelieving spouse. They will never be able to establish a "family altar," for the unbeliever does not have access to the Throne of Grace. The prospect of this spiritual division in the home should be enough to deter a Christian fellow or girl from marrying an unbeliever.

The couple in a mixed marriage is very likely to have in-law problems. "Inasmuch as no two people, no matter how much in love, live in a vacuum, the ideas, opinions and values of in-laws and family have a direct effect upon them, and that effect under circumstances

15. David H. Olsen, "Marriage of the Future: Revolutionary or Evolutionary Change?" in *The Family Coordinator*, October 1972, p. 384.

involving intermarriage is often negative."[16]   Marvin B. Sussman's survey of middle-class New Haven parents of married children revealed that 90 percent of the mixed marriages had encountered in-law difficulties as compared to only 18 percent of the unmixed marriages.[17]   "So mixed couples have more trouble and fewer rewards from their parents."[18]   Most parents of whatever faith or denomination desire that their children marry within the religious group. When the young person makes a choice outside the faith, they can expect a certain amount of opposition from the parents. If the convictions of the parents are very strong, the opposition may change to open hostility against the young person and his mate. Admittedly this is an unwise action on the part of the parents, but it does happen.

In many instances the parents will try to influence the religious education of the children born in a mixed marriage. "Interfaith marriages occasionally provoke a veritable tug of war between the two sets of parents for the souls of their grandchildren."[19]   Although the young parents may not feel it necessary for their baby to be baptized, yet where Roman Catholic in-laws are concerned, they may insist a baby be given this ritual. Later on they may try to influence the family to send the children to a Roman Catholic parochial school.

Likewise, the Protestant in-laws may insist the children be sent to the Sunday school and church of the Protestant parent. Similar potentials for conflict and unhappiness exist where a Protestant or Roman Catholic marries a person of the Jewish faith. Certain subcultural differences, such as dietary regulations and the close knit Jewish family, may increase the religious problems.

Christian in-laws will strive to make the best of an unfortunate and unhappy situation if their child should become involved in a mixed marriage. The parents cannot hold themselves responsible for the young person's decision to marry someone outside the faith, although they may sometimes unknowingly contribute to the situation. For example, the Protestant family that resides in a community where 80 to 90 percent of the population is Roman Catholic should be aware that a majority of the young people in the local high school will be Roman Catholic, and it is with these young people that their children will interact socially and be exposed to dating situations

16. Gordon, *Intermarriage*, p. 101.
17. Robert O. Blood, *Marriage* (New York: Free Press of Glencoe, 1962), p. 79.
18. Ibid.
19. Ibid.

which could lead to serious romantic involvement. The principle is "that the fewer fellow church members in the community, the higher the probability of intermarriage. This principle has been demonstrated for the Anglicans and Lutherans as well as Catholics (Bossard and Betts, 1956)."[20] A study in Canada showed that where 88 percent of the population was Catholic (Quebec), only 2 percent of the interfaith marriages involved Catholics. In British Columbia, only 14 percent of the population was Catholic, but 46 percent of the interfaith marriages involved Catholics.[21]

In a similar manner, the Christian parents who choose to send their son or daughter to a secular college or university, attended largely by unsaved students, because it costs "too much" to send the child to a Christian school, should be aware that many college students marry within the college group. They should not be surprised if the son or daughter marries an unbeliever, for these are the people they will associate with during the dating and courtship period of life. The parents may then realize that the Christian institution has some advantages in mate selection that cannot be measured in dollars and cents!

Even in such cases of poor judgment on the part of parents, or when parents have done everything possible to rear and educate their children according to God's will, there is nothing to be gained by feelings of remorse and guilt. They should make every effort to win the friendship of the unsaved son- or daughter-in-law and fervently pray for his salvation. The only way for the mixed marriage to be changed is for the unbeliever to accept Christ, so that the home may become a truly Christian home. The efforts of the believing parents should be directed to this end, and all their interaction with the young family should be motivated by this noble desire.

Some differences of religious beliefs may create conflict between the husband and wife in a mixed marriage. The saved fellow or girl who dates a Roman Catholic person may ignore during the courtship the question of family planning, but it must be faced realistically on the honeymoon. The Protestant and Roman Catholic churches hold opposing views on contraception, and this can become a continuing problem if each partner holds to the view of his own church.[22] If a wife is compelled to bear children she does not desire, it can have unhealthy effects upon her and also upon the unwanted children. There are great differences of opinion within the Roman Catholic

20. Ibid., p. 80.
21. Ibid., p. 81.
22. Landis and Landis, Successful Marriage, p. 187.

church itself on family planning, and many individual Roman Catholics disagree with the official position of their church.

Much unhappiness exists in the home where a spouse actively practices his or her faith and this is disliked by the partner. If the believing wife desires to attend all the services of the church, the unsaved husband may resent having to remain home alone. If she rears the children as active Christians, there will be a spiritual gulf between the father and children, just as there is between the mother and father. In cases of family conflict, the father may feel the mother has influenced the children against him, which can add to the unhappiness in the home. In some cases, the unsaved father may be able to turn the children against the mother and her faith. The children become confused. and may even become neurotics, because of the division and conflict in the home. Many reject Christ and the church because the home life has presented a perverted view of the Christian life.

In cases where the spouse does not object to the partner devotedly following the faith, it is possible for a Christian mother, for example, to rear her children as devout Christians. Such a woman assumes her place of submission in the home (I Peter 3:1-6), and attempts to win her husband by a "meek and quiet" spirit living a holy life to the glory of God. She is consistent in her Christian life and testimony, and has an eternal influence upon her children. She must depend more heavily upon the Lord in the spiritual training of her children, for she has the responsibilities usually shared by both the Christian mother and father.

The effects of an interfaith marriage upon children in such a family should be reason enough to avoid such a union. Gordon writes:

> Our personal histories [of persons interviewed] reveal the fact that no parent in a mixed marriage, however intelligent and capable he or she may otherwise be, can assure his children of the security in family and society they both want and need. Psychologically the children of mixed marriages are faced with more numerous emotional problems than we have a right to bequeath to them. It does not seem reasonable, therefore, to intensify the nature and quantity of the difficulties that mixed marriages and the children thereof are likely to face.[23]

These emotional problems apparently also lead to antisocial conduct. A greater percentage of children from mixed marriages are

23. Gordon, *Intermarriage*, p. 369.

involved in delinquency than are children from unmixed families. A study in Saint Louis found that "... arrests for juvenile crimes are more likely to occur when children are from religiously mixed homes by a factor of 1.9 for Protestants to 8.0 for Jews. These tables clearly suggest that child rearing, for example, in homes where parents have not married homogamously (by religion and nationality in these cases) is likely to be more of a problem."[24]

If the problems in the mixed marriage become insurmountable, the union may end in divorce. The stress and strain of such a union is too much for many families, and the resultant unhappiness is more than the couple can stand. Divorce is usually a traumatic experience, especially for the children involved. The believer has been taught that marriage is for life, and even though he does not believe in divorce, he may be forced into it by the unsaved spouse. The much higher rate of divorce for mixed marriages should be an effective warning to any Christian young person contemplating such a marriage.

INTERRACIAL MARRIAGES

An interracial marriage in America faces greater difficulties than an interfaith marriage because of the prejudice that is both overt and covert in American society. As recently as the end of World War II, thirty of the forty-eight states prohibited interracial marriage. In 1948, the California Supreme Court declared the California miscegenation law unconstitutional. Other states followed this lead. Finally, the United States Supreme Court in 1967 struck down the miscegenation laws of Virginia and fifteen other states.[25] These laws had legalized the prejudice existing in the West against whites marrying Indians or Orientals, and in the South against whites marrying blacks.

Although there are no longer laws forbidding such marriages, the prejudice against such unions still exists in all parts of the country. "Even though there are no legal prohibitions against interracial marriages in certain areas of this country, particularly the North and Northeast, there have been comparatively few such marriages. . . . From 1916 to 1937 the percent of Negro-white marriages in New York State exclusive of New York City was 2.9 percent."[26] This

24. David A. Schulz, *The Changing Family* (Englewood Cliffs, NJ: Prentice-Hall, Inc., 1972), p. 247. The factor for Catholics was 2.5.
25. Robert E. Cushman and Robert F. Cushman, *Cases in Constitutional Law* (New York: Appleton-Century-Crofts, 1968), pp. 1050-1056. The 1967 case was Loving vs. Virginia.
26. Gordon, *Intermarriage*, p. 265.

indicates that in the absence of laws forbidding miscegenation, the attitudes of individuals were sufficient to cause most persons to marry within their own race.

A recent article in *Jet* magazine states, "Interracial marriages in the United States have more than doubled since the 1968 Supreme Court decision which invalidated miscegenation laws. However, the number of the marriages is still very low compared to all marriages. In 1980, interracial marriages accounted for 1.9 percent of all marriages—up from 0.7 percent in 1968."[27] In a Roper Organization Poll, three-quarters of the women interviewed would accept a daughter marrying a man of a different religion, but only 23 percent would accept an interracial marriage.

However, it must be remembered that it is one thing to answer a poll question and approve of intermarriage, but a quite different situation when faced with the possibility of a child or friend entering such a marriage. Gordon writes:

> I believe that Negro-white marriages will increase slowly—but that they *will* [italics his] increase. . . . Negro-white marriages, however "reasonable" they may be, will in the forseeable future at least, prove difficult and problem-laden because the parents, family, and friends of the intermarried will continue to regard them with distress and anguish. They will, rightly or wrongly, be regarded as calamitous because the American people do not, to this date, accept them as proper. This has nothing whatever to do with their legal correctness. The mores of the American people are involved. Until they change— and I believe that ultimately they *will* [italics his] change to a degree—interracial marriage will continue to be severely frowned upon.[28]

WHY DO INTERRACIAL MARRIAGES OCCUR?

If there is such strong sentiment against interracial marriage, why do young people engage in such marriages? One reason is common to this type of marriage as well as to others, and that is "propinquity" or "nearness." With increased integration and more interaction between black and white young people, it is possible for romantic involvement to take place particularly at the college level. "The marriage of Charlayne Hunter, first Negro girl to enter the University of Georgia in 1961 and first of her race to graduate from it, to Walter Stovall, a white student at the University, has confirmed the belief held by some persons that interracial contacts on the school level must

---

27. *Jet*, 66:26, July 30, 1984, p. 26. The Roper Poll was in the *Dayton Daily News*, Dayton, OH, Oct. 20, 1985, p. 5-A.

28. Gordon, *Intermarriage*, pp. 270-271. Used by permission.

inevitably lead to some degree of interracial marriage. . . . Contact—whether it be in school, housing, or in employment—will have its effect upon the rate of interracial marriages."[29]

Another researcher, Jessie Bernard, analyzed the data on mixed couples who have married between 1950 and 1960, and "found that 60.3 percent of the black husbands who had white wives were in the same educational bracket as their wives. . . . Of those black husbands whose education differed from that of their white wives, 18.6 percent had *more* [italics hers] education than their wives; 21.1 percent less."[30] This seems to indicate that these interracial marriages were between partners with fairly equal educational and social standing.

The usual pattern in an interracial marriage is for a black man to marry a white woman. Vincent Herr studied statistics of interracial marriages kept by several states and his "data indicate that 'marriages between Negro men and white women are much more common than those between white men and Negro women.' "[31]

This phenomenon has several facets to it. For some Negroes, "the white person is the symbol of status and achievement, and is therefore desirable as a marriage partner. Marriage with a white woman or even a light-skinned Negro woman is thus viewed as 'status giving' and is highly desirable to some Negroes."[32] The marriage to a white woman may be a form of "status seeking" by the black man. With the advent of Black Nationalism, there may be a change in this attitude because of the "Black is beautiful" concept.

This may be evident in a Harris Poll taken in 1971, in which 40 percent of the blacks felt that a black man with "any pride" would marry a person from his own race.[33] Another report says, "Black college women report bitterness and resentment at being shunted aside by the black men on the campus for women who are white and blonde."[34]

Hugh Carter and Paul C. Glick suggest that some black males may seek a white wife because they think she may be less domineering than a Negro wife. They also remark that some are "motivated primarily by elementary attraction quite independent of other considerations."[35]

29. Ibid., p. 270.
30. Fullerton, *Survival in Marriage*, p. 318.
31. Ibid.
32. Gordon, *Intermarriage*, p. 269.
33. Fullerton, *Survival in Marriage*, p. 323. The poll was reported in *Life*, May 28, 1971, pp. 66-67.
34. Ibid.
35. Carter and Glick, *Marriage and Divorce*, p. 129.

Another reason for the black groom-white bride marriage is given by Robert K. Kelley. He points out that "the black man has always been forcibly prevented from having sexual relationships with white women; marriage to a white woman thus symbolizes his new freedom."[36]

For the white woman, such a marriage may be the result of failure in competing with white women for a white husband. There are not enough white men available as prospective husbands as indicated earlier in the chapter.

Interracial marriage for some may be the result of a liberal crusading spirit that identifies with the oppressed. Blacks in America have been oppressed and downtrodden, and many white young people are concerned with their social and economic lot. The young person is enamored with the civil rights movement and is active in organizations aimed at helping the blacks. Again "propinquity" comes into play and the young person is attracted to a black person and marriage results.

Some young people choose interracial marriages because of rebellion against their parents. "An individual who dislikes his parents may marry an outsider in order to hurt them or to prove his own independence."[37] Gordon gives the case history of a woman named "Ruth" who had a very unhappy home life with a mother and father who fought bitterly. Ruth says, "As I look back at it now it seemed that by marrying this Negro boy I could do two important things at the same time: first, prove that I believe all people are equal and that I was not a hypocrite; and second, get away from both my mother and father by marrying."[38] Needless to say, with such a shaky foundation, the marriage lasted only two years.

PROBLEMS OF INTERRACIAL MARRIAGES

The problems in an interracial marriage are similar to those faced by the interfaith couple, with the added burden of color prejudice and all that this includes. For example, the interfaith couple is not discriminated against in trying to rent or buy a home, but the interracial couple frequently encounters this difficulty. Although the Civil Rights laws prohibit such discrimination, the appearance of

36. Robert K. Kelley, *Courtship, Marriage and the Family*, 2nd ed. (New York: Harcourt Brace Jovanovich Inc., 1974), p. 281.
37. Blood, *Marriage*, p. 74.
38. Gordon, *Intermarriage*, p. 292.

cases in the newspapers where black individuals have filed suit with the Civil Rights boards indicate that such practices continue. Gordon records the case history of Doris: "That is one thing that happens to people of mixed racial marriages. We have had to work awfully hard to find a decent place to live. . . . There are a thousand different ways of saying the same thing, 'No, we don't want you!' But it all boils down to the same thing—people believe that interracial marriages are somehow a sign of decadence or something."[39]

Another problem faced by the interracial couple and not by the interfaith marriage is that of companionship with other families. If they live in a liberal community they may find other "mixed" couples. Judson T. and Mary G. Landis remark, "Young people who make mixed marriages while in a university community, where attitudes are likely to be more inclined toward acceptance of such marriages than in other communities, may encounter new problems if they leave the university community and settle elsewhere."[40] The couple may have to find more of their companionship with each other than the normal couple does. This can add strains to the relationship which it may not be able to bear.

Another area of potential difficulty for the interracial couple is discrimination in employment. This also is prohibited by the Civil Rights Act of 1964 but, like housing, employers are capable of finding subtle ways of avoiding compliance with the act.

The interracial marriage must also face in-law problems. According to Gordon's study, some families were able to accept with equanimity the announcement that a member was going to marry a person of another race. However, many families, including some who reared their children to be very liberal in racial attitudes, could not accept such a disclosure. Gordon writes concerning the case of Henry, a Jew, married for ten years to Violet, a Negro: "Friends of Henry's parents report that the marriage of their son to Violet has proved to be a great shock—one from which they haven't really recovered in all these years. The mother, a sensitive person, when she finds the strength to discuss this marriage often asks, 'Why did this happen to me?' . . . Friends have tried to reason with Henry's mother and father, but neither is inclined to listen."[41] In the case of Doris, who eloped to marry a Negro, her father never spoke to her again.[42] The disapproval of parents of an ordinary marriage is a minus factor, but

39. Ibid., p. 287.
40. Landis and Landis, *Successful Marriage*, p. 208.
41. Gordon, *Intermarriage*, p. 273.
42. Ibid., p. 286.

the negative influence of such disapproval in an interracial marriage is far more severe.

The greatest problem faced by an interracial couple is the difficulty of rearing children who are marginal to two different cultures. The adjustments faced by the couple in an interracial marriage pale into insignificance compared to those faced by children of such a marriage. Small writes,

> Not infrequently there is a very dark child and a very light one in the same family. The colored child loves the colored parent and dislikes the other. Or the parent takes to the child of the same color but rejects the other. This is aggravated when other children make fun of the fact that two children in the same family are different in color. Our cruel and competitive culture still brands such children as "half-breeds." So the crucial question is whether parents have a right to impose upon unborn generations a radical decision of their own.[43]

This truth is also stated by Gordon:

> Persons anticipating cross-marriages, however much in love they may be, have an important obligation to *unborn children* [italics mine]. It is not enough to say that such children will have to solve their own problems "when the time comes." Intermarriage frequently produces major psychological problems that are not readily solvable for the children of the intermarried. Living as we do in a world that emphasizes the importance of family and religious affiliations, it is not likely that the child will come through the maze of road blocks without doing some damage to himself.[44]

The case history of Helen Scott illustrates the kind of conflict that some children suffer because of their mixed parentage:

> *When I was a youngster, I definitely had certain problems because of my background. It is something you live with from the time you are first aware of the fact that you are something which you do not appear to be. All my life I have looked and lived (I think) like a white and yet all my life I have known I am a Negro. . . . I was brought up to regard myself as colored and it would have been an even greater conflict for me to think of myself as a white. Being colored is now natural to me. But I was a youngster. I hadn't found myself and I did have my problems. The problem would have been greatly aggravated had my parents not been divorced when I was quite a young child. . . . I lived with my mother. She regarded herself as colored so that made it easier for me. . . . the direct associations*

43. Small, *Christian Marriage*, p. 149. Used by permission.
44. Gordon, *Intermarriage*, p. 354. Used by permission.

*and identification with Negroes helped to stabilize me. It helped in a
measure to overcome my insecurities. . . . You may be sure that my
own personal insecurities, the attitude of Negroes toward me and
then the attitude of whites toward me made me a very unhappy
child.*[45]

Gail P. Fullerton devotes a chapter to a case study of a white
man-black woman marriage.[46] This couple has a child, and they tell
of their problems in finding black playmates for their daughter, since
they live in a white middle-class neighborhood. The author writes as
part of her conclusion to the chapter:

The parental roles in this interracial family are complicated by the
problems [italics mine] of raising a black child in a white, middle-
class milieu: the recurring necessity of interpreting—and helping the
child to interpret—the responses of others, the question of how
sensitized the child should be to racial identity, the difficulty of
finding playmates who will be like herself. . . . Even if these parents
are able to find black playmates for Laura, however, she will still
have the identity problems of a marginal individual, caught between
two racial subcultures.[47]

In view of the severe problems experienced by interracial marriages, it is no surprise to learn that they score lower on happiness
rating scales than do endogamous couples. Richard H. Klemer points
out that in one of the older studies (1937) they scored very low,
"—in fact lower than the total of all marriages of mixed nationality or
mixed religion."[48] He also states the following:

At least one recent study appeared to indicate that all interracial
marriages among well-educated people are more successful now than
they were in the past. However, the individual case reports cited in
the study give *small comfort* [italics mine] to those who would like
to believe that interracial marriages are something less than very
difficult. As the report put it: "Over and over again the comments
on the questionnaire drew a picture of sometimes hard times, rough
sledding."[49]

It is apparent from the evidence available that a couple contemplating an interracial marriage face great obstacles to adjustment and
happiness. The Christian couple may decide the Bible does not

45. Ibid., pp. 241-246. Used by permission.
46. Fullerton, *Survival in Marriage*, pp. 335-340.
47. Ibid., p. 340.
48. Klemer, *Marriage and Family Relationships*, p. 107.Used by permission.
49. Ibid., p. 108.

prohibit interracial marriage as it clearly prohibits interfaith marriage. There is at least one interracial marriage recorded which caused confusion and strife in the family. In Numbers 12:1, it is recorded, "And Miriam and Aaron spake against Moses because of the Ethiopian woman whom he had married: for he had married an Ethiopian woman." The following verses record the rebellion of Miriam and Aaron against the leadership of Moses. As a result God smote Miriam with leprosy which was only healed by Moses' direct intercession with God.

The Christian couple may rationalize that their faith will help them overcome the difficulties placed in their path by society. It is true that many difficulties faced in an ordinary marriage are solved by using spiritual resources. An interracial marriage is *not* an ordinary marriage because of the differences between the partners in such a relationship. As Henry R. Brandt observes, " 'Opposites attract' is a much believed axiom. Perhaps it is true in some phases of physical science, but not in marriage. Similarities in upbringing, education, religion, race and economic levels are to be desired for couples getting married."[50] When a couple disregards the need for similarity of racial background, they may encounter problems that are well-nigh insurmountable.

The fact that children of an interracial marriage bear the greatest hardship should deter any Christian young person from entering such a marriage. A Christian does not willingly inflict unnecessary pain, suffering, or mental anguish upon another. He is guided by the Golden Rule, " . . . whatsoever ye would that men should do to you, do ye even so to them" (Matt. 7:12). If the young person reads the evidence of the problems encountered by such children, he would never willingly or knowingly choose such a life for himself. Consequently, he should never enter a marriage that will beget children who will face such problems. Small writes,

> The fact that racial prejudice is a wicked and abhorrent thing does not alter the fact that it exists and influences social adjustment in the community. The mounting problems of personal insecurity in child life are grave enough without adding the possibility that children of interracial marriage will find themselves regarded as "outsiders" by the majority of youngsters. Overwhelming inferiority will make them curse the parents whose *selfish love* forced this unwanted life upon them.[51] (Italics added.)

50. Henry R. Brandt and Homer E. Dowdy, *Building a Christian Home*, (Wheaton, Scripture Press, 1960) p. 138.

51. Small, *Christian Marriage*, p. 148. Used by permission.

Landis and Landis make an interesting observation in relation to the children of an interracial marriage as contrasted with those of an interfaith marriage. They comment:

> Parents may possibly change their religion when they see that their differences are the cause of insecurity or confusion for their children, but they cannot change their race. The fact that there is no sound biological basis for the opposition to interracial marriages becomes merely an academic point; as long as prejudice against such marriages still exists, social attitudes are likely to create special difficulties for interracial marriages.[52]

Gordon, in the conclusion of his valuable book, *Intermarriage*, remarks, "Intermarriage, as I view it, holds no promise for a bright and happy future for individuals or for mankind. The evidence [373 pages of it], as I view it, is clear on this point. The facts speak for themselves."[53] The Christian young person must look clearly and objectively at the evidence before making a decision to enter an interracial marriage.

HOW CHRISTIAN YOUNG PEOPLE CAN AVOID MIXED MARRIAGES

Some saved young people will choose an unsaved mate in spite of the best efforts of their parents to give them a solid background in the Christian faith. However, there are some obligations that Christian parents have to their children which need emphasis. Every Christian couple should endeavor by the grace of God and the help of the indwelling Holy Spirit, to make their marriage so successful and joyous that their children will never settle for anything less than the prospect of having a similar Christian home. With all the aids of the Christian faith that the saved couple have at their disposal, there is no excuse for the disharmony and inconsistent Christian living found in so many homes.

Many young people reared in homes characterized by hypocrisy on the part of the parents have rejected the Christian faith as teen-agers. Christian parents must learn to yield themselves to the blessed Holy Spirit so that He can enable them to bear the fruits of the Spirit (Gal. 5:22-23) within the home. A happy home and a consistent Christian walk are not guarantees that the children will follow the Lord

52. Landis and Landis, *Successful Marriage*, p. 208. Used by permission.
53. Gordon, *Intermarriage*, p. 370.

always, but such parents will have a clear conscience before Him that they did everything possible to provide the right example and upbringing for their children.

Parents also have a responsibility to instruct their children in the important areas of dating, courtship, and mate selection. This includes the purpose of dating and the part it plays, either consciously or subconsciously, in choosing a mate. It is also imperative that the parents begin very early in the young person's experience to teach them never to have the first date with an unsaved boy or girl. C. W. Scudder observes, "The wisest policy is not to date or fall in love with one who is not a Christian."[54] This implies that the parents do everything possible to see that their children are in a church or school where they have opportunities to meet and to date other believers. Brandt suggests, "It is important that parents take an interest in their children's friends. The Christian, to be sure that his child will marry one of like faith, must see that his children associate with such people."[55] This also means the parents may have to move or change employment in order to provide these opportunities for their young people.

The parents should also supervise the choice of friends their children make, especially when they become interested in the opposite sex. The parents have an obligation to counsel their child when they feel he is choosing the wrong type of friends. This can be done easily and tactfully if the parent establishes good communication early in childhood. If the parent is living a consistent Christian life, and has good rapport with the young person, the advice probably will be well received.

HOW THE CHURCH CAN HELP YOUNG PEOPLE AVOID MIXED MARRIAGES

The pastor and church can also do much to instruct and encourage young people so that they marry in the will of God. The church must reinforce the teaching in the home concerning the spiritual standards and responsibilities in the areas of dating, courtship, mate selection, and morality. This can be done from the pulpit, and the various Bible classes conducted in the church. This obligation is greater than ever since the spread of the "new morality" in this generation.

54. C. W. Scudder, *The Family in Christian Perspective* (Nashville: Broadman Press, 1962), p. 56.
55. Brandt and Dowdy, *Building a Christian Home*, p. 139.

The church must also be very positive in the Biblical teaching concerning personal separation from the world. The apostle John wrote, "Love not the world, neither the things that are in the world. If any man love the world, the love of the Father is not in him" I John 2:15). The Hollywood movies and television programs are of the world, and present a distorted, and oftentimes perverted, view of love and marriage. It is unwise for young people to feed their minds with these perceptions, for they subtly influence their attitudes and actions. Many a young person has ended up in a mixed marriage, because he had been mixing with the world and had become romantically involved with someone in the world. This would not have happened had he not been violating the command, "Love not the world."

Young people are social beings by the creative act of God, and they should not be expected to live without social activities. If the church expects its young people to refrain from worldly amusements, parents and church must see to it that social activities are provided for them. Too many churches have been guilty of saying "Don't do this!" and "Don't go there," without giving the young person something to do or somewhere to go, activities pleasing to God and edifying to the young person. Large churches with full-time youth directors usually do not have this problem as enough social activities and opportunities for Christian service are planned to keep the young people busy.

If the churches of tomorrow depend on the youth of today, even small churches and their pastors may need to restudy their program and direct more of the pastor's energy and effort into working with the young people. If a church cannot afford a full-time youth director, and if it is concerned about its young people, the parents should insist that the church call a pastor who has demonstrated his concern for, and his effectiveness in working with the youth. If the premise is true that the young people are the greatest concern of the church, then the candidate's ability to work with the youth should be as important a criterion for calling a pastor as his ability to preach and "feed" the adults.

Parents should not be surprised if their young people become involved in the world if their church and pastor demonstrate little or no concern for the needs of the young people. They cannot expect strong, healthy young people to grow up in a social vacuum. Parents do have a responsibility to see that their young people are in a Bible-believing church with a strong youth program having a balance between Christian service and social activities.

It is also important that the local church have fellowship with other churches of like faith and order so there can be youth meetings including other churches. This gives Christian young people the opportunity to meet young people from other churches. Youth rallies and summer camps provide a social outlet as well as a spiritual challenge. They also encourage young people, especially those from smaller churches, to know they do not stand alone in their faith but that there are hundreds and thousands of other young people who have taken the same stand, and who are willing to bear the reproach of the cross of Christ.

Since mixed marriages are of great concern to Bible-believing churches, it is necessary that the pastor, Sunday school teachers, and youth leaders openly and frankly discuss the difficulties of such a home life. The young person should be instructed concerning what Roman Catholics, Jews, and the various sects believe. As the young person sees the great differences that exist between his beliefs as a born-again Christian and these various religions, he should find it easier to understand why happiness would be difficult to achieve if he marries a person with another religious background.

A Christian involved in a mixed marriage could give a testimony to a young people's class or youth meeting, or it could be tape recorded and played to the group without revealing the identity of the person.[56] If a fellow or girl is contemplating a mixed marriage, it might be well to arrange for them to talk to a believer who regrets his marriage.

Young people who plan to attend college should be encouraged by the parents and pastor to attend a Christian college or Bible institute. A latent function of these institutions is to provide social activities, and other opportunities for fellows and girls to get acquainted. Since most students in Christian colleges are saved, the possibility of an endogamous (within the group) religious marriage is very great. Not all young people who attend a Christian college or Bible institute find mates, but the chances of finding one of the same faith are far greater than if they go to a secular school.

With eternal values in view, it is far better for a Christian young person to attend a Christian college, even if by worldly standards it is nonaccredited, and find a good Christian mate, than it is for the person to attend a secular, highly accredited school, and end up in an unhappy mixed marriage. This is not to say that all marriages made between graduates of Christian schools are successful ones, nor that

---

56. See appendix for a tape recorded interview made by one pastor. This lady has been more unfortunate than many, but the manner in which she became involved, and the efforts to ameliorate the situation are typical of many such marriages.

it is impossible for a Christian to find a Christian mate in a secular school. However, it does say the possibilities of finding a Christian mate are far greater in a Christian school than in a secular one.

One of the greatest responsibilities that the pastor and church have toward their young people is to teach them the necessity of a close, daily walk with Christ in the power of the indwelling Holy Spirit. If a person submits to the leadership of the Holy Spirit in his life, he will make the good, acceptable, and perfect will of God supreme in his life. Such a fellow or girl will be able to resist the temptation to date unsaved individuals, and will never end up in a mixed marriage.

Contrary to the popular notion fostered by Hollywood and the mass media, the church needs to teach its young people that it is *not* a crime to remain unmarried. The person yielded to the Holy Spirit will recognize that it is far, far better to remain unmarried in the will of God than to be unhappily married out of the will of God. The sheer statistics of more Christian young women than Christian young men indicate that many will have to go through life unmarried, but if this is the will of God, it is better to accept it and find happiness in it, than to rebel and enter into a mixed marriage just for the sake of being married. It has always been true that the center of the will of God is the place of peace, blessing, and joy.

This chapter has dealt mainly with the mixed religious marriage and the interracial marriage, but many of the same problems and difficulties must be faced in the inter-class (e.g., between lower and upper-middle classes) or the inter-ethnic marriage (between different nationalities). Problems such as prejudice and discrimination are common to all of these, and yet there are difficulties that are unique to each type. The basic principle remains true in a mixed marriage of any kind: the greater the disparity of backgrounds between marriage partners, the greater the difficulties they will face in adjusting to each other; the risk of unhappiness and failure are consequently greater. Some people involved in mixed marriages rate their union as very successful and happy, but the question always remains as to how much happier they might have been had they engaged in an endogamous marriage. No amount of reasoning nor rationalizing can give the Christian young person the right to marry an unbeliever, for the Bible is clear in its prohibition against this type of union (II Cor. 6:14-18).

QUESTIONS FOR DISCUSSION AND REVIEW

1. Why are mixed marriages so frequent in American society?

2. Explain the statement, "Every date is a prospective mate."

3. Why do so many Christian girls marry unsaved men?

4. Describe how a "reference group" can help to prevent mixed marriages.

5. Is it wise for a saved young person to date an unsaved individual for the purpose of witnessing to him?

6. Discuss several problems that may be encountered in a mixed religious marriage.

7. What should be the attitude of Christian parents when their son or daughter enters a mixed religious marriage?

8. What are some of the problems unique to an interracial marriage?

9. How may Christian parents help their young people avoid mixed marriages?

10. What steps can be taken by a local church to influence Christian young people to marry within the faith?

15

THE SINGLE LIFE

Teach me to do thy will; for thou art my God. . . .
Psalm 143:10

THE SINGLE LIFE AND THE WILL OF GOD

God said, "It is not good that the man should be alone: I will make an help meet [fit] for him" (Gen. 2:18). The fact of man's loneliness resulted in the creation of Eve to be a companion for Adam, and the institution of marriage. Consequently, it is ordinarily the will of God that young people should marry and establish Christian homes and families. However, there are cases when it is not the will of God for some people to be married.

When our Lord commented on the beginning of marriage in Genesis (Matt. 19), His disciples were amazed that He would take such a firm stand against divorce, and they said to Him, "If the case of the man be so with his wife, it is not good to marry." The Lord Jesus replied, "All men cannot receive this saying, save they to whom it is given. For there are some eunuchs [born incapable of marriage] which were so born from their mother's womb; and there are some eunuchs, which were made eunuchs by men; and there be eunuchs which make themselves eunuchs for the kingdom of heaven's sake. He that is able to receive it, let him receive it" (Matt. 19:10-12). The Lord teaches here that some people, in order to do the will of God, choose not to marry. Clyde M. Narramore remarks, "To some has been given the gift of singleness that they may serve the Lord in that capacity (I Cor. 7). The most important thing, of course, is to be in the will of God, whether married or single. Everyone must determine this for himself before the Lord."[1] The will of God for his life should be the major concern of every Christian young person. He has been redeemed by the blood of Christ for this one purpose. The decision to marry is one of the most important decisions that a person ever makes, so it is most important that this decision be made according to the will of God.

If it is God's will for the person to remain unmarried, and if this is accepted as the will of God, the individual experiences far more blessing and happiness than they ever could if they married contrary to His will. Many young people have rebelled against God's will, and have married unsaved individuals just to be married. They have broken God's command, "Be not unequally yoked together with unbelievers . . . ," (II Cor. 6:14) and have forgotten that "complete harmony is impossible on any level when only one of the partners has been born again."[2] The happiness they expected was shortlived, and they regretted their rebellion a thousand times a day. They wish they had never married, but are now bound by marriage vows and children, so they must remain in an unpleasant union.

Narramore relates how nearly everyday he receives a letter from some single girl lamenting her situation in life. He proceeds to say, "But for every such letter, we receive several others from women who are married but wish they weren't."[3] Marriage is a wonderful and blessed experience, but only in the will of God. Walter Trobisch suggests that "those who find God, have found a place—regardless of where they are and regardless of whether they are married or single."[4]

An increasing number of young people also face the single life due to a larger number of divorces among Christians. Many a Christian young person has married another Christian in the will of God, but the marriage has been dissolved when the spouse sued for divorce for one reason or another. If the "innocent party" accepts the interpretation that marriage is for life and remarriage is forbidden by the Scriptures while the divorced spouse is living, then a single life is forced upon the individual by providential circumstances beyond his control. It is necessary to remember that the situation of these people is no different from that of the single individuals who, in the will of God, never marry.

1. Clyde M. Narramore, *Life and Love* (Grand Rapids: Zondervan Publishing House, 1956), p. 53.
2. Ibid.
3. Clyde M. Narramore, *The Unmarried Woman* (Grand Rapids: Zondervan Publishing House, 1963), p. 67.
4. Walter Trobisch, *I Married You* (New York: Harper and Row, 1971), p. 101.

A large number of accidents also leave many young widows to face life alone. Their situation is different from the divorced person, for Scripturally they are free to remarry. However, with the shortage of Christian fellows available as potential husbands, many young widows also face the problem of rearing children without a father.

REASONS WHY SOME DO NOT MARRY

There are some practical explanations why it is the will of God for some not to marry. There are still some areas of Christian service to which an individual may feel called where it would be very difficult to take a wife and children. Dwight H. Small suggests that normally it is the will of God for most young people to marry, but "God sometimes appoints an individual to a life of single status . . . and then evidently it is that one may conform to a special call of God for service where such a status is best suited to its fulfillment."[5] For some mission fields, the person may think it best to meet the challenge alone, and take the gospel to some very remote and primitive area. Life in those fields is very difficult and the person may be able to do more and take more risks to reach the people than if he had a wife and children to be concerned with. However, in most mission fields the wife and children are assets, for they provide the model of a Christian home for new converts.

Some persons remain unmarried because they become overly dependent upon their parents or siblings, and become too emotionally attached to them to break the home ties.[6] They may date during the young adult years, but they rarely become seriously involved. If they do, they find some rationalization for breaking the relationship as the marriage date approaches.

Unfortunately, there are parents in such situations who expect the son or daughter to care for them, and make every effort to prevent the son or daughter from marrying.[7] This is abnormal behavior, for usually the parents encourage their children to "leave the nest" and begin families of their own. One couple in Portugal was engaged thirty-five years until the fellow's mother died. As long as she lived, marriage was out of the question, for she would not give up her son, and he knew that it would not be wise to bring a wife in to live with

5. Dwight Hervey Small, *Design for Christian Marriage* (Westwood, NJ: Fleming H. Revell Co., 1959), p. 19.
6. Judson T. Landis and Mary G. Landis, *Building a Successful Marriage* (Englewood Cliffs, NJ: Prentice-Hall Inc., 1973), p. 72.
7. Narramore, *Unmarried Woman*, p. 67.

his mother! Where there are unmarried siblings, it is quite customary for them to maintain the family household after the death of the parents.

Some people do not marry because of poor personality development. They are just too shy and bashful to interact with the opposite sex. Some fellows can never get up the courage to ask a girl for a date, and if they do, they cannot carry on a conversation, and the experience is a failure. Some young women are so shy and afraid of the opposite sex they would not accept a date even if they were asked. This should not happen, for the Christian has a divine obligation to develop socially so that he can be a witness and testimony for His Savior. Occasionally a bashful person will ask or be asked for a date, and they rise to the situation, and a romance develops. In such cases the person asks for and receives from the Lord the ability to interact, and many times they develop lovely, warm personalities even though they would not qualify to teach a Dale Carnegie course.

Marriage demands that the individual give much of himself to satisfy the needs of the partner. When those who are too self-centered to meet the needs of others marry, they are unable to fulfill these personality needs, and the marriage results in failure because they cannot respond sufficiently to bring happiness and enjoyment to the union. They like to receive love but cannot give it in return. It is best for such persons not to marry, for they can be very happy if they have only themselves to think of and to care for. They become the model for the stereotypes of the "old maid" and "old bachelor" who are set in their ways, and who, very often, must have everything done their way, or there are problems.

It is unfair to intimate that all unmarried persons are personality misfits, for the majority are well-adjusted and reasonably happy in their single life. There are exceptions like the sixty-year-old spinster who is still anxiously seeking a husband. Most single men are single by choice (although there are some whom no one would live with), and most single women have had opportunities to marry, but for various reasons chose rather to remain unmarried. Many have sweet, likeable personalities, are very attractive physically, and are devoted Christians. They are unselfish and concerned for the needs of others, and are just the opposite of the stereotype of the "old maid" or "old bachelor." They enjoy good interpersonal relationships in their employment and in their church. Their Christian testimony is evident wherever they go. So they must not be judged as having inadequate personalities simply because they have chosen to remain single in the will of God.

There are some persons who are afraid of the responsibilities that accompany marriage. For the fellow, it means he must assume the responsibility of caring for, and providing for, a wife and possibly children. In American culture, he may be expected to take on these added duties while he is still trying to complete his education. If he waits until he completes the years of professional training, the best prospective mates near his age have already been chosen, and what young girl wants to marry an "old man thirty-five years old?"

For the girl, marriage means caring for a home and bearing and rearing children. Some girls have heard old wives' tales about the dangers and difficulties of childbirth, and are so frightened by the prospects of having children they avoid marriage altogether. If these kinds of people are not able or willing to take the responsibilities of marriage, it is better for them to remain single. One of the disadvantages of teen-age marriages is that so many of those involved are not old enough nor mature enough to carry the responsibilities they so often are eager to assume, and the marriage fails.[8]

The very poor home life that some young people are reared in turns them against marriage.[9] The parents are unhappy with each other and make life miserable for themselves and the children. The son or daughter resolves never to get married for fear of having the same disagreeable experience. It never occurs to them to examine their parents' relationship to find out what went wrong to produce such unhappiness. Was it poor mate choice to begin with? Does either have personality defects that would make it impossible for any mate to live with them? Is it a mixed marriage with built-in conflict situations? What happened to their Christian experience? Are they backslidden or hypocritical in their testimony? There are many reasons for such unhappiness so that the young person can avoid these problems if he is wise. He does not necessarily need to avoid marriage itself, but with a wise choice of partner, and real effort to make a marriage work, he can expect to duplicate the happiness he sees in well-adjusted married couples around him.

Many young women choose a career rather than marriage, for they do not feel adequate to combine the two. The availability of higher education to young women today enables them to prepare for careers in various types of employment.[10] They are no longer restricted to teaching, nursing, and library work. It takes years of time and much money to prepare for a career, and many young

8. Hugh Carter and Paul C. Glick, *Marriage and Divorce: A Social and Economic Study* (Cambridge, MA: Harvard University Press, 1970), p. 236.
9. Landis and Landis, *Successful Marriage*, p. 72.
10. Narramore, *Unmarried Woman*, p. 67.

women feel they must receive some benefit from all the effort spent in preparation. Since they are so strongly motivated toward a career, they will turn down a proposal for marriage. This is particularly true when the career is the type that reflects a call to full-time Christian service, such as that in a foreign mission field. Many a young lady has rejected the opportunity to marry and remain in the homeland because of obedience to the call of God to the foreign field.

Many young people do not marry because they are in a geographic area where they have little opportunity to meet compatible mates. This is particularly true of Christian girls who attend small churches where there are not enough Christian fellows to meet. A young lady in such a church who desires to be obedient to the Lord, and who will not date unbelievers, will face the possibility of living a single life. The situation can be just as difficult in a very large church where there are many fellows and girls to date. The girls usually outnumber the fellows, which makes the competition for husbands very stiff so that some young women will be unsuccessful.

Since propinquity is one of the greatest factors in mate selection, young persons need to be where the opposite sex are. They ought to plan on attending a Christian college. Jay E. Adams writes, " 'What? Go to college to find a husband? Isn't that an unworthy motive?' This motive should be high on the list of reasons for a woman to attend a Christian college."[11] Christian camps and Bible conferences are excellent places to meet other Christian young people. Employment in Christian organizations where there are opportunities to meet people has brought many couples together. Denominational conferences and youth rallies also provide possibilities of meeting persons of the same faith. The important thing for young people to remember is to be where other young people are if they desire to find a life partner.

Adams also makes several additional suggestions to young women who desire a Christian husband. He writes:

> Ask your pastor to help you discover where Christian men are. He may even know of Christian men who are looking for eligible Christian women. The word should be out among Christian families in your church. They may be able to invite you into their homes along with eligible young men. Speak to married women whose Christian witness you respect, especially those who married later in life; and ask them how they solved the problem. You may get some very helpful advice.[12]

11. Jay E. Adams, *Christian Living in the Home* (Nutley, NJ: Presbyterian and Reformed Publishing Co., 1972), p. 63. Used by permission.
12. Ibid. Used by permission.

There are some widowed persons who are eligible to remarry, but choose not to do so. Sometimes the marriage was so happy that the individual cannot bring himself to even think of marrying someone else. They live with the memories of the years spent together and do not wish for anyone to intrude into them. Others have children and are afraid there may be difficulties between the children and the new spouse, so they remain unmarried.

Some widowed persons have had the opposite experience where the marriage was so unhappy they resolve never to marry again. They do not desire to run the risk of repeating the unpleasant experience. They fail to see the many happy Christian marriages around them, and to realize there were reasons for the unhappiness in their marriage that could have been avoided. Many widowed persons do remarry, and are able to use the knowledge and experience of the previous marriage to help make the second more successful than the first.

Richard H. Klemer made a study of matched groups of single and married women. He made at least three significant findings:

> First, it was clear that the single women in the Florida sample were on the average as attractive physically as the married women. In fact, some of the single women were more attractive than most of the married women. Second, more of the single women were at the extremes of the personality characteristics for which they were measured. For example, more of the single women were extremely aggressive and extremely shy. The married women tended to cluster in the center of the continuum between aggressiveness and shyness. . . .
>
> Third, married women had been more social and more romantic in their growing-up years. The married women had more dates, love affairs, and romances than the single women had had.[13]

Klemer has devoted over two decades of study trying to find answers to the question. "How does one obtain love?"[14] He found several factors that provide some answers to the question. He believes that personality factors are usually more important than circumstantial factors. He summarizes:

> Your motivation to seek love and marriage, your flexibility, and your skill in relationships will determine your success. These are the major factors that control the number of friends (and consequently

13. Richard H. Klemer, *Marriage and Family Relationships* (New York: Harper and Row, 1970), p. 59. Professor Klemer has an excellent chapter entitled, *"Why Should They Fall in Love with You?"* Used by permission.
14. Ibid., p. 58.

opportunities for romance) in your own little social world. It is the size and composition of *that* social world that does have an important relationship to romance chances.[15]

It seems that all young people are motivated toward marriage, but Klemer discovered that many students had goals that were more important to them than love and marriage. He listed four reasons why they lacked motivation: (1) fears (either conscious or subconscious), (2) the lack of a sufficiently strong "goal-set," (3) substitute satisfactions, such as a strong companionship with a person of the same sex, and (4) failure to learn to love appropriately.[16] A young person desirous of marrying should examine his personality and motivation to see if there are areas that need improvement in order to improve his chances of "obtaining love."

ADVANTAGES OF THE SINGLE LIFE

There are some advantages to being single, even though the adult culture largely revolves around married couples and families. The single person is free to do the will of God as he sees fit. He is not hampered in his desire nor his decision making by the necessity of considering the wishes of a wife and children. Paul said, "He that is unmarried careth for the things that belong to the Lord, how he may please the Lord: but he that is married careth for the things that are of the world, how he may please his wife" (I Cor. 7:32-33). The single person can move and change his place of service if he feels this is the will of God for him.

The unmarried person also has more free time to serve the Lord than the married person.[17] Many churches have been blessed by some faithful single woman who was active in the church life, and who could always be depended upon to do the jobs that the married women were "too busy" to do. Many small churches would be without a bulletin if some dear unmarried lady did not give of her time to type one up and mimeograph it each week. The tasks such people perform are too numerous to be detailed, but the fact that these persons are single and therefore without all the demands of a family upon them gives them time to serve the Lord in these capacities. Often they are also able to do things for friends and

15. Ibid., p. 61. Used by permission.
16. Ibid., p. 61-68.
17. A. Donald Bell, *The Family in Dialogue* (Grand Rapids: Zondervan Publishing House, 1968), pp. 27-28.

neighbors that others do not have time for. They perform acts of kindness that enhance the testimony of Christ and the local church, such as carrying in meals to a sick person or a shut-in. They stay with small children when a neighbor becomes ill and is taken to a hospital in a distant city. They have an opportunity to serve others, and to glorify Christ because they are single and do not have the responsibility of a family of their own.

Although they are not as numerous in the local churches as single women, the single men also have more free time to make a real contribution to the Lord's work. Bell recites the case of Bill Elsey, a college graduate and businessman:

> He is one of those valuable church members who possess both maturity and youthful enthusiasm. The young people with whom he works are the most dedicated and useful the church has seen in a long time. In his position in life, he has more free time than do many church members with families, and he also has the ability to decide how he can best use his time. Because of this freedom, he has been able to serve untiringly in the Lord's work.[18]

Another advantage the single person enjoys is that of more free time for recreation and travel. Many times several unmarried individuals can travel together and share expenses, but even if they travel alone, the cost is much less than for a family making the same trip. They are able to go places and see things that the family cannot afford. Some mission boards are using short-term missionaries, and many single persons who are not called to full-time missionary service are able to fill critical needs in the areas of teaching and nursing. They are able to relocate more easily than a family, and the expenses of travel and maintenance are much less. Sometimes they are able to combine the return trip with an extensive sightseeing tour.

The single individual can enjoy a greater measure of financial security than the married person if he manages his money well. With the advent of "equal pay for equal work," single persons earn as much as the married man with a family. If the person is wise, the money the family man has to spend on a wife and children can be saved and invested. William M. Kephart points out that:

> At a yearly salary of $9,000 a single man can lead a reasonably comfortable life. With a wife, two or three children, and a home, this same man can hardly be characterized as free of economic worries. To a large extent, the same is true for the woman. An unmarried woman who makes a yearly salary of $9,000 can live rather well. But

18. Ibid. Used by permission.

if she were to marry and bear children, her husband would have to earn twice that amount to provide the level of living to which she was accustomed.[19]

The single person can achieve financial independence earlier, and provision can be made for an adequate income during retirement years. The same principles of money management as discussed in chapter 11 should be followed by the single person except in the area of life insurance. If the person has no dependents, it is only necessary to carry enough insurance for burial expenses. The exception to this would be the desire to make a church or other Christian institution the beneficiary of a sizable policy as discussed in chapter 12. On the other hand, since the single person has no one responsible for them in times of illness and incapacity, it is very necessary to have sufficient sickness and accident insurance to care for such contingencies. It is also important that the single person make a will as soon as he is of legal age. With good management, the single person may be able to do more for Christ in the area of Christian stewardship than the married couple can.

DISADVANTAGES OF THE SINGLE LIFE

One of the great disadvantages of the single life is loneliness.[20] It may not be as difficult if the person continues to live at home with parents. If he moves into an apartment of his own, and lives alone, he will experience loneliness. There are some people who are "loners" and are happiest when by themselves. Most individuals are sociable and, although they may enjoy times of solitude, they are not happy to spend the majority of their free hours alone. The problem is compounded if the single person moves to another state, and must establish a new group of friends. The Christian has an advantage here for he can locate a good local church where he can make friends, and enjoy Christian fellowship. A. Donald Bell makes the excellent suggestion that "a church and church friends can become 'the family' for these single adults."[21] The church cannot take the place of loved ones, and excruciating loneliness may be experienced especially on holidays such as Thanksgiving and Christmas, when the family is gathered back home.

19. William M. Kephart, *The Family, Society and the Individual* (Boston: Houghton-Mifflin Co., 1972), pp. 468-469. Used by permission.
20. Landis and Landis, *Successful Marriage*, p. 76.
21. Bell, *Family in Dialogue*, p. 27.

One solution for loneliness is for two or more unwed persons of the same sex to establish a joint household. If these persons are compatible, a relationship can be formed on the basis of friendship, common interests, and love for the Lord Jesus; providing companionship and preventing loneliness. There is also an economic advantage, for the cost of maintaining the household is shared by the group. If property is bought with joint ownership, the individuals need to have wills made that clearly define and protect the interests of all concerned. A clear agreement should be established as to the sharing of costs for maintenance. Such an arrangement can be very beneficial financially over the years, but it can also be the means by which good friendships are broken if misunderstandings develop.

The normal individual has a need to give and to receive affection, and in American culture this is done within the family between husband and wife, parents and children. The single person lacks this outlet, so the drive for affection must be sublimated and directed into other channels, such as creative work or avocations. If the person lives near enough to the family, or to the families of brothers and sisters, the affection can be shared with the parents and with nieces and nephews. There have been a few cases where single people have been permitted to adopt a child of the same sex, but this is very rare, and would ordinarily not be recommended. It is a difficult task for two parents to rear children, and although there are cases where a widow or widower has raised children without a mate, it is admitted that the task would have been much easier if they had had the help of a mate.

The unmarried person also has the disadvantage of a higher income tax rate. The federal government has always given a better rate to married persons and families. The theory is that the more dependents a person has, the less income tax he should pay. Demographers who are concerned about the population explosion are campaigning to have this situation reversed. The present system rewards those who have children, and penalizes those who do not marry or who do not have children. Some maintain the income tax rate should be highest on those who have children, and lowest on those who do not marry. Since it is unlikely that their views will be accepted by Congress, single persons can look forward to paying the higher tax rate. The unmarried Christian should be careful in his Christian stewardship to give sufficiently to Christian organizations in order to get the maximum benefit which the income tax laws allow.

Persons who choose not to marry also face the disadvantage of having to cope with friends who desire to see them married. Usually such friends find it difficult to understand that their single friends are happy without being married. One study of unmarried professional women discovered that 90 percent were satisfied with their way of life.[22] Another study indicated "there was some evidence to suggest that single, hard-driving, career-minded women probably would not make good marriage partners anyway," so it is best that some individuals remain unmarried.[23] The same is true for some men as "studies of hard-core bachelors previously cited indicate that many bachelors have habit patterns that wouldn't go well with marriage either."[24] This desire to see single adults enter marriage is part of the cultural pressure which results from the high esteem given to the state of matrimony.

No one can deny that there are tremendous blessings enjoyed by a happily married Christian couple, blessings that the unwed person can never know. It is only natural that such a couple would desire their single friends to marry so they might enjoy such blessings also. Consequently, if the happily married couple see the prospect of helping a single man and woman get to know each other, they cannot resist the temptation to play Cupid. Sometimes their efforts may be appreciated, and many happy marriages have eventuated from such efforts. However, in many cases they result in embarrassment to both the couple and the single persons.

If a couple feel led to introduce a fellow and a girl to each other, or to help along an already established friendship, it should only be done with the knowledge and consent of the individuals concerned. As indicated earlier in the chapter, there are persons who do not wish to be married. The happily married couple should recognize this and realize that some people do not need marriage in order to find happiness in the will of God. "Hortense Glenn and James Walters quite properly suggest that those who value marriage should also value a person's right to choose not to marry."[25] The unhappily married couple will not attempt such match-making, for they usually wish they were single again themselves and are not likely to encourage others to marry.

SELF-FULFILLMENT AND THE SINGLE LIFE

Single adults must face reality when they pass the age when most of their friends are married and they are not. In this situ-

22. Klemer, *Marriage and Family Relationships*, p. 70.
23. Ibid.
24. Ibid.
25. Ibid.

ation, reality may be the recognition that it is the will of God for the person to remain single. Many young people find it difficult to reconcile themselves to this fact and resist the will of God. The result is a continual spiritual battle that saps the person of spiritual vitality. The way to victory in this battle, as in any other, is a complete surrender to the will of God. The sooner the young person makes this decision, the sooner he or she will know peace, joy, and strength in life.

This resignation to the will of God does not mean that the young adult entirely gives up the idea of marriage and makes no effort to change his status. It does mean that the will of God becomes the goal. If the Lord sends a potential partner his way, he should still be open to this possibility. The young adult should continue to be as pleasant and attractive as possible, but should not be continually frustrated by the single status. This submission to the will of God is basic to a full and rich experience as a single person. As Adams puts it, "If she has been given the gift of living as a single person . . . she must not dread the future, looking at it apprehensively, but must recognize that the Lord never calls His children without providing them the help that they need to accomplish His will and the ability to be happy in doing it."[26] This truth also applies to the single man.

In order to have a full life, the young single adult must be actively involved in some form of Christian service in the local church. If a church is so "family oriented" that there is little opportunity for the single person to get involved, the individual must seek out a church where his services are needed and welcomed. Teaching a Sunday school class, leading a children's or youth group, helping in an Awana Club, Pioneer Girls, Boy's Brigade, Joy Club, Child Evangelism class, or church visitation are some of the activities that will enrich the life of the participant.

Elmer L. Towns lists other types of service that the young adult can perform in the local church. He suggests the formation of a group for young single people; helping maintain church property; performing such clerical jobs as writing a church paper, keeping Sunday school records or aiding in the church office, planning and directing recreational activities; assisting the pastor with technical skills such as architectural advice or construction supervision; and "serving through 'helping' jobs" such as ushering, music, or even directing traffic in the church parking lot. He concludes by writing, "As the young single adult 'gives' his life in service to God he usually finds 'abundant life.' This life is characterized by good personal and social

26. Adams, *Christian Living*, p. 61.

adjustment, once again giving truth to the statement, 'it is more blessed to give than to receive.' "[27]

The creative use of leisure time is a necessity if the single person is to have a well-rounded life. The short workweek and the longer vacation periods give the average person a lot of free time. Some of this can be used in Christian service, but there is time for other activities. For some, additional education can be acquired to better prepare the person for his vocation. Every individual ought to have one or more hobbies from which to receive personal enjoyment. Such activities as stamp or coin collecting, photography, music, art, reading, knitting, collecting and refinishing antiques of various kinds, restoring antique and classic autos, travel, and sports activities are illustrative of the types of hobbies engaged in by young single adults. The clubs formed by hobbyists provide opportunities to meet new friends, and occasionally a single person finds a mate through such propinquity. A person pursuing an interesting hobby usually does not have the time to be lonely nor to feel sorry for himself because of his unmarried state.

No life is complete without friends. The person with interesting employment, who is active in Christian service and enjoying a hobby probably will not lack for friends. Each of these provide opportunities for the cultivation of friendships on the basis of common interests. The Bible says, "A man that hath friends must shew himself friendly . . . " (Prov. 18:24). A person cannot expect others to be friendly if he himself does not exhibit a friendly spirit.

A single person can have a rich, full, victorious life if he accepts the will of God and proceeds to live for His glory. "His life can be a time of happiness and satisfaction or it can be a time of loneliness or despair."[28] Which it will be depends on the amount of yieldedness to the Lord, and how diligently the person seeks to live an abundant life. "Personal adjustment, not a marriage relationship, will ultimately determine the quality of life."[29]

THE SINGLE MISSIONARY

A difficulty faced by many mission boards is that of the single missionary, especially the single girl. Single men usually do not

27. Elmer L. Towns, *Ministering to the Young Single Adult*, (Grand Rapids: Baker Book House, 1967), pp. 112-118.
28. Ibid., p. 118.
29. Ibid., p. 24.

remain single long. On almost every mission field there is an abundance of eligible young women, and when the single man is placed among them, propinquity goes to work and a romance develops. Occasionally this process is hindered by over-zealous matchmaking efforts of the married couples on the field.

However, if left alone, it is rare for a fellow who went to the field single to return home without a wife. If he does not marry, he is faced with the suspicions of the nationals who do not believe it is possible for a young man to remain pure and chaste. He needs to take extra precautions to avoid any situation that might compromise his testimony and hinder his ministry for Christ. The mission boards would rather have a male candidate come to them with a wife, and the young man who feels the call of God to missionary service should make a diligent effort to seek a compatible mate among the many young women who share a similar calling in every Christian college and Bible institute.

The situation is different for the single girl who is called to the mission field. Since there are so many more girls than fellows who are obedient to the Great Commission, there are not enough fellows to go around. This means that a large number of girls will necessarily face life on the field alone. No one knows why fellows do not volunteer for service on the foreign field as the girls do. Perhaps it is because of the attitude many fellows have that a call to Christian service is a call to the pastorate, and consequently they never honestly face up to the needs of the world and the call of Christ to the foreign field. This attitude is reinforced by many sincere Christians who think a boy is destined to be a pastor, and a girl a missionary. When one young couple had a baby girl born into the family, a dear Christian lady said, "Now you have a little missionary."

Regardless of the cause, many more young women than men respond to the call for the missionary service. Sometimes a girl with such a call is led by the providence of God to a courtship with a young man who is not called to the field, or perhaps to a different field. She then has to make a decision whether to break the relationship and remain single, or to continue the relationship and marry. In such cases it is helpful for a young person to realize that his understanding of the will of God for his life changes from time to time. Many a missionary has gone to the field with the firm expectation that it was the will of God for him to spend his life on that particular field, only to be stricken with illness and have to return to a ministry here in the homeland. Many a man has started out in his first pastorate feeling the church ministry was to be his life work only to discover in a few years that God was leading him into a ministry of Christian publications, radio, or education. Other illustrations could be given how a person's perception of the will of God changes from time to time.

Consider the case of the young lady and the decision she has to make. In both cases she is responding to the will of God. She heard a call to the field and volunteered. Now, God, in His providence, brings a young man into her life with whom she is compatible and to whom she is drawn by cords of love. It would seem perfectly natural for her to say to her Lord whom she desires to obey, "Lord, when You spoke to my heart about the mission field, I was willing to go to the ends of the earth. Now You have brought this man into my life and I accept this as a further leading in my life. He does not feel called to the field (or to the same field), but since You have led us together, and as Your Word teaches, the wife is to be submissive to the husband, I accept Your call to him as Your leading in my life. May we serve Thee acceptably."

This may sound strange to some, but a little reflection will show this is precisely the way a wife is led *after* she is married. Suppose Jane is called to Liberia and meets Tom who is providentially called to the same field and they are married. They go to the field, but after three years Tom has to return home with a heart condition and the physician states he can never serve abroad again. Does Jane say to him, "Tom, I'm sorry you are ill and can't return to Liberia. However, you know God called me to Liberia so I must return without you. Please write at least once a week and send the letters airmail!" No, she accepts the will of God for her husband as His will for her life and will seek to be a helpmate here in the homeland.

In the same way, the wife of a pastor accepts the call to a new church as the will of God for her life as well as for her husband. It may be that in the hypothetical case God will call the young man to the field and this would be wonderful. On the other hand God does not bring two dedicated young persons together only to have them separate because the fellow does not accept the call of the girl as God's will for their lives.

The illustration may be reversed; a young man called to a missionary field meets and learns to love a girl who is not called to missionary service. Should they break the relationship or does the girl accept the call of the fellow as her call to service?

If, as in the previous illustration, these two young people are sincerely seeking to do the will of God, then the young lady could say a similar prayer, "Lord, You have brought this man into my life and I accept this as Your will for my life. He feels called to the mission field, and I do not, but I know You have led us together. Your Word teaches that the wife is to be submissive to the husband so I accept Your call to him as Your leading in my life. May we serve Thee acceptably." With such a yielded attitude, the Lord will give this young lady a burden for the field and when she is examined by a mission board, other things being in order, she will be considered a good prospect for the field.[30]

Many areas of the world are evangelized today because young women were willing to go and do the work that God called them to do. They have established churches, schools, hospitals, and dispensaries because there was no one else to do the task. The question of whether the single girl should go to the field would be unnecessary to ask if enough young men answered the call of God to the foreign field. Until enough men are willing to accept the responsibility of world evangelism, God continues to use women to spread the gospel to the ends of the earth.[31]

THE CHURCH AND ITS RESPONSIBILITY TO THE UNMARRIED

The average church is unaware of the needs of the single young adults in its congregation. It has a Sunday school class for the senior high youth, the young marrieds, and the adults. This leaves the young adult the choice of either staying home from Sunday school or else sitting in a class with the grandparents. The same is true of the Sunday evening youth groups. They usually stop at the senior high level with no provision for the young adults. With the large increase in the number of single young people, a church is not meeting its responsibility unless it has some program to help young adults.

Adams writes, "First, let the church acknowledge that far too little has been done to provide wide, significant contacts for young unmarried Christians. In her repentance the church should 'do works fitting for repentance' by beginning to do a great deal more for singles."[32]

Many churches have attempted to remedy some of these deficiencies by establishing a "college and career age" class to meet the needs

---

30. See *Love Is --* by Don Hillis (Moody Press, 1969) for a collection of 18 true love stories of how God directed the lives of each couple.

31. A single young woman planning to go to a mission field must read *Single and Satisfied* by Audrey Lee Sands, published by Tyndale House Publishers, Wheaton, IL, 1971. Miss Sands very ably deals with the problems faced by single women missionaries.

32. Adams, *Christian Living*, p. 60.

of the post-high-school age group. However, Towns indicates that these two groups should not be combined since their interests are different.[33] Some churches have started a youth group for the young adults that meets either before or after the evening service. These groups can help meet the social needs of this age group by means of parties, rallies, and retreats. They provide additional opportunities to teach the Word, and also for young people to meet each other.

Towns also makes several additional suggestions.[34] A coffee time thirty minutes before the Sunday school hour provides an opportunity for fellowship. Service projects such as teaching in a branch Sunday school, homes for the aged, hospitals, civic projects, and orphanages can be avenues of Christian service. Bell cites a survey made of young people, single and married, and their service in the local churches. The results showed that a high percentage of the Sunday school leadership was provided by the young single adult group.[35] Interest study groups and a lively sports program are other activities that single adults can enjoy together. A suggested program for an entire year is listed by Towns and includes some special emphasis each month.[36]

As a result of consulting over forty different young adult groups, Towns makes several valuable suggestions that a church and pastor should keep in mind when working with young single adults.[37] These include the idea that a church with less than five young single adults should not plan an organized meeting for them, but should utilize them in the regular work of the church and arrange for fellowship meetings on an interchurch basis. A new program for young adults should be given a two-month trial and if not a success, discontinued. Although college and career ages do not mix, an energetic and aggressive leader may be able to fuse the two groups. Providing fellowship meets one of the greatest needs of the young single adult since "becoming human through significant relationships" is characteristic of this group.

Other suggestions are that the programs for the young single adults be first class, as they have more disposable income than married couples and are attracted to quality programs. The final suggestion is, "Do not ask, 'Why aren't you married yet?' " since this question is the one that provokes them the most. It implies that the married

33. Towns, *Young Single Adult*, pp. 3-4.
34. Ibid., pp. 82-94.
35. Bell, *Family in Dialogue*, p. 29.
36. Towns, *Young Single Adult*, pp. 86-87.
37. Ibid. Introduction, pages not numbered.

state is right for all and that something is wrong with a person who has not married. Gene Getz remarks, "It is unfortunate when, particularly in Christian circles, there is criticism of the unmarried person. This is frequently done in the form of teasing but often creates deep feelings of hurt and anxiety. We must remember that one of the greatest problems faced by the single person is to accept his role in life in a society that is supercharged with 'marriage consciousness.' "[38] With the large increase in the number of single young people, a church is not meeting its responsiblity unless it has some program to help young adults.

CONCLUSION

It matters little whether a young person remains single by choice or by circumstances as long as he is in the center of God's will. Morris A. Inch points out that "to remain single is not an abnormality but, under certain circumstances, the ideal (I Cor. 7:32-40). The household of faith defines the limits, not the availability of a marriage partner."[39] If a marriage partner is not available in the will of God, then the sooner a person accepts this fact and adjusts to the idea of remaining single, the sooner the frustration departs and the life is filled with His peace and joy. God's will is the place of blessing, and here the greatest happiness is found.

Many books have been written to help the single person make the adjustment to their single status. Many of the larger churches are now having a ministry for singles and ofter employ a separate pastor to oversee the program.[40]

38. Gene Getz, *The Christian Home in a Changing World* (Chicago: Moody Press, 1972), p. 18.

39. Morris A. Inch, "Biblical Principles for Marriage and the Home," in *Adult Education in the Church*, eds. Roy B. Zuch and Gene A. Getz (Chicago: Moody Press, 1970), p. 272.

40. Additional books are G. Andrews, *Your Half of the Apple* (Grand Rapids: Zondervan Publishing House, 1972); M. Clarkson, *So You're Single* (Waco: Word Books, 1976); R. A. Dow, *Ministry with Single Adults* (Valley Forge: Judson Press, 1977); J. Fix and Z. Levitt, *For Singles Only* (Old Tappan, N.J.: Fleming H. Revell Co., 1978); A. Lum, *Single and Human* (Downer's Grove: Inter-varsity Press, 1976); M. McGinnis, *Single* (Old Tappan, N.J.: Fleming H. Revell Co., 1974); B. Sroka, *One Is a Whole Number* (Wheaton: SP Publications, 1978).

QUESTIONS FOR DISCUSSION AND REVIEW

1. Explain Matthew 19:10-12 and how it may be applied to young people today.

2. Discuss several reasons why some individuals do not marry.

3. Make a list of places where a Christian young person might meet a compatible mate.

4. What are some advantages and disadvantages of the single life?

5. How may a single person lead an abundant life?

6. How does an insurance program for a single person differ from that for a family?

7. What factors need to be considered by single people who set up a "joint household?"

8. Discuss the statement, "The individual's understanding of the will of God for his life will change from time to time."

9. What is the church's responsibility to the young unmarried adults and how may it meet this obligation?

16

PROBLEMS IN CHRISTIAN FAMILIES

He healeth the broken in heart
and bindeth up their wounds.
Psalm 147:3

RELATIONSHIP OF PROBLEMS TO GOALS IN MARRIAGE

Happiness is one of the goals of Christian marriage, but for some families this goal is blocked because of problems that arise in the home. Unhappiness results, and if it is severe, the couple may find that maintaining the relationship is too difficult, and separation or divorce takes place.

J. L. and Alma L. Hirning suggest that happiness in marriage can be arranged on a continuum with great happiness at one end and extreme unhappiness at the other.

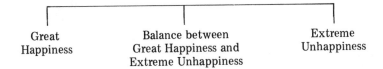

Great	Balance between	Extreme
Happiness	Great Happiness and	Unhappiness
	Extreme Unhappiness	

Other criteria of success such as great satisfaction and extreme dissatisfaction, or love and hate, can be substituted on the continuum. They point out that a marriage placed on the center or to the right of center indicates failure in the relationship. The idea of the continuum suggests that there are different degrees of failure.

The closer a marriage is placed toward the "extreme unhappiness" end, the more likely it is to be dissolved by separation or divorce.[1]

The Christian family is subjected to the same pressures toward disintegration as the average American family. Many of the changes in the society that have affected the family structure have also exerted strong influences upon the Christian home. As Jay E. Adams expresses it, "Is it possible to have a Christ-centered home in today's world of trouble and sin? . . . You may be concerned mostly because you recognize that your home falls far short of any such description. . . . You are in the company of many other Christians who, in their frank moments, will tell you that they are facing the same difficulty. Let's not fool ourselves. For the most part, Christian homes come pitifully short of the Biblical norms; and we are all aware of it."[2] As a result, there are many families with problems, and there seems to be an increasing number of Christian marriages on the right side of the continuum which are ending in divorce.

The Christian couple have spiritual resources to help them in the attempt to have a truly happy, successful Christian home. Gene Getz writes:

> There is only one perspective that will enable men and women to find answers to the perplexing problems facing them in their married and family life. It is the Biblical perspective. Apart from God's laws and principles as revealed in Scripture, there is no safe way to determine ultimate and enduring answers. . . . This new life in Christ not only gives meaning to individuals but in a special way provides purpose and resources for those "who have become one flesh."[3]

However, spiritual resources must be used in order to be helpful. When a Christian couple fail to utilize the provisions which God makes available for daily victorious living, they encounter many problems in the marriage. In some stages of the marriage cycle, the cultural pressures help to create the difficulties, such as rebellious teen-agers even though each spouse is living a life that is victorious.

Some problem areas of marriage have been covered in previous chapters, such as in-law difficulties, sex adjustment, and differences arising from the use of money. Consideration is given in the following pages to some other problems frequently encountered in family living.

1. J. L. Hirning and Alma L. Hirning, *Marriage Adjustment* (New York: American Book Co., 1956), pp. 341-343. Used by permission.
2. Jay E. Adams, *Christian Living in the Home* (Nutley, NJ: Presbyterian and Reformed Publishing Co., 1972), pp. 9-10.
3. Gene A. Getz, *The Christian Home in a Changing World* (Chicago: Moody Press, 1972), p. 9. Used by permission.

SUGGESTED SOLUTIONS FOR SOME
PROBLEMS IN CHRISTIAN FAMILIES

One of the main reasons for difficulties in a Christian marriage is that one or both partners get out of fellowship with God. This situation is peculiar to Christian marriage, for the unsaved individuals in a non-Christian marriage are not concerned about their relationship to God. One of the prime requisites for a successful Christian marriage is for the spouses individually and together to enjoy fellowship with their heavenly Father. If either one or both lose this fellowship, then problems can no longer be solved by bringing them to the Lord in prayer and seeking His solution to the difficulty. The severity of the problem can be vastly increased if one partner backslides to the extent that they return to the world and its values. This creates a wider gulf between the two partners, one that becomes difficult to bridge, for now each approaches the problem with a different frame of reference.

If the partners cannot resolve their problems alone, they should seek competent counsel. Sometimes a godly parent may give insights that can help the situation. (If the parent is part of an in-law problem this is not feasible.) Most of the time the couple turn to their pastor for his help. Other times it may be necessary to seek professional counseling as described below.

Cecil Osborne relates that it is usually the wife who seeks help for a marriage. In his experience as a counselor, he can "think of only two instances out of hundreds in which the husband first sought help."[4] However, none of these suggested counselors may be successful if one partner refuses to cooperate with the counselor. The most that can be done is that the concerned partner draws nearer to God, and prays and trusts that the Holy Spirit will convict the backslidden spouse of his sin, and bring him to a place of restoration of fellowship with God and the marriage partner. The opportunities for backsliding are numerous, and many a spouse has had to prayerfully and patiently wait for the partner to be brought back to a place of repentance and restoration, or else face the future alone—and yet not alone, for Jesus said, "Lo, I am with you always"(Matt. 28:20).

If there had been a poor choice in selecting a mate, the couple may have real problems because of their inability to adjust to each other. It is entirely possible for two sincere Christian young people to fail to thoroughly test their compatibilities during courtship and enter marriage without being compatible in many areas. It is very

4. Cecil Osborne, *The Art of Understanding Your Mate* (Grand Rapids: Zondervan Publishing House, 1970), p. 65.

easy for them when dating to be so infatuated with each other that they fail to discover, or refuse to discuss, the differences that exist between them because of psychological incompatibilities or emotional immaturities.

When the honeymoon is over, the problems of adjustment are very great. "It comes as something of a shock to most young couples to discover that marriages are not 'consummated,' they are worked at, hammered out, prayed through, suffered through."[5] If the marriage is to be saved, such a couple must realize that both must change and adapt to the other. A case history is given by Osborne of an overly possessive and domineering wife and a passive, noncommunicative husband who were on the verge of divorce. The husband was shown that he needed to communicate his feelings to the wife. When he did this, her behavior changed and the marriage was saved.[6]

For the unsaved couple, this may be impossible; but for the Christian couple, all things are possible with God's help. Although some personalities are more rigid and inflexible than others, yet it is possible for the Christian to seek God's help in overcoming deficiencies of personality that hinder the adjustments needed in a marriage. Adams takes the unusual position that compatibility is a "myth." He puts the emphasis, not upon similarity of background, but upon becoming "compatible by the sanctifying work of the Holy Spirit in their lives . . . that the two of you not only desire to but growingly give evidence of an ability to face, talk over, and solve problems together from God's Word in God's way. . . . With this capability, persons with quite diverse backgrounds find it possible to enrich their own lives profoundly."[7] While many authorities in the Family Life area disagree with his emphasis and suggest that young people seek compatible mates, his view is an encouragement to the couple who discover incompatible areas after marriage.[8] A couple can overcome incompatibilities with God's help. Daily the person can pray and ask the indwelling Holy Spirit to give victory in the area where change is desired. He can personally appropriate the precious promises of the Bible, such as Philippians 4:13, "I can do all things through Christ who strengtheneth me."

The change may be slow and gradual, but change there will be if the person or couple are sincere in their efforts to effect a change.

5. Ibid., p. 36.
6. Ibid., p. 88.
7. Adams, *Christian Living*, pp. 64-66. Used by permission.
8. Henry R. Brandt and Homer E. Dowdy, *Building a Christian Home* (Wheaton, IL: Scripture Press, 1960), p. 138. The authors state that "more than 100 studies show that the more alike two persons are, the better will be their chance for an enduring marriage."

There is no valid reason why two Christian young people cannot adjust to each other if they are sincerely willing to seek the help of God in making the necessary adjustments. Anytime a Christian couple state they are incompatible and cannot adjust to each other, it is an admission that they are not really desiring to let God help them to make the personality changes necessary for adjustment.

A crisis in the family can cause severe problems. A mate may be stricken with a chronic illness such as a crippling heart attack or rheumatoid arthritis that either suddenly or gradually incapacitates the person. Sometimes a spouse may become mentally ill and require long-term hospitalization. Many families have difficulties when the wife is going through the menopause. Henry R. Brandt and Homer E. Dowdy suggest that "change may bring a severe test of the family's inner strengths. At such a time, how well a family has integrated its values and beliefs into its day-to-day living will be demonstrated in its ability to cope with the change."[9]

The Christian must learn to accept such illness as being permitted in the providence of God, and to experience in reality the precious promises of God. He has said, "My grace is sufficient for thee." The tense of the verb here is such that the verse can be translated, "My grace is constantly, moment by moment, being made sufficient for thee." Multitudes of families have been drawn closer together, and have experienced the all-sufficient grace of God in their lives as they faced illness with all the changes in the family caused by that sickness. The wedding vows speak of caring for each other in "sickness and in health," and many couples have ample opportunity to demonstrate their love because of the illness of the spouse.

Other families face difficulties that arise upon the death of a child or a spouse. Judson T. and Mary G. Landis indicate that "death has been as taboo a subject as sex in our culture."[10] Death is never pleasant, but it appears unnecessarily cruel when a loved one is lost in an untimely death through accident or sudden incurable illness. Many parents are unable to accept the death of a child and adjust to the reality of the loss in the home. Sometimes when a spouse is taken in death, the surviving partner has difficulty in adjusting to the single state again. Often there are children to be reared without a mother, or a father, which makes the loss doubly severe.

Although it is difficult to understand, and many times impossible this side of heaven to fathom the reason for God's providence in such experiences, Romans 8:28 is still true, and the believer has the

9. Ibid., p. 78.
10. Judson T. Landis and Mary G. Landis, *Building a Successful Marriage* (Englewood Cliffs, NJ: Prentice-Hall, Inc., 1973), p. 498.

assurance that God makes no mistakes. He who knows the end from the beginning, and who holds the planets in their orbits, will not permit anything to enter the life of one of His children except His love deems it best. The Christian parent or spouse sorrows, but not as those who have no hope (I Thess. 4:13-18).

The believer also has inner spiritual resources to enable him to accept the will of God, and to help him reestablish his life without the loved one. If the unsaved can endure sorrow, how much more ought the child of God be able to adjust to the loss of a loved one. The Christian has the additional advantage of the fellowship and encouragement which other believers give to one in sorrow. "Whether one member suffer, all members suffer with it" (I Cor. 12:26). Such is Paul's description of the unity of the Body of Christ in a time of need. Other Christians are available to give spiritual help and lend practical assistance when necessary. The family who follows the term insurance program suggested in chapter 12 will not suffer financial need as do many families who are inadequately insured because they try to combine savings and an insurance program. Brandt and Dowdy suggest that "preparations other than economic ought also to be made. Some may be as commonplace as teaching the wife and the older children do-it-yourself jobs that usually wait on Dad's doing them."[11]

Some Christian families occasionally encounter problems because of temporary or chronic unemployment. In a time of rapid technological change and with the increasing use of automation in industry, even men who are highly educated and highly skilled are laid off and unable to secure employment.[12] Other breadwinners are employed in industries that are plagued by prolonged strikes that consume all the family's savings. Such experiences create tension in the home, for a major role of the husband and father is that of breadwinner for the family, and when he is unable to fulfill this role, he is apt to become discouraged, defeated, and perhaps even irritable.[13] It may also become necessary for the wife and mother to seek employment, even though she enjoys being in the home much more than holding down a job.[14] The family may have to accept a temporary, or even permanent reduction in their standard of living.

11. Brandt and Dowdy, *Building a Christian Home*, pp. 78-79.

12. See "The Uses of Adversity," *Newsweek*, January 18, 1971, p. 58, and "When the Brains Can't Get Work," *Business Week*, February 13, 1971, pp. 90-91.

13. Osborne, *Understanding Your Mate*, p. 36.

14. Brandt and Dowdy, *Building a Christian Home*, p. 81.

The family that has followed a systematic savings plan such as that suggested by George M. Bowman and described in chapter 11 (p. 220) will be able to adjust to these changes in the family's economic status much easier than the one which lives on the verge of bankruptcy each month. It is a value judgment, but it would seem to be a much better policy to accept a slightly lower standard of living each month in exchange for some financial security for the future. However, even in times of financial stress, the Lord has promised to supply the needs of His children (Phil. 4:19). Since no one can be totally secure in his job, the best the family can do is to plan prudently for the future, and leave the rest in the care of Him who holds the future in His almighty hands.

Problems are caused in some families by the neurotic needs of the spouses. The average couple have conflicting needs and drives, but these are resolved as they adjust to each other. The couple with neurotic needs cannot cope with them because they operate on the subconscious level of motivation.

Osborne gives the case of a young woman reared in a home with a domineering and brutal father. Her brothers followed his example. She married a man with a dominant personality, for "unconsciously, of course, she had chosen a mate who would recreate the only kind of emotional climate with which she was familiar."[15] The young wife developed a mental illness that required therapy. By means of group therapy she finally was enabled to see her hostility toward men and learned to relate to her husband in a satisfactory manner. The neurotic couple will very often require professional help in order to make a satisfactory adjustment in marriage.

Neurotic needs usually originate in childhood experiences.[16] Herbert Streeter lists several neurotic defenses that people use in marriage to protect their egos from being hurt. Bill is the "silent type" who agrees with everything his wife says, but who never does anything she wants. "Nagging Nellie" continually attacks her husband and children believing that the "best defense is a strong offense." In many persons, unfaithfulness is a neurotic defensive reaction. Some individuals, particularly men, are overly attached to their mothers. Other men, as Linus, have a security blanket: busyness in work. They retreat from the wife and lose themselves in their job. Streeter suggests that "one of the hardest persons to deal with in

---

15. Osborne, *Understanding Your Mate*, p. 15.

16. Herbert A. Streeter, *Help for Marital Hang-ups* (Anderson, IN: The Warner Press, 1970), p. 87.

marriage is the hypochondriac. . . . One gets far more sympathy when ill than when well."[17]

Streeter makes the point that "many neurotic defenses are sinful. They are our own immature, fleshly way of dealing with problems. They are, many times, a refusal to walk in God's way. . . . Defenses are our own attempts to neurotically avoid facing the hurts of life. Instead of overcoming hurts through spiritual insight from God, we trust the weak arm of flesh. It is true that neurotic defenses are but a poor substitute for the Christian way of life."[18] The neurotic Christian mate needs only to avail himself of the spiritual resources but also of professional counseling. After doing so, many neurotic individuals have gained insights into their personalities that enabled them to make a reasonably happy adjustment in marriage.

A family may experience real heartache, and sometimes actual grief, when a son or daughter deviates by choosing the way of the world rather than the way of the Cross. Every sincere Christian parent feels an obligation to rear his children in the "nurture and admonition of the Lord." His desire is for the child to love the Lord Jesus, and to be a faithful follower of Him. Leslie and Ruth Moser remark:

> Among the most meaningful things we can do as parents is to inculcate these Christian ideals in our youngsters. These ideals will have meaning throughout all areas of their lives, especially in the determination of success in marriage. But we must not be content to teach them Christian ideals; we must make every effort to insure that they accept Christ as their strength and constant companion. Christian ideals without the acceptance of Christ as Lord and Master of one's life fall far short of the mark.[19]

If, for some reason, a child does not make the right choice, the parents may experience guilt feelings because they realize they have failed in their aim of raising the child for Christ.

Feeling guilty after the child deviates does not help the situation, but it is one way that a person punishes himself for his failures. A parent who lives a nominal, or even a carnal, Christian life, and who is permissive in rearing his children, cannot expect them to grow up as dedicated Christians.

Paul A. Jongeward writes:

17. Ibid., p. 94. This paragraph is a condensation of Chapter 10, "What Are You Wearing for Armor?" Used with permission.
18. Ibid., p. 91. Used with permission.
19. Leslie E. Moser and Ruth Small Moser, *Guiding Your Son or Daughter Toward Successful Marriage*, (Grand Rapids: Baker Book House, 1967), p. 65.

My experiences over the past few years in working in public schools as a teacher and later as a psychologist, and in Christian youth programs, have led me to an inescapable conclusion: Jesus Christ is a "missing person" in the majority of "Christian" homes. His living presence and love have been replaced by a rigidly enforced, but largely meaningless, habit pattern.

During my years in the public schools, I saw little, if any, difference in moral behavior, attitudes, and values in the children of Christian parents. . . . In working with high school young people in the church [those who were still coming], I found Christianity had little relevance to the pressures and frustrations of their teen-age world. Most of them came because they were coerced by their parents. . . . Christ was not a reality to them and many termed Christianity a "real drag."[20]

Another writer, Larry Christensen, expresses the same idea:

Children are far more perceptive in spiritual matters than adults realize. They do not respond merely to the words and formal beliefs of their parents. . . . Oftentimes young people who rebel against the Christian faith are not rebelling against God at all. They have never had an actual encounter with the Living God to rebel against. They are rebelling against a dead religious formalism which merely imposed upon them a certain set of rules or rituals.[21]

Parents with a lukewarm Christian experience cannot expect their children to be ardent believers. Parents who sing loudly on Sunday morning, "Jesus is all the world to me," and then live worldly lives the rest of the week with no time for prayer and Bible reading in their lives or in the home cannot deceive their children by their singing. Young people are quick to see such inconsistency, and will be influenced by what their parents do rather than by what they say. "Children learn by what adults say and do. But if our words and actions are not consonant, our conduct will largely outweigh what we say. Christian standards are transmitted through the attitudes and actions of the parents and other significant family members, with verbal teaching serving to make those standards more incisive."[22] It could be stated, though difficult to prove, that more young people

20, Paul A. Jongeward, "Is Jesus at Home?" in *The Marriage Affair*, ed. J. Allen Petersen (Wheaton, IL: Tyndale House Publishers, 1971), p. 141. Used by permission of *Eternity* magazine, 1969, The Evangelical Foundation.
21. Larry Christensen, *The Christian Family* (Minneapolis: Bethany Fellowship, 1970), p. 159. Used by permission.
22. Jeanette Acrea, "Helping Parents Teach Christian Standards," in *Ventures in Family Living*, eds. Roy B. Zuch and Gene A. Getz (Chicago: Moody Press, 1971), p. 78.

are lost to the cause and service of Christ because of the inconsistent lives of their parents than from any other single cause.

Parents ought to be so conscious of setting an example of godly living for their children that they would fear to do anything that would be a stumbling block to them.

> The rule should be that I should live as I wish them to live. . . . That which I don't want them to do, I should not do. This is likely the most significant influence for success. . . . If I expect my children to go to church, then I will go to church. If they are to have faith, then I must have faith. If they are to be honest and generous, then I must set the pace.[23]

Jesus said, "Whosoever shall offend one of these little ones that believe in me, it is better for him that a millstone were hanged about his neck, and he were cast into the sea"(Mark 9:42). What solemn words! What a challenge for Christian parents to be completely dedicated to God as they seek to rear their little ones for His glory.

There are cases where parents have lived exemplary Christian lives, and still their child is lured away by the devil and his crowd. In this case the parents should not feel guilty, for they did their best to be consistent in their testimony and in their rearing of the young person. Narramore says, "The parents of a wayward child, when these parents have been faithful to the teaching of Scripture and have diligently brought up their children in the nurture and admonition of the Lord, *are not to be condemned* when the child grows up and goes his willful way"[24] (italics his). The parents' obligation is to be faithful in the rearing of the child and to see that he is given every opportunity to grow and mature in the Christian experience.

However, the time comes when the young person begins to make his own decisions, and he is responsible before God and society for those decisions. If he chooses not to follow Christ in spite of all the godly influences that have acted on his life, there is little the parents can do other than to pray and trust that like the Prodigal Son of Luke 15, he will someday return to the Father's house.

Some parents become Christians when their children are in late childhood or early adolescence. The years of ungodly influence are not easily overcome and the young people in such families sometimes fail to yield to the influences of the gospel. The parents in such circumstances must recognize the reason for such reluctance, and

23. Mark W. Lee, *Our Children Are Our Best Friends* (Grand Rapids: Zondervan Publishing House, 1970), pp. 212-213.
24. Clyde M. Narramore, "Disqualified for Service," in *Psychology for Living*, February 1971, p. 15.

must be very careful to live their newly found life in such a manner that the children will be attracted to Christ. Consistency must be the watchword in such homes. When the parent becomes a Christian, he should become a better parent with greater love, concern, and patience in dealing with the children. If a consistent life and prevailing prayer are not successful in winning the children to Christ, the parents can be consoled by the realization that they did their best and the results can be left with God.

RESTORATION OF A BROKEN CHRISTIAN MARRIAGE RELATIONSHIP

One of the most difficult problems a family ever faces is the threatened dissolution of the home. Many times the overt cause is stated as "incompatibility," but as indicated previously in this chapter, this is not a valid reason when Christians are involved because they have the help of God to enable them to make whatever adjustments are necessary to achieve happiness in marriage. They may experience some unhappiness during the time when they are learning to live harmoniously together, but there is no reason why they should not be able to eventually achieve a relationship which will bring great happiness to both partners.

Many marriages are threatened, and often broken, by the infidelity of one partner. God instituted marriage as monogamy and gave man a clear admonition to "cleave unto his wife." When the Law was given to Moses, the seventh and tenth commandments prohibited adultery (Exod. 20:14, 17). God knew that the greatest happiness of the home exists where there is faithfulness between the mates, and that His divine purposes for Israel and the church could be realized only in stable homes where the children could be reared according to His Word. C. W. Scudder remarks, "True marriage as God intends it, requires full commitment to fidelity."[25]

God so desired to protect the sanctity of the home that the Law specified the death penalty for anyone guilty of adultery (John 8:5). Many of the Corinthian Christians had lived very immoral lives before they were saved (I Cor. 6:9-11), and the apostle Paul exhorts the husbands and wives to be very careful in their relationships to fulfill each other's needs in order to avoid any temptation to infidelity (I Cor. 7:2-5).

25. C. W. Scudder, *The Family in Christian Perspective* (Nashville: Broadman Press, 1962), p. 39.

In today's "sex-suffused" society, Satan is able to present even the Christian with many stimuli and temptations to commit adultery.

> Affairs never just happen. They are usually born of neurotic frustrations in marriage. Some cases, of course, are the results of a momentary lapse under the pressure of temptation. All mankind is subject to the temptation of fornication, given the right set of circumstances. It can happen to anyone. There are times of weakness and vulnerability for each of us. The Bible says, "The heart is deceitful above all things, and desperately wicked: who can know it?" (Jer. 17:9).[26]

Unfortunately, many persons do yield to the temptation, and the family has to face the problem.

There are so many different situations where a mate may be unfaithful that it is impossible to deal with specific cases. However a general principle can be set forth: whenever possible, the chief concern should be the maintenance of the home. This principle should be practiced particularly where there are children involved. Streeter suggests that "the real question is not, 'Why did he do this to me?' The real question is, 'What should I do now?' As a marriage counselor, I often ask the question, 'Do you want to save your marriage?' In the majority of cases, the marriage is worth saving."[27]

If the erring mate repents, confesses his sin to God, and receives forgiveness from Him, He gives grace to the offended mate to forgive and to receive the offender back into the home. True forgiveness includes the forgetting of the offense, for God says, "Their sins and their iniquities will I remember no more" (Heb. 8:12), and "As far as the east is from the west, so far hath he removed our transgressions from us" (Ps. 103:12). It is difficult to forget the transgressions of a spouse, but if the person is sincere in the act of forgiving him, God gives the grace to erase, as far as possible, the sin from the mind of the forgiver. Extra grace will be needed to reenter into the sexual relationship with one who has been unfaithful, but God has promised that His grace is sufficient for every need (II Cor. 12:9), and that promise includes such a need.

Where a breach in the marriage has occurred, and restoration is attempted, the couple should seek to discover the cause of the waywardness, since all behavior has a cause. M. O. Vincent indicates that "infidelity is more often the result of a marriage breakdown

26. Streeter, *Marital Hang-ups, p. 96.*
27. Ibid.

than the *cause*"[28] (italics his). The possible causes are numerous, but if the marriage is to succeed the second time, the source of the problem which ruptured the relationship must be discovered and changed. Sometimes the cause will be obvious to the couple, such as a poor sexual adjustment, or problems over money management, and they themselves can take the necessary steps to change the situation. In other cases, the cause may not be readily ascertained, or the obvious cause may be only a symptom of a deeper problem. These couples need to seek professional counseling.

The possibility for much happiness exists if the couple will exert the effort to make their marriage a success. God forgives the sinner a whole lifetime of sin on the basis of the blood of Christ, and a mate ought to be willing and able to forgive on the same basis his erring spouse who repents. "Be ye kind one to another, tenderhearted, forgiving one another, even as God for Christ's sake hath forgiven you" (Eph. 4:32). God forgives the sinner not on the basis of how good he is, or how worthy he is, but He does it in grace for Christ's sake. In like manner, Christians are to forgive one another for Christ's sake, that His name might be exalted and glorified in their lives. Tim LaHaye expressed it very well when he wrote, "the Lord Jesus made it clear in Matthew 6:14-15 that you cannot be forgiven of your sins unless you are willing to forgive others for theirs. Therefore, forgiveness is a spiritual necessity. You can be sure that you Heavenly Father will enable you to do what he has thus commanded you to do—forgive one another regardless of the fault."[29]

There is no Christian marriage threatened with disruption by infidelity that cannot be restored if the couple are sincere in their attempts to be reunited, and are willing to ask God to help them make the adjustments necessary for success in their relationship. Dr. Wheat cites the case of Dean and Carol, one of whom had an extramarital affair, as an illustration of a marriage saved and strengthened through counseling that was accompanied by spiritual and emotional growth.[30]

Marriages can be broken by problems other than infidelity. Many couples have financial problems that lead to a break in the relationship. This difficulty in a Christian marriage can also be solved and the

28. M. O. Vincent, *God, Sex and You* (Philadelphia: J. B. Lippincott Co., 1971), p. 48.
29. Tim LaHaye, *How to Be Happy Though Married* (Wheaton, Tyndale House Publishers, 1968). p. 51.
30. Ed Wheat, M.D. *Love-Life for Every Married Couple* (Grand Rapids: Zondervan Publishing House, 1980), pp. 40-42.

relationship can be restored. The couple must seek professional counseling and change their habits of spending money before they can be happy together. This goal is attainable, but like other goals in life it requires each spouse to willingly and earnestly do his part in striving for happiness.

The preceding discussion may give the impression that marriages fail because of one big identifiable problem. This may be true in some cases, but in many others it is an accumulation of unresolved grievances that leads to a break in the relationship. J. M. and Alma L. Hirning state that couples often come to a marriage counselor but cannot give a reason for wanting to dissolve the relationship.

> When asked to state their problem, they may say that there are numerous little things which annoy them no end. They admit that the acts referred to are in themselves petty and unimportant, so much so that they are embarrassed to mention them. Nevertheless, the cumulative effect has become unendurable. Just as love may be the product of many small satisfactions, so hate may result from the combination of an increasing number of "inner" annoyances.[31]

This situation can be avoided in any marriage if the couple will communicate their feelings to each other. Petty grievances can only accumulate when a partner fails to inform the spouse of the thing that is annoying him. Adams emphasizes the need for daily communication by stating:

> Day by day, week by week, Christians ought to be dealing with interpersonal problems so that they do not pile up. Certainly this is needed preeminently in the Christian home, where there are the most intimate of human relationships, and also where as sinners we run into each other day by day. Like misguided automobiles, we collide and dent each other's fenders. . . . How important it is, therefore, to understand and practice the dynamics of Christian reconciliation in the home. Matters must be straightened out; we dare not ignore them—not even scratched fenders.[32]

Scudder offers the following helpful suggestions for solving problems:

> Many marriages could be saved and many broken homes avoided if husbands and wives would commit themselves to resolve their differences daily. Differences grow more difficult to resolve the longer they are allowed to exist; they should be settled early while they are small. Each couple should experiment with different ap-

31. Hirning and Hirning, *Marriage Adjustment*, p. 344.
32. Adams, *Christian Living*, p. 37.

proaches in solving problems and eliminating friction. If they will focus attention on the problem rather than upon each other, they can soon learn to deal effectively with their differences. They will find their marriage relationship growing stronger each time they are successful in eliminating tension and discord. . . . Christians should remember that they have at their disposal adequate resources for solving all their problems; they are uniquely qualified to resolve marital discord.[33]

SEPARATE MAINTENANCE

The question arises regarding the course of action to follow if a partner refuses a reconciliation. The answer is found in I Corinthians 7:10 and 11 where Paul writes, "And unto the married I command, yet not I, but the Lord, Let not the wife depart from her husband: But and if she depart, let her remain unmarried, or be reconciled to her husband; and let not the husband put away his wife." Joseph M. Stowell writes that "this might be thought to cover cases where, as a last resort after everything has been tried, a separation could be instituted."[34] If there is a separation, the wife or the husband is to seek a reconciliation, but if this is not possible, they are to remain in that state in order to be free for a reunion in the future. If there is a triangle situation where the spouse is infatuated with a third party, the situation may look very discouraging. However, there are many cases where the person has recovered from the infatuation and returned to his family, so such a situation is not hopeless.

If it is the husband who is unfaithful, the wife and family may be in need of support if he refuses to care for the family. Most states have some kind of "separate maintenance" law whereby the husband can be forced to support his family even though he is separated from them. If the wife has to take such a drastic step, it may widen the rift between the couple. If the husband wants a divorce and the wife does not believe in it, the situation is even more difficult. Even in these circumstances the wife and family have a right to support, and she is not obligated to consent to a divorce if it is against her convictions, and if she still desires a reconciliation. However, the erring partner may move to an area where he can secure a divorce against the wife's desire. This is illustrated in the following case:

Jim and Jane met while in college and married soon after their

33. Scudder, *Family in Christian Perspective*, p. 131.
34. Joseph M. Stowell, *Marriage Is for Keeps* (Des Plaines, IL: Living Reality, n.d.), p. 22.

graduation. Jane began work as a secretary and Jim went to work for a large corporation. His employment required him to spend a week or two from time to time in branch offices located in distant cities. After two years Jane gave birth to a lovely daughter and the marriage seemed happier than ever. When the baby was a year old, Jim went on one of his periodic trips to a city in another state. He usually called home in the middle of the week, but this time he failed to do so. Jane was worried so called him on Thursday to see what was wrong. He informed her that he had met another woman and was not returning to his home. Jane was shocked and stunned by such a revelation. She confided in her pastor and they both thought he would get over his infatuation for the other woman. Jim came back to town and rented an apartment, refusing even to see Jane or his pastor. He made frequent trips to see the other woman and eventually refused to support Jane and the baby. Jane was forced to ask for "separate maintenance" from the court. She refused to give Jim a divorce as she still hoped he would return home. Finally Jim quit his job, and he and the other woman moved to another state where, after a period of time, he was able to get a divorce from Jane on the grounds of "desertion" since he had not lived with her for a number of years.

DIVORCE AND REMARRIAGE

A major factor influencing the family in America is the alarming number of divorces. In 1974 there were 970,000 divorces but in 1982 there were 1.9 million. The number decreased in 1983 to 1.8 million — the first decrease in twenty years, but "the likelihood that marriages will end in divorce remains high: 50 percent now end in divorce; 20 years ago it was 30 percent."[35] Such statistics are often cited as evidence that monogamous marriage as an institution is failing in society and will be replaced by some alternate form of family structure.

Divorce statistics, however, are "a numbers jungle in which the explorer must pick his way with care," according to Lester Velie.[36] He asked Paul Glick of the U. S. Bureau of Census, an authority on marriage and divorce statistics, "How high, actually, is the divorce rate? Is it true that one-half of all marriages break up?" Mr. Glick replied:

> Definitely not. . . . Those who cite this high rate . . . are counting the marriages and the divorces in the same year, then comparing the

35. "Marriage, Divorce Down," *USA Today*, March 7, 1985, p. 1.
World Report, January 18, 1975, p. 43.
36. Lester Velie, "The Myth of the Vanishing Family," *Reader's Digest*, February 1973, p. 112.

two. But this is comparing apples with oranges—dealing with two different sets of people. In one set are the divorced, who may have married last year, or 10 or even 30 years ago. In the other set are the newly married. Suppose in a given community, you had 100 people who married during the year, and another 100, married in previous years, who get divorced. You obviously can't say that there is a 100 percent divorce rate, and predict that everyone of the new marriages will go on the rocks.[37]

Another factor which is seldom mentioned and which contributes to the high divorce rate as commonly used is the large number of people who marry and divorce several times. For example, "the highest incidence of divorce is found in the below 25 age group— three times that of the overall rate. . . . Wives under 20 are involved in almost half of all divorces recorded yearly. Indeed, marriages involving two teen-agers are so likely to fail that David M. Reed, of the Marriage Council of Philadelphia, calls such marriages 'a disaster area.' "[38]

The divorce rate also differs according to race. In research done for the 1967 Survey of Economic Opportunity, Paul Glick and Arthur J. Norton found that "among those who had entered marriage initially 20 or more years before the survey, approximately 30 percent of the Negroes had been married twice compared with only 17 percent of the whites, and four percent of the Negroes, but only two percent of the whites, had been married three or more times."[39]

The survey also discovered "that the great majority (four out of five) of those who had entered their first marriage at least twenty years before the survey date had been married only once. Moreover, among those married once, nine-tenths of the men and four-fifths of the women were still married after at least 20 years of marriage."[40] The logical conclusion drawn from these figures is that the divorce "rate" is inflated by the matrimonial activity of only a small percentage of men and women. The overwhelming majority of the persons in this study (92.5 percent of the men and 78.1 percent of the women) had never been divorced!

This is encouraging to those committed to monogamous marriage especially in view of the fact that the authors state that "the sample

37. Ibid., pp. 112-113.
38. Ibid., p. 113.
39. Paul G. Glick and Arthur J. Norton, "Frequency, Duration, and Probability of Marriage and Divorce," *Journal of Man and the Family*, May 1971, p. 308.
40. Ibid., pp. 308-309.

weights were adjusted to yield totals that were representative of the population as a whole."[41]

It is discouraging, however, when Christian couples head for the divorce court when problems develop between them. Once they head in that direction, they encounter no difficulty in dissolving the marriage for the most trivial reasons. The ease with which divorces are granted has been one of the greatest factors in the breakdown of the American family system. The states of California, Iowa, and Florida pioneered the concept of "no-fault divorce" (the word *divorce* itself is no longer used as marriages are now "dissolved") with "irreconcilable differences" and "incurable insanity" as the only grounds for "dissolution" of a marriage. The decree is final in six months.[42] The immediate effect of the new law in California was an increase of 46 percent in dissolutions in 1970 over the divorces of 1969. Part of this increase may have been due to the waiting period for a dissolution to become final being only six months in 1970 as compared to one year for a divorce in 1969. Many people in 1969 received annulments which were final on reception, rather than a divorce which required the year waiting period. There was a 32 percent decrease in annulments.[43] Most states now have "no-fault" dissolutions if the parties are in agreement, but permit divorces for contested cases.

Couples of the previous generation tried to work through their problems because of the negative social attitudes toward divorce, but it has become so common that there is no longer any social stigma attached to divorce. Wisconsin has gone against the trend to easier divorce laws, and requires the petitioners to submit to professional counseling before the petition is acted upon. "Milwaukee was the second city in the United States to establish a court of reconciliation (Cincinnati was first). In Milwaukee 60 percent of all divorce cases filed never go any further than filing. Much of this record is credited to the conciliation efforts of their own courts."[44]

They discovered that many marriages could be saved by having an impartial third party help to reestablish broken lines of communication. Paul Popenoe, founder of the American Institute of Family Relations and a pioneer in the field of marriage counseling, states that "most divorces are unnecessary and undesirable, and both

41. Ibid., p. 307.
42. Landis and Landis, *Successful Marriage*, pp. 373-374.
43. Robert W. Hansen, "Children of Divorce—What Rights Have They?" *Reader's Digest*, March 1967, pp. 181-186.
44. Evelyn Millis Duvall, David R. Mace, and Paul Popenoe, *The Church Looks at Family Life* (Nashville, Broadman Press, 1964), p. 145.

parties are worse off afterward than they were before. Divorce can be prevented with a moderate amount of effort—sometimes just a little delay."[45]

CONFLICTING VIEWS ON DIVORCE

This trend to easy divorce has had an unfavorable influence on the attitude of Christian people. It is not uncommon to encounter several divorced and remarried people within a church with a small membership. John Murray gives the following description of the situation:

> The Church of Christ is being increasingly perplexed by marital situations which in one way or another are related to divorce. Pastors and those in whom church government is vested know only too well how complex many of these cases are and what heart burning they entail for them. Any tendency to allow sociological considerations divorced from biblical teaching to dictate advice or solution is unworthy of the church of Christ. It is necessary to prize ever and anon the infallible rule of faith and practice provided for us in Holy Scripture.[46]

It is the attempt by Bible scholars to determine what is "the infallible rule of faith and practice provided . . . in Holy Scripture" that creates several views on divorce within evangelical churches. Much of the debate centers around the interpretation of Christ's teaching on divorce in Matthew 19:3-9:

> The Pharisees also came unto him, tempting him, and saying unto him, Is it lawful for a man to put away his wife for every cause?
> And he answered and said unto them, Have ye not read that he who made them at the beginning, made them male and female;
> And said, For this cause shall a man leave father and mother, and shall cleave to his wife, and they twain shall be one flesh?
> Wherefore, they are no more two, but one flesh. What, therefore, God hath joined together, let not man put asunder.
> They say unto him, Why did Moses then command to give a writing of divorcement, and to put her away?
> He saith unto them, Moses, because of the hardness of your hearts, permitted you to put away your wives, but from the beginning it was not so.
> And I say unto you, Whosoever shall put away his wife, except it be for fornication, and shall marry another, committeth adultery;

45. Ibid., pp. 145-146.
46. John Murray, *Divorce* (Philadelphia: The Presbyterian and Reformed Publishing Co., 1961), p. iii. Used by permission.

and whosoever marrieth her which is put away doth commit adultery.

Particular difficulty is found in trying to determine the meaning of the "exception clause" of verse 9, "except it be for fornication."

Some Bible scholars believe these verses permit divorce and give the "innocent party" the right to remarry. This view is represented by Harry Ironside who wrote:

> In these words Jesus affirmed the sacredness of the marriage relationship. It is intended by God to be a union for life. The subject believer will never break it. If one violates the tie by unchaste behavior—that is, by illicit relations with a third party—the innocent one is free to divorce the unfaithful one and to marry someone else. . . . While therefore affirming the high and holy character of marriage according to God's Word, Jesus does not put on the innocent divorced party the burden of going through life alone, because of the unfaithfulness of a wicked partner.[47]

A more recent writer, G. W. Peters states, "From these passages [Matthew 5:32; 19:9], I am compelled to draw the conclusion that the sin of fornication is of such devastating nature that it disrupts (in nature, but not necessarily legally) the most sacred and deepest human relationship and shatters the marriage bond. To say less is to regard this abominable sin more lightly than Christ did."[48] In reference to remarriage, he remarks, "Again we emphasize that forgiveness, reconciliation, and restoration are preferable and far more ideal. However, if these are not possible, divorce and remarriage cannot be forbidden on the basis of the words of Christ or Paul."[49] It is clear that many able Bible teachers believe that Jesus taught the possibility of divorce and remarriage for the "innocent party."

Other scholars believe that the entire tone of the passage teaches the permanency of marriage and prohibits divorce under any circumstances. They would be quick to point out the logical contradiction in Ironside's two statements, "It is intended by God to be a union for life" and ". . . the innocent one is free to divorce the unfaithful one and to marry someone else."

The view that divorce is forbidden under any circumstances is very well presented in a scholarly booklet, *Marriage and Divorce* by William J. Hopewell, Deputation Secretary of the Association of

---

47. H. A. Ironside, *Expository Notes on the Gospel of Matthew* (New York: Loizeaux Brothers, Inc., 1948), pp. 238-239. Used by permission.
48. G. W. Peters, *Divorce and Remarriage* (Chicago: Moody Press, 1970), p. 9.
49. Ibid., p. 24.

Baptists for World Evangelism, and formerly Professor of Missions at Baptist Bible College of Clarks Summit, Pennsylvania. He cites eight passages: (Gen. 2:24; Mal 2:14-16; Rom. 7:2-4, I Cor. 7:10; I Cor. 7:39; Matt. 19:3-8; Mark 10:1-12; and Luke 16:18) and states, "This aggregate of eight passages gives overwhelming and indisputable evidence for the permanency of God's institution of marriage . . ."[50]

Hopewell explains the "exception clause" of Matthew 19:9, "Whosoever shall put away his wife, except if be for fornication. . . " as referring to putting away a wife during the second stage or betrothal period of the Jewish marriage custom. The first stage was the "promise" to marry and the third the actual consummation. The betrothal period usually lasted a year to prove that the bride was not pregnant, and if so she could be put away by a bill of divorcement. [51] The decision of Joseph to "put away" Mary (Matt. 1:19) is the only Biblical example of the "exception clause." A consummated marriage, the third state, could never be broken. Such an interpretation of the "exception clause" agrees with Jesus' teaching in the passage on the permanency of marriage in verse 4-6, and with the passages in Mark 10:1-12 and Luke 16:18, where the exception clause does not appear.

Hopewell also makes an interesting observation concerning verse 6 of Matthew 19, "Wherefore they are no more twain, but one flesh. What therefore God hath joined together, let not man put asunder." He writes:

> Our Lord goes on in verse six to further emphasize this permanency of marriage when He says that they are no longer two, but one flesh. . . . Dr. Dwight D. Pentecost, head of the Bible Department of Dallas Theological Seminary, said that this emphasizes the indissolubility of marriage. *One* is the smallest indivisible unit there is, and *one* cannot be divided; so it is impossible to divide the unit of one flesh once it has been glued. . . . They are two individuals before marriage, but following marriage they become an indivisible unit of one in marital status that cannot be divided.[52]

Since divorce is not Biblical, it should not enter into the minds of Christian couples who face difficulties in their relationships. If one partner leaves the home, the Biblical exhortation is to seek recon-

---

50. William J. Hopewell, Jr., *Marriage and Divorce* (Cherry Hill, N.J., 1976), p. 9.

51. Ibid., p.12. See Gerald R. Leslie, *The Family in Social Context* (New York: Oxford University Press, 1973), pp. 158-59, for a description of the Hebrew marriage customs. In footnote 8 on p. 158 he states, "Sexual intercourse . . . after a betrothal was regarded as adultery and was punished as such."

52. *Ibid.*, p. 4. See also Wheat, *Love-Life*, pp. 34-38 for a clear presentation of the Biblical view of the permanence of marriage.

ciliation (I Cor. 7:11). If one partner deserts and secures a divorce, there is no Scriptural evidence for the privilege to remarry while the divorced mate is living, for Paul says in Romans 7:2, "For the woman which hath an husband is bound by the law to her husband so long as he liveth; but if the husband be dead, she is loosed from the law of her husband." Only when the divorced spouse dies is the partner free to marry again in the will of God (I Cor. 7:39).

This view stands in direct opposition to the trend toward easy divorce and remarriage found in our culture and in many churches. It is not easily received.

> People who set up personal happiness as the chief goal and purpose of marriage will find this intolerably severe. It is a question, however, whether God considers it too severe. God does not shy away from asking His people to endure hardship. It may well be that in order to preserve the stability of marriage as an institution of God, some people will have to endure an unhappy marriage. This is a lesser evil than the wholesale breakdown of marriage which we are witnessing in our own day. We may not be able to stem the tide of that in society at large. But Christian people can determine that they will live by God's laws, regardless of the prevailing standards in the world around them.[53]

The clear teaching of the Word of God on divorce needs to be vigorously presented so young people will be more careful in choosing a mate, and Christian couples will strive harder to make the adjustments needed to save their marriages. Louis H. Evans says that "we must remember this, that Cupid does not run a romantic 'ski-lift' which carries us to the top of the mountain of romance and then allows us to 'slalom' down with ease, across the steep slope that lies ahead. A marriage is a climb, and sometimes a steep climb. But, holding on to the hand of God, the sights are wonderful up there—if we learn to stay on the heights."[54] The family with problems must keep climbing and learning until they reach the top—where "the sights are wonderful."

Dr. Wheat reminds us that "Bible-believing Christians in *every* culture, in *every* age (italics mine) have found the wisdom and strength to move upstream against the current of prevailing lifestyles. Note that the Scriptural wisdom comes first; then the strength to go against popular opinion, no matter how powerful."[55]

53. Larry Christensen, *Christian Family*, p. 26. Used by permission.
54. Louis H. Evans, *Your Marriage—Duel or Duet* (Old Tappan, NJ: Fleming H. Revell Co., 1962), pp. 14-15.
55. Wheat, *Love-Life for Every Married Couple*, p. 24. An interesting case history of a couple whose marriage of ten years was dead, and then revived by following the suggestions in Dr. Wheat's book is found in *Rekindled*, by Pat and Jill Williams (with Jerry Jenkins), published by Fleming H. Revell Co.

QUESTIONS FOR DISCUSSION AND REVIEW

1. Why is a person's relationship to God so important in Christian marriage?

2. Discuss the statement, "Every pastor should have a good course in marriage counseling."

3. What steps to achieve compatibility should be taken by a married couple with many differences?

4. What should be the Christian attitude toward a death in the family?

5. Make several suggestions that will help a Christian family prepare for periods of unemployment.

6. What should Christian parents do when a young person deviates from the Christian faith?

7. What should be the chief concern when a home is threatened by the adultery of one spouse?

8. State the Scriptural grounds for separate maintenance.

9. List and discuss several Scripture passages that teach the indissolubility of the marriage bond.

10. Explain the "exception clause" of Matthew 19:9.

17

COUNSELING FOR FAMILY PROBLEMS

. . . he that hearkeneth unto counsel is wise.
Proverbs 12:15

COUNSELING SAVES MARRIAGES

Couples can solve many of the problems and conflicts of marriage if they seek the help of professional persons to aid them in finding solutions. They can avoid the unhappiness and often times the heartbreak such conflicts generate. "There is now plenty of evidence that, even after a marriage is in great difficulty, it may be reorganized and put back on the track by marriage counseling which will root out these harmful notions and show husbands and wives what to do and what not to do."[1]

Cecil Osborne, writing out of his years of counseling experience, states, "We often find marriages which seem so hopeless that there appears no way out but separation or divorce, the only answer to an intolerable situation which never should have existed. However, often seemingly insoluble conflicts do yield to an intelligent and persistent course of action."[2]

Another Christian marriage counselor states,

I do not think there are wrong marriages—only wrong people. There

1. Louis H. Evans, *Your Marriage—Duel or Duet?* (Old Tappan, NJ: Fleming H. Revell Co., 1962), p. 11.
2. Cecil G. Osborne, *The Art of Understanding Your Mate* (Grand Rapids: Zondervan Publishing House, 1970), p. 16.

is nothing final and unchangeable about the wrongness of people. Problems can be made right and when they are, the difficulties in marriage begin to melt away. . . . I've never seen a marriage *so desperately ill that it cannot be saved* [italics mine]. I have seen plenty that died needlessly because one or both of the partners did not want to pay the price to save their relationship. I've known of cases where couples have retired into such bitterness and hate that all communication has ceased. Yet these couples, in desperation, have begun to let the light through and have gone on to an experience of mutual love so thrilling that they could not have believed it possible.[3]

It is apparent from the testimonies of these marriage counselors that any marriage, no matter how great the difficulties, can be saved if the partners are willing to cooperate to help save the relationship.

REASONS FOR NOT SEEKING HELP

Some marriages fail because many people are unaware that there are professional counselors available to help them. "Most couples give at best only fleeting thought to that possibility. Even if they think about it or know of a person or agency not too far away, they probably have only a vague notion about what counseling can do—and they are not necessarily optimistic about it."[4] Leonard Benson also points out that "marriage counseling in America is a very young profession," and many counselors "handle their practice on a part-time basis." Thus, it is not the usual practice for a couple to seek a counselor when their marriage is sick in the same way they seek a doctor when physical illness strikes.[5]

When a couple is familiar with counseling, they may hesitate to visit a counselor because of the fear such an appointment engenders. "This can stem from many sources, but the main reason is that any badly corroded marriage is an extremely threatening and uncomfortable part of the person's life. Whoever has the job of probing around in this tormented area is potentially dangerous."[6] Even though the couple has a knowledge of the availability of counseling services, some do not use them because of fear.

3. James H. Jauncey, *Magic in Marriage* (Grand Rapids: Zondervan Publishing House, 1966), pp. 8-9. Used by permission.
4. Leonard Benson, *The Family Bond* (New York: Random House, 1971), p. 295.
5. Ibid., p. 297.
6. Ibid., p. 296.

The area of interpersonal relationship is one where people have not yet learned to seek help when they need it. When they have a plumbing problem, they call a plumber. When the car breaks down, they call a mechanic. When their body becomes ill, they call a physician. Osborne writes that a man will utilize all these services,

> ... but when his wife suggests they see a counselor about a marital problem, the typical response is "No! We're adults; we'll work this out ourselves. What can one of those head shrinkers tell us that we don't know already?" The human personality is roughly a hundred thousand times as complex as a television set, and the marriage relationship is much more complex than any other. It is a totally unrealistic, fear-ridden response on the part of the husband which causes him to reject professional help.[7]

When individuals encounter difficulties with other people, many do not realize that a whole science of counseling has been developed to help people with such problems.

This reluctance to seek help for personal problems may also stem from the fact that in American culture much emphasis is placed on being independent and self-reliant. People do not like to depend upon others, and they like to think they are sufficient in themselves. David R. Mace comments, "To ask outside help in our personal affairs seems somehow humiliating, a sign of weakness. It *is* good for us to stand on our own feet and solve our own problems *if we can*"[8] [italics his]. Louis Burke, Judge of the Los Angeles Conciliation Court, gives the case history of Ken Burns which illustrates how some people react to an offer of help. Ken said, "We don't need anybody's help. If Edna and me have got anything to talk about, we'll talk about it ourselves."[9] Two months later Ken and Edna were divorced since he could not bring himself to accept the proposed counseling.

Christian subculture also emphasizes the dependence upon the Lord for the solution of all a Christian's problems. Young people are taught to pray and seek the Lord's will in every matter, and to seek His help whenever faced with some difficulty or problem. Many times it does not occur to such individuals that a Christian counselor might be part of God's way of helping them find His solution to their problem.

7. Osborne, *Understanding Your Mate*, p. 66. Used by permission.
8. David R. Mace, *Success in Marriage* (Nashville: Abingdon Press, 1958), p. 145.
9. Louis H. Burke, *With This Ring* (New York: McGraw-Hill Book Co., Inc., 1958), p. 40.

WHEN COUNSELING IS NEEDED

The failure to seek counsel when it is needed may be due to the fact that people are unaware of their need for help from someone not involved in the situation. As a rule, a person or couple can use, and should use, the services of a counselor if they cannot find a solution to the problem after they have given it careful and prayerful consideration and discussion, and cannot resolve it. Mace suggests that "a point comes in marriage problems when the logical, sensible, mature, intelligent thing to do is to recognize that someone who is completely outside the situation can cope with it better than you can."[10] J. L. and Alma L. Hirning recommend if a couple "find that the problems they face are beyond their ability to solve, they will not hesitate to seek help from persons who can view their case objectively, who are qualified to recognize marital difficulties and recommend possible remedies."[11] Henry R. Brandt and Homer E. Dowdy state, "When crises arise repeatedly that cause friction, we must consider that marriage sick and outside help would be indicated."[12]

In marital difficulties, there are emotional overtones to most problems so that very intelligent people may not be able to solve a problem because the emotions hinder the reasoning process. "When your marriage is in trouble you seldom see things objectively. . . . That is why it pays to seek expert help from an adviser who is not at all emotionally involved. Again and again I have known of unhappy people desperately trying to resolve issues that do not even exist in the way they think they do. They have been fooled by their own emotions."[13] The principle restated is that the couple need counseling when they have made an honest effort to resolve their problem but cannot find a solution. When this fact is recognized, the services of an uninvolved, objective third party can often provide answers that the emotionally involved couple has overlooked.

Counseling is also needed when communication is broken between the two mates. Gary Collins says, "Marriage counselors consistently report that couples who aren't getting along are often unable to communicate. Sometimes there is open quarreling, sometimes sullen silence, but always there is inability to honestly share feelings and

10. Mace, *Success in Marriage*, p. 145.
11. J. L. Hirning and Alma L. Hirning, *Marriage Adjustment* (New York: American Book Co., 1956), pp. 345-346.
12. Henry R. Brandt and Homer E. Dowdy, *Building a Christian Home* (Wheaton, IL: Scripture Press, 1960), p. 54.
13. Jauncey, *Magic in Marriage*, p. 12.

ideas about significant issues."[14] Collins uses the illustration of a couple who could not communicate even to him during a joint interview. Then he separated them and talked to them individually. "When the spouse was absent, each spoke freely and gave the same message. 'We can't talk about anything. All we do is shout and scream or give each other the silent treatment.' "[15] Communication is needed long before this breakdown occurs, and usually such a situation can be avoided with wise counseling, but if it reaches this stage, it is imperative that a third party become involved.

The counselor can meet separately with each partner, and listen to both sides of the story, and enable them to express hostility without hurting the absent person. "By seeing the husband and wife separately it is possible for the counselor to get a more accurate idea of what each is like and to see how each views the marriage with its problems. The counselee feels freer to talk and has less of a need to defend himself against the accusations of a hostile mate."[16] As progress is made, the counselor will bring the couple together in his presence, and if all goes well, communication can be reestablished, problems can be solved, and the relationship resumed. If the counselor is able to help them resolve areas that have frequently caused conflict, the marriage may be reestablished on a firmer basis than it previously enjoyed. Evans says that "a broken bone may be stronger than before the breakage if it heals properly."[17] This was true in the case of Joe and Betty:

> *Joe and Betty had been married ten years when they arrived at the counselor's office. They had suffered frequent arguments over Joe's insistence of handling all the money. Another source of conflict was the harsh discipline that Joe used on the children. His whipping the seven-year-old son with a belt had been the cause of the argument which precipitated Joe's leaving home and refusal to return. The pastor suggested they see a Christian psychologist. The counselor worked with Joe and enabled him to see that his insistence on handling all the money was part of his role concept derived from his father, and that his sense of manhood could be maintained even if he permitted Betty to take charge of those items in a budget that pertained to the home and children. His harsh discipline of the children reflected his background, for his domineering father had known only how to use physical punishment. Joe was able to see the psychological harm that was being done to the son through such*

14. Gary Collins, *Effective Counseling* (Carol Stream, IL: Creation House 1972), p. 89. Used by permission.

15. Ibid.

16. Ibid., p. 95.

17. Evans, *Your Marriage*, p. 80.

> punishment, for the child was frequently involved in fights at school
> where he found an outlet for the hostility he held toward his father.
> Physical aggression was the way differences were settled between
> him and his father, and this was the only method he knew of settling
> differences with his playmates. Joe was taught severe punishment
> without love could be as harmful as no punishment at all. A budget
> was worked out and a division of roles made in the handling of
> money. Joe agreed to limit the use of physical punishment and to
> supplement it with other types of corrective measures. With these
> understandings Joe returned home for he really loved his wife and
> children. There were adjustments made, and some months later Joe
> confided in the pastor that they were happier than they had been for
> years.

There are other occasions when a couple experience such disharmony and conflict that they cannot attempt to solve their problems.
It is difficult to maintain spiritual fellowship with God under such a
situation, and often the couple is in no condition spiritually to seek
the Lord's help for their troubles. One counselee stated, "We started
out together in the Christian life but she has more time to study the
Bible than I have because she's home all day. Anyway, I feel a gap
between me and the Lord, for it seems all I get is criticism."[18] Little
by little the conflict generates hostility in the relationship, and the
love they once knew gradually becomes hatred. Just as love grows
and feeds on the pleasant emotional responses received in a relationship, so the opposite emotion of hate develops because of unpleasant
responses received from the mate.

Jay E. Adams cites the interesting case of a woman in a counseling
session who produced a "manuscript that was at least one inch thick,
on 8" X 11" size paper, single-spaced, typewritten on both sides. . . .
It turned out to be a thirteen-year record of wrongs that her husband
had done to her. They were all listed and catalogued."[19] This is an
extreme illustration, for most people never keep a list of the unpleasant emotional responses, but the effect of destroying the relationship is the same.

Whenever a couple senses that disharmony or conflict is damaging
their relationship, they should seek the help of a counselor. Since all
behavior has a cause, the training and experience of the counselor
enables him to find the cause of the difficulties and to make
suggestions as to how they may be eliminated. The couple should not
wait until irreparable harm has been done before seeking professional

18. Jeanette Acrea, "I Married a Lemon, " in *Psychology for Living*, September
1972, p. 4.
19. Jay E. Adams, *Christian Living in the Home* (Nutley, NJ: Presbyterian and
Reformed Publishing Co., 1972), p. 33.

help. It is much easier to restore a relationship before the couple has begun to hate each other. The fact that Christian couples do get divorces indicates that this process of love turning to hate can operate in Christian marriages as well as non-Christian marriages. As indicated earlier it is all so unnecessary if these couples would make a sincere effort to save their marriages with God's help. Love can never turn to hatred when His love dominates a relationship between two of His dear children.

A couple with a good overall marital adjustment may still be able to use the services of a professional person in some particular area of the marriage where there is maladjustment. The area of sex adjustment is one where help can be given to many couples. Numerous couples could resolve their occasional or frequent conflicts over money management if they would simply visit a counselor and let him work out a budget within the income limits of the family.

Sometimes it is the children who may need professional help. Much attention is being paid at the present time to neurologically impaired children.[20] No one knows the difficulties that parents have encountered in the past in trying to rear such children when neither physicians nor psychiatrists were able to pinpoint their problems. Now there is diagnosis and treatment for these children which solves many of the mysteries and difficulties other families have faced.

A limited amount of parent/teen-ager conflict may be normal as the youth attempts to reach adult independence, but severe conflicts may be eased if a professional counselor can give insight to both parties involved.[21]

SUCCESSFUL COUNSELING INVOLVES BOTH PARTNERS

Counseling is most successful when both partners cooperate with the counselor. Some agencies will not accept a case unless both mates agree to cooperate. However, there is evidence that wives consult a counselor more often than men, and even though the husband does not initially agree to cooperate, he may be induced to do so as the wife builds rapport with the counselor. Robert O. Blood quotes a study by The Marriage Council of Philadelphia which showed that in 65 percent of the cases where one partner made the initial contact, the counselor was able to secure the cooperation of the other

20. Clyde M. Narramore, *Children with Nervous and Emotional Problems* (Rosemead, CA: Narramore Christian Foundation, 1969), pp. 13-16.
21. Adams, *Christian Living*, p. 108.

spouse.[22] If the problem is not too severe, helping one partner may be sufficient to heal the relationship, and to restore it to a healthy condition.

A person should not refrain from seeking help just because the mate will not agree to it. Clyde M. Narramore suggests:

> Help is available for those who want it. But even with available counselors, there are those who refuse help. If your husband or wife is one, do not become discouraged. It is not the end of the road. . . . Give your mate time and keep on praying. He or she may be willing later on. For the time being, you have the responsibility to seek help anyway. And when you do, you may be paving the way for him to join you![23]

If the relationship has been broken by one mate leaving home, it becomes very difficult for the therapy given to one partner to influence the other. However, the mental condition of the one seeking help may be such that the therapy is necessary even if it cannot influence the absent partner.

Professional help for those with personal or interpersonal problems is becoming more and more available. Individuals and couples should learn to recognize when they need it, and where to find it.

THE PASTOR AS A COUNSELOR

Couples experiencing difficulties in their marriage most often turn to their pastor. Narramore feels that the pastor is "probably the nation's number one counselor" and is able to help so many couples "because problems often have a basis in or a relationship to spiritual maturity."[24]

Homer Kent writes:

> While physiological problems requiring medical attention sometimes lie at the base of difficulties which counselees bring to the minister, most of their problems issue from the fact of sin. The minister of the Gospel therefore should be the best counselor in the world, for he possesses the Gospel, which is the answer to the sin problem. This

22. Robert O. Blood, Jr., *Marriage* (New York: Free Press of Glencoe, 1962), p. 263.
23. Clyde M. Narramore, "See the Marriage Doctor," in *The Marriage Affair*, ed. J. Allan Petersen (Wheaton, IL: Tyndale House Publishers, 1971), p. 313.
24. Ibid., p. 310.

Gospel message includes not only a proclamation of salvation from the penalty of sin but also deliverance from its power.[25]

People know the pastor is there to help them in any way that he can, which accounts for their willingness to turn to him in times of stress and strain. An open ear, an empathetic heart, and kindly words of wisdom and counsel from the Scriptures in one counseling session may be all that are required to help the couple find the answer to their need. At other times, it may require several sessions and extensive probing and analyzing to find the source of the difficulty. A good counselor is always aware of his limitations, and is able to recognize behavior problems that are beyond his ability. He is also informed as to the resources of the community designed to deal with the various problems people have in today's society. There are those difficult cases where the pastor recognizes the couple's need for help from a person with more education and experience than he has. He then refers the couple to a counselor whom he thinks is capable of helping them in their distress.

Many a pastor is discovering in this day when individuals and couples are subjected to pressures from every side, that his greatest ministry is not in the pulpit, but in his office where he deals face to face with people and their problems. Paul Popenoe writes that "some ministers tell me they spend about a third of their time in counseling."[26] The Bible Institutes and seminaries are recognizing this fact, and more courses in psychology, sociology, and pastoral counseling are being offered to better equip the pastor for this important task of helping persons with their problems. Young men preparing for Christian service should take their undergraduate collegiate majors in such areas as psychology, sociology, and social work where they receive an excellent background for their future ministry of working with individuals. The post-graduate seminary training equips them for their public ministry.

A pastor may gain valuable new insights into pastoral counseling from *Competent to Counsel*, by Adams. He quotes O. Hobart Mowrer as asking, "Has Evangelical religion sold its birthright for a mess of psychological pottage?"[27] The answer, according to Adams, is that it has. He then states:

25. Homer A. Kent, Sr., *The Pastor and His Work* (Chicago: Moody Press, 1963), p. 288. Used by permission.
26. Evelyn Millis Duvall, David R. Mace, Paul Popenoe, *The Church Looks at Family Life* (Nashville: Broadman Press, 1964), p. 139.
27. Jay E. Adams, *Competent to Counsel* (Grand Rapids: Baker Book House, 1970), p. 17.

This book strikes an entirely new note, a note which is long overdue. Rather than defer and refer to psychiatrists steeped in their humanistic dogma, ministers of the gospel and other Christian workers who have been called by God to help his people out of their distress, will be encouraged to reassume their privileges and responsibilities. Shall they defer and refer? Only as an exception, never as the rule, and then only to other more competent Christian workers. Their task is to confer. The thesis of this book is that qualified Christian counselors properly trained in the Scriptures are competent to counsel—more competent than psychiatrists or anyone else.[28]

According to Adams a good knowledge of the Scriptures is an important qualification for a counselor. He remarks, "This is one reason why properly equipped ministers may make excellent counselors. A good seminary education rather than medical school or a degree in clinical psychology, is the most fitting background for a counselor. . . . The Holy Spirit uses counselors to right wrongs by the application of God's Word to human problems."[29] Every pastor and Christian worker should consider the issues raised by Adams. He sets forth a thoroughly Biblical method of counseling which has proven highly successful.[30]

There is an organization for pastors who have had specialized training in counseling. The American Association of Pastoral Counselors "requires extensive clinical training in addition to a Masters degree for full-time specialists, doctorate for fellows, and supervised counseling experience for ministers who counsel only as part of their pastoral duties."[31] The group encourages the establishment of pastoral counseling centers to help individuals in need of counseling. In 1964 there were 164 centers operating, but "since then there have been numerous others opening up throughout the country."[32]

Some pastors are not equipped either by education or by personality to be good counselors. They lack an understanding of the basic elements of human behavior, or their personalities are the type that do not relate well to individuals on a face-to-face basis. They do well in the pulpit, but they cannot share the burdens of individuals.

Other pastors who faithfully preach the sufficiency of the grace of God to save sinners, seem to forget that the same grace operates to

28. Ibid., p. 18.
29. Ibid., p. 61.
30. Ibid., p. 57.
31. "When a Marriage Is in Trouble," *Changing Times*, May 1965, p. 45. Additional information may be secured by writing the American Association of Pastoral Counselors, 31 W. 10th St. New York, NY 10011.
32. Doris McGuire, personal letter, August 25, 1971, Administrative Secretary, American Association of Pastoral Counselors.

restore sinning saints. When a member transgresses by being unfaithful to his wife, they want to immediately dismiss the man rather than try to work to reestablish a Christian home. This is not to say that church discipline is not to be invoked, but it should be a last resort rather than an immediate reaction to the erring brother's (or sister's) conduct. The statement of Paul in Galatians 6:1, "Brethren, if a man be overtaken in a fault, ye which are spiritual, restore such a one in the spirit of meekness, considering thyself, lest thou also be tempted," puts a divine obligation upon the pastor and spiritual leaders to try diligently to mend the home broken by the waywardness of a husband or wife.

One of the fundamental rules of counseling is that the privacy of the client must be protected. "Private conversations must not be repeated in any way to anybody, without the expressed consent of the person concerned. Each person should feel that his secret is absolutely safe with his pastor, and he is therefore free to tell whatever may be necessary for his emotional release."[33] Unfortunately, there are pastors who cannot, or who do not, keep the confidence that is placed in them when a parishioner comes for help. Either they or their wives spread the private information to other church members to the embarrassment of the person concerned. Needless to say, not many individuals will seek the help of a pastor who behaves in this fashion.

Many pastors do share with their wives the burdens of their people so that they can pray for them together. However, if a man has a wife who cannot be trusted with confidential information, he must not share it with her. The privacy of the client must be protected if the pastor is to have a successful counseling ministry.

CHRISTIAN PSYCHOLOGISTS AND PSYCHIATRISTS AS COUNSELORS

Another source of counseling is the psychologist or the psychiatrist, preferably a Christian one. There are elements of Christian behavior that the unsaved person does not understand, so it is best to seek out a Christian in these professions. Adams asks:

> Why are Christians without peace turning to men who themselves know nothing of the "peace of God that passes all understanding?" How is it that Christian ministers refer parishioners who lack self-control to a psychiatrist who has never been able to discover the

33. Stanley E. Anderson, *Every Pastor a Counselor* (Wheaton, IL: VanKampen Press, 1949), p. 84.

secret of self-control in his own life? Outwardly he may appear calm and assured, mature, patient, and ever suave. Can this be his actual inward condition if he does not know Jesus Christ? Can he have the fruit of the Spirit apart from the Spirit?[34]

Kent makes a smilar statement:

Many people with problems are seeking out those who are expert in these matters to help them. Sad to say, many such "experts" have not vital Christian faith. They do not approach the solution in a Biblical way. They fail in many cases to deal adequately with the problem of sin, which is basic to all human difficulty. Their efforts are humanistic, laying emphasis upon man's potentiality instead of upon God's power.[35]

The tragedy is that there are so few believers practicing in these areas. The education required is long, extensive, and expensive, and Christian young people have not had either the dedication or the resources to acquire it. It is hoped that this generation of students will recognize the opportunities for a Christian ministry that counseling affords, and large numbers of them will be attracted to this field. Many Christian colleges now offer undergraduate majors in the behavioral sciences which prepare the student for graduate work. Narramore, a pioneer in the field of Christian psychology, has established the Rosemead Graduate School of Psychology, to help increase the number of well-trained Christian psychologists.[36]

Narramore has also established the Narramore Christian Foundation which sponsors various activities in the field of Christian psychology. Many of these activities are designed to help the individual directly, such as a daily national radio broadcast; a monthly magazine, *Psychology for Living*; Bible-centered literature dealing with problems Christians face; and Christian counseling clinics.

Other programs aim to prepare more individuals to help others such as the Rosemead Graduate School of Psychology, or short-term training for ministers and missionaries. These short-term institutes last about a month and the pastor and missionary are given some background on the dynamics of human behavior, and how to deal with the problems developed by such behavior.[37] These pastors and

34. Adams, *Competent to Counsel*, p. 21.

35. Kent, *Pastor and His Work*, p. 288. Used by permission.

36. Rosemead is now a graduate school of Biola University, 13800 Biola University, LaMirada, CA 90639.

37. Additional information on the ministries and the location of the counseling clinics can be obtained by writing to the Narramore Christian Foundation, Rosemead, CA 91770.

missionaries are better equipped to offer sound counsel when they return to their ministries.

Narramore has also authored *The Psychology of Counseling*, which will be of great help to all who seek to counsel from a Christian viewpoint. The book contains a very useful section listing Scripture references to use when dealing with individuals having different problems.

Individuals living near a Christian college or Bible institute may find qualified counselors available who serve on the faculties of those institutions. Many Christian colleges offer courses in psychology, and many Bible institutes have courses in pastoral counseling. These courses are usually taught by men who have had considerable education and training in the field. Although they may not have a professional practice of counseling services, yet they are men of God, and if called upon in a time of great need, they would attempt to help the individual with his problem.

CHRISTIAN SOCIAL WORKERS AS COUNSELORS

The professionally trained social worker with a master's degree in social work (M.S.W.) has been called the "poor man's psychiatrist." They are educated in the dynamics of human behavior, and are able to help solve many kinds of problems. The Christians in this field have started their own organization called "The National Association of Christians in Social Work." They hold an annual meeting for fellowship and discussion of problems concerning the Christian and the social work profession. A directory of members is published biannually and the members holding the Masters degree in Social Work are so indicated.[38] Again, if a Christian psychologist or psychiatrist were not available, a person living near one of these dedicated Christian social workers could find help or a referral to someone who could help with the problem.

There is a trend in the field of social work for social workers to enter private practice, and the supply of Christian counselors could be increased if Christian social workers were to begin to offer their services on a fee basis. There are many in the social work profession who do not approve of this trend toward private practice, but it must be recognized that the dearth of competent counselors makes such a

---

38. Further information may be secured by writing the National Association of Christians in Social Work, Box 90, St. Davids, PA 19087.

practice possible for there are many who could afford this service but
not the services of a psychiatrist.

SOURCES OF COUNSELING IN THE SECULAR WORLD

If the person with a problem cannot find a source of competent
Christian counseling, then he must turn to the secular realm. In every
community of any size there is a private, nonprofit, community
supported Family Service Agency. These agencies exist to help families with problems. If the difficulty is mainly financial, they will
refer the individual to the proper agency where such aid is available.
The Family Service Agency is mainly concerned with nonfinancial
problems, and the social workers usually are very well trained, and
can provide excellent help, although they do not have the Christian
perspective. Most couples with marital problems *that are not
essentially spiritual in nature* could benefit greatly from the services
offered by a Family Service Agency. Since it is supported by the
community, its fees are usually correlated with the ability of the
individual to pay, and no one is refused service because of inability
to pay. The social worker in such an agency can deal with the
problems that people usually face, and are taught how to recognize
the deep-seated psychological problems that require the services of a
psychiatrist.

The national government is very concerned about the availability
of mental health services to the American people. Consequently, it is
channeling large sums of tax money back to the states to help them
establish comprehensive mental health centers that include counseling services on an out-patient basis. It is the plan for every area to
have such facilities available to help meet the needs of people with
problems. At the present time there is a shortage of qualified people
to staff many of these centers, especially in the area of psychiatry.

These centers are primarily concerned with emotional and psychological problems, but many times these may be related to a marital
problem. "One-half of the families who seek help from family service
agencies, and nearly one-half of those who seek professional help for
mental or emotional problems say that their problems center around
their marriage."[39] The treatment of the person includes dealing with
the environmental factors such as the marriage problems. Where such
mental health centers have been established, there are qualified
counselors to help. However, the ability to aid a person with a

39. "When a Marriage Is in Trouble," *Changing Times*, May 1965, p. 43.

basically spiritual problem may be limited because the unsaved therapist does not understand spiritual concepts.

Families with children who have problems may find help for them at a "Child Guidance Center" or at a similar clinic established to help such children. The federal government has also been active in helping such clinics, for it realizes that today's problem children very often become tomorrow's problem adults. Many children can be helped if the problems are treated before they become too deep-seated. If a qualified Christian counselor is not available, a Christian parent should not hesitate to take a child with a problem to such a center, for the counselors are dedicated to serving children and are able to effect some very remarkable changes in behavior. Usually, the center requires the cooperation of the parents in the treatment process since it is impossible to help the child unless the environmental factors contributing to his problem also are changed.

PRIVATE MARRIAGE COUNSELORS

There is a growing number of well-educated individuals who engage professionally in a full-time practice of marriage counseling. They are usually located in larger cities where there is sufficient demand for their services. They charge a fee and many middle-class people prefer to seek this kind of help where they are expected to pay, rather than seeking help from an agency supported by the United Fund. Many of the individuals who engage in full-time marriage counseling belong to the American Association of Marriage and Family Counselors. This group was organized in 1942 and has provided the leadership to establish the standards for a profession of marriage counselors. The association is "working closely with other professional groups to establish and revise state laws pertaining to marriage, divorce, licensing of marriage counselors and related subjects."[40]

The Association also has been active in the movement for state licensing of marriage counselors. This has become a necessity since any person who wishes to call himself a "marriage counselor" may do so in most states. Unscrupulous individuals with no specialized education in counseling have set themselves up in business and have

---

40. *The American Association of Marriage and Family Counselors, What It Is . What It Does* (Dallas: American Association of Marriage and Family Counselors, n.d.), p. 2. For information write to the American Association of Marriage and Family Counselors, 6211 W. Northwest Highway, Suite 2900, Dallas, TX 75225.

harmed many marriages, and brought disrepute on the whole area of marriage counseling. This has led to the desire to have state laws governing who may enter the practice of marriage counseling. Some states such as California, Michigan, and New Jersey already have laws regulating the practice.[41] An article in *Changing Times*, May 1965 states, "Almost any reputable, well-qualified practitioner will belong to some nationally recognized group such as the American Association of Marriage Counselors, American Psychological Association, American Psychiatric Association, or the Academy of Certified Social Workers. Be leery of any counselor who calls himself a doctor but ducks when asked, 'doctor of what?' "[42]

The person who seeks help from a marriage counselor in private practice should investigate the qualifications of the counselor before visiting him, since "quacks" will be in business until all states have laws regulating the profession. A person needing medical help does not refuse the help of a physician even though there are "quacks" and incompetents in the medical profession. In like manner, a person needing counseling should not refuse to seek out a qualified counselor even though there are the unscrupulous persons calling themselves "counselors."

NECESSITY OF SEEKING HELP EARLY

The important thing for a family to remember is to seek help when it is needed. Counselors are unanimous in their opinion that the earlier help is sought for a problem, the easier the solution can be found. Mace suggests the following:

> It is always best to take a marriage problem to a counselor before it has become very serious. Many people adopt the attitude that they should try everything else first, and then if all else fails, they can call in a marriage counselor. This is a mistaken attitude, because while less experienced people are tinkering with the problem, valuable time is being lost and the situation may be deteriorating rapidly. The right time to seek marriage counseling is *immediately when the couple become aware that they have a problem which they seem unable to solve by themselves*[43] (italics his).

If a couple waits until all communication lines are down between them, or waits until a child is emotionally disturbed before seeking

41. Clyde O. McDaniel, Jr., "Toward a Professional Definition of Marriage Counseling," in *The Family Coordinator*, January 1971, p. 35.
42. *Changing Times*, May 1965, p. 45.
43. Mace, *Success in Marriage*, p. 148. Used by permission.

aid, the task of restoration becomes far greater. But even when the problem is attacked early, "the counselor offers no magic formula. Their role is helping you to see the problem. Solving it is up to you."[44] The Christian, of course, has resources that the average person does not possess so that he does not have to solve the problem alone. However, it is still true that he must cooperate with the counselor while seeking divine help and comfort.

CONCLUSION

It is hoped that the young person who reads this book will be able to face realistically the choosing of a life partner, and be aware of the necessity to continually strive to improve the marital relationship. Successful Christian marriages do not just "happen"; they are created with God's help by selecting the right mate, and then the two partners work to build the best relationship possible. Norman Williams writes that:

> Marriage is a rich and satisfying experience to those who are willing to sacrifice selfish ideas and patterns of action and work together to please Christ and each other. In the adjusting of two lives into a relationship of creative harmony, there are many trials, tears, heartaches and conflicts. Christian marriage is full of happiness but it is a happiness given by the Lord Jesus Christ to those who are willing to pay the price and deny themselves.[45]

Modern marriage makes many demands upon those who choose to enter into the bonds of matrimony, but none of these demands are too great for those who seek the help of the "God of all grace." He is able to enrich and to bless the lives of those who put their trust in Him. A. Donald Bell makes the following suggestion:

> Only with the help of God could a couple expect to succeed in this serious business of building a Christian home. Only God can take the raw materials of two personalities, a house, furnishings, friends and neighbors, and remake these into a Christian home. . . . Like many miracles, building a Christian home is a long range process. Over a period of years of working and playing and praying the God-blessed institution evolves. . . . The young man and woman who wants a Christian home must pay a high price to secure it.[46]

44. *Changing Times*, May 1965, p. 45.
45. Norman V. Williams, *The Christian Home* (Chicago: Moody Press, 1952), pp. 50-51. Used by permission.
46. Bell, *The Family in Dialogue*, pp. 25-26, 37.

The task of achieving such a successful marriage will be easier if the mates are well chosen, but even where incompatibilities exist, there are no problems that cannot be solved between a Christian husband and wife who honestly seek His help. "Problems can be made right and when they are, the difficulties in marriage begin to melt away. This brings us back to the principle . . . that it is possible for all marriages to be happy and satisfying, if both husband and wife agree."[47]

The great number of happy Christian families indicates that the miracle of marriage is still possible. The fine, dedicated Christian young people that are products of these homes are evidence that Biblical principles of child rearing are still effective when conscientiously and consistently followed.

47. Jauncey, *Magic in Marriage*, p. 8.

QUESTIONS FOR DISCUSSION AND REVIEW

1. Why are people in American society reluctant to seek help for problems in interpersonal relationships?

2. When should a couple seek counseling?

3. Explain the process by which love turns to hatred in a marriage.

4. Suggest some areas where a couple with good overall adjustment may be able to use counseling services.

5. Why is counseling with both marriage partners more successful than with only one partner?

6. How should a pastor's undergraduate education differ from his graduate seminary education?

7. Where may a person find a Christian counselor?

8. Why is the social worker called "the poor man's psychiatrist?"

9. What are some sources of counseling in the secular field?

10. How may a person determine whether a counselor is genuine or a fraud?

SELECTED
BIBLIOGRAPHY

This list of books is only a small sampling of the material available on marriage and the family. *The International Bibliography of Research in Marriage and the Family, 1900–1964* contains 12,850 references, and should be consulted by the reader when a more extensive bibliography is needed.

Certain periodicals regularly review books in the field. *The Family Coordinator*, published quarterly by the National Council on Family Relations, utilizes about twenty pages of each issue in reviewing current literature in the area of marriage and the family.

Included are titles that are published by secular and Christian companies or organizations. The listing of a title, either secular or Christian, *does not indicate the approval of every idea presented in the book*, but merely signifies the work contains some helpful information. As is the case in reading any literature, what is acceptable or helpful to one person may not be to another.

Most of the books have been published within the last few years, but some older titles have been included, especially those that are classics in their field such as Annette Garrett's *Interviewing—Its Principles and Methods*.

The section on Counseling has been extended so that those who work with young people and families may be informed about the large amount of material available to help increase their knowledge and ability to help individuals or families who have problems.

GENERAL

Adams, Jay E. *Solving Marriage Problems*. Phillipsburg, N.J.: Presbyterian and Reformed Publishing Co., 1972.

Aldous, J., and Hill, R. *The International Bibliograph of Research in Marriage and the Family*, 1900-1964. Minneapolis: University of Minnesota Press, 1967.

Amstutz, H. Clair. *Growing Up to Love*. Scottdale, PA: Herald Press, 1966.

Andrews, G. *Your Half of the Apple*. Grand Rapids: Zondervan Publishing House, 1972.

Andrews, G. H. *Sons of Freedom: God and the Single Man*. Grand Rapids: Zondervan Publishing House, 1975.

Arledge, Byron W. *Laugh With Your Teenagers*, Wheaton, IL: Tyndale House Publishers, 1985.

Augsburger, David A. *Caring Enough to Hear*. Glendale, CA: Regal Books, 1982.

Beardsley, L. *A Family Love Story—Between Parent and Teenager*. Irvine, CA: Harvest House Publishers, 1975.

Beardsley, Lou, and Spry, Toni. *The Fulfilled Woman*. Irvine, CA: Harvest House Publishers, 1975.

Bell, A. Donald. *The Family in Dialogue*. Grand Rapids: Zondervan Publishing House, 1970.

Benson, Dan. *The Total Man*. Wheaton, IL: Tyndale House Publishers, 1977.

Berry, J. *The Happy Home Handbook*. Old Tappan, NJ: Fleming H. Revell Co., 1976.

Besancenez, Paul H. S. J. *Interfaith Marriages: Who and Why*. New Haven, CT: College and University Press Services, Inc., 1971.

Birkey, V., and Turnquist, J. *A Mother's Problem Solver*. Old Tappan, NJ: Fleming H. Revell Co., 1978.

Blood, Robert O. *Marriage*, 3rd ed. New York: Free Press, 1978.

Bock, L. and Working, M. *Happiness Is a Family Time Together*, Old Tappan, NJ: Fleming H. Revell Co., 1975.

———. *Happiness Is a Family Walk with God*. Old Tappan, NJ: Fleming H. Revell Co., 1977.

Bontrager, Frances. *The Church and the Single Person*. Scottsdale, PA: Herald Press, 1969.

Bowman, George M. *Here's How to Succeed with Your Money*. Rev. ed. Chicago: Moody Press, 1974.

Brandt, H., and Landrum, P. *I Want My Marriage to Be Better*. Grand Rapids: Zondervan Publishing House, 1976.

———. *I Want to Enjoy My Children*. Grand Rapids: Zondervan Publishing House, 1975.

Brandt, Henry R. *Balancing Your Marriage*. Wheaton, IL: Scripture Press, 1966.

———. *Building a Christian Home*. Wheaton, IL: Scripture Press, 1960.

———. *Build a Happy Home with Discipline*. Wheaton, IL: Scripture Press, 1965.

Calkin, R. H. *Two Shall Be One*. Elgin, IL: David C. Cook Publishing Co., 1977.

Carlson, C. C. *Established in Eden*. Old Tappan, NJ: Fleming H. Revell Co., 1978.

Carlton, Anna Lee. *Guidelines for Family Worship*. Anderson, IN: Warner Press, 1965.

Carter, Hugh, and Glick, Paul C. *Marriage and Divorce: A Social and Economic Study*. Cambridge: Harvard University Press, 1970.

Champion, M. A. *Especially for Husbands*. Minneapolis: Bethany Fellowship, Inc., 1978.

Chapman, G. *Hope for the Separated.* Chicago: Moody Press, 1982.

Child Study Association of America. *You, Your Child and Drugs.* New York: Child Study Press, 1971.

————. *And Then There Were Two: A Handbook for Mothers and Fathers of Twins.* Rev. ed. New York: Child Study Press, 1971.

Christensen, L. and N. *The Christian Couple.* Minneapolis: Bethany Fellowship, 1977.

Christensen, L. *The Christian Family.* Minneapolis: Bethany Fellowship, 1970.

Clarkson, M. *So You're Single.* Wheaton, IL: Harold Shaw Publishers, 1978.

Coble, H. H. *Man: Responsible and Caring.* Nashville: Broadman Press, 1977.

Cole, Edwin L. *Maximized Manhood.* Springdale, PA: Whitaker House, 1982.

Cook, Wm. H. *Success, Motivation and the Scriptures.* Nashville: Broadman Press, 1974.

Cooper, D. B. and Carroll, A. K. *Happy Husband Book.* Wheaton, IL: Victor Books, 1980.

Crawford, John and Dorathea. *Being the Real Father Now That Your Teenager Will Need.* Philadelphia: Fortress Press, 1968.

Crabb, Lawrence J. Jr. *The Marriage Builder: A Blueprint for Couples and Counselors.* Grand Rapids: Zondervan Publishing House, 1982.

Dahl, Gerald L. *Why Christian Marriages are Breaking Up.* New York: Thomas Nelson Publishers, 1979.

Deal, William, *God's Answer for the Unequally Yoked.* Westchester, IL: Good News Publishers, 1980.

Dayton, H. L., Jr. *Your Money, Frustration or Freedom.* Wheaton, IL: Tyndale House Publishers, 1979.

————. *Marriage: Duet or Discord.* Grand Rapids: Zondervan Publishing House, 1971.

Demarest, G. *Christian Alternatives Within Marriage.* Waco: Word Books, 1977.

Dobson, James, *Love Must Be Tough.* Waco, TX: Word Publishers, 1983.

————. *Preparing for Adolescence.* New York: Bantam Books, 1978.

————. *The Strong-willed Child.* Wheaton, IL: Tyndale House Publishers, 1978.

————. *Straight Talk to Men and Their Wives.* Waco, TX: Word Publishers, 1984.

Dow, R. A. *Ministry with Single Adults.* Valley Forge: Judson Press, 1977.

Drakeford, John W. *Games Husbands and Wives Play.* Nashville: Broadman Press, 1971.

————. *How to Manipulate Your Mate.* New York: Thomas Nelson, Inc. 1974.

————. *Made for Each Other.* Nashville: Broadman Press, 1973.

Duty, Guy. *Divorce and Remarriage.* Minneapolis: Bethany Fellowship, 1967.

Duvall, Evelyn Millis. *Parent and Teenager, Living and Loving.* Nashville: Broadman Press, 1976.

————. *The Art of Dating.* New York: Association Press, 1967.

Engelsma, D. *Marriage—The Mystery of Christ and His Church.* Grand Rapids: Reformed Free Publishing Association, 1975.

Edmund, E. *Sex, Love and Life.* Grand Rapids: Zondervan Publishing House, 1973.

Engel, Louis and Wood, Brendan, *How to Buy Stocks.* New York: Bantam Books, 7th Rev. ed., 1983.

Epp, Theodore H. *Marriage and Divorce.* Lincoln, NB: Back to the Bible Broadcast.

Erb, Alta Mae. *Christian Education in the Home*. Scottdale, PA: Herald Press, 1963.

Erdahl, L. and C. *Be Good to Each Other*. New York: Hawthorne Books, Inc., 1976.

Evans, Colleen Townsend and Evans, Louis, Jr. *Bold Commitment*. Wheaton, IL: Victor Books, 1983.

Exel, G. W. *Live Happily with the Woman You Love*. Chicago: Moody Press, 1977.

Fennema, Jack. *Nurturing Children in the Lord*. Grand Rapids: Baker Book House, 1977.

Feucht, Oscar E., ed. *Family Relationships and the Church*. St. Louis: Concordia Publishing House, 1971.

Fix, J., and Levitt, Z. *For Singles Only*. Old Tappan, NJ: Fleming H. Revell Co., 1978.

Fooshee, George and Marjean. *You Can Beat the Money Squeeze*. Old Tappan, NJ: Fleming H. Revell Co., 1980.

Ford, George. *All the Money You Need*. Waco: Word Books, 1974.

Foster, Richard J. *Money, Sex and Power: The Challenge of the Disciplined Life*. San Francisco: Harper and Row, 1985.

Fritze, Julius A. *The Essence of Marriage*. Grand Rapids: Zondervan Publishing House, 1971.

Fryling, Alice and Robert. *A Handbook for Married Couples*. Downers Grove, IL: Inter-Varsity Press, 1984.

Galloway, D. E. *We're Making Our Home a Happy Place*. Wheaton, IL: Tyndale House Publishers, 1976.

Getz, Gene. *The Measure of a Man*. Glendale, CA: Regal Books, 1980.

Gordon, Albert I. *Intermarriage*. Boston: Beacon Press, 1964.

Grulan, Stephen A. *Marriage and Family, A Christian Perspective*. Grand Rapids: Zondervan Publishing House, 1984.

Gundry, Patricia. *Heirs Together*. Grand Rapids: Zondervan Publishing House, 1980.

Hardisty, George and Margaret. *Successful Financial Planning*. Old Tappan, NJ: Fleming H. Revell Co., 1978.

Harrell, J. *Good Marriages Grow*. Waco: Word Books, 1968.

Hefley, James. *Sex, Sense and Nonsense*. Elgin, IL: David C. Cook Publishing Co., 1971.

Heidebrecht, P., and Rohrbach, J. *Fathering a Son*. Chicago: Moody Press, 1979.

Hendricks, Howard and Jeanne. *Footprints: Walking Through the Passages of Life*. Portland, OR: Multnomah Press, 1978.

Herr, E. L. *Growing Up Is a Family Affair*. Chicago: Moody Press, 1978.

Hess, Bartlett and Margaret. *How Does Your Marriage Grow?* Wheaton, IL: Victor Books, 1983.

Hinson, Ed. *The Total Family*. Wheaton: Tyndale House Publishers, 1981.

Hocking, D. *Love and Marriage*. Eugene, OR: Harvest House, 1981.

Huffman, George W. *How to Inspect a House*, Reading, MA: Addison Wesley Publishing Co., 1985.

Hugget, Joyce. *Growing Into Love*. Downers Grove: Inter-Varsity Press, 1982.

Hunter, Brenda. *Where Have All the Mothers Gone?* Grand Rapids: Zondervan Publishing House, 1982.

Jacobsen, M. B. *What Happens When Children Grow*. A revision of *The Child in the Christian Home*. Wheaton, IL: Victor Books, 1977.

Jacobsen, M. L. *How to Keep Your Family Together and Still Have Fun*. Grand Rapids: Zondervan Publishing House, 1972.

Johnson, Rex. *At Home with Sex*. Wheaton, IL: Victor Books, 1979.

————. *Communication—Key to Your Parents*. Irvine, CA: Harvest House Publishers, 1978.

Joy, Donald M. *Bonding: Relationships in the Image of God*. Waco, TX: Word Books, 1985.

Kelser, Jay. *Too Big to Spank*. Glendale, CA: Regal Books, 1978.

Ketterman, Grace H., M.D. *The Complete Book of Baby and Child Care*. Old Tappan, N.J.: Fleming H. Revell Co., 1985.

Kilgore, J. *Being a Man in a Woman's World*. Irvine, CA: Harvest House Publishers, 1975.

Knight, G. W., III. *The New Testament Teachings on the Role Relationship of Men and Women*. Grand Rapids: Baker Book House, 1977.

Kolb, Erwin J. *Parents Guide to Christian Conversation about Sex*. St. Louis: Concordia Publishing House, 1967.

Krutza, William J. *101 Ways to Enrich your Marriage*. Grand Rapids: Baker Book House, 1982.

Kuntzelman, Charles. *The Well Family Book*. San Bernandino: Here's Life Publishers, Inc., 1985.

Lackey, Camilla Dayton. *You Can Live on Half Your Income*. Grand Rapids: Zondervan Publishing House, 1982.

LaHaye, Tim. *The Battle for the Family*. Old Tappan, NJ: Fleming H. Revell Co., 1982.

————. *How to Develop Your Child's Temperament*. Irvine, CA: Harvest House Publishers, 1977.

————. *Spirit Controlled Family Living*. Old Tappan, NJ: Fleming H. Revell Co., 1978.

————. *Understanding the Male Temperament*. Old Tappan, NJ: Fleming H. Revell Co., 1977.

Lanez, Carl J. *The Divorce Myth*. Minneapolis: Bethany House Publishers, 1981.

Larson, Bruce, ed. *Marriage Is for Living*. Grand Rapids: Zondervan Publishing House, 1968.

Leaman, D. R. *Making Decisions—A Guide for Couples*. Scottdale, PA: Herald Press, 1979.

Leman, Kevin. *Making Children Mind Without Losing Yours*. Old Tappan, NJ: Fleming H. Revell Co., 1984.

————. *Parenthood Without Hassles*. Irvine, CA: Harvest House Publishers, 1979.

LePeau, A. T. *One Plus One*. Downers Grove, IL: Inter-Varsity Press, 1981.

Lessin, Roy. *How to Be the Parents of Happy and Obedient Children*. Van Nuys, CA: Bible Voice, Inc. 1978.

MacArthur, John F. *The Family*. Chicago: Moody Press, 1982.

MacDonald, Gordon. *Magnificent Marriage*. Wheaton, IL: Tyndale House Publishers, 1976.

————. *The Effective Father*. Wheaton, IL: Tyndale House Publishers, 1977.

Mace, David R. *Love and Anger in Marriage*. Grand Rapids: Zondervan Publishing House, 1982.

McFarland, Robert L., and Burton, John David. *Learning for Loving*. Grand Rapids: Zondervan Publishing House, 1969.

McGinnis, M. *Single*. Old Tappan, NJ: Fleming H. Revell Co., 1974.

McLean, Gordon. *Let God Manage Your Money*. Grand Rapids: Zondervan Publishing House, 1977.

Martin, O. Dean. *Good Marriages Don't Just Happen*. Old Tappan, NJ: Fleming H. Revell Co., 1984.

Mason, Mike. *The Mystery of Marriage*. Portland, OR: Multnomah Press, 1985.

Mayhall, Jack and Carole. *Marriage Takes More Than Love*. Colorado Springs: Navpress, 1978.

Meier, Paul D. *Christian Child-rearing and Personality Development*. Grand Rapids: Baker Book House, 1977.

Meredith, D. *Becoming One*. New York: Thomas Nelson, Inc., 1979.

Merrill, Dean. *The Husband Book*. Grand Rapids: Zondervan Publishing House, 1977.

Miles, H. J. *The Dating Game*. Grand Rapids: Zondervan Publishing House, 1975.

————. *Singles, Sex and Marriage*. Waco, TX: Word Books, 1983.

Moore, Louis and Kay. *When You Go to Work: How Two Paycheck Families Can Stay Active in the Church*. Waco, TX: Word Books, 1982.

Murphy, Cecil. *The Encyclopedia of Christian Marriage*. Old Tappan, NJ: Fleming H. Revell Co., 1984.

Myra, H. L. *Love Notes to Jeanette*. Wheaton: Victor Books, 1979.

Narramore, Bruce. *An Ounce of Prevention: A Parent's Guide to Moral and Spiritual Growth of Children*. Grand Rapids: Zondervan Publishing House, 1973.

————. *Parenting with Love and Limits*. Grand Rapids: Zondervan Publishing House, 1979.

————. *You're Someone Special*. Grand Rapids: Zondervan Publishing House, 1978.

————. *Why Children Misbehave*. Grand Rapids: Zondervan Publishing House, 1980.

Narramore, Clyde M. *Discipline in the Christian Home*. Grand Rapids: Zondervan Publishing House, 1961.

————. *How to Succeed in Family Living*. Glendale, CA: Gospel Light Publications, 1968.

————. *How to Tell Your Children about Sex*. Grand Rapids: Zondervan Publishing House, 1958.

————. *Improving Your Self-confidence*. Grand Rapids: Zondervan Publishing House, 1961.

————. *The Unmarried Woman*. Grand Rapids: Zondervan Publishing House, 1961.

Nederhood, Joel. *The Holy Triangle*. Grand Rapids: Baker Book House, 1970.

Nida, C. *Before You Marry—Written Especially for Men*. Chicago: Moody Press, 1977.

O'Kane, M. Lauen. *Living with Adult Children*. St. Paul: Diction Books, 1982.

Ortlund, R. and A. *The Best Half of Life*. Glendale, CA: Regal Books, 1976.

Parson, Martin. *Toward the Senior Years*. Chicago: Moody Press, 1966.

Pedrick, B. *The Confident Parent*. Elgin, IL: David C. Cook Publishing Co., 1979.

Peters, G. W. *Divorce and Remarriage*. Chicago: Moody Press, 1972.

Petersen, Evelyn, and Petersen, J. Allan. *For Women Only*. Wheaton, IL: Tyndale House Publishers, 1974.

Petersen, J. Allan. *Conquering Family Stress*. Wheaton, IL: Victor Books, 1978.

Sell, Charles M. *Achieving the Impossible: Intimate Marriage*. Portland, OR: Multnomah Press, 1982.

———. *Family Ministry, the Enrichment of Family Life Through the Church*. Grand Rapids: Zondervan Publishing House, 1981.

Shedd, Charles W. *You Can Be a Great Parent*. Waco, TX: Word Books, 1982.

Small, Dwight Hervey. *After You've Said I Do*. Old Tappan, NJ: Fleming H. Revell Co., 1968.

———. *Your Marriage Is God's Affair*. Old Tappan, NJ: Fleming H. Revell Co., 1979.

Sroka, B. *One Is a Whole Number*. Wheaton, IL: Scripture Press, 1978.

Staples, Robert. *The Black Family: Essays and Studies*. Belmont, CA: Wadsworth Publishing Co., 1971.

Start, Clarissa. *Never Underestimate the Little Woman*. St. Louis: Concordia Publishing House, 1969.

———. *First Aid for Faltering Families*. Lincoln, NB: Back to the Bible, 1978.

Petersen, J. A., and Smith, E. and J. *Two Become One*. Wheaton, IL: Tyndale House Publishers, 1973.

Portnoy, Louis, and Saltman, Jules. *Fertility in Marriage: A Guide for the Childless*. New York: Crowell-Collier Publishing Co., 1962.

Poure, Ken. *It's All in the Family*. Denver: Baptist Press Publications, 1975.

Poure, Ken, and Stoop, Dave. *Parents, Give Your Kid a Chance*. Irvine, CA: Harvest House Publishers, 1977.

Public Affairs Committee, Barman, A., and Cohen, L. *Help for Your Troubled Child*. Bienvenu, M. J., Sr. *Parent-Teenager Communication*. Bienvenu, M. J., Sr. *Talking It Over at Home*. Schiller, A. *Drug Abuse and Your Child*. Public Affairs Committee, 381 Park Ave. S., New York 10016.

Queen, Stuart A., Habenstein, Robert W., and Adams, John B. *The Family in Various Cultures*. Philadelphia: J. B. Lippincott, 1967.

Ray, Bruce A. *Withhold Not Correction*. Grand Rapids: Baker Book House, 1978.

Reese, Harold. *Overcoming Financial Bondage*. Stone Mountain, GA: Crossroads Publications, Inc., 1975.

Reiss, Walter. *Before They Start to Leave*. St. Louis: Concordia Publishing House, 1967.

———. *The Teen-Ager You're Dating*. St. Louis: Concordia Publishing House, n.d.

Richards, Larry. *How Far Can I Go*. Chicago: Moody Press, 1969.

Rickerson, W. E. *Good Times for Your Family*. Glendale, CA: Regal Books, 1976.

Ridenour, Fritz. *It All Depends*. Glendale, CA: Gospel Light Publications, 1969.

Roberts, Wes, and Wright, H. Norman, *Before You Say, "I Do."* Irvine, CA: Harvest House Publishers, 1978.

Roberts, Wes and Judy, and Wright, H. Norman. *After You Say, "I Do."* "Irvine, CA: Harvest House Publishers, 1979.

Rock, S. A. *This Time Together*, Grand Rapids: Zondervan Publishing House, 1980.

Roper, G. *Wife, Mother, Mate, Me*. Grand Rapids: Baker Book House, 1975.

Sala, Harold J. *They Shall Be One Flesh*. Denver: Accent Books, 1978.

———. *Train Up a Child and Be Glad You Did*. Denver: Accent Books, 1978.

Salter, D. *One Is More Than Un*. Grand Rapids: Baker Book House, 1978.

Sanders, J. Oswald. *Spiritual Maturity*. Chicago: Moody Press, 1967.

Sandmel, Samuel. *When a Jew and Christian Marry*. Philadelphia: Fortress Press, 1977.

Scalan, B. *The Family Bible Study Book*. Old Tappan, NJ: Fleming H. Revell Co., 1975.

_____ . ed. *The Family Bible Study Book 2*. Old Tappan, NJ: Fleming H. Revell Co., 1977.

Schaeffer, Edith. *What Is a Family*. Old Tappan, NJ: Fleming H. Revell Co., 1975.

Schlesinger, Benjamin. *The Jewish Family*. Toronto: University of Toronto Press, 1970.

Schrum, D. *Creating Love and Warmth for Our Children*. Nashville: Broadman Press, 1977.

Sears, William, M. D. *Christian Parenting and Child Care*. New York: Thomas Nelson Publishers, 1985.

_____ . *When You're a Widow*. St. Louis: Concordia Publishing House, 1968.

Stedman, E. *A Woman's Worth*. Waco: Word Books, 1975.

Steven, Norma. *What Kids Katch from Parents*. Irvine, CA: Harvest House Publishers, 1976.

Strafford, Tim. *A Love Story*. Grand Rapids: Zondervan Publishing House, 1977.

_____ . *The Trouble with Parents*. Grand Rapids: Zondervan Publishing House, 1978.

Stowell, Joseph M. *Marriage Is for Keeps*. Des Plaines, IL: Living Reality, n.d.

Strauss, R. L. *Living in Love*. Wheaton, IL: Tyndale House Publishers, 1978.

_____ . *Marriage Is for Love*. Wheaton, IL: Tyndale House Publishers, 1973.

Sutton-Smith, B. and S. *How to Play with Your Children (and When Not To)*. New York: Hawthorne Books, Inc., 1974.

Swindoll, Charles R. *Strike the Original Match*. Portland, OR: Multnomah Press, 1980.

Taylor, J. R. *One Home Under God*. Nashville: Broadman Press, 1974.

Thurmond, Nancy Moore. *Happy Mother, Happy Child*. Wheaton, IL: Tyndale House Publishers, 1982.

Timmons, Tim. *Maximum Marriage*. Old Tappan, NJ: Fleming H. Revell Co., 1976.

_____ . *Stress in the Family*. Eugene, OR: Harvest House, 1982.

Treadwell, M. A. *The Discipline of Raising Children*. Irvine, CA: Harvest House Publishers, 1977.

Triton, A. N. *Living and Loving*. Downer's Grove, IL: Inter-Varsity Press, 1972.

Tournier, Paul. *To Understand Each Other*. Richmond: John Knox Press, 1967.

Towns, Elmer. *Ministering to the Young Single Adult*. Grand Rapids: Baker Book House, 1967.

Trobisch, Walter. *I Married You*. New York: Harper and Row, 1971.

VanKooten, Tenis. *Building the Family Altar*. Grand Rapids: Baker Book House, 1969.

Vaughn, R. *To Be a Mother*. Nashville-New York: Thomas Nelson, Inc., 1978.

Vetter, B. and J. *Jesus Was a Single Adult*. Elgin, IL: David C. Cook Publishing Co., 1978.

Wakefield, N. *You Can Have a Happy Family*. Glendale, CA: Regal Books, 1977.

Walker, G., ed. *The Celebration Book*. Glendale, CA: Regal Books, n.d.

Ward, Ted. *Values Begin at Home*. Wheaton, IL: Victor Books, 1973.

_____. *Personal Involvement Workbook for Values Begin at Home*. Wheaton, IL: Victor Books, 1979.

Watts, V. *The Single Parent*. Old Tappan, NJ: Fleming H. Revell Co., 1976.

Weinstein, Grace W. *Children and Money*. New York: Schocken Books, 1975.

Welch, R. *We Really Do Need Each Other*. Nashville: Impact Books, n.d.

Whitehead, John W. *Parents' Rights*. Westchester, IL: Crossway Books, 1985.

Wiersbe, Warren. *Creative Christian Living*. Westwood NJ: Fleming H. Revell Co., 1967.

Whiting, Ellis W. *The Story of Life*. Grand Rapids: Baker Book House, 1972.

Williams, Norman V. *The Christian Home*. Chicago: Moody Press, 1952.

Wise, Francis. *Youth and Drugs: Prevention, Detection and Cure*. New York: Association Press, 1971.

Wonderly, Gusta M. *Training Children*. Lincoln, NB: Back to the Bible Broadcast, n.d.

Wrage, Karl. *Man and Woman*. Philadelphia: Fortress Press, 1969.

_____. *Communication, Key to Your Marriage*. Glendale, CA: Gospel Light Publications, 1974.

_____. *In-laws, Outlaws; Building Better Relationships*. Irvine, CA: Harvest House Publishers, 1977.

Wright, H. Norman, and Inmon, Marvin. *Dating, Waiting, and Choosing a Mate*. Irvine, CA: Harvest House Publishers, 1978.

Wright, H. Norman, *Seasons of a Marriage*. Glendale, CA: Regal Books, 1982.

Wright, H. Norman and Johnson, Rex. *Communication, Key to Your Teens*. Irvine, CA: Harvest House Publishers, 1978.

Wright, H. Norman. *The Family That Listens*. Wheaton, IL: Victor Books, 1978.

_____. *The Living Marriage*. Old Tappan, NJ: Fleming H. Revell Co., 1975.

Wynn, John Charles, ed. *Sexual Ethics and Christian Responsibility: Some Divergent Views*. New York: Association Press, 1970.

Wyrtzen, Jack. *Sex Is Not Sinful*. Grand Rapids: Zondervan Publishing House, 1970.

Zuck, Roy B., and Getz, Gene A. *Adult Education in the Church*. Chicago: Moody Press, 1970.

_____. *Christian Youth—An In-depth Study*. Chicago: Moody Press, 1968.

COUNSELING

Adams, James Frederick. *Counseling and Guidance: A Summary View*. New York: Macmillan Co., 1965.

Adams, Jay E. *The Christian Counselor's Casebook*. Grand Rapids: Baker Book House, 1974.

_____. *The Christian Counselor's Manual*. Grand Rapids: Baker Book House, 1973.

_____. *Competent to Counsel*. Grand Rapids: Baker Book House, 1970.

_____. *The Use of the Scriptures in Counseling*. Nutley, NJ: Presbyterian and Reformed Publishing Co., 1977.

Adolph, Paul E. *Release from Tension*. Wheaton, IL: Scripture Press, 1969.

Aldrich, C. Knight, and Nighswonger, Carl. *A Pastoral Counseling Casebook*. Philadelphia: Westminster Press, 1968.

Anderson, Stanley E. *Every Pastor a Counselor*. Wheaton, IL: Van Kampen Press, 1949.

Babbage, Stuart Barton. *Christianity and Sex*. Chicago: Inter-Varsity Press, 1963.

Bassett, William. *Counseling the Childless Couple*. Philadelphia: Fortress Press, 1969.

Benjamin, Alfred. *The Helping Interview*. Boston: Houghton-Mifflin Co., 1969.

Blees, Robert A. *Counseling with Teen-agers*. Philadelphia: Fortress Press, 1968.

Bracher, Marjory. *Love, Sex and Life*. Philadelphia: Fortress Press, 1964.

Brown, Kristi, ed., *Family Counseling: An Annotated Bibliography*. Cambridge, MA: Oelgeschlager, Gunn and Hain, 1981.

Bustanoby, A. *You Can Change Your Personality*. Grand Rapids: Zondervan Publishing House, 1976.

Chandler, E. R. *Budgets, Bedrooms and Boredom*. Glendale, CA: Regal Books, 1976.

Clinebell, Howard J., Jr. *Basic Types of Pastoral Counseling*. Nashville: Abingdon Press, 1966.

Clinebell, Howard J., Jr., and Clinebell, Charlotte H. *The Intimate Marriage*. New York: Harper and Row, 1970.

Collins, Gary. *Effective Counseling*. Carol Stream, IL: Creation House, 1972.

————. *Family Talk—Getting Along Together*. Santa Ana: Vision House Publishers, 1978.

————. *The Rebuilding of Psychology*. Wheaton, IL: Tyndale House Publishers, 1977.

Cosgrove, Mark P., and Mallory, James D., Jr. *Mental Health: A Christian Approach*. Grand Rapids: Zondervan Publishing House, 1977.

Crabb, L. J., Jr. *Basic Principles of Biblical Counseling*. Grand Rapids: Zondervan Publishing House, 1975.

————. *Effective Biblical Counseling*. Grand Rapids: Zondervan Publishing House, 1977.

Dahl, G. L. *Why Christian Marriages Are Breaking Up*. New York: Thomas Nelson, Inc.

Dicks, Russell L. *Premarital Guidance*. Philadelphia: Fortress Press, 1967.

Eyrich, Howard A. *Three to Get Ready*. Grand Rapids: Baker Book House, 1979.

Fisher, Esther Oshiver. *Help for Today's Troubled Marriages*. New York: Hawthorne Books, 1968.

Fletcher, Peter. *Understanding Your Emotional Problems*. New York: Hart Publishing Co., 1966.

Frame, John Davidson. *Psychology and Personality Development: Case Studies in Emotional Problems and Their Implications for the Christian Life*. Chicago: Moody Press, 1967.

Garrett, Annette. *Interviewing:—Its Principles and Methods*. New York: Family Service Association of America, 1942. Revised by T. Zahi and Margaret M. Mangold, 1972.

Grounds, Vernon. *Emotional Problems and the Gospel*. Grand Rapids: Zondervan Publishing House, 1977.

Hamilton, James D. *The Ministry of Pastoral Counseling*. Grand Rapids: Baker Book House, 1972.

Hardisty, M. *Forever, My Love*. Irvine, CA: Harvest House Publishers, 1975.

Hirning, J. L., and Hirning, Alma L. *Marriage Adjustment*. New York: American Book Co., 1956.

Hulme, William Edward. *How to Start Counseling; Building the Counseling Program in the Local Church*. New York: Abingdon Press, 1955.

Hyder, O. Quentin. *The Christian's Handbook of Psychiatry*. Old Tappan, NJ: Fleming H. Revell Co., 1971.

Jacobson, Margaret Bailey. *The Child in the Christian Home*. Wheaton, IL: Scripture Press, 1959.

Jauncey, James H. *Above Ourselves*. Grand Rapids: Zondervan Publishing House, 1964.

Jeeves, Malcolm. *Psychology and Christianity: A View Both Ways*. Downer's Grove, IL: Inter-Varsity Press, 1976.

Kent, Homer A., Sr. *The Pastor and His Work*. Chicago: Moody Press, 1963.

Kesler, J. *I Want a Home with No Problems*. Waco: Word Books, 1977.

Kent, Homer A., Sr. *The Pastor and His Work*. Chicago: Moody Press, 1963.

Kettering, Grace H. M.D. *How to Teach Your Child about Sex:* Old Tappan, NJ: Fleming H. Revell Co., 1981.

Little, L. Gilbert. *Nervous Christians*. Chicago: Moody Press, 1956.

Mace, David R. *Youth Considers Marriage*. Camden, NJ: Thomas Nelson, Inc., 1966.

Metcalfe, J. C. *The Bible and Counseling*. Fort Worthington, PA: Christian Literature Crusade, 1966.

Morris, J. Kenneth. *Premarital Counseling: A Manual for Ministers*. Englewood Cliffs, NJ: Prentice-Hall, Inc. 1965.

Narramore, Clyde M. *Counseling with Youth at Church, School, and Camp*. Grand Rapids: Zondervan Publishing House, 1966.

_____. *A Woman's World*. Grand Rapids: Zondervan Publishing House, 1963.

_____. *Encyclopedia of Psychological Problems*. Grand Rapids: Zondervan Publishing House, 1966.

_____. *The Psychology of Counseling*. Grand Rapids: Zondervan Publishing House, 1960.

_____. *This Way to Happiness: Psychology for Living*. Grand Rapids: Zondervan Publishing House, 1967.

Nelson, Marion H. *Why Christians Crack Up*. Chicago: Moody Press, 1967.

Oates, Wayne E. *New Dimensions in Pastoral Care*. Philadelphia: Fortress Press, 1970.

_____. *Pastoral Counseling in Social Problems*. Philadelphia: Westminster Press, 1966.

_____. *Premarital Pastoral Care and Counseling*. Nashville: Broadman Press, 1958.

_____. *Protestant Pastoral Counseling*. Philadelphia: Westminster Press, 1962.

Olford, Stephen F., and Lawes, Frank A. *The Sanctity of Sex*. Westwood, NJ: Fleming H. Revell Co., 1963.

Osborne, C. G. *The Art of Learning to Love Yourself*. Grand Rapids: Zondervan Publishing House, 1976.

_____. *The Art of Understanding Yourself*. Grand Rapids: Zondervan Publishing House, 1968.

_____. *The Art of Understanding Your Mate*. Grand Rapids: Zondervan Publishing House, 1970.

Patterson, Cecil Holden. *Theories of Counseling and Psychotherapy*. New York: Harper and Row, 1966.

Perez, Joseph Francis. *The Initial Counseling Contact*. Boston: Houghton-Mifflin, 1968.

Popenoe, Paul, and Disney, Dorothy Cameron. *Can This Marriage Be Saved?* New York: Macmillan Co., 1960.

Rozell, Roy. *The Sunday School Teacher as Counselor*. Grand Rapids: Zondervan Publishing House, 1965.

Rutledge, Aaron L. *Premarital Counseling*. Cambridge: Schenkman Publishing Co., 1966.

Sala, Harold J. *Guidelines for Successful Living*. Grand Rapids: Baker Book House, 1972.

Sall, Millard J. *The Emotions of God's People*. Grand Rapids: Zondervan Publishing House, 1978.

————— . *Faith, Psychology and Christian Maturity*. Grand Rapids: Zondervan Publishing House, 1975.

Schoen, S. J. *Please Love Them*. Ardmore, PA: Dorrance and Co., 1979.

Shedd, Charlie W. *Letters to Karen*. Old Tappan, NJ: Fleming H. Revell Co., 1965.

————— . *Letters to Philip*. Old Tappan, NJ: Fleming H. Revell Co., 1968.

Skoglund, E. *Your Troubled Child*. Elgin, IL: David C. Cook Publishing Co., 1974.

————— . *You Can Be Your Own Child's Counselor*. Glendale, CA: Regal Books, 1978.

Stewart, Charles W. *The Minister as Marriage Counselor*. Nashville: Abingdon Press, 1961.

Streeter, Herbert A. *Help for Marital Hang-ups*. Anderson, IN: Warner Press, 1970.

Terkelsen, Helen E. *Counseling the Unwed Mother*. Philadelphia: Fortress Press, 1967.

Trobisch, Walter. *Love Is a Feeling to Be Learned*. Downers Grove, IL: Inter-Varsity Press, 1971.

Vincent, M. O. *God, Sex and You*. Philadelphia: J. B. Lippincott Co., 1971.

Wagner, M. E. *The Sensation of Being Somebody: Building an Adequate Self-concept*. Grand Rapids: Zondervan Publishing House, 1975.

Walter, P. *Family Problems and Predicaments: How to Respond*. Wheaton, IL: Tyndale House Publishers, 1977.

Watson, Tom, Jr., and Hillis, Don W. *Sex Is a Four-letter Word (Love)*. Carol Stream, IL: Creation House, 1971.

White, J. *Parents in Pain*. Downer's Grove, IL: Inter-Varsity Press, 1979.

Wright, H. Norman. *Premarital Counseling*. Chicago: Moody Press, 1977.

MARRIAGE MANUALS

Butterfield, Oliver W. *Sexual Harmony in Marriage*. New York: Emerson Books, 1967.

Chesser, Eustace. *Love and the Married Woman*. New York: New American Library, 1970.

Ketterman, Grace H. M.D. *Before and After the Wedding Night*. Old Tappan, NJ: Fleming H. Revell Co., 1984.

LaHaye, Tim and Beverly. *The Act of Marriage*. Grand Rapids: Zondervan Publishing House, 1976.

Mace, David. *Sexual Difficulties in Marriage*. Philadelphia: Fortress Press, 1972.

Miles, Herbert J. *Sexual Happiness in Marriage*. Grand Rapids: Zondervan Publishing House, 1967.

————— . *Sexual Understanding Before Marriage*. Grand Rapids: Zondervan Publishing House, 1971.

Penner, Clifford and Joyce. *The Gift of Sex*. Waco, TX: Word Books, 1981.

Small, Dwight H. *Christian, Celebrate Your Sexuality*. Old Tappan, NJ: Fleming H. Revell Co., 1974.

Wheat, Ed and Gaye. *Intended for Pleasure*. Old Tappan, NJ: Fleming H. Revell Co., 1975.

Wright, Rusty and Linda Raney. *Dynamic Sex*. San Bernadino, CA: Here's Life Publishing Co., Inc., 1979.

Terkelsen, Helen E. *Counseling the Unwed Mother.* Philadelphia: Fortress Press, 1967.

Trobisch, Walter. *Love Is a Feeling to Be Learned.* Downers Grove, IL: Inter-Varsity Press, 1971.

Vincent, M. O. *God, Sex and You.* Philadelphia: J. B. Lippincott Co., 1971.

Wagner, M. E. *The Sensation of Being Somebody: Building an Adequate Self-concept.* Grand Rapids: Zondervan Publishing House, 1975.

Walter, P. *Family Problems and Predicaments: How to Respond.* Wheaton, IL: Tyndale House Publishers, 1977.

Watson, Tom, Jr., and Hillis, Don W. *Sex Is a Four-letter Word (Love).* Carol Stream, IL: Creation House, 1971.

White, J. *Parents in Pain.* Downer's Grove, IL: Inter-Varsity Press, 1979.

Wright, H. Norman. *Premarital Counseling.* Chicago: Moody Press, 1977.

MARRIAGE MANUALS

Butterfield, Oliver W. *Sexual Harmony in Marriage.* New York: Emerson Books, 1967.

Chesser, Eustace. *Love and the Married Woman.* New York: New American Library, 1970.

Henry, Joseph B. *Fulfillment in Marriage.* Westwood, NJ: Fleming H. Revell Co., 1966.

LaHaye, Tim and Beverly. *The Act of Marriage.* Grand Rapids: Zondervan Publishing House, 1976.

Mace, David. *Sexual Difficulties in Marriage.* Philadelphia: Fortress Press, 1972.

Miles, Herbert J. *Sexual Happiness in Marriage.* Grand Rapids: Zondervan Publishing House, 1967.

———. *Sexual Understanding Before Marriage.* Grand Rapids: Zondervan Publishing House, 1971.

Narramore, Clyde M. *A Christian View of Birth-control.* Grand Rapids: Zondervan Publishing House, 1961.

Small, Dwight H. *Christian, Celebrate Your Sexuality.* Old Tappan, NJ: Fleming H. Revell Co., 1974.

Wheat, Ed and Gaye. *Intended for Pleasure.* Old Tappan, NJ: Fleming H. Revell Co., 1975.

Wright, Rusty and Linda Raney. *Dynamic Sex.* San Bernadino, CA: Here's Life Publishing Co., Inc., 1979.

APPENDIX I

CASE STUDY OF A
MIXED MARRIAGE

UNEQUALLY YOKED

"My life is a mess." The woman sitting across the table brushed tears from her eyes. "It's hard to believe the situation is as bad as it is."

"Could you go back and tell us when it all began?"

"It began in my teens. I was introduced to a man older than I. I really didn't pay any attention to him, but to my surprise he called me the next day and asked me to go out with him. I knew it was wrong for a number of reasons. First of all, I knew he was not a Christian. I knew he gambled. He came from a family that had entirely different standards than my family had. I knew he was a Catholic, a Catholic by tradition rather than by conviction; but I've discovered that Catholic tradition to be about the strongest thing in the world."

"Were you a Christian at the time?"

"Oh, yes. All the time I went with him I felt uncomfortable. The Holy Spirit gave me no peace, but I blundered on without paying attention to the Lord. Soon there was talk of marriage. At first I said no.

"Suddenly I found myself surrounded by pressure—not only from him, but from his family and from some acquaintances who had always, more or less, ridiculed my stand for Christ. There was a certain appealing glamor to it all; being courted in an expensive car, going to the finest restaurants, and—I'm ashamed to admit it—going to a number of places I had no business visiting. The pressure grew, and while I knew it was wrong—absolutely wrong—I shut my eyes and stumbled on. After eight months the pressure reached a peak.

"I can still remember the bad advice I heard from my friends. 'He's devoted to you. He'll never interfere with your religion.' 'Look, you marry him and after awhile he'll go along with you.' 'He's not a strong Catholic, he hasn't been in the church in five years.' A number of people said that I was lucky to have a man interested in me who had so much money. Even a Christian friend of mine said, 'Some Christians make too much fuss about marrying outside of the faith. It's not really important if you love the man.' I finally surrendered to marriage. How wrong they all were!"

"Were you happy at all after you were married?"

"Oh, no. I discovered almost at once that while my husband made enormous amounts of money, he spent more than he made. He was in debt to such an extent I never believed we could escape. Now, after thirteen years, it's worse than ever."

"Could you sum up the reason why you fell into this situation?"

"Disobedience to the direct revelation of the Lord. I knew then, as well as I know now, this marriage did not have God's blessing. How well I remember the marriage ceremony. I wouldn't get married in a Catholic church and he wouldn't get married in my church, so we compromised and were married in a liberal church.

"Another building had been rented for the reception. I had no idea what my husband's family planned to do. They brought in liquor and a wild dance band. The amount of liquor consumed was shocking. I remember feeling so sorry for my parents and the handful of Christian friends who came. They stood to one side and watched the turmoil with shock. Because of my foolishness, I had put them in a most embarrassing position; and I am sure they never experienced a sadder moment.

"You asked before if I ever had happiness in my marriage. I said, no, and that's true; yet for a time, I prayed and began to entertain great hopes my husband would become a Christian. I expected it, but I've learned since there has to be a willingness on the part of the person for whom you are praying before the prayer can be answered. My husband was not willing then, and he's more unwilling now to listen than ever before, but I keep praying."

"What area of your life has this affected most?"

"There isn't one area of my life that hasn't been disturbed. I hate to admit it, but there was a time I became so desperate I even tried drinking. But that didn't help the problem; it complicated it.

"I shed more tears over the children than anything else. You know we have four. My girls and boys are completely confused. My husband has always treated me brutally; and even though my boys are young, I can't control them. They treat me the way he does. My husband swears and uses foul language constantly. The boys pick this up and there's nothing I can do. Even my girls say things I wouldn't dare let pass my lips. We're a ruined home.

"After our second child was born, I went to pieces because my husband didn't want children. Well, I went to the doctor and he discovered I had an ulcer. I've been under the doctor's care ever since. What can I do? I'm desperate. I don't believe in divorce. I don't believe in separation. What can I do? I know it's all my fault. You think of the few minutes a marriage takes. Then you think of the whole life you have to spend with the person you married.

"The situation has also affected the children in their schoolwork. I'm constantly being called in; and while all the children are unusually bright, the three in school barely pass their subjects. I have had a series of conferences with the school psychologist. He blames everything on the home life. The psychologist keeps telling me that unless he can counsel with my husband, he can't do a whole lot. When I tell my husband this, he gets furious and tells me it's my fault because I emphasize religion and we would be better off if the children were raised Catholic.

"The school authorities suggested I make an appointment with a psychiatrist. I went with the children a few times, but my husband refused to go and I gave up. The boys tend to follow their father's footsteps; and while the girls are a little closer to me, they're always confused because my husband plays them against me. The other day he came in and asked at the supper table, 'Who's the biggest complainer in this house?' I won the vote on the basis of my attempt to make Christ the Head of our household."

"Have you ever tried to talk to your husband about spiritual things?"

"Oh, yes, but I get absolutely nowhere. You wouldn't believe how far apart we are. He claims he believes there is a God; but he says if he accepted Christ the way I want him to, he'd have to change his entire way of life. He's in a business field where the politicians have to be paid off, and one year he had to pay $20,000 to the syndicate. I think he's afraid to make a break from them.

"Then there's his family. They're not church-going Catholics, but it's like a social organization and no one dares break out of it.

"He gambles; just about everything he does is a gamble. He goes to the racetrack every week. Even in his business, it's always the investment type of opportunity to make a large amount or lose a large amount. He hasn't told me, but I think he's paying off gambling debts every week."

"Do you think he still loves you?"

"One day he said, 'You're not the girl I married, you're different.' I insisted I wasn't. Then he blamed me for being a hypocrite for hiding what I was when he first met me. He said if he had known what I really believed, he wouldn't have married me. He's right about that. He always calls me a phony.

"It's funny; no, it's not funny; it's sad. I've tried everything. I've tried keeping quiet about Christ. I've tried going my husband's way. I've tried living all out for the Lord. Nothing works. Look at me now. I'm a nervous wreck—trembling, tears. What can I do? I can't blame the Lord. I got myself into this mess and I just don't see any way out.

"There have been times when my children have responded to spiritual things, but my husband puts a quick end to that by ridiculing and tearing them down. He gets them crying, and the next thing you know they're going his way."

"Is there a verse that has sustained you at all?"

"Galatians 2:20 helps. But when I look at the future, I have to admit I'm discouraged and blue. I have dishonored Christ and I know it's my fault. I can't change things now. Every now and then I see some Christian boy or girl marrying an unsaved person and I feel like screaming. If they could only see what they are doing to themselves and to any children they may have. I wish I could warn them, but there's one thing I know—My life has been one large tragedy. My heart is broken. My family life is a wreck. My children are neurotics. Where do I go from here?"

This is an actual tape-recorded conversation of a problem. As a pastor, I am involved in counseling, but this family is so divided it is difficult to know where to start. I can only say to young people, don't be trapped into marrying a non-Christian. The Lord said, "Can two walk together, except they be agreed?" (Amos 3:3).

"Be ye not unequally yoked together with unbelievers: for what fellowship hath righteousness with unrighteousness? . . . or what part hath he that believeth with an infidel? And what agreement hath the temple of God with idols? for ye are the temple of the living God. . . . Wherefore come out from among them, and be ye separate, saith the Lord . . . " (II Cor. 6:14-17).

One mistake can ruin your life. It's not worth it!

—Craig Massey

(Taken from *Conquest,* Regular Baptist Press, October 6, 1968. Used by permission.)

APPENDIX II
HOW SAVINGS GROW

This schedule, showing how weekly savings accumulate, is based on the rate of 5% a year, compounded daily.

HOW SAVINGS GROW	$1 Weekly	$2 Weekly	$3 Weekly	$5 Weekly	$10 Weekly	$20 Weekly
1 yr.	53.33	106.68	160.00	266.68	533.36	1066.68
2 yrs.	109.40	218.83	328.21	547.04	1094.08	2188.08
3 yrs.	168.34	336.74	505.05	841.78	1683.57	3367.01
4 yrs.	230.30	460.69	690.95	1151.65	2303.29	4606.42
5 yrs.	295.45	591.01	886.40	1477.41	2954.81	5909.41
10 yrs.	674.86	1349.98	2024.72	3374.70	6749.39	13498.28
15 yrs.	1162.11	2324.65	3486.54	5811.20	11622.40	23243.92
20 yrs.	1787.83	3576.33	5363.83	8940.16	17880.32	35759.29

This chart shows how given amounts grow at the rate of 5% a year, compounded daily, when left in a savings account for various periods of time.

HOW SAVINGS GROW	$50	$100	$500	$1,000	$5,000	$10,000
6 months	51.27	102.54	512.69	1025.38	5126.92	10253.84
1 year	52.56	105.13	525.63	1051.27	5256.35	10512.70
2 years	55.26	110.52	552.60	1105.20	5526.00	11052.00
3 years	58.09	116.19	580.95	1161.90	5809.48	11618.97
4 years	61.08	122.15	610.75	1221.50	6107.51	12215.02
5 years	64.21	128.42	642.08	1284.17	6420.83	12841.65
10 years	82.46	164.91	824.56	1649.13	8245.64	16491.27
20 years	135.98	271.97	1359.85	2719.70	13598.49	27196.99

Use this chart to plan your college fund. This chart is based on the rate of 5% a year, compounded daily.

Starting at Child's Present Age	Here's how various monthly amounts build up by the time your child is 18					
	$5 monthly	$10 monthly	$20 monthly	$25 monthly	$50 monthly	$100 monthly
0	1756.12	3511.95	7024.18	8780.30	17560.32	35120.92
1	1611.76	3223.27	6446.79	8058.56	16116.85	32233.97
2	1474.45	2948.67	5897.58	7372.03	14743.82	29487.89
3	1343.84	2687.47	5375.16	6719.01	13437.80	26875.81
4	1219.61	2439.02	4878.24	6097.85	12195.50	24391.19
5	1101.44	2202.69	4405.56	5507.00	11013.82	22027.81
6	989.03	1977.90	3955.95	4944.98	9889.80	19779.76
7	882.11	1764.07	3528.28	4410.39	8820.63	17641.41
8	780.40	1560.68	3121.48	3901.88	7803.64	15607.40
9	683.66	1367.21	2734.53	3418.19	6836.27	13672.64
10	591.64	1183.18	2366.46	2958.10	5916.10	11832.29
11	504.11	1008.13	2016.35	2520.46	5040.83	10081.75
12	420.85	841.63	1683.33	2104.17	4208.28	8416.63
13	341.65	683.25	1366.55	1708.20	3416.35	6832.76
14	266.32	532.60	1065.23	1331.55	2663.07	5326.17
15	194.66	389.30	778.62	973.28	1946.54	3893.11
16	126.50	252.99	505.99	632.50	1264.98	2529.97
17	61.67	123.33	246.67	308.34	616.67	1233.35

Retiring at age 65? Here's what you can accumulate by age 65 if you save weekly, based on the rate of 5% a year, compounded daily.

Begin Saving at Age	AMOUNT SAVED WEEKLY					
	$1	$2	$3	$5	$10	$20
20	8835.82	17674.94	26509.10	44184.05	88368.10	176729.57
30	4948.51	9898.87	14846.45	24745.32	49490.64	98977.57
40	2591.38	5183.74	7774.64	12958.38	25916.75	51831.56
50	1162.11	2324.65	3486.54	5811.20	11622.40	23243.92
60	295.45	591.01	886.40	1477.41	2954.81	5909.41

SUBJECT INDEX